RECENT

AMERICAN FOREIGN POLICY

Conflicting Interpretations

LAWRENCE S. KAPLAN

Kent State University

1968 • THE DORSEY PRESS

Homewood, Illinois

Library of Congress Catalog Card No. 67–30244

PRINTED IN THE UNITED STATES OF AMERICA

For Jan

PREFACE

This book owes its origins to thoughts about the history of American foreign policy that occupied my mind during a Fulbright year as lecturer at the University of Louvain in Belgium in 1964 and 1965. It was a pleasure for me as a visiting professor to observe the interest, and even enthusiasm, for American studies displayed by Belgian university students representing many disciplines. Though student interest ranged widely over American history, its focus was on the years after World War II when American foreign policy played so large a role in world affairs and when the fate of countries such as Belgium seemed to rest on American decisions. I quickly discovered that student interest outran understanding. Belgian students thought in terms of clichés, half-truths, and outright slanders about the motives and conduct of American foreign policy. This discovery forced me, without resorting to propaganda or apologies, to recast my presentation in an attempt to give meaning to American foreign policy without violating its materials.

The approach I developed in Belgium and have used in this volume emphasizes America's emergence after World War II from a long and useful, if obsolete, tradition of isolationism into a position of international responsibility. The change was fundamental, its execution inevitably painful, and its conduct frequently inept. My major assumption is that the period from 1946 to 1949 were the seminal years that produced the concept of containment, which in expanded or attenuated form has dominated American relations with the Communist powers for the past 20 years. The practice of containment since the war has yielded an almost annual harvest of "great" and "little" debates over the wisdom of the policy.

The 15 chapters in the volume represent selected issues in recent American diplomatic history. Although the most numerous concern Europe, since this was the scene of the major change in American policy, the selections attempt to offer some perspective on the American role in the Far East, Middle East, Africa, and Latin America. Each problem is related to the other as the focus shifts from Washington to Europe or to the Far East.

The general plan of each chapter consists of: (1) an introductory section that links in narrative and analytical fashion the major problems and major arguments; (2) one or two major documents—treaty, presidential statement, administrative decision—from which the debates spring; (3) representative views of participants in the policy, with as many views as possible shown in conflict; and (4) critical views of observers—historians, journalists, and

others—who can view the problem with the advantage of relative detachment, even though they may reflect particular biases. My purposes are to
excite in the student a sense of the drama implicit in the confrontation of
men and ideas, an awareness of the variety of interpretations that the historical record affords, and an understanding of the changes and challenges
facing the United States in the present era.

Most of the documents are of major significance in the record of the
period. I have included some ephemeral items, however, which illustrate
special problems. The interplay of familiar materials with recondite, scholarly
with journalistic, is deliberate, and I hope useful. I have separated primary
from secondary materials in order to give the student an opportunity to see
the complexity of the historical records, and then to note the shapes the
critic has given them. Some of the juxtapositions are admittedly forced, and
a few of the confrontations were less dramatic than here presented. But this
volume will provide the student with a narrative of events from 1946 to
1967 that reflects the development of American foreign policy in our time.
He may also see how the policies themselves are debated and resolved
under the influence of the many competing pressure groups which shape
public opinion and decision making in a democracy.

    Kent, Ohio   LAWRENCE S. KAPLAN
    December, 1967

TABLE OF CONTENTS

1

ISOLATIONISM IN
AMERICAN HISTORY
Nature of the Tradition

I. EDITORIAL INTRODUCTION

There was no more honorable tradition in American history than isolationism. The "great rule of conduct" suggested by George Washington in his Farewell Address of 1796 (Selection II–A.) was enshrined as an article of faith by succeeding generations of Americans. America represented a new order of society which could only be damaged by excessive contact with the sick and evil Old World. American history and geography both conspired to make this a viable doctrine. Americans were transformed Europeans who had partially escaped their Old World tradition in the New World, separated from the Old by an ocean that was God's way of ensuring the purity of the American. Europe's way was that of war and corruption, of disease and starvation; and while a commercial connection was welcome, a political tie could drag America down to the level of Europe. And history pointed to the dangers. All the British dynastic wars had sucked America into the European maelstrom; the very alliance which had helped to win freedom from Europe was in Washington's day "an artificial tie" that might by its obligations compromise America's freedom.

The history of the nineteenth century seemed to confirm the wisdom of Washington's advice. The United States severed the alliance with France in 1800, but found itself caught up once again in Europe's wars in 1812. Eleven years later the Monroe Doctrine announced clearly the separation of the two spheres and the intention of the United States to abstain from European politics and to keep Europe out of the American hemisphere. England's fortuitous sharing of America's view of Europe's territorial ambitions in America and the presence of an unexploited continent to absorb America's attention permitted the nation to pursue a foreign policy of continental expansion which ignored the European balance of power, and virtually ignored Europe itself. The United States prospered under the aegis of isolationism. But isolationism as an ideology was never equated in practice with isolation from the world. Even in Washington's and Jefferson's dicta commercial relations were distinguished from political ties, and while foreign commerce compared unfavorably with domestic in the nineteenth century it was not because of ideological aversion to foreign trade.

Coexisting and compatible with isolationism were two subsidiary sentiments in foreign affairs which governed American behavior in the nineteenth century and which, like isolationism, occasionally manifested themselves in the twentieth century. One of them is embodied in the Monroe Doctrine and suggests a hemispheric solidarity in which the Americas shared common destiny and presumably a common outlook toward the rest of the world. Throughout much of the nation's history this special relation with Latin America took the form of supporting Latin independence from European conquest or reconquest, to the point where under Theodore Roosevelt the Monroe Doctrine appeared to justify an American intervention in one form or another in parts of Latin America to maintain Latin freedom from European control. Inevitably, this interference, accompanied by economic penetration and political manipulation of power, bred a resentment against the United States far surpassing any fears Latin Americans had about German, British, Spanish, or Japanese dangers to the hemisphere. As in the case of isolationism the United States was forced to reevaluate the meaning of the Monroe Doctrine in the 1930's.

The second important subsidiary strain in American foreign policy concerned a romantic and economic attachment to the Far East which went back to the China trade of the late eighteenth century. In East Asia and in the Pacific Americans nourished memories of a successful economic challenge to British power and the apparently successful transplantation of American religious denominations through the respective efforts of traders and missionaries. The United States regarded itself as the only Western country concerned with the territorial integrity of China or Japan. The idea of the "Open Door" had appeared long before it was formulated in 1900, and it had always connoted to Americans more than merely equal opportunity for trade in the Far East. What linked the Open Door policy to the Monroe Doctrine and both to isolationism was the assumption of American moral superiority over Europe in Latin America and in the Far East and the identification of European nations as hostile to the welfare of both the Asian and American worlds. Experience with those areas served to confirm the wisdom of America's isolation from European affairs.

It is frequently argued that the Spanish-American War introduced the United States as a world power and consequently marked the end of its isolationist period. Such was not quite the case. Admiral Alfred Thayer Mahan, the leading spokesman for a "large" foreign policy, urged America to continue to abstain from the politics of Europe even as he demanded a navy to fulfill America's mission as a great power in Asia, the Pacific, and Latin America. Although it was impossible to separate Latin America or China from European quarrels and the European balance of power, the United States reaffirmed the distinction. Theodore Roosevelt's dabbling in Morocco at the time of the Algeciras Conference in 1905–06 was a by-product of his personal energies rather than a portent of a new view of American foreign policy. America's involvement in China and in the Caribbean in the first decade of the twentieth century was not to be connected with the power struggles of Europe.

When the United States finally entered Europe directly, it was not a consequence of a new sophistication but a reflection of its own tradition; Wilson brought America into European affairs only on the assumption that the traditional European balance-of-power system would thereby be destroyed. After Wilsonian expectations were exploded, the United States continued its isolationist sentiments and if they seemed deeper than before, it was simply because America in the twentieth century could have made a far greater impact upon the balance of power than in the nineteenth. In this sense American isolationism in the interwar period of 1919 to 1939 was a contributing factor to the holocaust of World War II.

The war transformed the conduct of American diplomacy almost as much as it did foreign policy. The close association of President Roosevelt with Prime Minister Churchill was matched by unprecedented forms of Anglo-American cooperation on both military and political levels. Old departments, such as the Army and Navy, received responsibilities in statecraft, and new ones, such as the Office of War Information, were involved in policy making. With the memory of 1919 to guide it, the America of 1945 was prepared to assume at last the burden of leadership, symbolized by membership in the United Nations, which it had not anticipated in 1939. The wartime hopes of an America in crisis found an expression in the Connally Resolution in which the Senate of the United States resolved that the United States "with free and sovereign nations in the establishment and maintenance of international authority with power to prevent aggression and to preserve the peace of the world." (Selection II–B.)

In the new world that lay at the end of the war, President Roosevelt foresaw the end of isolationism. In his last State of the Union address, only a few months before the final defeat of Nazi Germany, he warned Europeans and Americans alike not to allow the difficulties of reconstruction to divide the world again. While he condemned the term, "power politics," he urged Americans to accept an imperfect world and take up the responsibilities of power. The alternative could be another world war. (Selection III–A.)

Far more passionate in its demands of Americans was the voice of Wendell Willkie, Roosevelt's opponent in the Presidential campaign of 1940, who dramatized the new role of the United States in his book, *One World,* written in the midst of war. He saw only three courses open to the United States after the war: "narrow nationalism," "international imperialism," or the creation of a new world with "equality of opportunity" for every nation. There was a strong note of Wilsonian messianism in the mission he assigned to Americans. There was also no recognition of the "power" factor pointed out by Roosevelt. (Selection III–B.)

Isolationism, even as a term, had fallen from favor by 1945. Yet, its message had not wholly disappeared. Former President Herbert Hoover still used the language of the past clearly and unequivocally. In 1951, in the midst of the Korean conflict, Hoover was able to point to the United States recognition of the Soviet government in 1933 as the first step in the wrong direction, a step taken only after he had left office. The end result was the bleeding of American strength through land wars in Europe and Asia. He implied that while Europe or Asia might well fall to the present enemy, the maintenance of American naval and air and economic strength would defend America against all enemies. (Selection III–C.)

Historians have been almost as disturbed as policy makers over the issue of isolationism after World War II. Charles Beard, the most influential American historian of the interbella period, lamented the passing of isolationism on at least two major grounds. One was the pursuit of an illusion which could easily destroy the nation. To him it was incredible that America could achieve peace and security in the world by involving itself in European wars. Roosevelt himself had to dissemble to the American people in pushing them into a war they would not otherwise have joined. And for what end? World War II merely raised another despot in Europe to make a mockery of the goals of the United Nations and the Atlantic Charter. (Selection IV–A.)

A more benign view of the changes in American foreign policy was expressed by Professor Alexander DeConde who saw isolationism in the twentieth century as more complicated than in the nineteenth since it was fed by more sources. It also acquired a bad odor that led its leaders to abandon even its name. America's entry into World War II, unlike World War I, was a response to the changes in the balance of power, and its leadership after the war made isolationism an impossibility (Selection IV–B.)

Professor Samuel Flagg Bemis, dean of American diplomatic historians, agreed that World War II had changed America's role in the world, and credited Franklin Roosevelt, with some severe reservations, with understanding the relation of American security to the balance of power. But in view of the rise of the Soviet Union and the familiar American postwar disillusionment, the United States might have to act alone as it had in the nineteenth century, not because of isolationist sentiment, but because there was no other power in the world to help maintain the international equilibrium (Selection IV–C.)

II. DOCUMENTS

> ### SELECTION II–A
>
> This is an excerpt from Washington's "Farewell Address" first printed in the *American Daily Advertiser*, September 17, 1796. It remains the classic statement of American isolationism.

The great rule of conduct for us in regard to foreign nations is, in extending our commercial relations to have with them as little *political* connection as possible. So far as we have already formed engagements let them be fulfilled with perfect good faith. Here let us stop.

Europe has a set of primary interests which to us have none or a very remote relation. Hence she must be engaged in frequent controversies, the causes of which are essentially foreign to our concerns. Hence, therefore, it must be unwise in us to implicate ourselves by artificial ties in the ordinary vicissitudes of her politics or the ordinary combinations and collisions of her friendships or enmities.

Our detached and distant situation invites and enables us to pursue a different course. If we remain one people, under an efficient government, the period is not far off when we may defy material injury from external annoyance; when we may take such an attitude as will cause the neutrality we may at any time resolve upon to be scrupulously respected; when belligerent nations, under the impossibility of making acquisitions upon us, will not lightly hazard the giving us provocation; when we may choose peace or war, as our interest, guided by justice, shall counsel.

Why forego the advantages of so peculiar a situation? Why quit our own to stand upon foreign ground? Why, by interweaving our destiny with that of any part of Europe, entangle our peace and prosperity in the toils of European ambition, rivalship, interest, humor, or caprice? . . .

> ### SELECTION II–B
>
> The Connally Resolution, reproduced here from the *Congressional Record— Senate*, 78th Congress, 1st sess., November 5, 1943, p. 19222, was passed by a vote of 85 to 5. It gave evidence that the new United Nations would not meet the fate of the League of Nations a quarter of a century before.

So Senate Resolution 192, as modified, was agreed to, as follows:

Resolved, That the war against all our enemies be waged until complete victory is achieved.

That the United States cooperate with its comrades-in-arms in securing a just and honorable peace.

That the United States, acting through its constitutional processes, join with free and sovereign nations in establishment and maintenance of international authority with power to prevent aggression and to preserve the peace of the world.

That the Senate recognizes the necessity of there being established at the earliest practicable date a general international organization, based on the principle of the sovereign equality of all peace-loving states, and open to membership by all such states, large and small, for the maintenance of international peace and security.

That, pursuant to the Constitution of the United States, any treaty made to effect the purposes of this resolution, on behalf of the Government of the United States with any other nation or any association of nations, shall be made only by and with the advice and consent of the Senate of the United States, provided two-thirds of the Senators present concur.

III. VIEWS OF PARTICIPANTS

SELECTION III–A

This excerpt is taken from President Roosevelt's "Annual Message on the State of the Union" of January 6, 1945 as it appeared in the *New York Times*, Jan. 7, 1945. The President's hopes for a "brave new world" are outlined here.

In the field of foreign policy, we propose to stand together with the United Nations not for the war alone but for the victory for which the war is fought.

It is not only a common danger which unites us but a common hope. Ours is an association not of Governments but of peoples—and the peoples' hope is peace. Here, as in England; in England, as in Russia; in Russia, as in China; in France, and through the continent of Europe, and throughout the world; wherever men love freedom, the hope and purpose of the people are for peace—a peace that is durable and secure.

It will not be easy to create this peoples' peace. We delude ourselves if we believe that the surrender of the armies of our enemies will make the peace we long for. The unconditional surrender of the armies of our enemies is the first and necessary step—but the first step only.

We have seen already, in areas liberated from the Nazi and the Fascist tyranny, what problems peace will bring. And we delude ourselves if we attempt to believe wishfully that all these problems can be solved overnight.

The firm foundation can be built—and it will be built. But the continuance and assurance of a living peace must, in the long run, be the work of the people themselves.

We ourselves, like all peoples who have gone through the difficult processes of liberation and adjustment, know of our own experience how great the difficulties can be. We know that they are not difficulties peculiar to any continent or any Nation. Our own Revolutionary War left behind it, in the words of one American historian, "an eddy of lawlessness and disregard of human life." There were separatist movements of one kind or another in Vermont, Pennsylvania, Virginia, Tennessee, Kentucky, and Maine. There were insurrections, open or threatened, in Massachusetts and New Hampshire. These difficulties we worked out for ourselves as the peoples of the liberated areas of Europe, faced with complex problems of adjustment, will work out their difficulties for themselves.

Peace can be made and kept only by the united determination of free and peace-loving peoples who are willing to work together—willing to help one another—willing to respect and tolerate and try to understand one another's opinions and feelings.

The nearer we come to vanquishing our enemies the more we inevitably become conscious of differences among the victors.

We must not let those differences divide us and blind us to our more important common and continuing interests in winning the war and building the peace.

International cooperation on which enduring peace must be based is not a one-way street.

Nations like individuals do not always see alike or think alike, and international cooperation and progress are not helped by any Nation assuming that it has a monopoly of wisdom or of virtue.

In the future world the misuse of power, as implied in the term "power politics," must not be a controlling factor in international relations. That is the heart of the principles to which we have subscribed. We cannot deny that power is a factor in world politics any more than we can deny its existence as a factor in national politics. But in a democratic world, as in a democratic Nation, power must be linked with responsibility, and obliged to defend and justify itself within the framework of the general good.

Perfectionism, no less than isolationism or imperialism or power politics, may obstruct the paths to international peace. Let us not forget that the retreat to isolationism a quarter of a century ago was started not by a direct attack against international cooperation but against the alleged imperfections of the peace.

In our disillusionment after the last war we preferred international anarchy to international cooperation with Nations which did not see and think exactly as we did. We gave up the hope of gradually achieving a better peace because we had not the courage to fulfill our responsibilities in an admittedly imperfect world.

We must not let that happen again, or we shall follow the same tragic road again—the road to a third world war.

We can fulfill our responsibilities for maintaining the security of our own country only by exercising our power and our influence to achieve the principles in which we believe and for which we have fought.

. . . .

We and our allies have declared that it is our purpose to respect the right of all peoples to choose the form of government under which they will live and to see sovereign rights and self-government restored to those who have been forcibly deprived of them. But with internal dissension, with many citizens of liberated countries still prisoners of war or forced to labor in Germany, it is difficult to guess the kind of self-government the people really want.

During the interim period, until conditions permit a genuine expression of the people's will, we and our allies have a duty, which we cannot ignore, to use our influence to the end that no temporary or provisional authorities in the liberated countries block the eventual exercise of the peoples' right freely to choose the government and institutions under which, as freemen, they are to live.

It is only too easy for all of us to rationalize what we want to believe, and to consider those leaders we like responsible and those we dislike irresponsible. And our task is not helped by stubborn partisanship, however understandable on the part of opposed internal factions.

It is our purpose to help the peace-loving peoples of Europe to live together as good neighbors, to recognize their common interests and not to nurse their traditional grievances against one another.

But we must not permit the many specific and immediate problems of adjustment connected with the liberation of Europe to delay the establishment of permanent machinery for the maintenance of peace. Under the threat of a common danger, the United Nations joined together in war to preserve their independence and their freedom. They must now join together to make secure the independence and freedom of all peace-loving states, so that never again shall tyranny be able to divide and conquer.

International peace and well-being, like national peace and well-being, require constant alertness, continuing cooperation, and organized effort.

International peace and well-being, like national peace and well-being, can be secured only through institutions capable of life and growth.

Many of the problems of the peace are upon us even now while the conclusion of the war is still before us. The atmosphere of friendship and mutual understanding and determination to find a common ground of common understanding, which surrounded the conversations at Dumbarton Oaks, gives us reason to hope that future discussions will succeed in developing the democratic and fully integrated world security system toward which these preparatory conversations were directed.

We and the other United Nations are going forward, with vigor and resolution, in our efforts to create such a system by providing for it strong and flexible institutions of joint and cooperative action.

The aroused conscience of humanity will not permit failure in this supreme endeavor.

> ## SELECTION III–B
>
> An excerpt from *One World* (New York, 1943), p. 202–6 by Wendell Willkie. Reprinted by permission of Philip H. Willkie. The Republican presidential candidate of 1940 was a leading spokesman for a new world order that should develop from World War II. His book was a byproduct of his wartime travels abroad.

If our withdrawal from world affairs after the last war was a contributing factor to the present war and to the economic instability of the past twenty years—and it seems plain that it was—a withdrawal from the problems and responsibilities of the world after this war would be sheer disaster. Even our relative geographical isolation no longer exists.

At the end of the last war, not a single plane had flown across the Atlantic. Today that ocean is a mere ribbon, with airplanes making regular scheduled flights. The Pacific is only a slightly wider ribbon in the ocean of the air, and Europe and Asia are at our very doorstep.

America must choose one of three courses after this war: narrow nationalism, which inevitably means the ultimate loss of our own liberty; international imperialism, which means the sacrifice of some other nation's liberty; or the creation of a world in which there shall be an equality of opportunity for every race and every nation. I am convinced the American people will choose, by overwhelming majority, the last of these courses. To make this choice effective, we must win not only the war, but also the peace, and we must start winning it now.

To win this peace three things seem to me necessary—first, we must plan now for peace on a world basis; second, the world must be free, politically and economically, for nations and for men, that peace may exist in it; third, America must play an active, constructive part in freeing it and keeping its peace.

When I say that peace must be planned on a world basis, I mean quite literally that it must embrace the earth. Continents and oceans are plainly only parts of a whole, seen, as I have seen them, from the air. England and America are parts. Russia and China, Syria and Turkey, Iraq and Iran are also parts. And it is inescapable that there can be no peace for any part of the world unless the foundations of peace are made secure throughout all parts of the world.

This cannot be accomplished by mere declarations of our leaders, as in an Atlantic Charter. Its accomplishment depends primarily upon acceptance by the peoples of the world. For if the failure to reach international under-standing after the last war taught us anything it taught us this: even if war leaders apparently agree upon generalized principles and slogans while the war is being fought, when they come to the peace table they make their own interpretations of their previous declarations. So unless today, while the war is being fought, the people of the United States and of Great Britain, of Russia and of China, and of all the other United Nations, fundamentally agree on their purposes, fine and idealistic expressions of hope such as those of the Atlantic Charter will live merely to mock us as have Mr. Wilson's Fourteen Points. The Four Freedoms will not be accomplished by the decla-rations of those momentarily in power. They will become real only if the people of the world forge them into actuality.

When I say that in order to have peace this world must be free, I am only reporting that a great process has started which no man—certainly not Hitler—can stop. Men and women all over the world are on the march, physically, intellectually, and spiritually. After centuries of ignorant and dull compliance, hundreds of millions of people in eastern Europe and Asia have opened the books. Old fears no longer frighten them. They are no longer willing to be Eastern slaves for Western profits. They are beginning to know that men's welfare throughout the world is interdependent. They are resolved, as we must be, that there is no more place for imperialism within our own society than in the society of nations. The big house on the hill surrounded by mud huts has lost its awesome charm.

Our Western world and our presumed supremacy are now on trial. Our boasting and our big talk leave Asia cold. Men and women in Russia and China and in the Middle East are conscious now of their own potential strength. They are coming to know that many of the decisions about the future of the world lie in their hands. And they intend that these decisions shall leave the peoples of each nation free from foreign domination, free for economic, social, and spiritual growth.

Economic freedom is as important as political freedom. Not only must people have access to what other peoples produce, but their own products must in turn have some chance of reaching men all over the world. There will be no peace, there will be no real development, there will be no eco-nomic stability, unless we find the method by which we can begin to break down the unnecssary trade barriers hampering the flow of goods. Obviously, the sudden and uncompromising abolition of tariffs after the war could only result in disaster. But obviously, also, one of the freedoms we are fighting for is freedom to trade. I know there are many men, particularly in America, where our standard of living exceeds the standard of living in the rest of the world, who are genuinely alarmed at such a prospect, who believe that any such process will only lessen our own standard of living. The reverse of this is true.

Many reasons may be assigned for the amazing economic development of the United States. The abundance of our national resources, the freedom of our political institutions, and the character of our population have all undoubtedly contributed. But in my judgment the greatest factor has been the fact that by the happenstance of good fortune there was created here in America the largest area in the world in which there were no barriers to the exchange of goods and ideas.

And I should like to point out to those who are fearful one inescapable fact. In view of the astronomical figures our national debt will assume by the end of this war, and in a world reduced in size by industrial and transportation developments, even our present standard of living in America cannot be maintained unless the exchange of goods flows more freely over the whole world. It is also inescapably true that to raise the standard of living of any man anywhere in the world is to raise the standard of living by some slight degree of every man everywhere in the world.

Finally, when I say that this world demands the full participation of a self-confident America, I am only passing on an invitation which the peoples of the East have given us. They would like the United States and the other United Nations to be partners with them in this grand adventure. They want us to join them in creating a new society of independent nations, free alike of the economic injustices of the West and the political malpractices of the East. But as partners in that great new combination they want us neither hesitant, incompetent, nor afraid. They want partners who will not hesitate to speak out for the correction of injustice anywhere in the world.

Our allies in the East know that we intend to pour out our resources in this war. But they expect us now—not after the war—to use the enormous power of our giving to promote liberty and justice. Other peoples, not yet fighting, are waiting no less eagerly for us to accept the most challenging opportunity of all history—the chance to help create a new society in which men and women the world around can live and grow invigorated by independence and freedom.

SELECTION III–C

An excerpt from the original text of "We Should Revise Our Foreign Policies," by Herbert Hoover, as it appeared in *Addresses upon the American Road, 1950–55* (Stanford, 1955), pp. 11–15, 22. Reprinted by permission of the Herbert Hoover Foundation. Portions of this article were aired in a nationwide broadcast on February 9, 1951. Former President Hoover was a respected national sage 20 years after his defeat for re-election. The trials of American policy in the cold war confirmed his fears of danger in any departure from the isolationist past.

Fellow Americans:

I have been urged by many thousands of you to again discuss with you our foreign policies.

A responsibility rests upon me to speak out from fifty years of personal experience with most of the peoples of the free world and with Russia and China. I have been entrusted during thirty-five years with high responsibilities by my countrymen.

I should like to address you through the rose-colored spectacles of idealism and the need of free nations to defend free men.

But I would be doing my country a disservice if I did not take into account the realities in this endangered world.

There is nothing sacrosanct about foreign policies, as witness the tombstones which have been erected over many of them in the last ten years. They bear the inscriptions Undeclared War, The Alliance with Stalin, Teheran, Yalta, Potsdam, Dismantling of German Peacetime Industry, The Promoting of Mao Tse-tung.

Many men, including myself, have demanded the revision of these policies at each wrong turning.

The rightness of our many proposals has been proved by time. I shall recall only two of them for your test.

Seventeen years ago, as President, I refused recognition of the Soviet Government. I knew from ample experience, and their own documents, that this bloody conspiracy against mankind would flood our country through this open door with Fifth Columns and spies; that they would sabotage our national life and government. Every American knows they have done just that.

About ten years ago, on June 29, 1941, in a great crisis I urged the revision of our policies to meet the greatest danger that had come to the American people.

Mr. Roosevelt had proposed a tacit alliance of the United States with Stalin and his Communist Russia. Britain was then safe because of the diversion of Hitler's armies to an attack on Russia. A few sentences from my address were:

. . . Now we find ourselves promising aid to Stalin and his militant Communist conspiracy against the whole democratic ideals of the world. . . .

It makes the whole argument of our joining the war to bring the four freedoms to mankind a gargantuan jest. . . .

If we go further and join the war and we win, then we have won for Stalin the grip of Communism on Russia and more opportunity for it to extend in the world.

I said these two dictators—Stalin and Hitler—were locked in deadly combat, that statesmanship required the United States to stand aside in watchful waiting, armed to the teeth; that the day would come when these nations

. . . will be sufficiently exhausted to listen to the military, economic, and moral powers of the United States and at that moment and that moment only can the United States promote a just and lasting peace.

Remember this was in June 1941, almost ten years ago. Need I remind you that the grip of Communism in this decade has spread slavery from 200,000,000 to 800,000,000 people? And we have no peace.

I could recall a dozen more instances, some within the past twelve months.

OUR PROBLEMS NOW

In order to reach any conclusions as to the wise course for America to pursue in the critical issues which confront us we must again and again appraise the constantly shifting forces moving in the world.

The problems which we face are of far larger dimensions than the current discussion on sending contingents of American boys to Europe.

Their appraisal must also include:

1. Land war strengths.
2. The defense of the American people and the Western Hemisphere.
3. Our economic capacity over a long period.
4. The United Nations.
5. Our policies in the Far East.
6. The North Atlantic Military alliance.

Policies in these six categories cannot be separated from each other—they are all interlocked.

We must appraise the somber facts around these points before we can map a national direction. We must not shrink from clear-minded appraisal of our strengths, our weaknesses and the attainment of the purposes to which the Congress has committed us.

LAND WAR STRENGTHS

The first grim reality is the military strengths for land war in the world.

I am fully aware of the shortcomings of the term "divisions" as a measuring device for comparative military strength, but it is the nearest to a common descriptive unit that we have.

The Kremlin-directed horde has under arms and in reserves probably 300 combat divisions, with 30,000 tanks. I am now told they have over 20,000 mostly tactical planes and they have with their satellites 50,000,000 men available for cannon fodder.

In World War II, when Russia was without satellites, the Germans failed with 240 well-equipped divisions to overcome her. With her allies of General Manpower, General Space, General Winter, and General Scorched Earth, she had stopped the Germans even before Lend-Lease had reached her.

The nations of Europe in the Atlantic Pact have at the present moment less than 20 equipped and trained combat divisions available for European action.

There is here a stark reality upon which our foreign policies must be based. With any seeable land forces from non-Communist nations, even including the United States, a land offensive against the Communist could bring no military victory, no political conclusion. But that does not mean that there are no other methods of stopping the Kremlin's ambitions.

THE DEFENSE OF OUR GIBRALTAR
OF WESTERN CIVILIZATION

The second stark realism upon which our foreign policies must be based is the defense of the Western Hemisphere. Its defense is not only in our interests but in the interests of free men everywhere.

Much criticism is offered even to a discussion of this question. An atmosphere of hurry, rush, anxiety is being developed, the effect of which is to make it difficult, if not impossible, for the American people to judge their own situation.

I may say at once that with proper economic action this Hemisphere can be made self-contained in critical raw materials. From a long professional career and from years as Secretary of Commerce dealing with such questions, I might qualify as something of an expert in this field.

Also, unless we so dissipate our strength as to become a beaten and crushed people, we will be able to keep sea lanes open.

Moreover, this Hemisphere can be defended from Communist armies come what will. It is still surrounded with a great moat. To transport such invading armies either 3,000 miles across the Atlantic or 6,000 miles across the Pacific would require transport ships and naval protection which the Russians do not possess and could not build or seize, no matter what further countries they occupy. If we have a proper naval and air strength, we could sink them in mid-ocean. With somewhat more attention paid to our defense, this would apply to invasion by way of the Bering Straits. Hitler's armies could not even cross the English Channel. Bering Straits are much wider. Atomic bombs can do us damage but they do not transport troops over the ocean.

Communist armies can no more get to Washington than any allied armies can get to Moscow.

No responsible military man denies these two conclusions.

The American people should not be frightened into rash action by fear that we cannot survive. I am not advocating isolationism. But if other nations should fail, we may be isolated by force of circumstance and against our will.

We might go into a period hard to endure, but this nation can stick it out.

.   .   .   .

IN CONCLUSION

I have proposed no retreat, no withdrawal. I have proposed no repudiation of treaties or obligations. Rather I have proposed that the pledges to the Congress and the American people be kept. I have proposed that we stop, look, and listen before we start on a road of land war that risks the loss of all civilization.

I propose no good to Stalin. His greatest hope is to get us into a land war.

Before we go off the deep end of steps toward another land war in Europe, let us remember that we fought two such wars hoping to bring peace and we have no peace. We should be prepared to make heavy sacrifices to help. But we should do it with common sense, within our strength, with the long view of history in our minds.

The essence of the program I have proposed is to effectively restrain our enemies from attack upon our allies or ourselves. It is the best chance of peace—even if it is an uneasy peace.

If we pursue the lines of our own genius and resources, we can meet this —the greatest menace of a century.

And being in the right the Almighty is on our side.

IV. VIEWS OF OBSERVERS

SELECTION IV–A

From Charles A. Beard, *President Roosevelt and the Coming of the War, 1941: A Study in Appearances and Realities* (New Haven, 1948), pp. 573–77. Copyright © 1948. Reprinted by permission of the Yale University Press. Charles Beard was perhaps the most influential American historian of the 1930's—a progressive at home, an isolationist abroad.

The discrepancies between official representations and official realities in the conduct of foreign affairs during the year 1941, until the coming of war, stand out starkly in documents already available. Other documents that bear on the subject, running into the thousands, are known to exist, but they are still under the seal of secrecy. What they will reveal, if all of them are ever unsealed, can only be a matter of conjecture for the general public and students of history. But in any event several primary discrepancies are established beyond question by the documents now published.

In the nature of things human and political, these established discrepancies may be and are being turned to account in various ways by politicians, publicists, and commentators. They may be, for example, formulated into a bill of indictment against President Roosevelt and his Administration. Or they may be incorporated in a brief of defense which, like a demurrer in a court of justice, concedes the facts and denies that they make a true case under superior and overriding principles, taken for granted in advance. Or they may appear to reflective minds as furnishing precedents material and relevant to the future and fortunes of constitutional and democratic government in the United States.

THE MAIN BRIEF OF DEFENSE—TESTED
BY CONSEQUENCES

For these discrepancies a favorable interpretation has been and is still being offered by many American publicists in the following form. The great end which President Roosevelt discerned and chose justified the means which he employed. As a farsighted statesman he early discovered that unless the United States entered the war raging in Europe, Hitler would be victorious; and the United States, facing alone this monstrous totalitarian power, would become a victim of its merciless ideology and its despotic militarism. According to this interpretation, it was a question of democracy, the Four Freedoms, the noble principles of the Atlantic Charter, and world security on the one side; of totalitarianism, consummate despotism, and military subjugation on the other side. Since the American people were so smug in their conceit, so ignorant of foreign affairs, and so isolationist in sentiment that they could not themselves see the reality of this terrible threat to their own safety and a necessity to meet it by a resort to war, President Roosevelt had to dissemble in order to be reelected in 1940 as against Wendell Willkie, then the antiwar candidate of the Republicans on an antiwar platform. Furthermore, as members of Congress, Democrats and Republicans alike, continued throughout the year, until December 7, their vigorous opposition to involvement in war, President Roosevelt, in conducting foreign affairs, had to maintain the appearance of a defensive policy until the Japanese attack on Pearl Harbor. But the means which President Roosevelt actually employed in the conduct of foreign affairs were justified by the great end which he, with peculiar clairvoyance, had early discerned and chosen for himself and his country.

Oblique but evident support for this interpretation was provided by the Department of State in Chapter I of its publication, *Peace and War, 1931–1941*, issued in July, 1943, prepared by or for Secretary Hull. In that chapter, the President and the Secretary of State are represented as convinced at some time "early" in that decade that "the idea of isolation as expressed in 'neutrality' legislation" was untenable, as having information about foreign affairs or foreseeing developments in foreign relations of which the public was not aware, and as compelled to move gradually "to a position in the forefront of the United Nations that are making common cause against an attempt at world conquest unparalleled alike in boldness of conception and in brutality of operation."

The interpretation that the end justified the means, like all other interpretations, depends upon the point of view of those who make or accept it; and though it be proclaimed as the settled truth, its validity is nonetheless open to tests of knowledge. Even a cursory examination of the thesis raises questions of time and consequences, foreign and domestic.

When did the end that justified the means actually come? With the surrender of Italy, Germany, and Japan? If not, when did it come or is it to come—in what span of time, short or long? By whom and according to what criteria is the question of time to be answered beyond all reasonable doubt?

If the time for the achievement of the end be postponed to some point in the indefinite future, the confirmation of the thesis must likewise be postponed indefinitely. In that case an effort to confirm it now becomes a matter of calculating probabilities, ponderable and imponderable. If, however, the results of the war—foreign and domestic—thus far known be taken into the reckoning, a question both logical and historical may be asked: Does it now appear probable that President Roosevelt did in fact so clearly discern the end—the consequences to flow from his actions in 1941—that he was in truth justified in his choice and use of means?

With regard to consequences in foreign affairs, the noble principles of the Four Freedoms and the Atlantic Charter were, for practical purposes, discarded in the settlements which accompanied the progress, and followed the conclusion, of the war. To the validity of this statement the treatment of peoples in Estonia, Lithuania, Poland, Rumania, Yugoslavia, China, Indo-China, Indonesia, Italy, Germany, and other places of the earth bears witness. More significant still for the fortunes of the American Republic, out of the war came the triumph of another totalitarian regime no less despotic and ruthless than Hitler's system, namely, Russia, possessing more than twice the population of prewar Germany, endowed with immense natural resources, astride Europe and Asia, employing bands of Quislings as terroristic in methods as any Hitler ever assembled, and insistently effectuating a political and economic ideology equally inimical to the democracy, liberties, and institutions of the United States—Russia, one of the most ruthless Leviathans in the long history of military empires.

> ### SELECTION IV–B
>
> Excerpts from *Isolation and Security* edited by Alexander DeConde (Durham, North Carolina, 1957) pp. 6–10. Reprinted with permission of the author and of the Duke University Press. DeConde is professor of history at the University of California at Santa Barbara and an authority on the diplomatic history of the early national period.

While isolation as a doctrine has always been complex and made up of many ideas, the isolationist ideology of the nineteenth century was relatively simple when compared with that of the twentieth century. By stressing that their ideas were anchored in the revered past, isolationists of the present century identified them with Americanism and self-interest. To some they were nothing more than that. Yet twentieth-century isolationism was different from the isolation of the nineteenth. It was different, we shall see, because it was a complex of emotions and ideas; because some of its ideas and vocabulary had changed; because the world of the nineteenth century was no more; and because the United States of the twentieth century was ethnically and culturally different from what it had been in the preceding century.

That the first vigorous critics of traditional isolation made themselves heard at the end of the nineteenth century and in the beginning of the twentieth was not accidental. Their criticisms reflected changes in the world and in the United States. By the turn of the century the United States was a world power; a powerful Germany had forced Great Britain to abandon her "splendid isolation" by challenging her maritime and industrial supremacy; Great Britain began a new *rapprochement* with the United States a *rapprochement* stronger than a formal alliance; and streams of "new immigrants" accelerated the change in the ethnic, social, and political composition of the United States started earlier by Germans and Irish. Externally and internally those developments changed or modified traditional American values. In particular they made isolationism different from the isolation of the past.

The world of the nineteenth century, in which American isolation was a political fact and served the nation well, was a world policed by the British fleet, a world in which Englishmen grew rich and Americans pospered peacefully. "America lives in a world of peace," wrote Lord Bryce of the nineteenth-century United States. "Safe from attack, safe even from menace, she hears from afar the warring cries of European nations and faiths. For the present at least—it may not always be so—America sails upon a summer sea." The summer sea became a storm-churned one because the balance of power in Europe, and in the world, shifted. This European balance of power Americans considered evil, an evil they shunned.

Our victory over Spain and the possession of the Philippines made us a weighty factor in the shifting power balance. We participated in European rivalries through the back of door of Asia. In Asia, too, Japan successfully challenged the old power status and the traditional hegemony of the Western World. Her victory over Russia in 1904–5 marked the beginning of the end of Europe's nineteenth-century dominance over colored peoples. In Europe, Germany challenged English pre-eminence, which for a century had commanded peace and stability. England responded by reversing her traditional diplomatic commitments on the Continent and by seeking an alliance or close understanding with the United States.

When Germany's challenge in the First World War almost succeeded in destroying the English-dominated and French-supported *status quo,* it changed the thinking of many Americans on foreign policy, particularly on isolationism. Even in defeat Germany had destroyed the old balance of power. England was no longer the balancer; the United States was.

Many Americans wedded to the ideas of nineteenth-century isolation now realized, as perhaps they had not before, that they had profited from

England's manipulation of the balance of power. The things they considered important and wished to preserve, Germany endangered. Woodrow Wilson stressed this when he urged the nation on that fateful April 2, 1917, "to spend her blood and her might for the principles that gave her birth and happiness and the peace that she has treasured."

Americans held most of those principles, political, institutional, social, and cultural, in common with England, and France shared some of them. Essentially, their peaceful enjoyment had rested on England's maritime and diplomatic ascendancy in the nineteenth century. To preserve these common institutions and ideals when England seemed no longer capable of holding a commanding influence in world politics, or even of maintaining the nineteenth-century equilibrium, many Americans had urged participation in the First World War and rejoiced when we entered it. They forsook the traditional principles of isolationism and saw with satisfaction that American intervention tipped the balance in favor of France and England.

But the balance of power was not the same, the old nineteenth-century detachment of the United States could not be regained. America had become the decisive weight in the balance. As Theodore Roosevelt had told a German friend before the war (1911), the United States, because of its geographical position and great strength, was becoming more and more the most important power in the world's balance of power. Yet even after the World War most Americans persisted in thinking that the balance of power was evil and should be shunned. Cordell Hull, an internationalist Secretary of State who favored participation in world politics, was, if not typical, at least representative of this kind of thinking. He never believed in the balance of power as a means of keeping the peace. During the First World War, he explained in his memoirs, he studied the balance of power and was convinced it was iniquitous. "The conclusions I then formed in total opposition to this system," he said, "stayed with me."

When after the war the victors established a world organization predicated on maintaining the *status quo* of the wartime Allied coalition it failed. The League of Nations failed, many Americans reasoned, because the United States, the fulcrum in the new balance of power, would not participate in collective action to uphold the balance. For reasons germane more to internal developments than to international affairs the United States tried to slip back into the comfortable isolation of the past. Actually, while the words and some of the ideas sounded the same, isolationism too had changed.

It was no longer a doctrine of self-preservation on which almost all Americans agreed. Opponents argued that it was the unthinking defensive posture of the ostrich; it did not fit the facts of international affairs in the twentieth century. The true doctrine of self-preservation, they argued, was collective security. While agreeing that the world and America's relationships with other nations had changed, isolationists contended that their doctrine was still best for self-preservation. In the 1920's and 1930's most Americans seemed to agree.

In less than two decades after the First World War Germany again challenged the international *status quo*. This time Japan and Italy were also challengers. Again the United States entered the war to tip the balance in favor of England; again Americans, more of them than in 1917, believed ultimately that American intervention was essential to preserve important Anglo-American values.

When the United States entered the Second World War it did not do so as an outsider interested primarily in preserving the dominant status of a close friend with the idea of returning home after the peace and leaving the friend once more responsible for the balance of power. This time, as had not been clearly the case in the First World War, the challenge to the upholders of the established balance threatened American security.

Although England for a while held off Germany alone, the United States, not she, became the main defender of the old international *status quo*. At the same time a new and powerful ally, Soviet Russia, helped destroy the German-Japanese challenge. But Communist Russia did not value the ideals Americans, Englishmen, and Frenchmen shared.

With the end of the Second World War a newly polarized distribution of power emerged. At one end was Russia, determined to destroy what remained of the old international *status quo*. At the other pole was the United States, a firm opponent of Communist power but a reluctant defender of remnants of England's nineteenth-century world hegemony. Whether or not most Americans like it, the United States had inherited Great Britain's role as the pivot of the Western World; it became the main defender of Anglo-American values. America's security, particularly after Russia had penetrated the secret of the atom, was now linked with that of Europe and of all the world. Not even a Procrustes could force those facts to fit the doctrine of nineteenth-century isolation.

SELECTION IV–C

From Samuel F. Bemis, "The Shifting Strategy of American Defense and Diplomacy," XXIV (Summer, 1948), *Virginia Quarterly Review*, pp. 332–35. Reprinted with permission of the author and publisher. Samuel Bemis, professor emeritus at Yale University, is the dean of American diplomatic historians. In this essay he defended the deviation from isolationism produced by World War II from the attacks of the new revisionists.

It will be Franklin D. Roosevelt's claim to statesmanship as compared with that of Woodrow Wilson, that, whatever his initial vacillations and his campaign deceptions, he came to see the American *raison d'état*, the vital relation of the United States to the balance of power at the advent of the Second World War. He protected that relation at the risk and fact of a double war, rather than permit Japan to destroy the British Empire in the Pacific while the United States was striving to preserve it for our defense in the Atlantic. Despite Pearl Harbor, the greatest humiliation of American history, for which Roosevelt seems as much responsible as any one, he was right in taking on the double war: with the help of the British Commonwealth we licked Japan left-handed while our right arm was busy together with so many other arms in Europe.

Roosevelt's understanding of the vital interests of the United States in the new shift of the balance of power after the defeat of Germany and Japan was, I suggest, more questionable.

Now, after the Second World War, the geographical basis of American defense and foreign policy is shifting again with the balance of power, shifting back to the north.

Three unexpected political phenomena of victory are: (1) the rise of a new colossus, in the potential supremacy of Russia in the world; (2) the disintegration of the British Empire; (3) the demoralization, at least temporary, of the United States in the Great Let-Down of 1945-1947.

These three phenomena have perturbed international politics and the prospect of world peace almost as profoundly as the sudden birth of three new world powers at the advent of the twentieth century. None of them offsets the others: on the contrary they all supplement each other in favor of Russia. What does that bode for the balance of power and the traditional principles of American foreign policy?

There is increasing reason to believe that the leaders of Russia for reasons of domestic policy fear the *friendship* of the Western World, particularly of the United States, much more than they do its enmity. In fact, given the phenomena of victory just mentioned, and the perfect security of Russian frontiers brought about by the complete defeat of Germany and Japan, they do not fear our *enmity* at all. It is we who fear *their* enmity and want their friendship.

We have extended an eager hand of friendship to Russia to grasp, for the rights of man, for the principles of non-intervention, democracy, self-determination, and freedom; freedom of speech, freedom of religion, freedom from fear (including the fear of atomic warfare); freedom (hopefully) from want, freedom from the crushing burden of armaments, freedom of trade, freedom of the international rivers and straits; in short, the things we have traditionally stood for in the world and still stand for. We had hoped that Russia would grasp that hand, for on such a sincere handclasp is the only hope for world peace. But these are not the things that Russia stands for in the world. What she wants rather is the extension of her opposite principles, by revolution if necessary, to the rest of the world: a W.U.S.S.R., that kind of a United Nations.

What is the strategy of American security and defense now that collective security has failed and the balance of power has turned against us?

It consists, I submit, in three lines of defense: a first line, in Europe; a second line, in the New World, south; a third line in the New World, north; along the Arctic Circle, perhaps south of it. That third line may become, at any moment, the first line, in a new Pearl Harbor.

In respect to Europe, the foreign policy of the United States, since Pearl Harbor, would seem to have undergone nothing less than a diplomatic revolution, but, on second historical thought, it is still the problem of maintaining a safe balance of power. Before the Second World War it was the policy of Great Britain first, and of the British Commonwealth of Nations and the United States behind Great Britain, to rest upon a balanced Europe and a balanced Asia. Now that that balance has been lost, by defeat in victory, at Yalta, at Potsdam, and at home in London, Ottawa, and Washington, in the will and morale of our people, we have had to reform our ideas of the balance. We are making a desperate effort short of war itself to encourage not the division but the union of Western Europe in a new balance before the present precarious situation leads to war. We have sluiced money and munitions, to say the least, into Turkey and Greece to hold back the weight of totalitarian power pressing down upon the Dardanelles. If the plug is pulled, so to speak, at the Dardanelles, Soviet power will pour unobstructed through the Near East into Africa, as Japanese power did through the straits of Singapore in 1942, into Micronesia and Australasia, only more devastatingly: on the one hand into Persia and India, on the other hand flowing into Africa to occupy a springboard for a jump across to sedulously prepared ground in South America.

In addition to sustaining Greece and Turkey, the people of the United States have expended eleven billions of dollars worth of economic aid and loans for the peaceful rehabilitation of an exhausted Western Europe, and are preparing to expend twice as much more in a mammoth program, the Marshall Plan, put together by the free governments in consultation, to rehabilitate the economy of those countries 25 per cent above their prewar level as a means of firming them to resist the threat of revolution from within and aggression from without.

If I were a member of Congress, I would have voted for these aids, but with misgivings. I would vote for them because the American people, still not fully recovered from their postwar demoralization and disillusion, are not yet willing to take other measures more resolute in nature. I would have misgivings because such devices are essentially mercenary in character. If history teaches any lesson, it is that no great people has ever been able safely to rely on mercenaries, on foreign legions, on subsidies, to maintain its liberties. They may help but they cannot be a substitute for valor. The hope of the Marshall Plan is that it may transfuse enough health into Western Europe to enable those peoples to regain a consciousness of liberty, and health to defend it. But it cannot be a substitute for our own right arm and resolution. If it does not work, we shall have to fall back on our second line of defense—in South America; and, perhaps simultaneously, on our third and last line of defense in North America. Here I venture to think the line will eventually be drawn; and we had better use what little time there may be gained by the Marshall Plan, resolutely to prepare for the worst, in order that the best may be saved.

These successive lines of defense are also the lines of defense of those other countries which lie behind them, first, second, and third. People may grieve to find their countries a possible battleground between two great potentials of power; they may wish, they may strive, they doubtless will strive to be neutral. But as they do so, they cannot but realize that the battleground, if such it becomes, is one of liberty against slavery in a struggle for the rights of English freemen, for those fundamental freedoms which flowered in the recent British Century. To be neutral in any final Armageddon means surrender of those priceless human rights, of all the long constitutional log of freedom from Magna Carta to the Statute of Westminster and the Charter of the United Nations. It is inconceivable to me that Britons, Canadians, and Americans, nay before them that Swiss, Frenchmen, Belgians, or Dutchmen, should lie down without a struggle and accept the yoke of Moscow in a W.U.S.S.R. Suppose then that these three lines of defense left for Anglo-Saxon liberty did not remain? Suppose that back of the last there were left no final power for the defense of freedom? Where could free men look for life? The Iron Curtain would be an Iron Cover closed down over all the globe, and no man could tell, no man would be permitted to tell, how many centuries must pass before it could be lifted.

2

ONSET OF THE COLD WAR

America's Responsibility?

I. EDITORIAL INTRODUCTION

The United States entered the postwar era determined not to repeat the errors made following World War I. Never again would Americans withdraw from the world in a fashion that would sow the seeds of wars. Even before Pearl Harbor, President Roosevelt had conceived of a new league, with America as a central force, which would keep the peace that the old League of Nations had been unable to enforce. Together with Winston Churchill and then with other allies the United States expanded the scope of the Atlantic Charter to embrace a United Nations in which the United States would play a major role. He succeeded magnificently as he won bipartisan support for the international organization which had its base in New York.

But American acceptance of the United Nations was not immediately equated with abandonment of isolationism. Isolationist attitudes remained: demand for morality in place of the balance of power in international affairs, the reduction of American forces in Europe regardless of the political or social or economic situations of European countries, the use of the United Nations as a substitute for an American foreign policy. Indeed, the war ended with many Americans expecting the "Four Policemen" of the Security Council to maintain the peace of the world by patrolling the behavior of the smaller countries. Russian communism and American democracy seemed to share the same fundamental goals of world peace. Evil had been defeated and normality should return.

Many of America's postwar difficulties emerged from wartime behavior. The deferring of political decisions until the war was over, while failing to recognize the concurrent movement of communist ideology and Russian power into the vacuum left by Germany's defeat, inevitably strengthened the Soviet's hopes for a communized Europe. It required more than a year and a half before the United States could respond effectively to Soviet hostility. President Truman and Secretary of State Byrnes employed the weapons of American politics, which included a large dosage of moralistic rhetoric, in their futile attempts to force the Russians to abide by agreements made at Yalta and Potsdam.

Did the naiveté of American arguments combined with the widely publicized popular American demand for demobilization of the war economy induce the Russians to push their advantage in Europe? Or was the logic of communist ideology such that no matter which course the United States had taken, the Soviet Union would use the weakness of Europe as a vehicle for the expansion of communism?

The clearest call to Americans came from Winston Churchill, who in a famous speech at Westminster College as early as March, 1946, pointed to an "iron curtain" that separated freedom from slavery in Europe. Behind that curtain the Soviet Union was building power to undo the liberation so recently won in Europe, with the aid of agents preparing to subvert the democratic governments lying west of the curtain. Only the association of the United States with the United Kingdom could redress the balance of power and preserve the harassed United Nations.

Ultimately, the lines drawn by Churchill in 1946 were to be followed and expanded upon by the Truman administration, but in the spring of 1946 even the reference to the United Nations and the experience of Soviet intransigence concerning their control over Eastern Europe were insufficient incentives for Truman or his aides to accept the implications of Churchill's Fulton speech. Indeed, the President's initial reaction had been to ignore the subject. The idea of an Anglo-American alliance was still much too difficult for Americans to accept. (Selection II.)

Yet, the implications of Churchill's speech deeply affected American behavior in 1946. The Soviet Union was not honoring its promises, was not fulfilling the hopes of the United Nations, and since American blandishments met with repeated rebuffs, something more should be done. Even before the Churchill speech Senator Arthur H. Vandenberg of Michigan, the leading Republican authority on foreign policy and the nation's most famous convert from isolationism, had scored Secretary Byrnes' attempts at appeasement, and urged the country to stand up for its interests. But in the same speech Vandenberg dwelt upon the United Nations assigning it a role inconsistent with his recognition of the realities of power. (Selection III–A.)

But even the relatively mild stand of Vandenberg toward the Soviet Union at the Paris Conference of Foreign Ministers in 1946 was too much for such friends of the Soviet Union as Secretary of Commerce Henry A. Wallace, former Secretary of Agriculture and Vice President under Franklin D. Roosevelt. Wallace was appalled at the American behavior, which in its annoyance over Russian actions, had forgotten so quickly the sacrifices of Russia in World War II. Much of the animosity to the Soviet Union he attributed to the machinations of British imperialists and to former Axis elements influencing American policy. If only the Soviet Union could be made to understand that America wanted only peace and cooperation, not to rescue British Empire or to secure oil in the Near East, a genuine accommodation could be made under the aegis of the United Nations. (Selection III–B.)

The man in the middle was the Secretary of State, who was obliged to bow to administration and Republican charges of vacillation in the face of Soviet action as well as charges of provoking the Russians by his harshness. His bruised feelings were reflected in his memoirs written shortly after his resignation in 1947. Convinced that he was unfairly attacked by both the left and right, his major antagonist emerged inferentially as the President who did not give him sufficient backing. Even the resignation of Secretary Wallace did not remove his insecurity. The one major note of satisfaction was his successful service in the cause of a bipartisan policy, but it was bipartisanship without a policy during his tenure. (Selection III–C.)

The origins of the Cold War are no mystery to some critics. Professor D. F. Fleming, for example, saw in Churchill's Fulton speech the origins also of World War III, as the former British Prime Minister, no longer checked by Roosevelt or Hull, summoned the West to a crusade against world communism. The fact that Truman sat on the platform with Churchill, and applauded the speech, gave the lie to the President's disclaimers about approving it. The consequence, according to Fleming, was Russian recognition of American hostility and encouragement to those Germans who wanted to divide the conquerors. Nothing that Vandenberg or Byrnes had said before could be compared to this blow to Soviet-American relations. (Selection IV–A.)

Historian Staughton Lynd found an answer to the cold war in the attitudes and decisions of wartime diplomacy toward the future of Eastern Europe. By insisting on the doctrines of self-determination and on the abstractions of American democratic thought, American diplomats promised the peoples of Eastern Europe what the Soviet government would never have provided: namely, freedom from Russian hegemony. Beyond this, Americans convinced themselves that Stalin had accepted their view of a postwar Europe. While Britain saw the situation with realism, it lacked the strength to influence the Soviet; while the United States had the potential strength to win Russia over to some of its aspirations, its behavior, particularly with respect to withdrawal of troops, suggested that American precepts might be ignored with impunity. (Selection IV–B.)

In defense of Secretary Byrnes, biographer George Curry pointed out in 1945 that Byrnes and Truman, with full American support, did all in their power to avoid the division of the world into two armed camps. Byrnes, the able politician, did as much as any American could do, given the lack of bargaining power in his dealing with Stalin. It was Byrnes who saw the bankruptcy of accommodation, and pushed Truman to take a firm stand by the summer of 1946. The President was manifestly unfair in his criticism of Byrnes for failure or for weakness in his dealings with the Soviet Union. If he did nothing else, he exposed the purposes of Soviet policy and laid the groundwork for others to build a new policy that recognized the futility of compromise. (Selection IV–C.)

II. DOCUMENT

SELECTION II

From Winston Churchill's "Iron Curtain" speech at Fulton, Missouri on March 5, 1946 as published in *Vital Speeches of the Day*. Used with permission of the publisher. XII (March 15, 1946), pp. 331–32.

A shadow has fallen upon the scenes so lately lighted by the Allied victory. Nobody knows what Soviet Russia and its Communist international organization intends to do in the immediate future, or what are the limits, if any, to their expansive and proselytizing tendencies. I have a strong admiration and regard for the valiant Russian people and for my war-time comrade, Marshal Stalin. There is sympathy and good will in Britain—and I doubt not here also—toward the peoples of all the Russias and a resolve to persevere through many differences and rebuffs in establishing lasting friendships. We understand the Russians need to be secure on her western frontiers from all renewal of German aggression. We welcome her to her rightful place among the leading nations of the world. Above all we welcome constant, frequent and growing contacts between the Russian people and our own people on both sides of the Atlantic. It is my duty, however, to place before you certain facts about the present position in Europe—I am sure I do not wish to, but it is my duty, I feel, to present them to you.

From Stettin in the Baltic to Triest in the Adriatic, an iron curtain has descended across the Continent. Behind that line lie all the capitals of the ancient states of central and eastern Europe. Warsaw, Berlin, Prague, Vienna, Budapest, Belgrade, Bucharest and Sofia, all these famous cities and the populations around them lie in the Soviet sphere and all are subject in one form or another, not only to Soviet influence but to a very high and increasing measure of control from Moscow. Athens alone, with its immortal glories, is free to decide its future at an election under British, American and French observation. The Russian-dominated Polish government has been encouraged to make enormous and wrongful inroads upon Germany, and mass expulsions of millions of Germans on a scale grievous and undreamed of are now taking place. The Communist parties, which were very small in all these eastern states of Europe, have been raised to pre-eminence and power far beyond their numbers and are seeking everywhere to obtain totalitarian control. Police governments are prevailing in nearly every case, and so far, except in Czechoslovakia, there is no true democracy. Turkey and Persia are both profoundly alarmed and disturbed at the claims which are made upon them and at the pressure being exerted by the Moscow government. An attempt is being made by the Russians in Berlin to build up a quasi-Communist party in their zone of occupied Germany by showing special favors to groups of Left-Wing German leaders. At the end of the fighting last June, the American and British armies withdrew westward, in accordance with an earlier agreement, to a depth at some points 150 miles on a front of nearly 400 miles to allow the Russians too occupy this vast expanse of territory which the western democracies had conquered. If now the Soviet government tries, by separate action, to build up a pro-Communist Germany in their areas this will cause new serious difficulties in the British and American zones, and will give the defeated Germans the power of putting themselves up to auction between the Soviets and western democracies. Whatever conclusions may be drawn from these facts—and facts they are—this is certainly not the liberated Europe we fought to build up. Nor is it one which contains the essentials of permanent peace.

.   .   .   .

WAR NOT INEVITABLE

On the other hand I repulse the idea that a new war is inevitable; still more that it is imminent. It is because I am so sure that our fortunes are in our own hands and that we hold the power to save the future, that I feel the duty to speak out now that I have an occasion to do so. I do not believe that Soviet Russia desires war. What they desire is the fruits of war and the indefinite expansion of their power and doctrines. But what we have to consider here today while time remains, is the permanent prevention of war and the establishment of conditions of freedom and democracy as rapidly as possible in all countries. Our difficulties and dangers will not be removed by closing our eyes to them. They will not be removed by mere waiting to see what happens; nor will they be relieved by a policy of appeasement. What is needed is a settlement and the longer this is delayed the more difficult it will be and the greater our dangers will become. From what I have seen of our Russian friends and allies during the war, I am convinced that there is nothing they admire so much as strength, and there is nothing for which they have less respect than for military weakness. For that reason the old doctrine of a balance of power is unsound. We cannot afford, if we can help it, to work on narrow margins, offering temptations to a trial of strength. If the western democracies stand together in strict adherence to the principles of the United Nations Charter, their influence for furthering these principles will be immense and no one is likely to molest them. If, however, they become divided or falter in their duty, and if these all-important years are allowed to slip away, then indeed catastrophe may overwhelm us all.

III. VIEWS OF PARTICIPANTS

> *SELECTION III—A*
>
> Portions of a speech by Arthur H. Vandenberg as it appeared in the *Congressional Record*—Senate, 79th Congress, 2d sess., v. 92, February 27, 1946, pp. 1694–95. As chairman of the Senate Foreign Relations Committee in the 80th Congress, Vandenberg was the most influential Republican supporter of Truman's foreign policy. This speech showed his ambivalence toward the U.N. He wanted the United States to defend its own interests much as the U.S.S.R. had done; at the same time he called for the renunciation of 'power politics.'

Mr. President, I confess that I was proud of western democracy that night. And the life of the United Nations took on new assurance and new expectancy, in the pattern of their attitudes. On the other hand, I trust I am not unfair in also confessing that it seemed to me the distinguished Soviet delegate—one of the ablest statesmen I have ever seen in action—seemed to be less interested in helping Lebanon and Syria than he was in baiting France and Britain—less interested in peace at this point than he was in friction. I am certain it posed the same question in all our minds which I am now finding almost every day, in one form or another, in every newspaper I read —"What is Russia up to now?" It is, of course, the supreme conundrum of our time. We ask it in Manchuria. We ask it in eastern Europe and the Dardanelles. We ask it in Italy where Russia, speaking for Yugoslavia, has already initiated attention to the Polish legions. We ask it in Iran. We ask it in Tripolitania. We ask it in the Baltic and the Balkans. We ask it in Poland. We ask it in the capital of Canada. We ask it in Japan. We ask it sometimes even in connection with events in our own United States. "What is Russia up to now?" It is little wonder that we asked it at London. It is less wonder that the answer—at London and everywhere else—has a vital bearing on the destiny of the United Nations. And, Mr. President, it is a question which must be met and answered before it is too late.

It would be entirely futile to blink the fact that two great rival ideologies— democracy in the west and communism in the east—here, find themselves face to face with the desperate need for mutual understanding in finding common ground upon which to strive for peace for both. In the final analysis this means that the two greatest spokesmen for these rival ideologies— Soviet Russia and the United States—find themselves face to face with this same need for mutual understanding, both in and out of the United Nations.

Indeed, if this does not oversimplify the problem, it might even be said that the future of the United Nations itself is wrapped up in this equation.

If this be so, Mr. President, I assert my own belief that we can live together in reasonable harmony if the United States speaks as plainly upon all occasions as Russia does; if the United States just as vigorously sustains its own purposes and its ideals upon all occasions as Russia does; if we abandon the miserable fiction, often encouraged by our own fellow travelers, that we somehow jeopardize the peace if our candor is as firm as Russia's always is; and if we assume a moral leadership which we have too frequently allowed to lapse. The situation calls for patience and good will; it does not call for vacillation.

Let me make it wholly clear that I do not complain because Russia speaks —indeed, Mr. Vishinsky probably spoke in this Security Council more than the spokesmen of all the other powers combined. I am glad she speaks. She ought to speak. That is what this forum is for. But it is for others, too, Mr. President—just as Mr. Bevin used it upon more than one eloquent and courageous occasion. It is, I repeat, for others, too. All should feel an equal freedom, an equal duty, and an equivalent responsibility. The governments of the world suddenly find themselves in the presence of a new technique in international relations. It is in this forum of the United Nations where the most dominant of all debates and decisions are hereafter calculated to occur. It would be impossible to overemphasize the importance of our own role and our own performance in such epochal events, and the need for positive foreign policies as our consistent guide therein.

I confess that in this first meeting of the United Nations I missed the up-lifting and sustaining zeals for a great, crusading, moral cause which seemed to imbue the earlier Charter sessions at San Francisco. Perhaps it was because the agenda was so largely confined to the humdrum routine of organizational details. Perhaps it was the burden of anxiety over the misgivings that are inevitable in launching a peace project which never yet has succeeded in the history of civilization; or, on the other hand, perhaps it was the accumulated tiredness which dampens ardor and easily surrenders to the expedient notion that "all's well." Perhaps it was because, in the aftermath of war, we confront too many grim realities that are utterly at odds with the precepts of justice which we presume to defend. In any event, and whatever the cause, we are on notice that the peoples of the earth must never cease to evangelize this struggle for peace if it shall reach full flower.

Again, Mr. President, I sensed at London what seemed to be too great a tendency to relapse into power politics, in greater or less degree, and, as someone has said, to use the United Nations as a self-serving tribune rather than as a tribunal. It will require constant, consistent, courageous guidance to keep the United Nations within the main channel of its obligations—and here again is a clear call to America always to act in its traditional character for liberty and justice, and not to lapse, as I fear we may have done on some occasions.

Mr. President, I have endeavored faithfully to report both the credits and the debits on the United Nations' ledgers as a result of the first meeting of the General Assembly. I fear it has been illy and inadequately done. But I want to leave the positive and emphatic conclusion that the credits utterly preponderate with a heavy, a significant, a wholesome and an encouraging balance.

Those, sir, were 37 vital days in London. They are freighted with hope—solidly justified hope—in respect to collective security in this atomic age. In such an age there can be no security which is not collective. With unwavering fidelity we must carry on the great adventure. If there be any failure, let not the blood be upon our hands nor the tragedy upon our souls.

The United States has no ulterior designs against any of its neighbors anywhere on earth. We can speak with the extraordinary power inherent in this unselfishness. We need but one rule. What is right? Where is justice? There let America take her stand.

> SELECTION III–B
>
> From a speech by Henry A. Wallace, September 12, 1946, as published in *Vital Speeches of the Day*. Used with permission of the publisher. XII (October 4, 1946), pp. 739–41. Wallace was Secretary of Commerce under Truman after having served the New Deal as Secretary of Agriculture and Vice President. In this speech he revealed his sympathy for the problems of the Soviet Union and urged a detente with communism.

I plead for an America vigorously dedicated to peace—just as I plead for opportunities for the next generation throughout the world to enjoy the abundance which now, more than ever before, is the birthright of man.

To achieve lasting peace, we must study in detail just how the Russian character was formed—by invasions of Tartars, Mongols, Germans, Poles, Swedes, and French; by the czarist rule based on ignorance, fear and force; by the intervention of the British, French and Americans in Russian affairs from 1919 to 1921; by the geography of the huge Russian land mass situated strategically between Europe and Asia; and by the vitality derived from the rich Russian soil and the strenuous Russian climate. Add to all this the tremendous emotional power which Marxism and Leninism gives to the Russian leaders—and then we can realize that we are reckoning with a force which cannot be handled successfully by a "Get tough with Russia" policy. "Getting tough" never brought anything real and lasting—whether for schoolyard bullies or businessmen or world powers. The tougher we get, the tougher the Russians will get.

Throughout the world there are numerous reactionary elements which had hoped for Axis victory—and now profess great friendship for the United States. Yet, these enemies of yesterday and false friends of today continually try to provoke war between the United States and Russia. They have no real love of the United States. They only long for the day when the United States and Russia will destroy each other.

We must not let our Russian policy be guided or influenced by those inside or outside the United States who want war with Russia. This does not mean appeasement.

We most earnestly want peace with Russia—but we want to be met half way. We want cooperation. And I believe that we can get cooperation once Russia understands that our primary objective is neither saving the British Empire nor purchasing oil in the Near East with the lives of American soldiers. We cannot allow national oil rivalries to force us into war. All of the nations producing oil, whether inside or outside of their own boundaries, must fulfill the provisions of the United Nations Charter and encourage the development of world petroleum reserves so as to make the maximum amount of oil available to all nations of the world on an equitable peaceful basis—and not on the basis of fighting the next war.

For her part, Russia can retain our respect by cooperating with the United Nations in a spirit of openminded and flexible give-and-take.

The real peace treaty we now need is between the United States and Russia. On our part, we should recognize that we have no more business in the *political* affairs of Eastern Europe than Russia has in the *political* affairs of Latin America, Western Europe and the United States. We may not like what Russia does in Eastern Europe. Her type of land reform, industrial expropriation, and suppression of basic liberties offends the great majority of the people of the United States. But whether we like it or not the Russians will try to socialize their sphere of influence just as we try to democratize our sphere of influence. This applies also to Germany and Japan. We are striving to democratize Japan and our area of control in Germany, while Russia strives to socialize eastern Germany.

In the United States an informed public opinion will be all-powerful. Our people are peace-minded. But they often express themselves too late—for events today move much faster than public opinion. The people here, as everywhere in the world, must be convinced that another war is not inevitable. And through mass meetings such as this, and through persistent pamphleteering, the people can be organized for peace—even though a large segment of our press is propagandizing our people for war in the hope of scaring Russia. And we who look on this war-with-Russia talk as criminal foolishness must carry our message direct to the people—even though we may be called communists because we dare to speak out.

I believe that peace—the kind of peace I have outlined tonight—is the basic issue, both in the Congressional campaign this fall and right on through the Presidential election in 1948. How we meet this issue will determine whether we live not in "one world" or "two worlds"—but whether we live at all.

SELECTION III–C

From pp. 230–40, 242–43 *Speaking Frankly* by James F. Byrnes. Copyright © 1947 by Donald S. Russell, Trustee. Reprinted by permission of Harper & Row, Publishers. Byrnes was Secretary of State in 1946 after serving as senator from South Carolina, as Supreme Court Justice and "assistant president" to FDR. Caught between Vandenberg and Wallace, he provided a vigorous apologia immediately upon his retirement.

My experience with the Moscow agreements demonstrated that in the pursuit of a truly national foreign policy one has to be prepared for criticism from both the right and the left. Had these agreements been as favorable to the Soviet Union as some critics have charged, the Soviets would not have violated them. And the fact that ever since then we have been protesting against these violations indicates that they were in the best interests of the liberated states.

However, the person or persons inspiring the stories of dissension between the President and myself continued their efforts. In at least one press conference the President denied such dissension, but the stories persisted. A man who holds public office learns to disregard misrepresentations, but I admit these untrue stories did not make life any easier for me in the strenuous days of early 1946.

My hope for united support of our foreign policies received a serious setback when, on September 12, 1946, while I was in Paris, Secretary of Commerce Henry A. Wallace made a speech at Madison Square Garden contending that the policy which had been approved by the President, and carried out by me, was too harsh to the Soviet Union and that a more conciliatory approach to them was necessary. I was not greatly surprised by the Secretary's action. Previously, he had made a statement to the New York *Times* referring to our negotiations with Iceland for the use of the airfield we had built there. His statement was effectively used by the Communists in Iceland and it had obstructed the efforts of the State Department to secure an agreement important to the defense of this hemisphere.

In Paris, the importance of Mr. Wallace's Madison Square Garden speech was magnified in the minds of the representatives of foreign governments by newspaper reports quoting President Truman as saying at a press conference that he approved the Wallace speech in its entirety. This report stimulated widespread discussion among the governmental representatives attending the peace conference; it inspired inquiries to our representatives in various capitals. Foreign Ministers wondered whether in my various public statements I had correctly presented American policy.

Senator Vandenberg issued a statement saying that he wanted to cooperate with the administration but he could co-operate with only one Secretary of State at a time.

Senator Connally declared that he supported the policy we had announced and had been following.

I concluded that I should not make a public statement; that the matter called for correction by the President.

Of course, the position of our delegation was a very unhappy one. So far as possible, I tried to avoid delegates to the conference or the other Foreign Ministers because I wanted to avoid answering questions about whether the policy of our government had changed. Our difficulties were increased rather than lessened when Mr. Wallace announced on the White House steps that he and the President had agreed that the Secretary of Commerce would make no more speeches until after the peace conference. To the delegates in Paris, this implied that the President had not objected to a later renewal of his attacks on our foreign policy.

While I had no direct communication with the White House, I learned of developments from the press and from several messages sent to me by Assistant Secretary of State Donald Russell. As a result, on September 18, I sent the President a message, reminding him that, on the advice of a physician, I had given him my resignation in April. By agreement, my resignation would take effect upon the completion of the treaties. My message further stated:

> If it is not possible for you, for any reason, to keep Mr. Wallace, as a member of your Cabinet, from speaking on foreign affairs, it would be a grave mistake from every point of view for me to continue in office, even temporarily. Therefore, if it is not completely clear in your own mind that Mr. Wallace should be asked to refrain from criticizing the foreign policy of the United States while he is a member of your Cabinet, I must ask you to accept my resignation immediately. At this critical time, whoever is Secretary of State must be known to have the undivided support of your administration and, so far as possible, of the Congress.

> I shall, of course, remain here until my successor arrives. In case you are not ready to make that appointment promptly, you can, of course, appoint someone other than the Secretary of State to head the United States delegation at the Peace Conference.

.   .   .   .

It is not proper for me to quote the President's statements. But I think it is proper to say that, as a result of the conversation, I knew he did not intend to change his policies or leave any doubt about his views. He did not tell me what action he would take. However, the following day the President settled the matter in a manner satisfactory, I hope, to the overwhelming majority of the people of the United States.

With the resignation of Secretary Wallace, confidence in the American policy was restored. Senators Connally and Vandenberg continued to serve in support of our foreign policy with unswerving loyalty. The Wallace incident took place during a national campaign which resulted in the shifting of the majority rule in Congress from the Democrats to the Republicans. Senator Connally met opposition in his primary election, but would not abandon his work in Paris where he was helping his country and come home to help himself. Senator Vandenberg, who also was a candidate for re-election, not only took no part in the campaign but was barely able to get back to Michigan to vote; he urged other Republicans to support the bi-partisan foreign policy.

The results of our efforts to maintain a bipartisan foreign policy were clearly indicated by the overwhelming approval of the Senate in its vote on June 5, 1947, ratifying the five treaties thus far concluded. When I was informed of the vote, I could not help but recall again the unhappy months after World War I when President Wilson struggled with a disgruntled and determined Senate that finally defeated his efforts for peace. And I renewed my hope that never again would our policy makers repeat President Wilson's mistake; that hereafter the responsible leaders of both parties would be kept informed of our policies from the beginning of their formulation to their ultimate conclusion.

IV. VIEWS OF OBSERVERS

> SELECTION IV–A
>
> From D. F. Fleming, *The Cold War and Its Origins, 1917–1960* (2 volumes, New York, 1961), I, pp. 348–51. Copyright © 1961. Reprinted by permission of Doubleday & Co., Inc. Fleming, professor emeritus of political science at Vanderbilt University, was a vigorous dissenter to Truman's foreign policies.

Stalin's February Address. On February 9, 1946, Premier Stalin made a speech which stirred fears in some quarters. He opened with the Marxist explanation of world wars, monopoly capitalism fighting for markets and raw materials. He did distinguish sharply between the two world wars, the latter having become an anti-fascist people's war, during which the Soviet social system had shown itself the best and strongest. It had survived because the Communist Party had reversed the usual development and built heavy industries first. Now the fundamental task was to restore the devastated areas, to increase goods for mass consumption, to surpass the world in scientific achievements and to organize "a new mighty upsurge of national economy." Three or four five-year plans might be necessary to raise production to, among other things, 60,000,000 tons of steel annually.

This figure was at once said to be ominous, since it was coupled with

Stalin's warm praise of the Red Army, but any belligerent intent in his speech had to be deduced by implication and by somewhat strained interpretation.

Preliminary Conference. The same could hardly be said of Winston Churchill's famous speech at Westminster College, Fulton, Missouri—in President Truman's home state—on March 5, 1946. During several weeks spent in Florida he carefully matured his blast, after flying to Washington on February 10 for a conference with President Truman which was reported to concern his speech. That the content of the speech was discussed hardly admits of doubt, since it was to be a world-shaking event.

As the momentous day approached, Churchill returned from Florida to Washington and the President journeyed with him to Fulton to present him to his audience and to bless the occasion. As Churchill said in opening his speech: "The President has travelled a thousand miles to dignify and magnify our meeting here today."

The Address. The urgency of the occasion was soon evident. In the grand prose cadences which had thrilled so many millions of Americans during the war, Churchill declared that "Opportunity is here now, clear and shining, for both our countries. To reject it or ignore it or fritter it away will bring upon us all the long reproaches of the aftertime." Constancy of mind was essential and persistency of purpose.

What for? "Our over-all strategic concept" was to protect the myriad cottages or apartment homes of the wage earners "from the two gaunt marauders—war and tyranny." The Missouri folk had not been conscious that these two monsters were about to attack them until Churchill described "the frightful disturbance in which the ordinary family is plunged when the curse of war swoops down upon the bread-winner and those for whom he works and contrives."

It was evident that the situation was serious, for Churchill went on to urge that the UN "must immediately begin to be equipped with an international armed force" and a certain number of air squadrons. He asserted that it would be "criminal madness" to cast the atomic bomb adrift "in this still agitated and ununited world." No one would be able to sleep so soundly if some Communist, or Neo-Fascist state had invented the bomb. God had willed that this should not be.

Then he came to the second danger which threatened "the cottage home," tyranny, the "police governments" of Eastern Europe. It was "not our duty at this time, when difficulties are so numerous, to interfere forcibly in the internal affairs of countries whom we have not conquered in war," but we must "never cease to proclaim in fearless tones the great principles of freedom. . . ."

The inference was clear that we could not go to war to drive the Communists out of Eastern Europe *at this time*, but we must keep the matter in mind and we must keep on insisting that "the people of any country have the right and should have the power" to exercise all the rights of Englishmen and to enjoy all of the governmental processes and freedoms of the Anglo-Saxon world, which Churchill enumerated in full.

Then "at this sad and breathless moment" he came to "the crux of what I have travelled here to say"—no prevention of war or successful UN without an alliance of the English-speaking peoples, continuance of the Joint Chiefs of Staff, joint use of all naval and air force bases all over the world, doubling our mobility.

Otherwise, "The Dark Ages may return, the Stone Age." "Beware, I say: Time may be short. Do not let us take the course of letting events drift along until it is too late." A shadow had fallen. Nobody knew "what Soviet Russia and its Communist international organization intends to do in the future, or what are the limits if any to their expansive and proselytizing tendencies." From Stettin to Trieste there was "an iron curtain." He saw enormous and wrongful inroads into Germany.

Turkey and Persia were profoundly alarmed. And in front of the iron curtain "Communist Fifth Columns" were everywhere, "a growing challenge and peril to civilization." In the Far East there was anxiety, especially in Manchuria.

Having built up this picture of a terrible juggernaut operating all over the world which had to be tamed, Churchill then repulsed "the idea that a new war is inevitable, still more that it is imminent." He did not believe that Russia desired war, only "the fruits of war and the indefinite expansion of their power and doctrines." Therefore "while time remains" he demanded the "establishment of conditions of freedom and democracy as rapidly as possible in all countries." Since nothing except overwhelming force could rapidly eliminate communism from East Europe and Russia herself, he did not explain how this was to be done.

In the meantime, what was needed was a "settlement and the longer that is delayed, the more difficult it will be and the greater our dangers will become" (i.e. our atomic monopoly would disappear). Therefore no balance of power, no working "on narrow margins," no "quivering precarious balance of power to offer its temptation to ambition or adventure." What was needed was a great preponderance of power against Russia.

Then he drew on the great prestige which he had won before 1939. The last time he "saw it all coming and cried aloud," but "no one paid any attention." Surely we "must not let that happen again." There must be "a good understanding," that is, a showdown, with Russia "now, in 1946."

The old warrior and world strategist was off again, and with a terrifying start. He had waged war on the Reds in Russia to the limit of British tolerance during 1919 and 1920. Then throughout the twenties he had preached the menace of the Red revolution, never losing an opportunity to refer to the Bolshevik leaders "as murderers and ministers of hell."

Forced to welcome their aid in 1941 to save Britain, he had incessantly attempted the impossible feat of using them to beat Germany while denying them the fruits of victory. Now he would mobilize the might of the United States to achieve what he had never been able to do before.

A Master Stroke. If, too, there is a Third World War, Churchill's Missouri speech will be the primary document in explaining its origins. His was the first full-length picture of a Red Russia out to conquer the world. Backed by the immense authority of his war record, and by the charm of his great personality, it pre-conditioned many millions of listeners for a giant new *cordon sanitaire* around Russia, for a developing world crusade to smash world communism in the name of Anglo-Saxon democracy. In print Churchill's battle cry became the bible of every warmonger in the world. It said all they had wanted to say and with his great name behind it, it could be used endlessly with great effect.

At Fulton, Churchill also prevailed over Roosevelt and Hull, the great American leaders who had checkmated him in all the later stages of the war, preventing him from creating a gulf between East and West. At Fulton he did it. Had Roosevelt lived, Churchill would never have dared to propose that he come to the United States and issue a call for a world alliance to encircle the Soviet Union and establish Western democracy in Eurasia. If he had ventured to make such a speech in the United States he would have been sharply disavowed. But with Roosevelt dead he was able not only to do that, but to carry President Truman along in his baggage.

Whether the idea of the speech originated with Churchill or Truman is not yet known. In the light of Truman's strongly hardened determination to quit "babying" the Soviets, he was probably the originator. It seems a little odd that in his *Memoirs* there is only one casual reference to an event of such outstanding importance, one of the chief landmarks of the Cold War.

SELECTION IV–B

An excerpt from Staughton Lynd, "How the Cold War Began," Commentary, XXXX (November, 1960), pp. 386–89. Reprinted from Commentary, by permission; copyright © 1960 by the American Jewish
Committee. Lynd, an assistant professor of history at Yale University, is a
leader in the "new left" movement of the 1960's.

In the absence of firm tripartite agreements, particularly about Poland, the British government, hitherto the advocate of realistic acceptance of a Soviet sphere of influence in Eastern Europe, at war's end found itself imploring American military assistance to contain the expansion of Soviet power. The upshot was as paradoxical as it was tragic. A sequence of events familiar in Anglo-American diplomatic history then took place. As in the formulation of the Monroe Doctrine, as in the formulation of the Open Door policy, the British government suggested to America a joint declaration of policy for reasons altogether in the realm of *Realpolitik*. As in the two preceding instances, so in 1945–47 the United States government proclaimed the policy as its own and lent it the panoply of a moral crusade. Ten years later, in consequence, England was in the position of trying to restrain the partner which but yesterday it had to prod.

Looking back, it is still difficult to assign responsibility with any sureness for this critical turn of events. America, which realized the importance of creating the United Nations before the bonds of wartime partnership were relaxed, failed to see the comparable importance of more humble agreements about governments and frontiers, and this failure complicated the already inherent difficulty where two men so different in their points of view as Churchill and Stalin had to reach firm agreements. A number of prominent Americans, including Roosevelt and Hopkins, were deeply impressed by England's determination to retain its empire: this made them slow to accept Churchill's growing fear of Russian expansion, just as it blinded them to the truth that, in actual hard fact, America had always depended on the English empire to shield it from potential aggressors. Had the Soviet leaders been less suspicious and dogmatic than they were, they might well have been confused in responding to an England which did not have the strength to enforce its realism, and an America which did not seem to realize that idealism must be supported by something more than documents.

For the Soviets, such indecision on the part of the West must have encouraged the hope, championed by Trotsky after World War I, of carrying revolution westward on the bayonets of the Red Army. Advocates of the Russian interpretation of these events have quoted the Forrestal diaries to show that military leaders in the West did not really fear Soviet attack: but these quotations begin no earlier than 1946, when the readiness to mobilize military force to deter such attack had already shown itself. Feis and Mc-Neill reiterate that we possess very little material with which to interpret Soviet intentions in the spring of 1945. But there seems no good reason to doubt that the Russians were ready to carry their influence as far westward as they could safely go without risking the danger of war.

The inertia acquired by supposedly temporary military arrangements, their tendency then to turn into a political status quo unless deflected by new agreements for which, after Yalta, the Big Three alliance suddenly seemed no longer capable, posed for the West a genuinely "agonizing reappraisal." It seemed that to keep on a friendly footing with Russia it was necessary to betray (as it appeared to the West) the Polish people on whose behalf England had gone to war. Roosevelt and Truman were not as different in their reactions to this problem as extremists of both the right and the left would have one think: the President who sent the two most pro-Soviet men in American governmental circles (Davies and Hopkins) as his first envoys to Churchill and Stalin cannot have been, initially, bitterly anti-Soviet.

The course ultimately adopted was, of course, containment, and its error lay, surely, in making such a "posture" the *whole* of one's foreign policy. In itself, containment was simply the normal practice of diplomacy which sought to maintain a balance of power, and supported this effort with the threat of force; England has certainly never practiced anything else, and when the United States has tried to follow another course—as between 1801 and 1812 in our dealings with England and France—it has altogether failed. Containment was startling only in contrast with the Wilsonian idealism, today almost hard to remember, which preceded it.

What was novel and alarming was the exaltation of containment from one of many normal means to the entire substance of a policy. There was nothing in the idea of containment itself which would have precluded, for example, long-term credits for postwar reconstruction to the Soviet Union. Even if this had seemed impossible for domestic political reasons, such loans might have been offered to Eastern Europe. When in the Marshall Plan proposals the offer was finally made, the international atmosphere had become embittered, Communist parties had strengthened their hold throughout Eastern Europe, and it was too late. In a sense, Eastern Europe was the first underdeveloped area where we failed.

In its sudden, totalistic shift for a reliance on ideals alone to a reliance only on the threat of war, American policy after 1945 exhibited a characteristic tendency to go from one-sided solution to its opposite, equally one-sided. The Darlan and Badoglio deals, the unconditional surrender formula, the dropping of the atom bomb, also suggest an extremism of expendiency and violence which all too frequently was the sequel to the benevolent extremism of America's first intentions.

.   .   .   .

If then, we return to the question, Why did the cold war start? the most fundamental answer might be: Because for the first time the challenge of authoritarian socialism to democratic capitalism was backed by sufficient power to be an ever-present political and military threat. It is a far more complicated and potent challenge than that represented by Germany in 1914 or Japan in 1941; it is the kind of challenge associated with the break-up of empires and the transformation of whole societies rather than with the ordinary jostling of diplomatic intercourse. In this sense, those who now speak of negotiation and disarmament as simple nostrums are being superficial, and those who invoke the American way of life are more nearly correct.

Yet containment, while recognizing the seriousness of the problem, would appear to be an inadequate response. Even before the possession of atomic weapons by both sides made reliance on military reprisal archaic, containment was a one-sidedly negative policy which could lead only to slow defeat, and, by way of the frustration and fear thereby engendered, to war. It involved and still involves an identification of the United States with governments whose only qualification for our friendship is their anti-Communism, and which in every other respect go against rather than with the grain of worldwide aspiration. Only a narrow and superficial realism can look to such alliances for strength in the long run.

SELECTION IV–C

From George Curry's "James Francis Byrnes," in *The American Secretaries of State and Their Diplomacy*, Robert H. Ferrell and Samuel F. Bemis, eds., XIV (New York, 1965), pp. 305–17. Copyright © 1965 by Cooper Square Publishers, Inc. Reprinted by permission. Curry is professor of history at the University of South Carolina and the author of a biography of Byrnes.

What then, one might ask in conclusion, was Byrnes' contribution as Secretary of State? Judgment of his effectiveness centers on his efforts to help his country fill the new role in international affairs which the Truman Administration inherited and on his endeavors to conclude treaties of peace, an overwhelming preoccupation of his eighteen months of service. In historical perspective his great opportunity—for thus would someone as energetically ambitious as he view his appointment—came in the concluding phase of the most destructive and politically unsettling of world conflicts which ended the traditional power structure of both Europe and Asia. It sprang from the advent of power of a Chief Executive who was almost devoid of experience in foreign affairs. By contrast Roosevelt had not only overshadowed his Secretaries of State but, as Byrnes well knew, regularly used other intermediaries to pursue his personal diplomacy. With Churchill, Roosevelt had nurtured the "strange alliance" between Stalin's Russia and the Western democracies, a collaboration which however difficult had made possible the destruction of the Axis powers and which, the two leaders felt, should continue in the uncertain postwar world. This alliance was already faltering when Roosevelt's death and Churchill's forced retirement, added to the new factor of an atomic weapon, further complicated the uneasy relationship between East and West.

Byrnes hoped to sustain and sometimes to guide the new President as the latter assumed his heavy burdens. A proven talent for personal contact, private negotiation and practical compromise, together with natural optimism, encouraged him to believe that sensible accommodation could be made between the wartime partners and he looked forward to achieving a peace settlement which would crown his career. Unwilling to be a mouthpiece or, as he would say, a "messenger boy," Secretary Byrnes expected to control his own Department and to be in fact the President's principal aide in the making and execution of foreign policy. This view is revealed in a letter of April, 1946, to Bernard Baruch when the "adviser to Presidents" was concerned as to what personal initiative he would retain as U.S. representative to the United Nations Atomic Energy Commission. Byrnes reminded Baruch that "under the law the President determines the policy and transmits such policy through me. . . . You will be acting toward me just as I act toward the President. I know what his basic policies are. Knowing that, I do not hesitate to take positions as to matters which could not be anticipated. If they are matters of great importance I try to communicate with him. We have never had any difference in views that was not quickly reconciled. I am sure that will be your experience. In short, Byrnes felt that he should function creatively under the President and, if events demanded, exercise initiative, subject to final approval. Also he thought that presidential aims and policies, which he would largely help determine, would seldom differ markedly from his own.

What were these aims and policies as Byrnes began his service? Baldly stated, they were to restore peace and prosperity to the world as quickly as possible along the lines laid down by President Roosevelt. This goal, felt Byrnes and his advisers, could best be pursued by the rapid conclusion of peace treaties with the lesser enemy states, the disarmament and control of Germany and Japan prior to the formation of free governments therein, and promotion of an effective United Nations organization. These policies sought to preserve American interests: for example, the restored countries of Europe would be open to U.S. political and economic influences; and the occupation of Japan, in whose defeat the United States was primarily involved, would be almost exclusively an American affair. The approach was basically a liberal one, much in the Wilsonian tradition, for the United States as the most powerful member of the victorious coalition had fewer territorial ambitions and sought less in reparations than its associates in peacemaking. Byrnes also wanted to promote open agreements in which a large number of states would participate. Moreover, the American view in July, 1945, and long afterwards was that the United States, while fulfilling its occupation duties and supporting the United Nations, would largely disband its tremendous military machine.

Years later memoir writers, affected by the atmosphere of the Cold War, took pains to emphasize the negative side of U.S.-Russian relations during their miliary alliance and thereafter. In July, 1945, neither Truman nor Byrnes believed that the end of the great conflict should be followed by a massive confrontation between the Soviets and the West, with a prospect of further hostilities over the ravaged lands of Europe and Asia. In this they were fully supported by the American people. In fact, during Byrnes' secretaryship and during that of his successor hope lingered that the division of the world into two enemy camps could be avoided and therefore every effort should be made to convince the Russians of the good will of those who did not share their economic and political views.

.   .   .   .

This assessment closes with a final word on the Byrnes-Truman relationship. Since the break in their friendship, dating from the period after Byrnes' retirement, it has often been assumed that there was disharmony between them from the outset and that they never worked well together. This seems to be a distortion of the facts which unfortunately the general tone of the Truman memoirs encouraged. From the first President Truman expected to use Byrnes' alert mind as a catalyst to be applied to many of the different situations which confronted him. Circumstances, however, often took Byrnes away from Washington and emphasized his natural tendency to act independently. Understandably, during much of his early period as President, Truman's touch was frequently unsure; aware that the country required leadership he was anxious to appear no less decisive than his great predecessor and he sometimes acted on impulse. This made for some uncertainty in policy which is not reflected in his memoirs. It also left the President open to the influences of those around him who urged, doubtless with sincere intentions, that he make himself master in his own house. Since the period was one of new situations and difficult adjustments, many wished to advise the President on foreign affairs. This advice sometimes took the form of warning the President that his Secretary of State was too "soft" or too "hard," or what became worse in Mr. Truman's eyes, too "independent." One interpretation of the memorandum-letter addressed to Byrnes in January, 1946, is that the Chief Executive was deeply frustrated by the overwhelming problems he faced, that he was listening to the troublemakers and that he was resorting to a paper protest to relieve his feelings. If Byrnes was as difficult a subordinate as was claimed, he was cured very rapidly of his fault, for the President writes in his memoirs that on the strength of one conversation with his Secretary of State he had no further trouble whatsoever over the problem of failure to keep him informed. The Truman version of the January, 1946, incident cannot be accepted without serious qualification, nor in justice to Byrnes can it be held that the President's phrase "I'm tired of babying the Soviets" really constituted at the time a new departure in U.S. policy.

As to the circumstances of Byrnes' resignation, it is sometimes implied that he was forced out by President Truman and that his ill health was more diplomatic than real. The facts are that in mid-April, 1946, the Secretary genuinely feared that he had developed cardiac weakness, a condition from which his sister was suffering acutely at the time. Intent on finishing the minor treaties he decided to resign after their completion. With undue optimism it was thought they could be negotiated by July; work on them was to continue until the year's end. Further medical examination showed the Secretary's condition was not grave, though he was suffering from a distressing stomach complaint, which tension aggravated. Through General Eisenhower, Truman had warned General Marshall early in May that he was Secretary-designate. When it appeared that Byrnes would carry on beyond the July deadline, the President decided to keep this transaction confidential. Meanwhile he remained in touch with Marshall over developments in China, using Dean Acheson as intermediary. Acheson, Byrnes' trusted deputy, had been told by the latter of his intention to resign for health reasons. The Secretary apparently felt his replacement would not be easy and would be at the President's leisure. With Byrnes absent in Paris, preoccupied with the peach conference, Acheson heard from Truman that Marshall was virtually already appointed. Acheson was not happy to be privy to a secret known only to the two generals and to the Chief Executive. As he wrote of his position, "Complications in relationships, dimly foreseen in November [1945, when he became Marshall's link with the White House], were now becoming all too apparent. They did not grow less in the months preceding the change in Secretaries in January, 1947.

Friends of Byrnes believe that he was deeply hurt when he finally learned of the early commitment to Marshall though he admired the latter and endorsed his appointment. They also hold that Byrnes, aware of his detractors around the President, was glad to be rid of the complications as well as the strains of office. Doubtless Byrnes' self-assurance bothered the President at times just as his tendency to operate rather independently disturbed some departmental professionals and at least one prominent Senator. But on the whole the Truman-Byrnes relationship was easier during Byrnes' term of office than is generally supposed, and their parting was cordial. Their "moment of truth" came perhaps during the Wallace episode of September, 1946 —their teletype conversation at the time, which was not for public consumption, being significant. "You have done an excellent job. Nobody appreciates it more than I do and I shall continue to support you with everything I have," signalled Truman. To which Byrnes answered, "You certainly have done it up to this time and your statement makes me feel good." This exchange more truly reflects the spirit of their collaboration than the acidity of the Truman memoirs: otherwise how can the President's repeated expressions of confidence in Byrnes during the latter's period in office be explained except as examples of gross insincerity?

Leaving office Secretary Byrnes ruefully remarked, "Any man who would want to be Secretary of State would go to hell for pleasure." High hopes of 1945 had not been realized, for his central task, that of peacemaking, had proved slow, strenuous, frustrating and incomplete. There had been irritating complications in his relationship with President Truman, who had also been subjected to the pressures of the hour. Repeated absences from Washington had weakened the personal control he liked to exercise and accounted for much unfinished business. But, as has been seen, there had been real accomplishments. A start had been made on State Department reorganization, with the United Nations, on control of the atom, while Japan and that part of Europe not under Soviet arms had been saved. Successful cooperation with Vandenberg had encouraged bipartisanship in a period of difficult readjustment. If in the months of strain he had not found a basis of agreement with Stalin, Byrnes in his diplomacy had exposed the nature and purpose of

Soviet policy. The judgment of his friend, the soldier-diplomat Lucius D. Clay, bears repeating: "He had given from his high intelligence and his broad experience of government his utmost effort to allay Soviet suspicions and to create a world of peace by agreement. When he found this impossible he had made clear our firm intent to yield no further in our views in the hope of compromise." Byrnes' short period of service charted the way to the future, and again in his remarkable career he had, in President Truman's friendly parting words of January, 1947, "earned the thanks of the Nation."

3

TRUMAN DOCTRINE AND

MARSHALL PLAN

The Question of Compatibility

I. EDITORIAL INTRODUCTION

Action rather than words challenging the Soviet Union's vision of the world was the United States response to communism early in 1947. All through the previous year the administration had contested control over areas occupied by the Soviet Union in the course of World War II. Suddenly, America was faced with the fact of communist expansionism beyond these areas, most notably in Greece and Turkey. It was given dramatic emphasis by Great Britain's announcement in February that its strength was insufficient to help anticommunist forces in the eastern Mediterranean. Britain appealed to the United States to assume the major burden.

President Truman's response was the Truman Doctrine in which the President announced to the Congress that the very existence of both Greece and Turkey was threatened by communist activities. Britain's limited resources were overburdened; the United Nations was not in a position to give the necessary assistance. Only the United States could provide the means of saving Greece and Turkey from the same kind of tyranny that had overtaken the countries of Eastern Europe. Having been given evidence of the will of these countries to maintain freedom, Truman asked for military and economic aid to support the Greek and Turkish efforts to preserve their independence. The purpose, however, was not only to help deserving peoples defend themselves, but also to recognize "that totalitarian regimes imposed upon free peoples, by direct or indirect aggression, undermine the foundations of international peace and hence the security of the United States." (Selection II–A.)

Here at last was action, not merely words, since the United States was making a commitment not anticipated in 1945 in the organization of the United Nations or during the rapid national demobilization of 1946. Within a few months time, the Truman Doctrine was followed by the Marshall Plan, conceived by such able State Department officials as Dean Acheson and William Clayton, and popularized by Secretary of State Marshall at the Harvard commencement exercises of June 5, 1947. The Marshall Plan, according to the administration, was an extension of the purposes of the Truman Doctrine. If the United States was to support effectively the military efforts of other European nations as it had rallied to Greece and Turkey in the Truman Doctrine, it was necessary that the economic base of the beneficiary be strong enough to use the military assistance. In this sense the Marshall Plan represented a significant underpining of the Truman Doctrine. Where the latter applied only to two countries, the former served a continent; where the former emphasized military protection, the latter underscored economic reconstruction. Even in the Truman Doctrine the President had pointed out that "the seeds of totalitarian regimes are nurtured by misery and want." This view was expanded in the Marshall Plan into an offer of large scale assistance to restore Europe to its former prosperity. Europe was facing bankruptcy, and only the United States could provide the means for recovery. In essence, if the chaos of Greece and Turkey was not to be repeated in France or in Italy, where already large communist parties were flourishing, the United States must help Europeans create economic conditions which would permit them to cope with the promises of communism. (Selection II–B.)

The complementary features of the Truman Doctrine and the Marshall Plan were always apparent. Both attempted to help Europeans organize themselves against communist pressures.

But to many critics it was also apparent that there were differences between the two programs which appeared to be irreconcilable. The suddenness of the Truman message to the Congress suggested almost a reflex action, a policy based on the exigency of the moment, rather than a carefully worked out plan within the larger frame of foreign policy. Aid to Greece and Turkey represented the plugging of a leak in a corner of Europe, primarily a military operation despite Truman's reference to economic rehabilitation. Basically, the Truman Doctrine was a major strike in the cold war.

The Marshall Plan, on the other hand, could be interpreted as a more mature expression of the assistance America gave Europe after World War I, but without the taint of a loan. The United States recognized in this program that its own welfare, economic and otherwise, depended on the restoration of Europe. Furthermore, it was a program that was dependent on evidences of Europe's involvement in its own recovery, and on the creation of a European institution to receive the assistance and guarantee its proper use. And in encompassing all of Europe, including communist Europe, it was designed to reduce the tensions of the cold war. Therefore, critics of administration policy deplored the increasing ties after 1947 between economic and military recovery, between a European community of cooperation and a defense alliance with the United States.

Most spokesmen for the administration could see no such conflict. Both the Truman Doctrine and the Marshall Plan fitted easily into the program of containment identified by George Kennan in a seminal article written anonymously for *Foreign Affairs* in 1947. Kennan at this time was chairman of the Policy Planning Committee of the Department of State and had been expounding some of the views expressed in his articles months earlier. Kennan had made clear that the goals of Soviet communism and American democracy could not be reconciled at that moment. Soviet hostility and Soviet expansionism were a product of ideology and Russian history, and must be accepted as facts of international life. The United States must show its ability to contain this force with patience and with vigor until the dynamism of communism had been drained. Given an America willing to develop a coherent policy toward the Soviet Union, the West could expect the strains and tensions and contradiction within an authoritarian society to force ultimately a revision of its current revolutionary goals. (Selection III–A.)

In opposing this reasoning, Henry Wallace, Presidential candidate of the liberal internationalist Progressive Party, spoke frequently and eloquently. Arraigning the Truman doctrine as nothing more than cynical support of reactionary militarists, he professed initial optimism about the Marshall Plan. As the European Recovery Program developed, however, it appeared as another instrument in the cold war as self-defeating as the Truman Doctrine. His recommendation was to employ the United Nations as a vehicle for economic aid to Europe with a Reconstruction Fund modeled after UNRRA. (Selection III–B.)

Senator Kenneth Wherry of Nebraska, a conservative isolationist spokesman of the Republican Party, was equally disturbed about the meaning of the Truman Doctrine. He was worried about two vital features of the Doctrine. The first was the monetary drain involved in aiding the two countries, since he saw no assurance that such aid as planned would serve its purpose. And if it did not, what recourse would the United States have then? Would America be bound to enter a war against Russia in Greece, Turkey or elsewhere to contain communism? His answer made clear his opinion that America's strength would be spread too thin to serve either herself or the client country (Selection III–C.)

Scholars and pundits from the beginnings of the containment policy saw something new in American foreign policy. To such a distinguished isolationist as Edwin Borchard of the Yale Law School, both the Truman Doctrine and the Marshall Plan were dismal signs of the times. The Truman Doctrine, which he noted had been compared with the Monroe Doctrine, was precisely the kind of commitment the Founding Fathers would never have made: an open-ended promise to intervene in European feuds. As for the Marshall Plan, he accepted the claim that its intentions were economic and not political, as in the case of the Truman Doctrine, but the Marshall Plan was equally subversive of United States interests. If the money was not utterly wasted, its effect would be to finance the development of state socialism in the name of recovery. Or it could be converted into a military measure that would make a mockery of "recovery." (Selection IV–A.)

Walter Lippmann, the most prestigious of American journalists, based his objections on what he felt to be fundamental weakness in the containment philosophy. Devoting a book challenging Kennan's views as expressed in the *Foreign Affairs* article, Lippmann condemned Kennan for basing his policy on unproven assumptions. Was Soviet power inherently weak and impermanent, and was the containment of its power at every point the way of exposing this weakness? Rejecting the Truman Doctrine, Lippmann saw hope in the Marshall Plan which unlike the former was essentially a European plan enabling Europe to save itself. It would be tragic in his opinion if the Marshall proposals were converted to the purposes of the Truman Doctrine (Selection IV–B.)

If there was a question about the connection between the two programs on the part of the administration, Joseph Jones, one of the draftsmen of the Truman Doctrine and the Marshall Plan, clarified them by the very title of his book, *The Fifteen Weeks.* To him it was a period of excitement, of America's sudden acceptance of responsibility as a world leader. The Truman Doctrine and the Marshall Plan were the central features of a "national conversion" that permitted the development in later years of NATO, Point IV, and the defense of the Republic of Korea. (Selection IV–C.)

II. DOCUMENTS

SELECTION II–A

The Truman Doctrine originated in the President's message to the Congress on March 12, 1947 in which he asked for emergency aid to Greece and Turkey. A portion of the message appears here as excerpted from the Department of State *Bulletin,* XVI (March 23, 1947), pp. 536–37.

At the present moment in world history nearly every nation must choose between alternative ways of life. The choice is too often not a free one.

One way of life is based upon the will of the majority, and is distinguished by free institutions, representative government, free elections, guaranties of individual liberty, freedom of speech and religion, and freedom from political oppression.

The second way of life is based upon the will of a minority forcibly imposed upon the majority. It relies upon terror and oppression, a controlled press and radio, fixed elections, and the suppression of personal freedoms.

I believe that it must be the policy of the United States to support free peoples who are resisting attempted subjugation by armed minorities or by outside pressures.

I believe that we must assist free peoples to work out their own destinies in their own way.

I believe that our help should be primarily through economic and financial aid which is essential to economic stability and orderly political processes.

The world is not static, and the *status quo* is not sacred. But we cannot allow changes in the *status quo* in violation of the Charter of the United Nations by such methods as coercion, or by such subterfuges as political infiltration. In helping free and independent nations to maintain their freedom, the United States will be giving effect to the principles of the Charter of the United Nations.

.   .   .   .

In addition to funds, I ask the Congress to authorize the detail of American civilian and military personnel to Greece and Turkey, at the request of those countries, to assist in the tasks of reconstruction, and for the purpose of supervising the use of such financial and material assistance as may be furnished. I recommend that authority also be provided for the instruction and training of selected Greek and Turkish personnel.

Finally, I ask that the Congress provide authority which will permit the speediest and most effective use, in terms of needed commodities, supplies, and equipment, of such funds as may be authorized.

If further funds, or further authority, should be needed for purposes indicated in this message, I shall not hesitate to bring the situation before the Congress. On this subject the Executive and Legislative branches of the Government must work together.

This is a serious course upon which we embark.

I would not recommend it except that the alternative is much more serious.

The United States contributed $341,000,000,000 toward winning World War II. This is an investment in world freedom and world peace.

> SELECTION II–B
>
> The Marshall Plan was embodied in a commencement address of Secretary of State George C. Marshall at Harvard University on June 5, 1947. It urged a program of European and American cooperation in securing the economic revival of Europe. A portion of the address is here reprinted from the Department of State *Bulletin* XVI (June 15, 1947), pp. 1159–60.

I need not tell you gentlemen that the world situation is very serious. That must be apparent to all intelligent people. I think one difficulty is that the problem is one of such enormous complexity that the very mass of facts presented to the public by press and radio make it exceedingly difficult for the man in the street to reach a clear appraisement of the situation. Furthermore, the people of this country are distant from the troubled areas of the earth and it is hard for them to comprehend the plight and consequent reactions of the long-suffering peoples, and the effect of those reactions on their governments in connection with our efforts to promote peace in the world.

In considering the requirements for the rehabilitation of Europe, the physical loss of life, the visible destruction of cities, factories, mines, and railroads was correctly estimated, but it has become obvious during recent months that this visible destruction was probably less serious than the dislocation of the entire fabric of European economy. For the past 10 years conditions have been highly abnormal. The feverish preparation for war and the more feverish maintenance of the war effort engulfed all aspects of national economies. Machinery has fallen into disrepair or is entirely obsolete. Under the arbitrary and destructive Nazi rule, virtually every possible enterprise was geared into the German war machine. Long-standing commercial ties, private institutions, banks, insurance companies, and shipping companies disappeared, through loss of capital, absorption through nationalization, or by simple destruction. In many countries, confidence in the local currency has been severely shaken. The breakdown of the business structure of Europe during the war was complete. Recovery has been seriously retarded by the fact that two years after the close of hostilities a peace settlement with Germany and Austria has not been agreed upon. But even given a more prompt solution of these difficult problems, the rehabilitation of the economic structure of Europe quite evidently will require a much longer time and greater effort than had been foreseen.

.   .   .   .

Aside from the demoralizing effect on the world at large and the possibilities of disturbances arising as a result of the desperation of the people concerned, the consequences to the economy of the United States should be apparent to all. It is logical that the United States should do whatever it is able to do to assist in the return of normal economic health in the world, without which there can be no political stability and no assured peace. Our policy is directed not against any country or doctrine but against hunger, poverty, desperation, and chaos. Its purpose should be the revival of a working economy in the world so as to permit the emergence of political and social conditions in which free institutions can exist. Such assistance, I am convinced, must not be on a piecemeal basis as various crises develop. Any assistance that this Government may render in the future should provide a cure rather than a mere palliative. Any government that is willing to assist in the task of recovery will find full cooperation, I am sure, on the part of the United States Government. Any government which maneuvers to block the recovery of other countries cannot expect help from us. Furthermore, governments, political parties, or groups which seek to perpetuate human misery in order to profit therefrom politically or otherwise will encounter the opposition of the United States.

It is already evident that, before the United States Government can proceed much further in its efforts to alleviate the situation and help start the European world on its way to recovery, there must be some agreement among the countries of Europe as to the requirements of the situation and the part those countries themselves will take in order to give proper effect to whatever action might be undertaken by this Government. It would be neither fitting nor efficacious for this Government to undertake to draw up unilaterally a program designed to place Europe on its feet economically. This is the business of the Europeans. The initiative, I think, must come from Europe. The role of this country should consist of friendly aid in the drafting of a European program and of later support of such a program so far as it may be practical for us to do so. The program should be a joint one, agreed to by a number, if not all, European nations.

An essential part of any successful action on the part of the United States is an understanding on the part of the people of America of the character of the problem and the remedies to be applied. Political passion and prejudice should have no part. With foresight, and a willingness on the part of our people to face up to the vast responsibility which history has clearly placed upon our country, the difficulties I have outlined can and will be overcome.

III. VIEWS OF PARTICIPANTS

SELECTION III–A

Although at the time of its publication the author was identified only as X, the following was actually written by George F. Kennan who was then the Director of Policy Planning Staff, Department of State. The policy of containment is usually associated with the ideas presented in this article. Excerpted by special permission from *Foreign Affairs,* XXV (July, 1947), pp. 566–67; 580–82. Copyright by the Council on Foreign Relations, Inc., New York.

The political personality of Soviet power as we know it today is the product of ideology and circumstances: ideology inherited by the present Soviet leaders from the movement in which they had their political origin, and circumstances of the power which they now have exercised for nearly three decades in Russia. There can be few tasks of psychological analysis more difficult than to try to trace the interaction of these two forces and the relative rôle of each in the determination of official Soviet conduct. Yet the attempt must be made if that conduct is to be understood and effectively countered.

It is difficult to summarize the set of ideological concepts with which the Soviet leaders came into power. Marxian ideology, in its Russian-Communist projection, has always been in process of subtle evolution. The materials on which it bases itself are extensive and complex. But the outstanding features of Communist thought as it existed in 1916 may perhaps be summarized as follows: (a) that the central factor in the life of man, the factor which determines the character of public life and the "physiognomy of society," is the system by which material goods are produced and exchanged; (b) that the capitalist system of production is a nefarious one which inevitably leads to the exploitation of the working class by the capital-owning class and is incapable of developing adequately the economic resources of society or of distributing fairly the material goods produced by human labor; (c) that capitalism contains the seeds of its own destruction and must, in view of the inability of the capital-owning class to adjust itself to economic change, result eventually and inescapably in a revolutionary transfer of power to the working class; and (d) that imperialism, the final phase of capitalism, leads directly to war and revolution.

The rest may be outlined in Lenin's own words: "Unevenness of economic and political development is the inflexible law of capitalism. It follows from this that the victory of Socialism may come originally in a few capitalist countries or even in a single capitalist country. The victorious proletariat of that country, having expropriated the capitalists and having organized Socialist production at home, would rise against the remaining capitalist world, drawing to itself in the process the oppressed classes of other countries." It must be noted that there was no assumption that capitalism would perish without proletarian revolution. A final push was needed from a revolutionary proletariat movement in order to tip over the tottering structure. But it was regarded as inevitable that sooner or later that push be given.

For 50 years prior to the outbreak of the Revolution, this pattern of thought had exercised great fascination for the members of the Russian revolutionary movement. Frustrated, discontented, hopeless of finding self-expression—or too impatient to seek it—in the confining limits of the Tsarist political system, yet lacking wide popular support for their choice of bloody revolution as a means of social betterment, these revolutionists found in Marxist theory a highly convenient rationalization for their own instinctive desires. It affored pseudo-scientific justification for their impatience, for their categoric denial of all value in the Tsarist system, for their yearning for power and revenge and for their inclination to cut corners in the pursuit of it. It is therefore no wonder that they had come to believe implicitly in the truth and soundness of the Marxian-Leninist teachings, so congenial to their own impulses and emotions. Their sincerity need not be impugned. This is a phenomenon as old as human nature itself. It has never been more aptly described than by Edward Gibbon, who wrote in "The Decline and Fall of the Roman Empire": "From enthusiasm to imposture the step is perilous and slippery; the demon of Socrates affords a memorable instance how a wise man may deceive himself, how a good man may deceive others, how the conscience may slumber in a mixed and middle state between self-illusion and voluntary fraud." And it was with this set of conceptions that the members of the Bolshevik Party entered into power.

.   .   .   .

It is clear that the United States cannot expect in the foreseeable future to enjoy political intimacy with the Soviet régime. It must continue to regard the Soviet Union as a rival, not a partner, in the political arena. It must continue to expect that Soviet policies will reflect no abstract love of peace and stability, no real faith in the possibility of a permanent happy coexistence of the Socialist and capitalist worlds, but rather a cautious, persistent pressure toward the disruption and weakening of all rival influence and rival power.

Balanced against this are the facts that Russia, as opposed to the western world in general, is still by far the weaker party, that Soviet policy is highly flexible, and that Soviet society may well contain deficiencies which will eventually weaken its own total potential. This would of itself warrant the United States entering with reasonable confidence upon a policy of firm containment, designed to confront the Russians with unalterable counterforce at every point where they show signs of encroaching upon the interests of a peaceful and stable world.

But in actuality the possibilities for American policy are by no means limited to holding the line and hoping for the best. It is entirely possible for the United States to influence by its actions the internal developments, both within Russia and throughout the international Communist movement, by which Russian policy is largely determined. This is not only a question of the modest measure of informational activity which this government can conduct in the Soviet Union and elsewhere, although that, too, is important. It is rather a question of the degree to which the United States can create among the peoples of the world generally the impression of a country which knows what it wants, which is coping successfully with the problems of its internal life and with the responsibilities of a World Power, and which has a spiritual vitality capable of holding its own among the major ideological currents of the time. To the extent that such an impression can be created and maintained, the aims of Russian Communism must appear sterile and quixotic, the hopes and enthusiasm of Moscow's supporters must wane, and added strain must be imposed on the Kremlin's foreign policies. For the palsied decrepitude of the capitalist world is the keystone of Communist philosophy. Even the failure of the United States to experience the early economic depression which the ravens of the Red Square have been predicting with such complacent confidence since hostilities ceased would have deep and important repercussions throughout the Communist world.

By the same token, exhibitions of indecision, disunity and internal disintegration within this country have an exhilarating effect on the whole Communist movement. At each evidence of these tendencies, a thrill of hope and excitement goes through the Communist world; a new jauntiness can be noted in the Moscow tread; new groups of foreign supporters climb on to what they can only view as the band wagon of international politics; and Russian pressure increases all along the line in international affairs.

It would be an exaggeration to say that American behavior unassisted and alone could exercise a power of life and death over the Communist movement and bring about the early fall of Soviet power in Russia. But the United States has it in its power to increase enormously the strains under which Soviet policy must operate, to force upon the Kremlin a far greater degree of moderation and circumspection than it has had to observe in recent years, and in this way to promote tendencies which must eventually find their outlet in either the break-up or the gradual mellowing of Soviet power. For no mystical, Messianic movement—and particularly not that of the Kremlin—can face frustration indefinitely without eventually adjusting itself in one way or another to the logic of that state of affairs.

Thus the decision will really fall in large measure in this country itself. The issue of Soviet-American relations is in essence a test of the over-all worth of the United States as a nation among nations. To avoid destruction the United States need only measure up to its own best traditions and prove itself worthy of preservation as a great nation.

Surely, there was never a fairer test of national quality than this. In the light of these circumstances, the thoughtful observer of Russian-American relations will find no cause for complaint in the Kremlin's challenge to American society. He will rather experience a certain gratitude to a Providence which, by providing the American people with this implacable challenge, has made their entire security as a nation dependent on their pulling themselves together and accepting the responsibilities of moral and political leadership that history plainly intended them to bear.

> ### SELECTION III–B
>
> From Henry A. Wallace's "My Alternative for the Marshall Plan," as it appeared in the *New Republic*, XXXVIII (January 12, 1948), pp. 13–14. Reprinted by permission of the New Republic, © 1948, Harrison-Blaine of New Jersey, Inc. Wallace ran for President as the candidate of the Progressive Party in 1948, opposing the cold war.

In an address in Milwaukee, Wisconsin, on December 30, I laid down the principles which seem to me essential for a genuine plan for world recovery. I think the best use I can make of my space in the *New Republic* this week is to repeat what I said then, especialy in view of the hostile reception and inadequate report given my ideas by most of the American press.

Yesterday I announced that there would be a new party, and to that end

I announced that I am an independent candidate for the presidency in 1948.

My final decision was made solely on the basis of giving the American people a chance to vote for peace and security. I fear the die was cast when Truman came out for military aid to Greece and Turkey last March. Steadily during 1947 our help to foreign lands has been in the spirit of fighting Russia, not in the spirit of helping starving humanity. Steadily the military, the Wall Street press and the State Department have been waging psychological warfare against the American people to blind them to the fact that our unilateral help to Europe intervenes in the internal politics of nearly every Western European nation, that the ordinary European worker looks on it as naked imperialism—or even worse, in the case of Greece—and that in the end the cold war will end in bombs and expeditionary forces across Canada and the Scandinavian peninsula.

There are no more tragic victims of our insane policy, which will bankrupt us morally and financially, than the Greek people. Our first loan has been spent. Greek children still cry for milk, while the American-trained Greek army parades the severed heads of guerrillas through the streets, and a corrupt government decrees the death penalty for legitimate trade-union activities. The people of the world must see that there is another America than this Truman-led, Wall Street-dominated, military-backed group that is blackening the name of American democracy all over the world.

The original Marshall Plan speech sounded good to me when it was delivered. The principles of self-help, mutual aid and American support were the same that I had suggested on many occasions. The differences now are clear. They are fatal differences. When the Marshall Plan was announced, I declared that the Truman Doctrine would have to be scrapped to give it meaning. It has not been scrapped. With the Truman Doctrine as its core, the so-called European Recovery Program is a plan to interfere in the social, economic and political affairs of countries receiving aid. We are saying, "We will help you if you have our kind of government and subordinate your economy to ours."

We have invested $400 million in Greece and Turkey; $2 billion in China and $25 billion for our armed forces to support a foreign policy which leads to war, not peace. We *can* afford to invest in European reconstruction, *but* our policy must not require billions of dollars for arms, and millions of men in arms to back it up.

We can't stop communism or any other idea in Western Europe with military might or by supporting undemocratic government. The bipartisan coalition has allied the American people with kings, fascists and reactionaries.

The Russians certainly aren't blameless for the cold war. But even if we should accept every charge made against the Russians, it does not excuse an American policy which runs contrary to American principles.

A practical policy must begin with genuine support forthe United Nations.

We have been ignoring the UN. We circumvented the UN in the name of "emergency" to send military help to Greece and Turkey. We killed UNRRA, which had Europe on the road to recovery. We ignored the UN in proposing the Marshall Plan. We must reaffirm our faith in the UN. It cannot succeed if the most powerful nation in the world destroys confidence in the principle of world organization and operates in direct violation of that principle. We can't talk the language of one world and use our economic and political power to split that one world in two.

Today, when there is almost unanimous agreement on the necessity for helping Europe, is the time to "get practical."

If we reject the Marshall Plan as it is now proposed to apply it, this does not mean that we are without a plan. We propose a plan based on world unity and friendship that will lay the foundation of peace, not a plan based on world division and conflict that sows the seeds of war. We propose a plan that will effectuate the fine words spoken by Secretary Marshall at Harvard last June—not a plan whose deeds contradict those words.

The experience of UNRRA proved that such a plan is eminently practical —that such a plan will work. That experience showed indeed that *only* such a plan will work for peace—not war.

In the past 15 months I have repeatedly indicated the elements of such a plan. Let me restate them in brief and concrete terms:

My plan calls for a proposal from the U.S. to the UN for the establishment of a UN Reconstruction Fund, modeled after UNRRA, for the rehabilitation and reconstruction of the war-devastated lands in Europe and Asia to the end that their industry and agriculture may be restored and placed on a self-sustaining basis at the earliest possible moment.

I propose that this Reconstruction Fund be administered by an agency of the UN established for that purpose.

The Reconstruction Fund should be made up of contributions appropriated by our Congress and other nations possessed of the means, in an amount sufficient to finance an over-all five-year plan. A part of the fund may be in the form of loans and the balance in the form of a grant.

The UN agency should be directed to give priority in the allocation of funds to those nations which suffered most severely from Axis aggression. Allocations must be based solely on these considerations of merit and need, without regard to the character of the politics and social institutions of the recipient nations.

The allocation of funds by the UN agency must be made with scrupulous respect for the national sovereignty of all beneficiary countries. There must be no political or economic conditions attached to loans or grants. In particular, the UN agency must not make aid conditional upon conformity by any nation with an over-all economic plan, but must leave each nation free fully to develop its own national economic plan. Aid must not be coupled with any restrictions upon the development by recipient nations of expanded or new industries, or any attempt made to require restrictions on full and free economic development as price of assistance. Provision should be made that the funds, made available with due regard for sovereignty, are not wasted by graft and inefficiency, and that the expenditures are subject to review by a UN authority to make sure that there is not such graft and inefficiency.

The entire fund shall be used exclusively for peaceful purposes, and no monies shall be available to finance the purchase of military supplies, armaments or war preparations.

Finally, the German industrial heartland in the Ruhr Valley should be placed under international administration and control by the Big Four, in order, first, that its resources may be made available to aid in the reconstruction of Europe and second to guarantee that Germany shall never again be in a position to threaten the security of her neighbors or the peace of the world.

These are essentially for world peace. The greatest, richest, most powerful nation in the world can afford to take leadership on such constructive proposals. We must take leadership as well on a program of disarmament which will outlaw all mass methods of destruction and permit the efforts of workers and farmers the world over to be used in creating the abundance our resources, science and know-how make possible.

> ### SELECTION III–C
>
> Excerpts from an address by Senator Kenneth Wherry as printed in the *Congressional Record*—Senate, 80th Congress, 1st sess., v. 93, April 21, 1947, p. 3742–43. The Senator from Nebraska was a spokesman for the Republican isolationists in the 80th Congress.

If we accept the President's own statement of why these funds for Greece and Turkey are needed, we can trace the pattern which they will set for the future, a pattern from which we cannot possibly escape.

On March 12, in speaking of the need for maintaining the independence of Greece and Turkey, the President said:

That integrity is essential to the preservation of order in the Middle East.

The Senator from Michigan [Mr. Vandenberg] goes even further by saying:

If the Middle East falls within the orbit of aggressive Communist expansion, the repercussions will echo from the Dardanelles to the China Sea and westward to the rims of the Atlantic.

Then, at least, let us be honest about the nature and extent of the commitments for which these Greek and Turkish gifts will set a precedent. We will, by taking this step, serve notice on all the nations of the world which are still left outside of the Russian sphere of influence, that they have become our first line of defense. Naturally these nations will be only too glad to unload their burdens on us if by that means they can get us to use our own resources and our own finances and manpower to supplant theirs.

The President, in declaring an all-out offensive against the spread of communism, must realize that the economies of these nations which lie in the path of Russian expansion cannot support adequate military defense against such threats.

It is admitted by the Senators who have returned from abroad that Turkey has an economy which excels even our own, yet they cannot continue to arm themselves to meet the advances of Russia. There is the story. They cannot support adequate military defense against Russia.

Thus we will be undertaking to rehabilitate the peacetime economies, raise standards of living, encourage economic reconstruction, and at the same time superimpose on all of these requirements military establishments which cannot be maintained except through endless drains on American resources and raw materials.

For instance, if we underwrite Greece and Turkey, what about Syria? Syria will need perhaps $150,000,000 next year. Then there is Palestine where the British kept 100,000 troops last year at the cost of $340,000,000. Conditions in Palestine are steadily deteriorating into civil war and anarchy. Surely we will have to underwrite the British commitments here. Then there is Egypt which guards the entrance to the Suez Canal. The Egyptian economy will certainly call for a financial shot-in-the-arm from Uncle Sam in the very near future.

.   .   .   .

Most of the emphasis in the President's message has been placed on the economic aspects of these grants. But these economic aspects cannot be divorced from the total offensive against communism, which is the essence of the Truman doctrine.

The President has asked that we first use financial and political force to implement his policy. But if that fails, what does he say? He has said he will not hesitate to ask for further authority.

At the outset $300,000,000 of the $400,000,000 being asked is being made available for military purposes. That is admitted. This leaves no doubt that the President is going to attempt to revive economic standards of nations that stand in the path of communistic aggression, and yet superimpose on these economies military establishments which neither they nor we can possibly continue to maintain.

On November 17, 1946, the New York Times reported the official Government policy toward foreign trade which was revealed at the thirty-third foreign trade convention at the Waldorf-Astoria.

The conference report approved by all the foreign traders present and concurred in by our State Department officials, is as follows, and I quote:

Our foreign economic policy is seen to embrace the responsibility for promoting and safeguarding the interests of American foreign traders—this responsibility lies in the area of assuring the safety and security of American investments abroad, and of providing conditions which will make possible the receipt of an adequate volume of useful goods and services in return for our exports of goods and capital.

Mr. President, such a revival of dollar diplomacy of necessity requires that American armed forces shall follow the American dollar all over the world.

That such a dependence on military force is uppermost in the mind of this administration is nowhere better revealed than in the memorandum submitted by Secretary of State Marshall accompanying the detail of military missions bill in which Secretary Marshall states:

The United States Government has received requests from several foreign governments for the detail of military and/or naval missions with which, in the opinion of the interested departments, it would be in the advancement of the public interest to comply, but with which it cannot comply for the lack of the legislative authority which is being requested herewith. There are also a number of other missions now serving with foreign governments which, in the absence of such legislation, may have to be terminated before they have accomplished their task—

Iran is one of them—

should the present state of war or of national emergency be officially declared terminated. It is also anticipated that additional requests will be received from other countries with which it would be in the national interest to comply.

Mr. President, there is no good purpose to be served by ignoring the military implications of the Truman doctrine. On March 2, 1947, Mr. Hanson Baldwin, military analyst for the New York Times, wrote:

Today the United States and Russia are face to face in a struggle for the world, a conflict short of war, but a struggle nevertheless that will alter world history. . . . The United States alone is capable of sustaining western civilization.

On March 25, 1947, General Eisenhower, for whom I have the highest regard, issued a grave warning to the Nation to prepare for troubled times ahead. And in his plea for more adequate military power, he said:

Weakness cannot cooperate in the world today. All it can do is beg.

Mr. President, this raises the whole question of the advisability of endorsing the Truman doctrine just from the point of military preparedness alone. It would be suicidal for the United States in such a critical hour to undertake the impossible task of adding the unbearable weight of military establishments to the national economies which it seeks to revive. We would spread ourselves so thin across the world, even while we are bleeding ourselves of our finances and resources, that we would become vulnerable on every front. We would set up conditions where Pearl Harbors and Corregidors could be repeated simultaneously in a score of places.

IV. VIEWS OF OBSERVERS

SELECTION IV—A

Text of Edwin Borchard's "Intervention—the Truman Doctrine and the Marshall Plan," reprinted by permission from the *American Journal of International Law,* XLI (October, 1947), pp. 885–88. Professor Borchard of the Yale School of Law was a major ideologue of isolationism in the period between World War I and World War II.

While the Marshall proposal for aid by the United States toward European recovery is often called a corollary of the Truman Doctrine, they differ essentially in their aims. While both are directed against the expansion of Soviet Russia the Truman Doctrine looks to military aid to Greece and Turkey, and the outcome is unknown. The Marshall proposal, on the other hand, looks purely to economic aid for the countries of Western Europe and professes to disregard political considerations.

The so-called Truman Doctrine is often called an extension of the Monroe Doctrine. But this is surely an error. The Monroe Doctrine was limited geographically to this continent. It announced that American arms would protect the Continent against any effort of Europe to extend its system across the Atlantic. Several efforts at European intervention were made during the nineteenth century, efforts which always failed. The Truman Doctrine has no geographical limits and promises American intervention in places where the United States has little or no interest. One of the major premises of the Monroe Doctrine was the traditional American policy of not intervening in European feuds. The bottom has, therefore, been taken out of the Monroe Doctrine by American intervention abroad, so that the United States has now little moral claim to ask Europe to refrain from extending its political philosophy to this continent. Moreover the Truman Doctrine is not a self-denying ordinance but a promise to use American dollars, if not more, to stop Communism. Apart from the fact that Soviet Russia exemplifies not Communism but National Socialism—the Communist Utopia not having yet arrived—it remains to be proved that dollars can stem the advance of a doctrine which finds its major source and soil in poverty and misery. President Truman recently announced, in describing the Potsdam Declaration, that chaos had been brought to Germany by the Nazi Party. Regardless of the accuracy of his ascription, the fact is that chaos prevails in most of Europe and that American money, which European peoples naturally are delighted to spend, can hardly shore up countries that surrender to the inevitable. It shows how fantastic was the half-truth of the idea of "One World." As Senator Root said to Senator Bacon of Georgia in a famous debate on Mexico, many ideas, like world government, are logical, but not practical.

One of the primary interests of the founders of this country, who are entitled to be heard in such a dilemma as now confronts the United States, is that European ideology must not be imported into this heterogeneous population. The founders' warning was prophetic. The major opposition to the Italian Treaty comes from Italian-American societies who resent the fate meted out to Italy. In that opposition they have a good ground for protest, but it seems pitiful to transfer European problems to this soil in the alleged interests of an unachievable Utopia.

The Marshall Proposal. The so-called Marshall Plan is no plan at all but merely undertakes to finance some plan satisfactory to Secretary Marshall and the United States Congress if the European countries can come to agreement. Russia and her satellites have already declined American aid and profess to see in it danger to the aided. They promise to defeat the proposal.

If we should advance any money to Europe in addition to the twenty billions already devoted to relief and other purposes it will show that the United States is the only country really paying reparations in addition to what Russia has looted out of Germany and Austria and her satellites, mostly private property. It may be questioned why the United States should pay reparations, but it is a result of failing to think about what will happen after a war. The psychology of merely defeating an enemy is manifestly inadequate. Yet the mores of war forbid thought beyond this point. First we spend billions, not, it is true, with a view to destroying Europe but having that effect. Now we are to spend new billions to restore Europe with the promise that it will be interpreted as American imperialism. It may also have that result, since Secretary Marshall promises to supervise the expenditure of any funds which Congress may advance. But that is not the initial intention. The Russians are wrong in charging that it positively will have that result. We can accept Secretary Marshall's statement that he, at least, has no such intention. He may, however, find himself in the position of the British in Egypt after 1882; then the United States, already a Balkan power, will become an imperialist power. It is simply too early to forecast all future developments. The chances are not weak that the reparations of Italy and other countries payable to Russia and her satellites may be siphoned off from American loans to Italy and other reparation paying countries.

The Marshall Plan seems particularly to lack consideration because no one can tell what it may cost the United States. We have seen figures mentioned of three billions for three years, five billions for four years, and seven billions for ten years. The President states that we have already contributed twenty billions to Europe since the end of hostilities in 1945. Europe is now based on the unsound political plan of Potsdam, and no amount of American money can change that fact. So long as that basis stands any American money raised, as it must be on credit, will be the sheerest palliative and can serve no purpose of recovery.

There are other dilemmas that must be faced. Europe's condition is not only due to the unfortunate features of the Potsdam agreement, of which Russia seems to have taken full advantage, but Eastern Europe has also been separated from the West to a considerable extent by the so-called Iron Curtain. Eastern Europe normally exports foodstuffs and raw materials, as does Russia, but they are not getting in exchange industrial goods from the West, goods which they badly need. Although Russia hurries to make agreements with her satellites, they can hardly make good the deficiency. Eastern Europe, therefore, seems likely to suffer an industrial famine, although the Marshall proposal does not contemplate a termination of the bilateral treaties made between Eastern countries and the West.

The Marshall proposal seems more likely to finance state socialism, although the word "recovery" is frequently employed. At this writing (September, 1947), it is unsafe to predict developments, but since Russia and her satellites have declared war on the plan, the financing of Western Europe might turn into a military measure, leaving recovery an unachieved aim.

We now learn that France objects to increasing the German output, though the joint chiefs-of-staff have already issued a directive to that effect. Great Britain is also said to protest against part of the program. Perhaps this is the most significant trend of recent years, since it throws light on the origins of the war in 1914, however justified the protest. If Europe is not to be allowed full production, it seems idle to throw American money into the breach. The plan is stymied at the source.

The countries which possess the fifteen billion dollars of gold and foreign exchange that the National City Bank reports are not the countries with which the bulk of American trade is done, but some exchange is possessed by those countries. Should Secretary Marshall insist first on their spending their assets on American goods before receiving American bounty? Or will they say, as a British cabinet minister threatened the other day, that default in certain loans will follow or that the United States in its own interest must finance exports up to eight billions a year—the difference between exports and imports—since otherwise unemployment will result in the United States?

There are thus many obstacles which the Marshall proposal must overcome. Will the proposal founder on one or more of these obstacles? Only the future can give an answer.

> ### SELECTION IV–B
>
> An excerpt from pp. 52–57 *The Cold War: A Study in U.S. Foreign Policy* by Walter Lippmann. Copyright © 1947 by Walter Lippmann. Reprinted by permission of Harper & Row, Publishers. Lippmann is America's most distinguished journalist and a critic in 1947 of the containment policy.

In the introduction to this essay, I said that Mr. X's article* on "The Sources of Soviet Conduct" was "a document of primary importance on the sources of American foreign policy" in that it disclosed to the world the

* Excerpts from this article are reproduced in Selection III–A.

estimates, the calculations, and the conclusions on which is based *that part* of American foreign policy which is known as the Truman Doctrine. Fortunately, it seems to me, the Truman Doctrine does not have a monopoly. Though it is a powerful contender for the control of our foreign policy, there are at least two serious competitors in the field. One we may call the Marshall line, and the other is the American commitment to support the United Nations.

The contest between the Truman Doctrine on the one hand, the Marshall line and the support of the U.N. on the other is the central drama within the State Department, within the Administration, within the government as a whole. The outcome is still undecided.

The real issue is hidden because the Truman Doctrine was promulgated shortly after General Marshall became Secretary of State, and because he made the decision to go to the support of Greece and Turkey, which was a concrete application of the Truman Doctrine. The issue is confused by the fact that Mr. Molotov and the Soviet propaganda abroad and many publicists here at home are representing the Marshall proposals to Europe as an application of the Truman Doctrine. The confusion is compounded still more because the Director of Secretary Marshall's Planning Staff is now known, through the publication of Mr. X's article, to have been the leading expert upon whose observations, predictions, and hypotheses the Truman Doctrine is based.

Nevertheless, if we look at the two main theatres of American diplomatic interest—at China and at Europe—and if we fix our attention on Secretary Marshall's approach, we can see a line of policy developing which is altogether different from the line of the Truman Doctrine. General Marshall's report on China, which has now been reviewed and confirmed by General Wedemeyer, made it quite clear that in his judgment we could not, and should not, attempt the kind of intervention in China which we are carrying on in Greece. The Marshall and Wedemeyer reports do not argue that we can contain the Soviet Union and erect unassailable barriers in its path by participating in the Chinese civil war, as we are in the Greek civil war, and by underwriting Chiang Kai-shek's government as we are underwriting the Athens government. The Marshall line in China is not an application of the Truman Doctrine, but of an older American doctrine that we must not become entangled all over the world in disputes that we alone cannot settle.

Yet the Marshall line in China is not isolationist. It would not end in our ceasing to interest ourselves in China and in giving Russia a free hand. But it is emphatically not the line of the Truman Doctrine which would involve us as partisans in the Chinese conflict and as patrons of one faction.

The line of the Marshall policy in China is to disentangle the United States, to reduce, not to extend, our commitments in Asia, to give up the attempt to control events which we do not have the power, the influence, the means, and the knowledge to control.

The proposal which Secretary Marshall addressed to Europe in his Harvard speech last June was animated by the same fundamental conception— as China's problem has to be dealt with primarily by the Chinese, so European problems have to be dealt with primarily by Europeans. Thus there was no "Marshall Plan" for Europe: the essence of his proposal was that only a European plan for Europe could save Europe, or provide a basis on which the American people could prudently and fairly be asked to help Europe save itself. The Marshall proposal was not, as Mr. Molotov and many Americans who do not understand it have tried to make out, an extension to Europe as a whole of the experiment in Greece. Quite the contrary. In Greece we made an American plan, appropriated the money, entered Greece and are now trying to induce the Greek government to carry out our plan. In the Harvard speech Secretary Marshal reversed this procedure. He told the European governments to plan their own rehabilitation, and that then he would go to Congress for funds, and that then the European governments would have to carry out their plans as best they could with the funds he could persuade Congress to appropriate.

The difference is fundamental. The Truman Doctrine treats those who are supposed to benefit by it as dependencies of the United States, as instruments of the American policy for "containing" Russia. The Marshall speech at Harvard treats the European governments as independent powers, whom we must help but cannot presume to govern, or to use as instruments of an American policy.

The Harvard speech was delivered about three months after President Truman's message. Much had happened in those three months, and all of it had gone to show that while Congress and the people were willing to applaud the Truman Doctrine, because they are exasperated with Russia, they were not going to support it with the funds and blanket authority which it requires. Though the President got the funds he asked for in order to apply his doctrine in Greece and Turkey, he got them after a long delay and in circumstances which were tantamount to telling him not to come back too soon for much more. The plans which existed for extending the Truman Doctrine to Korea and then to a series of impoverished, disordered and threatened countries on the perimeter of the Soviet Union were discreetly shelved.

Yet a crisis, enormously greater than that in Greece or Korea or Iran or Turkey, was developing. It was a crisis of the British Empire, and of France, and of Italy, and indeed of the whole western world. Extraordinary measures of American assistance were obviously going to be needed. After Congress had showed its attitude last spring, there was no possibility that this assistance would be provided by applying the principles, the procedure, and the precedent of the Truman Doctrine, as it had been revealed in the

Greek affair. A wholly different conception and a radically different approach were necessary if the crisis of the western world was to be dealt with.

Out of the knowledge that the Truman Doctrine was unworkable in Europe, that Congress would not support it anyway, and that a constructive revival of European collaboration was imperatively necessary, the policy of the Harvard speech was conceived. And I think it is true to say that those who conceived it were concerned not only to devise a way by which Europe could be saved from economic disaster, but also to devise a graceful way of saving the United States from the destructive and exhausting entanglements of the Truman Doctrine.

They may not succeed. If the planning of policy in the Truman Administration were to be dominated by the conclusions propounded by Mr. X, the Marshall proposals would fail. For the European crisis is insoluble if Europe remains divided by the iron curtain, raised by the Russians, and by the containing wall which we are supposed to construct.

But there are reasons for thinking that the Russians will not be able to maintain the iron curtain and that we cannot construct western Europe as a containing wall. They are that the vital needs of the people of Europe will prevail: the economic interdependence of western and eastern Europe will compel the nations of the continent to exchange their goods across the military, political and ideological boundary lines which now separate them.

The great virtue of the Marshall proposal is that it has set in motion studies abroad and in this country which will demonstrate conclusively that the division of Europe cannot be perpetuated. And since the division of Europe came about because the Red Army and the Anglo-American armies met in the middle of Europe, the withdrawal of these armies is necessary if Europe is to be reunited. The Harvard speech calls, therefore, for a policy of settlement, addressed to the military evacuation of the continent, not for a policy of containment which would freeze the non-European armies in the heart of Europe.

The Marshall studies will show that the industrialized areas of western Europe cannot be supported, except to relieve their most pressing immediate needs, from North and South America. They must revive their trade with the agricultural regions of eastern Europe and with European Russia. If they do not do that, the cost of maintaining a tolerable standard of life in western Europe will be exorbitant, and the effort to meet it will require a revolutionary adjustment of the economic life of the whole Western Hemisphere.

At the same time studies made in Warsaw, Prague and in Moscow will show that the problems of eastern Europe are insoluble without increasing economic intercourse with western Europe. Thus from all quarters in eastern Europe and in western Europe, in Washington and in Moscow, the pressure will increase to reunite the divided economy of Europe—and perhaps to go on towards a greater unity than ever existed before.

SELECTION IV–C

Selected passages from *The Fifteen Weeks*, copyright © 1955 by Joseph M. Jones. Reprinted by permission of Harcourt, Brace & World, Inc. Jones, a former member of the State Department who was involved in the preparation of the Marshall Plan, offers this analysis presented from the perspective of observer rather than participant.

The Fifteen Weeks was one of those rare times in history when shackles fall away from the mind, the spirit, and the will, allowing them to soar free and high for a while and to discover new standards of what is responsible, of what is promising, and of what is possible. It was a time when men thought not in terms of what could be done but of what should be done, when only the timid idea was banished and all others welcomed a time of courage, of bold decision, of generous response. It was a time when American democracy worked with unexampled efficiency and inspiration to produce national agreement. It was a great time to be alive.

The *avant-scène* was as dreary and unpromising as any in our history: a little-respected Democratic President, a Republican-controlled Congress bent on political mayhem after fourteen years in the wilderness, and an apathetic and heedless public. How then could the sudden transformation of the Fifteen Weeks possibly have occurred? The convergence of historical trends was compelling, but this cannot be the whole answer, for the lost compelling moments recorded in history would add up to quite a respectable span of time. The remainder of the answer must therefore be found in the qualities displayed by the nation's leaders and in the processes that enabled statesmanship to emerge and to prevail.

There is no way of getting around the fact that it was the courage, decisiveness, clear-thinking, and informed judgment of President Truman that opened the doors to the progress made during the Fifteen Weeks. It detracts none at all from the credit due him that he had exceptionally good advice, for his advisers were his appointees selected for qualities he admired and respected, and they operated in the climate of his administration and within the boundaries of what they thought he would support. Without considering its possible effect upon his personal popularity or re-election prospects, or whether it would mean an increase in taxes or the national debt, he made his decision on the basis of what the security of the nation seemed to require, and boldly confronted Congress and the people with their responsibilities. Moreover he knew what many men who find themselves in positions of power never learn, and that is that Americans respond more freely to big ideas than to small ones.

There is no substitute for this kind of courageous leadership. Most men are prisoners of their own limited conception of what is possible, and except in the most extraordinary circumstances most men involved in the foreign policy-making process in the government, from bottom to top, deliver their opinions and make their recommendations according to their own private estimate of what Congress and the American people will support. That estimate is usually low, somewhere near what Congress and the people have demonstrably supported in the past. There is nothing reprehensible in this. It is natural, if not inevitable, that practical men in subordinate positions should act in terms of what they consider possible. Unless, therefore, the President and the Secretary of State, drawing upon a faith in the capacity of their fellow men for clear thinking and sacrifice, add the element of statesmanship, unless they proclaim the policy of the United States in terms of bold, moving concepts and projects, whether or not they are fully and immediately attainable, the whole government process rocks along at a low level, policy planning is an exercise in futility, and the security and well-being of the nation may very well be jeopardized. But if with full candor and in accents of leadership they open new vistas of what is necessary and what is possible, they automatically raise the sights of the nation and release powerful ideas in the government departments, in Congress, and among the citizenry. In the ensuing public and official discussions great and practicable projects may emerge, with broad public support. This is what happened during the Fifteen Weeks.

The conservative prefers a balance-sheet approach to world affairs even in an age when his ledgers, the metal filing cases that enclose them, and the concrete and steel buildings that house them have a remarkably good prospect of being reduced to radioactive dust during his lifetime: add up the nation's revenues and armed forces in one column, and then figure out what can be done to build toward peace and security! There are legislators who profess to see the difference between national solvency and bankruptcy in the addition of several wings to the Air Force, even at a time when our margin of air-atomic superiority is disappearing. There are Cabinet officers who oppose a "Marshall Plan" for Asia at a time when that continent is in the balance between the free world and the slave, on the grounds that we are already "scraping the bottom of the financial barrel." There are writers on foreign policy who are considered sages for parading on appropriate occasions the neat homily (so obviously true!) that a nation's world commitments should not exceed its power to carry them out. During the Fifteen Weeks there were some who profesed to be horrified at the President's announcement of an open-end policy of aiding free peoples. Where would it lead? There were some who urged a balance-sheet approach at a time when most of the world, hungry and desperate, seemed on the point of bargaining away freedom for food and coal. And of course the 80th Congress was busily engaged in building a smaller financial barrel so that they could publicly scrape the bottom of it. The whole nation was in a psychological barrel of its own construction.

What, indeed, are the limits of United States power? And what are the limits of United States foreign policy? Are they what we can accomplish with an existing budget, an existing level of armed force, an existing program of world economic development, an existing tax rate? Are they what we could accomplish were these increased, or decreased, by 10 per cent, or 50 per cent? Is our power what we can mobilize to fight a war once we are engaged? By what standard, and whose, can we measure our power to help build around the world in time of peace the economic, social, political, and military conditions that protect freedom and diminish the danger of war? The answer is that the limits of our foreign policy are on a distant and receding horizon; for many practical purposes they are what we think we can accomplish and what we think it is necessary to accomplish at any given time.

President Truman, Secretary Marshall, and Undersecretary Acheson rejected an approach to world problems based upon an existing financial statement and upon what the American Congress and people considered possible and necessary before the situation had been explained to them. Instead they figured out what needed to be done, explained their bold projects publicly in frank terms, and had faith that the American people would back them up. The Fifteen Weeks demonstrated the tremendous capacity of the American people to respond to courageous leadership with clear thinking, constructive ideas, and personal sacrifice. The people did not demand to know what was at the end of the road before responding, or the total cost, or the full extent of possible dangers. They wanted only to be satisfied that the direction in which their leaders pointed was good and necessary, and they pitched in with ideas, intellectual support, and with money to help get a big show on the road. This generous response, in turn, encouraged the nation's leaders to new acts of statesmanship.

Without making extravagant claims, and without forgetting that many complex factors enter in any major policy decision, it is reasonable to suggest that a number of other bold policies and actions, beyond aid to Greece and Turkey and the Marshall Plan, had their roots in the national conversion of the Fifteen Weeks: The North Atlantic Alliance and the North Atlantic Treaty Organization, the Military Defense Assistance Program, the Far Eastern programs of the Economic Cooperation Administration, the Mutual Security Program, the Point IV Program, the prompt commitment of American power against Communist aggression in Korea, the Manila Pact, the other defensive alliances that link our destiny with countries around the globe. And the process of drawing together and strengthening the free world continues, will probably continue far into the future. No doubt the greatest stimulus to our policy development since 1947 has been the Soviet-Communist challenge. But as was evident in the debates of the Fifteen Weeks and has been so often demonstrated since, the generous impulse, the humanitarian motive, the sense of responsibility for protecting freedom, the business instinct, the common-sense conclusion as to how peace and prosperity might best be secured in a world grown small and highly explosive—all these have played a powerful part, leavening, controlling, what might otherwise have been a foreign policy that sought security in a revolutionary age by purely military means.

. . . .

Only a beginning, of course, has been made. Brilliant early successes have been achieved. But we have yet to to build in Western Europe and in the Atlantic Community more than a partial foundation for that organic unity of our economies, political systems, and armies which is necessary if we are to resist the persistent and prolonged efforts that will be made to divide, weaken, and destroy us. And although in Asia and other underdeveloped regions we have made a start with economic-development programs, technical assistance, and military aid, we have traveled only a few steps down a long, long road.

The responsibility that rests upon the United States to lead, inspire, and aid free men and free nations to draw ever closer together, and together to build ever stronger the conditions of freedom, is heavier than any that has ever rested upon any nation. It is also the greatest challenge and opportunity ever offered to any nation to save its own life and its own soul.

4

NORTH ATLANTIC TREATY

End of Isolationism?

I. EDITORIAL INTRODUCTION

On April 4, 1949, the United States signed a treaty of military alliance with eleven nations. By this act the nation made nothing less than a military and political commitment to preserve the territorial integrity of its new allies, an apparent reversal of a tradition that went back at least one hundred and forty-nine years. The one and only entangling alliance made by the United States with a European power had been with France in 1778, and this was concluded with relief in 1880. Indeed, the unhappy experience with the French alliance was an important factor in deeping the isolationism that had its roots in colonial times.

It is questionable if an Atlantic alliance as it developed in 1949 had been in the minds of American policy-makers involved in the shaping of the Truman Doctrine and the Marshall Plan. It was obviously far from the thinking of the optimists of 1944 and 1945 who had seen in the United Nations a substitution for such alliances and the ending of the old balance-of-power system of international relations that had brought the world the holocaust of World War II. The only articulate spokesmen for alliance were those followers of Clarence Streit who had embraced a "Union Now" movement with Great Britain which conceivably could extend to other Atlantic democracies. Similarly, the hopes of the United World Federalists encompassed a supranationalism in which NATO might fit, given the apparent impossibility of converting the United Nations into a world government. Yet, the military aspects and other traditional attributes of alliances found in NATO troubled these groups and created doubts about the compatibility of NATO with their respective ideals.

It seems reasonable to conclude that the need of an alliance, even one that appeared to flout the lessons of American history, reflected the evolution of the containment doctrines of the Truman administration and the bipartisan marjority of the 80th Congress. Once the nation realized that the existence of the United Nations alone was no guarantee of peace for the future, it looked for means that could deter Soviet expansionism without at the same time undermining the United Nations. America's presence in the eastern Mediterranean in 1947 and massive economic assistance to the failing economies of Europe were both parts of this effort; but they were neither meshed clearly together nor very promising of success by themselves. Military aid to Greece and Turkey under the Truman Doctrine held the line for the moment, but the economic and social problems of these countries would continue to invite communist activity in the future. Economic assistance to all Europe under the Marshall Plan could create a climate of confidence in the future that would make the price of communism too high to pay, but this would be achieved only if Europe felt militarily secure. How could the West achieve prosperity while paralyzed by anxiety over subversion from communist minorities or fear of invasion by Soviet armies? It became apparent even before the machinery of the Marshall Plan had been set in motion that a sense of military security was a prerequisite for recovery from the ravages of war.

The communist coup d'état in Czechoslovakia in February 1948 underscored the need for further American involvement in Europe. Czechoslovakia was a westernized country even if it had been subjected to greater Soviet influences than the countries of western Europe which had been liberated by Anglo-American arms. Its fall to a Stalinist regime—coinciding with the mysterious death of Thomas Masaryk, a hero of the West as well as of democratic Czechoslovakia—revealed to western Europeans the implications of their military weakness. Their response to this danger was the establishment of the Western Union, a military alliance signed in Brussels in March, 1949 by France, the United Kingdom, and the Benelux countries. In creating a new community with military, economic, and cultural bonds they hoped to create a psychological climate that would assure the success of the Marshall Plan. If there were doubts about the hostility and bellicosity of the Soviet Union in the minds of some Western leaders the Berlin blockade, begun in April, 1948, removed them.

Where did the United States stand as it observed rapidly shifting events in Europe in the winter and spring of 1948? Certainly there was concern that the immediate yield of the developing Marshall Plan was increased insecurity as the Soviet Union struck in Czechoslovakia and in Berlin. The most obvious answer from the vantage point of Europeans would have been an American membership in the Brussels Pact, since it was understood from the beginning that even the pooled resources of the five nations were insufficient to deter communist advance. It was as if the Brussels Pact was an earnest of intention, to show Americans that Europe was willing to sacrifice for the sake of survival. In return they expected American support.

But the tradition of isolationism was a factor which no American politician could disregard. While membership in the Western Union was a logical response to the problem, the most the country could do in that period was to put forth the Vandenberg Resolution of June, 1948, in which the Senate resolved to associate itself "by constitutional process, with such regional and other collective arrangements as are based on continuous and effective self-help and mutual aid." (Selection II–A.) Such was the broad hint given to Europe that the United States would "join" the Brussels Pact in America's interests as well as Europe's. It required the presidential election of 1948 and a cautious, careful rewording and recasting of the Brussels Pact before the United States could openly proclaim its new policy. With some apprehension the administration finally approached the nation in the spring of 1949 with the Treaty of Washington. (Selection II–B.)

The makings of a "Great Debate" were there. Announcement that the United States was abandoning the policy of Washington, Jefferson, and Monroe, could unleash emotions that might destroy the effectiveness of the country's containment system. Anticipating opposition, Secretary of State Dean Acheson addressed the nation in a radio broadcast, in which he attempted to assure public opinion of the necessity of the Treaty, two weeks before it was to be signed. With great care he pointed out that the goals were peace and security, that the association with Europe was not in fact an "alliance," since determination of military action rested with the Congress, and that the treaty was in full accord with the United Nations. (Selection III–A.)

Senator Robert A. Taft, the leader of Senate Republicans and of isolationist thinking in America, clearly opposed the administration's reasoning, and proclaimed that it would encourage excessive European dependence upon the United States while at the same time forcing American adherence to the dangerous foreign policies of Europe. Although the Soviet threat was genuine, he felt that the American response should be to maintain the traditions of independence, and to protect Europe through a new Monroe Doctrine which would serve Europeans just as the Monroe Doctrine had served Latin Americans over the century. (Selection III–B.)

Scott Keyes, a spokesman for a Quaker group from State College, Pennsylvania, was equally disturbed over the meaning of the Atlantic Pact for different reasons. Whatever the intentions, its only result would be to exacerbate the tensions of the cold war, and place the United States in the midst of the dangerous European balance-of-power system. Its inevitable aftermath would be the war it was designed to prevent. (Selection III–C.)

Yet, the passions of a pacifist witness at the Senate Hearings or the voice of a distinguished critic on the Senate floor were not reflected in the country at large. The Pact was regarded at the time as just another American measure of response to the Soviet challenge, an example of America's assumption of Britain's old responsibilities.

To some observers of the time and to many more later, the significance of the Treaty as a milestone in the evolution of American policy became increasingly obvious. Numerous analyses of the Treaty quickly followed its signing. They ranged from its defense on the grounds that the Constitution (Selection IV–A.) makes allowances for just such commitments to vehement criticism on the grounds that the language of the Treaty and of its defenders was so vague that no one could know exactly the nature of America's commitment. (Selection IV–B.) It may be noted, however, the confusion over the definition of the Treaty's responsibilities was not altogether unwelcome to NATO planners. American policy-makers in particular were mindful of the radical place of the Treaty in American diplomatic history. The Aesopian terms they used to defend the Treaty reflected the administration's concern that the nation would only accept the imperatives of the present if they were couched in the familiar language of the past. (Selection IV–C.)

II. DOCUMENTS

SELECTION II–A

The following text of the Vandenberg Resolution (S. Res. 239) is excerpted from *The Congressional Record,* 80th Cong., 2d sess. v. 94, June 11, 1948, p. 7791. The resolution was the evidence that Europe needed of America's willingness to identify the defense of western Europe with the defense of the United States. It opened the way for the North Atlantic Treaty.

Whereas peace with justice and the defense of human rights and fundamental freedoms require international cooperation through more effective use of the United Nations: Therefore be it

Resolved, That the Senate reaffirm the policy of the United States to achieve international peace and security through the United Nations, so that armed force shall not be used except in the common interest, and that the President be advised of the sense of the Senate that this Government, by constitutional process, should particularly pursue the following objectives within the United Nations Charter:

(1) Voluntary agreement to remove the veto from all questions involving pacific settlements of international disputes and situations, and from the admission of new members.

(2) Progressive development of regional and other collective arrangements for individual and collective self-defense in accordance with the purposes, principles, and provisions of the Charter.

(3) Association of the United States, by constitutional process, with such

regional and other collective arrangements as are based on continuous and effective self-help and mutual aid, and as affect its national security.

(4) Contributing to the maintenance of peace by making clear its determination to exercise the right of individual or collective self-defense under article 51 should any armed attack occur affecting its national security.

(5) Maximum efforts to obtain agreements to provide the United Nations with armed forces as provided by the Charter, and to obtain agreement among member nations upon universal regulation and reduction of armaments under adequate and dependable guaranty against violation.

(6) If necessary, after adequate effort toward strengthening the United Nations, review of the Charter at an appropriate time by a general conference called under article 109 or by the General Assembly.

SELECTION II–B

Reprinted from *Hearings, North Atlantic Treaty,* Senate Committee on Foreign Relations, 81st Congress, 1st sess., Part 1, pp. 1–3. The North Atlantic Treaty of 1949 marked the first time since 1800 that the United States had entered into an entangling alliance with a European country. In this case the alliance encompassed eleven other nations, American and European.

NORTH ATLANTIC TREATY

The Parties to this Treaty reaffirm their faith in the purposes and principles of the Charter of the United Nations and their desire to live in peace with all peoples and all governments.

They are determined to safeguard the freedom, common heritage and civilization of their peoples, founded on the principles of democracy, individual liberty and the rule of law.

They seek to promote stability and well-being in the North Atlantic area.

They are resolved to unite their efforts for collective defense and for the preservation of peace and security.

They therefore agree to this North Atlantic Treaty:

ARTICLE 1

The Parties undertake, as set forth in the Charter of the United Nations, to settle any international disputes in which they may be involved by peaceful means in such a manner that international peace and security, and justice, are not endangered, and to refrain in their international relations from the threat or use of force in any manner inconsistent with the purposes of the United Nations.

ARTICLE 2

The Parties will contribute toward the further development of peaceful and friendly international relations by strengthening their free institutions, by bringing about a better understanding of the principles upon which these institutions are founded, and by promoting conditions of stability and well-being. They will seek to eliminate conflict in their international economic policies and will encourage economic collaboration between any or all of them.

ARTICLE 3

In order more effectively to achieve the objectives of this Treaty, the Parties, separately and jointly, by means of continuous and effective self-help and mutual aid, will maintain and develop their individual and collective capacity to resist armed attack.

ARTICLE 4

The Parties will consult together whenever, in the opinion of any of them, the territorial integrity, political independence or security of any of the Parties is threatened.

ARTICLE 5

The Parties agree that an armed attack against one or more of them in Europe or North America shall be considered an attack against them all; and consequently they agree that, if such an armed attack occurs, each of them, in exercise of the right of individual or collective self-defense recognized by Article 51 of the Charter of the United Nations, will assist the Party or Parties so attacked by taking forthwith, individually and in concert with the other Parties, such action as it deems necessary, including the use of armed force, to restore and maintain the security of the North Atlantic area.

Any such armed attack and all measures taken as a result thereof shall immediately be reported to the Security Council. Such measures shall be terminated when the Security Council has taken the measures necessary to restore and maintain international peace and security.

ARTICLE 6

For the purpose of Article 5 an armed attack on one or more of the Parties is deemed to include an armed attack on the territory of any of the Parties in Europe or North America, on the Algerian departments of France, on the occupation forces of any Party in Europe, on the islands under the jurisdiction of any Party in the North Atlantic area north of the Tropic of Cancer or on the vessels or aircraft in this area of any of the Parties.

ARTICLE 7

This Treaty does not affect, and shall not be interpreted as affecting, in any way the rights and obligations under the Charter of the Parties which are members of the United Nations, or the primary responsibility of the Security Council for the maintenance of international peace and security.

ARTICLE 8

Each Party declares that none of the international engagements now in force between it and any other of the Parties or any third state is in conflict with the provisions of this Treaty, and undertakes not to enter into any international engagement in conflict with this Treaty.

ARTICLE 9

The Parties hereby establish a council, on which each of them shall be represented, to consider matters concerning the implementation of this Treaty. The council shall be so organized as to be able to meet promptly at any time. The council shall set up such subsidiary bodies as may be necessary; in particular it shall establish immediately a defense committee which shall recommend measures for the implementation of Articles 3 and 5.

ARTICLE 10

The Parties may, by unanimous agreement, invite any other European state in a position to further the principles of this Treaty to contribute to the security of the North Atlantic area to accede to this Treaty. Any state so invited may become a party to the Treaty by depositing its instrument of accession with the Government of the United States of America. The Government of the United States of America will inform each of the Parties of the deposit of each such instrument of accession.

ARTICLE 11

This Treaty shall be ratified and its provisions carried out by the Parties in accordance with their respective constitutional processes. The instruments of ratification shall be deposited as soon as possible with the Government of the United States of America, which will notify all the other signatories of each deposit. The Treaty shall enter into force between the states which have ratified it as soon as the ratifications of the majority of the signatories, including the ratifications of Belgium, Canada, France, Luxembourg, the Netherlands, the United Kingdom and the United States, have been deposited and shall come into effect with respect to other states on the date of the deposit of their ratifications.

ARTICLE 12

After the Treaty has been in force for ten years, or at any time thereafter, the Parties shall, if any of them so requests, consult together for the purpose of reviewing the Treaty, having regard for the factors then affecting peace and security in the North Atlantic area, including the development of universal as well as regional arrangements under the Charter of the United Nations for the maintenance of international peace and security.

ARTICLE 13

After the Treaty has been in force for twenty years, any Party may cease to be a party one year after its notice of denunciation has been given to the Government of the United States of America, which will inform the Governments of the other Parties of the deposit of each notice of denunciation.

ARTICLE 14

This Treaty, of which the English and French texts are equally authentic, shall be deposited in the archives of the government of the United States of America. Duly certified copies thereof will be transmitted by that Government to the Governments of the other signatories.

In witness whereof, the undersigned plenipotentiaries have signed this Treaty.

Done at Washington, the fourth day of April, 1949.

III. VIEWS OF PARTICIPANTS

SELECTION III–A

Excerpted from the text of a radio address, "The Meaning of the North Atlantic Pact," presented by Dean Acheson on March 18, 1949, as printed in Department of State *Bulletin* XX (March 27, 1949), pp. 384–86. Acheson was Secretary of State from 1949 to 1952 and a major contributor to the Truman foreign policy.

The text of the proposed North Atlantic pact was made public today. I welcome this opportunity to talk with my fellow citizens about it. It has taken many months to work out this text with the representatives of the other nations involved. First Mr. Lovett, and then I, met with the Ambassadors of Canada, Britain, France, Belgium, the Netherlands, and Luxembourg. Recently the Ambassador of Norway joined in these discussions. These talks had to be conducted in private and in confidence, so that each of us could speak frankly and fully on matters of vital importance to our countries. It is for this compelling reason that public discussion of the text of the pact by your representatives has not been possible up to this time.

That restraint no longer applies. The treaty and its implications can now be fully discussed. Public opinion can now be formed on the basis of complete information. Only in this way can your Government have what former Secretary of State Stimson has termed "the understanding support . . . of the American people," which is essential to the success of any policy.

I think the American people will want to know the answers to three principal questions about the pact: How did it come about and why is it necessary? What are its terms? Will it accomplish its purpose?

The paramount purposes of the pact are peace and security. If peace and security can be achieved in the North Atlantic area, we shall have gone a long way to assure peace and security in other areas as well.

The achievement of peace and security means more than that in the final outcome we shall have prevented war and brought about the settlement of international disputes by peaceful means. There must be conviction of people everywhere that war will be prevented and that disptues will be settled peacefully. In the most practical terms, true international peace and security require a firm belief by the peoples of the world that they will not be subjected to unprovoked attack, to coercion and intimidation, to interference in their own affairs. Peace and security require confidence in the future, based on the assurance that the peoples of the world will be permitted to improve their conditions of life, free from fear that the fruits of their labor may be taken from them by alien hands.

These are goals of our own foreign policy which President Truman has emphasized many times, most recently in his inaugural address when he spoke of the hope that we could help create "the conditions that will lead eventually to personal freedom and happiness for all mankind." These are also the purposes of the United Nations, whose members are pledged "to maintain international peace and security" and to promote "the economic and social advancement of all peoples."

These purposes are intimately related to the origins of the United Nations. As the second World War neared its end, the peoples who bore the brunt of the fighting were sick of the horror, the brutality, the tragedy of war. Out of that revulsion came the determination to create a system that would go as far as humanly possible in insuring international peace and security.

The United Nations seeks to maintain peace and security by enjoining its members from using force to settle international disputes. Moreover, it insists that they acknowledge tolerance and cooperation as the guiding principles for the conduct of nations.

The members are expected to settle differences by the exercise of reason and adjustment, according to the principles of justice and law. This requires a spirit of tolerance and restraint on the part of all the members.

But, as in any other institution which presupposes restraint, violence or obstruction can be used to defeat the basic undertaking. This happens in personal relations, in families, communities, churches, politics, and everywhere in human life. If the system is used in ways it was not intended to be used, there is grave danger that the system will be disrupted.

That applies to the United Nations. The system is not working as effectively as we hoped because one of its members has attempted to prevent it from working. By obstructive tactics and the misuse of the veto, the Soviet Union has seriously interfered with the work of the Security Council in maintaining international peace and security.

But the United Nations is a flexible instrument. Although the actions of the Soviet Union have disturbed the work of the United Nations, it is strong enough to be an effective instrument for peace. It is the instrument by which we hope world peace will be achieved. The Charter recognizes the importance of regional arrangements consistent with the purposes and principles of the Charter. Such arrangements can greatly strengthen it.

The Atlantic pact is a collective self-defense arrangement among the countries of the North Atlantic area. It is aimed at coordinating the exercise of the right of self-defense specifically recognized in article 51 of the United Nations Charter. It is designed to fit precisely into the framework of the United Nations and to assure practical measures for maintaining peace and security in harmony with the Charter.

It is the firm intention of the parties to carry out the pact in accordance with the provisions of the United Nations Charter and in a manner which will advance its purposes and principles.

Already one such arrangement under the Charter has been established with United States participation. The 21 American republics in reorganizing their regional system have specifically brought it within the framework of the United Nations Charter. We are now joining in the formation of a second arrangement, pertaining to the North Atlantic area, likewise within the framework of the United Nations.

It is important to keep in mind that the really successful national and international institutions are those that recognize and express underlying realities. The North Atlantic community of nations is such a reality. It is based on the affinity and natural identity of interests of the North Atlantic powers.

The North Atlantic treaty, which now formally unites them, is the product of at least three hundred and fifty years of history, perhaps more. There developed on our Atlantic coast a community, which has spread across the continent, connected with Western Europe by common institutions and moral and ethical beliefs. Similarities of this kind are not superficial, but fundamental. They are the strongest kind of ties, because they are based on moral conviction, on acceptance of the same values in life.

The very basis of western civilization, which we share with the other nations bordering the North Atlantic, and which all of us share with many other nations, is the ingrained spirit of restraint and tolerance. This is the opposite of the Communist belief that coercion by force is a proper method of hastening the inevitable. Western civilization has lived by mutual restraint and tolerance. This civilization permits and stimulates free inquiry and bold experimentation. It creates the environment of freedom, from which flows the greatest amount of ingenuity, enterprise, and accomplishment.

These principles of democracy, individual liberty, and the rule of law have flourished in this Atlantic community. They have universal validity. They are shared by other free nations and find expression on a universal basis in the Charter of the United Nations; they are the standards by which its members have solemnly agreed to be judged. They are the elements out of which are forged the peace and welfare of mankind.

Added to this profoundly important basis of understanding is another unifying influence—the effect of living on the sea. The sea does not separate people as much as it joins them, through trade, travel, mutual understanding, and common interests.

For this second reason, as well as the first, North America and Western Europe have formed the two halves of what is in reality one community, and have maintained an abiding interest in each other.

It is clear that the North Atlantic pact is not an improvisation. It is the statement of the facts and lessons of history. We have learned our history lesson from two world wars in less than half a century. That experience has taught us that the control of Europe by a single aggressive, unfriendly power would constitute an intolerable threat to the national security of the United States. We participated in those two great wars to preserve the integrity and independence of the European half of the Atlantic community in order to preserve the integrity and independence of the American half. It is a simple fact, proved by experience, that an outside attack on one member of this community is an attack upon all members.

We have also learned that if the free nations do not stand together, they will fall one by one. The stratagem of the aggressor is to keep his intended victims divided, or, better still, set them to quarreling among themselves. Then they can be picked off one by one without arousing unified resistance. We and the free nations of Europe are determined that history shall not repeat itself in that melancholy particular.

SELECTION III–B

Portions of an address by Senator Robert A. Taft, as printed in the Congressional Record—Senate, 81st Congress, 1st sess. vol. 95, July 11,
1949, p. 9206. Senator Taft was the most important Republican spokesman in the country after World War II, and remained an outspoken
isolationist while such major figures as Senator Vandenberg joined the
Democrats in much of the foreign policy planning between 1946 and
1949. Taft was one of the small minority of 13 to vote against the Atlantic
Pact on the Senate floor.

It is said that the Atlantic Treaty is simply another Monroe Doctrine. I
wish it were. That would be much more acceptable to me than the Atlantic
pact, arms or no arms. Let me point out the vital differences. The Monroe
Doctrine was a unilateral declaration. We were free to modify it or withdraw
from it at any moment. This treaty, adopted to deal with a particular emergency today, is binding upon us for 20 years to cover all kinds of circumstances which cannot possibly be foreseen. The Monroe Doctrine left us free
to determine the merits of each dispute which might arise and to judge the
justice and the wisdom of war in the light of the circumstances at the time.
The present treaty obligates us to go to war if certain facts occur. The
Monroe Doctrine imposed no obligation whatever to assist any American
Nation by giving it arms or even economic aid. We were free to fight the
war in such a manner as we might determine, or not at all. This treaty imposes on us a continuous obligation for 20 years to give aid to all the other
members of the pact, and, I believe, to give military aid to all the other
members of the pact.

All kinds of circumstances may arise which will make our obligation
most inconvenient. The government of one of these nations may be taken
over by the Communist Party of that nation. The distinguished Senator from
Michigan says that we are then released from our obligation, but I see no
basis whatever for such conclusion. If that were true of a Communist government, it might also be true of a Socialist government if we did not happen
to approve of socialism at the time. Presumably, it could be true of a Fascist
government, one similar, perhaps, to that existing in Spain which has been
denounced recently by the Secretary of State, and which is not very different
from the dictatorship of Portugal, which is a member of the pact and which
has not a truly democratic form of government.

I cannot find anything in this treaty which releases us because we do not
happen to like the officials in charge of the member nations at the particular
moment.

Obviously, any help we give one of these nations today may be used later
for aggressive purposes, against Russia or its satellites, or neutrals, or members of the pact, or it may even be used against us when we try to fulfill our
obligation to other members of the pact. Except for the warning conveyed to

Soviet Russia, this treaty does not bear the slightest resemblance to the Monroe Doctrine.

It is said that the treaty is in strict accordance with Senate Resolution 239 adopted by the Senate in June 1948. I did not vote upon that resolution, but I believe this treaty goes far beyond the advice there given by the Senate. That resolution approved the general theory of a treaty to exercise the right of individual or collective self-defense in case of an armed attack in accordance with the purposes, principles, and provisions of the Charter, but I do not think it suggested the providing of arms to members of the pact, or even the obligations of article 5. Paragraph 4 of the resolution, which is the closest one to authorizing the present treaty, sounds more like a new Monroe Doctrine than it does like a treaty. It does not refer to a treaty of any kind. It says that one of our objectives should be contributing to the maintenance of peace by making clear our determination to exercise the right of individual or collective self-defense under article 51 should any armed attack occur affecting our national security. This looks far more like a warning to Russia than it does like a defensive military alliance of the present type. The distinguished Senator from Michigan, in explaining the resolution at that time, said:

It declines automatically military alliances. It declines all peacetime renewals of the old, open-ended lend-lease formula. It declines unilateral responsibility for the fate of western Europe. It is none of those things. It is the exact opposite.

The present treaty is a military alliance. The present treaty does contemplate a peacetime renewal of the old, open-ended lend-lease formula. The present treaty assumes unilateral responsibility for the fate of western Europe. We are obligated to go to the defense of any nation whether the other members of the pact do so or not, or whatever their consultation may advise.

> ## SELECTION III–C
>
> Text of a statement by Scott Keyes, as published in *Hearings, North Atlantic Treaty*, Senate Committee on Foreign Relations, 81st Congress, 1st sess. An assistant professor of economics at Pennsylvania State College in 1949 Keyes appeared for himself and as a representative of the Peace Committee of State College Friends Committee. He presented a pacifist objection to NATO.

I wish to comment on only two questions: First whether the pact, by its very nature, can achieve its own purposes; and second, the relation of the pact to the United Nations.

THE PACT AND PRESERVATION OF THE PEACE

With regard to the first question, I think it is a fair and a hopeful thing to say that we are all agreed upon one larger objective—the attainment of peace. The proposed treaty itself, and Secretary Acheson's defense of it, both stress this objective repeatedly. Nevertheless, in view of the long record of failure of armed preparedness as a means of preserving peace—in view of the positive record of armament races culminating in war, the question of whether the pact can achieve its purpose must receive the careful attention of the committee.

As Secretary Acheson has pointed out, no one can say with certainty that the pact will succeed in its purpose. Likewise, no one can say with certainty that it will not achieve its aims. Nevertheless, there are good grounds for believing that it will not achieve its own objectives because of the very logic of the circumstances.

The pact has been developed in response to tensions that exist in the world today. These tensions arise out of differences of opinion on certain basic social, economic, and political issues. They can only be eliminated by the admittedly difficult process of negotiation, seeking constantly to widen areas of agreement, and to narrow areas of disagreement. When one group of nations, therefore, undertakes armament, and establishes machinery for joint military planning, such action must inevitably call forth parallel action elsewhere. It takes two sides, each of somewhat comparable strength, each believing in the justice of its cause, to create tension in the first place. In the process of the armaments race, the belief grows, however erroneously it may be, and however eloquently and sincerely the several foreign ministers of the respective countries plead their peaceful intentions, the belief grows that the die is irrevocably cast for war.

Thus the elimination of the tensions, the only basis upon which peace can be established, become difficult, if not impossible, and war, the very occurrence the pact seeks to avoid, almost inevitable.

There is another sense, also, in which it is questionable whether the pact can or will achieve its own larger objectives. The purpose of this pact is not merely to achieve peace; it is to preserve the free institutions which are part of the cultural heritage of the signatory nations. Yet, we must ask ourselves very frankly whether these free institutions can be maintained in the midst of an armed society. National defense, in these days of atomic warfare, as the President's Committee on Universal Military Training pointed out so clearly 2 years ago, is a far-reaching concept. Not only must the Nation have armed forces ready for instant action; it must likewise be prepared industrially, socially, scientifically. It must carry on, also, extensive intelligence operations at home and abroad, to promote its own philosophy in other countries, to learn of the actions of potential enemies, to counteract espionage, to prevent the infiltration of subversive ideas.

The effects of these needs of national defense on our social and economic institutions are plain. Economically, the needs of national defense stimulate that concentration of control over business and industry which the Federal Trade Commission and Senate investigating committees tell us is destroying the very system we seek to maintain. Governmentally, the needs of national defense lead to situations such as that in Washington today, where secret military organizations conduct operations of unknown scope and magnitude with budgets which are not matters of public record. Scientifically, the needs of national defense lead to a barren preoccupation with the problems of warfare. Socially, the needs of national defense lead to increasing interference with civil liberties—that phase of our society on which we pride ourselves most highly. Increasingly, people who out of an honest concern for the welfare of their country question any social or economic policy find themselves regarded as subversive, as traitors, frequently being deprived of their livelihoods.

Where is the logic of this situation? Do we preserve our free institutions by turning our own and our neighbors' countries into armed camps; by promoting the concentration of economic control which is destroying free competitive enterprise; by increasing the magnitude and scope of secret operations in the Government; by increasingly violating civil liberties, and instilling fear into all who would protest? Furthermore, if our objective is to encourage the growth of civil liberties in nations outside the pact, can we hope to accomplish this aim by a policy of military containment, particularly in view of the effects of such a policy in our own free society? These questions will, I hope, receive your earnest consideration.

THE PACT AND THE UNITED NATIONS

Secondly, I should like to comment briefly on the relationship of the proposed pact to the United Nations. On this matter I speak with diffidence, recognizing that some of the members of this committee were among the architects of that organization. Nevertheless, every person who believes, as I do, heart and soul, in the cause of the United Nations has a responsibility to examine to the best of his ability the contention which has been made repeatedly that the proposed North Atlantic Treaty is consistent with the spirit as well as with the letter of the United Nations Charter.

We are told that the Charter recognizes the importance of regional arrangements consistent with its purposes and principles. Can the proposed treaty be said in the largest sense to fit this definition? This, I think, is a debatable point. For better or for worse, the Charter establishes an association of nations which can only function effectively when its principal members are on friendly terms with each other. The regional arrangements which are recognized in article 51 and the several articles of chapter VIII must be construed in the light of this fundamental prerequisite of the organization as a whole. Thus, any regional arrangement by which some members arm themselves against other members is not consistent with the basic philosophy of the organization. By their solemn ratification of the Charter, the several nations have not only expressed their intent to make such a step unnecessary but have made it out of keeping with the spirit of the organization. The rearmament that is countenanced is against former enemies which are not members of the United Nations. Furthermore, any arrangement which divides the members into armed camps only renders it more difficult to achieve in practice the unanimous agreement of the major powers which, for all its shortcomings, is the one principle which makes an international organization possible at this stage in the world's development. Pursued to its logical conclusion, any other argument culminates in the ultimate question whether the United Nations can and should continue to exist, and I cannot believe that the American people are willing even to entertain the thought of abandoning their participation in that organization.

The very fact that the proponents of the treaty have been at considerable pains to square it with the United Nations—and I am not making any charge of bad faith—indicates, I think, the deep-seated concern the American people have for the success of the United Nations. Finally, I think our people will also become increasingly disturbed if they find our Nation committed to continue spending more per day to maintain our own and other military establishments than the United Nations is spending per year to achieve peace.

In view of these arguments, therefore, that there are grave doubts whether the pact can, by the very logic of the circumstances achieve its own larger objectives of attaining peace and protecting our free institutions, and that it is inconsistent with the larger philosophy of the United Nations. I respectfully urge that the members of this committee recommend the rejection of the proposed North Atlantic Treaty.

IV. VIEWS OF OBSERVERS

> SELECTION IV–A
>
> Lyman B. Burbank's "NATO and the U.S. Constitution," *Social Education*, XVI (May, 1952), pp. 207–9; 221. Reprinted with permission of the author and the National Council for the Social Studies. Professor Burbank, formerly a member of the History Department at Danbury (Connecticut) State Teachers College, is presently Director of Teacher Education at Vanderbilt University. He affirmed the compatibility of the Treaty with the Constitution.

It is standard educational practice to require prerequisites for advanced courses. That is as it should be. It would seem that for an intelligent discussion of the North Atlantic Alliance in a course on the history of modern Europe, students should have some understanding of western Europe and its problems. The question immediately arises as to what prerequisites, if any, are the most advantageous and desirable.

Because twelve of the fourteen NATO nations are outside this hemisphere, and because most of NATO's problems are essentially those of rearming Europe and finding the resources with which to do it, one would assume that a study of NATO is more pertinent for a course on western Europe than on the history of the United States. However, there is something to be said for the fact that a proper understanding of the drafting and subsequent development of the pact cannot be had without a proper understanding of the Constitution of the United States.

One of the factors which delayed negotiation of the pact was the conflict between the French idea, that each signatory should pledge itself to come to the immediate aid of a member-nation under attack, and the American realization that such a pledge would be a violation of Article I, Section 8 of our Constitution, granting to Congress the power to declare war.

It has been my experience that most college students have little understanding of the Constitution. Their minds are cluttered with a series of half-truths and false assumptions. They may be dimly aware that the President cannot declare war, but it should not be the function of an instructor in a course on the history of modern Europe to take the time of the class to explain the history of the war-making power of the Constitution. That Article I, Section 8 was decisive in determining the language of the pact—and the commitments under it—is supported by abundant evidence.

Article II, Section 2 was of equal importance in drafting the pact. This section says the President shall have power, by and with the advice and consent of the Senate, to make treaties. It is clear that the Truman administration has interpreted this section much different from the interpretation given it by Woodrow Wilson. But here again, it should not be the business of the instructor to take class time to discuss the constitutional history of Article II, Section 2.

Taken together, the two above sections were very important. They were both responsible for determining the language of the pact, and the former section was a consideration of great importance in determining the manner in which the North Atlantic Treaty Organization was negotiated.

Senate Resolution 239, often called the "Vandenberg Resolution," passed in the summer of 1948 after the Communist seizure of Czechoslovakia, had "advised" the President to pursue six objectives within the framework of the United Nations Charter. This "advice," worked out in cooperation with the State Department, devoted three points to United Nations reform and three points to developing "regional and other collective self-defense arrangements under Article LI" of the UN Charter. Following this "advice," secret conferences were held with representatives of five European nations and Canada, and from these conferences eventually came the North Atlantic Treaty.

From the early days of Senate Resolution 239 to the ratification of the treaty there was close cooperation between the executive branch of the government and the Senate. This was a far cry from the opinion of Woodrow Wilson that Article 2, Section 2 of our Constitution meant that the President might, *if he wished,* consult the Senate during the negotiation of a treaty. The Truman administration made it clear from the beginning that it felt, either for political or constitutional reasons, or both, that the executive branch was *required* to consult with the Senate in negotiating treaties. Senator Connally said that Dean Acheson and Under-Secretary of State Levett were "the chief architects for the United States in building the treaty structure." He added, however, the significant statement that the Foreign Relations Committee and the Senate as a whole "furnished some of the stone and mixed some of the mortar to complete its symmetry and strength."

According to Article V of the North Atlantic Treaty, an attack on one member is considered to be an attack on all. The signatories agree that if a member nation should be under attack, they will assist "by taking action forthwith." This action may be individual or collective, as each member "deems necessary," and it may include the use of armed force. The origins of this phraseology are interesting, although secrecy has prevented us from knowing the entire story.

On January 28, 1949, James Reston reported in *The New York Times* that the seven nations negotiating the pact had reached agreement on many items. It was agreed, for example, that nations ratifying the treaty would be obligated to take "military or other action forthwith" in case of armed attack against one of the signatories. Reston also reported agreement on the idea that meeting obligations by constitutional processes would either be written into the pact, or implied. Further, he reported that the conferees had decided the pact should not come up for renewal during a presidential election year.

On February 10, 1949, the *Times* reported that the United States had recommended two changes in the draft proposal. As it was, it apparently provided that the treaty was to take effect when ratified by one half the signatories. We recommended that the "one half" be changed to "all" the signatories. We further recommended that there should be no direct or specific reference to "military" aid in the pact. Secretary Acheson is said to have told the negotiators that these two changes would simplify the task of getting Senatorial approval of the pact.

It was apparently after consultation with Senators Connally and Vandenberg that the key words "such action as it deems necessary" appeared in Article V of the treaty. It was also after consultation with the Senate Foreign Relations Committee that the obligation of signatories to carry out the treaty "in accordance with their respective constitutional processes" was transferred from the preamble to Article XI.

The results of the rather close teamwork between the executive and legislative branches of government were rewarding. The Senators were apparently satisfied that the power to declare war had not been handed to the executive. During the debate, thirty-one Senators spoke for the treaty and twelve against it, but the opposition centered around the inappropriateness of the pact, rather than its language. There were those in Europe who pointed out that Article IV of the Brussels Pact (between Belgium, France, the Netherlands, Luxembourg and the United Kingdom) was much stronger than Article V of the North Atlantic Treaty. But when the Brussels Pact was negotiated, there was no United States Constitution involved.

When the North Atlantic Treaty reached the Senate floor, an interesting constitutional question arose regarding the admission of a new nation. Would such admission be a legislative or an executive act? Secretary Acheson stated categorically that no new nation would be admitted without the advice and consent of the Senate. Senator Vandenberg thought this pledge was binding upon the present President's successors. "In my opinion," said he, "any Presidential successor who might do otherwise would be impeached." The most that can be said constitutionally, is that both Greece and Turkey were admitted to NATO according to Mr. Acheson's formula.

Less than a year and a half after the pact had taken effect, its purposes and achievements came under close scrutiny in the Congress. The subject was the troops-for-Europe issue. Senator Taft, speaking to a packed Senate for more than an hour on January 15, 1951, clearly disapproved of our use of ground troops in Korea, as well as of the commitment of other troops to Europe, without the consent of Congress. After several weeks of debate, a compromise resolution was passed, approving the sending of four more divisions to Europe but asking that Congress be consulted if more were to be sent. One has the feeling, however, that if the political atmosphere had been different the North Atlantic Treaty might then and there have been struck a death blow with the constitutional argument that the President was exceeding his authority. Clearly, our constitutional history supported the President in this argument. But, equally clearly, our constitutional history has on more than one occasion done a sudden about-face.

At the Ottawa meeting of the members of the pact, in October, 1951, a committee, known as the "three wise men," was created, the purpose of which was to survey the financial capacities of the NATO countries and report on how the rearmament program could best be met.

The committee's report criticized Belgium rather severely. Specifically, the Belgians were asked to increase their defense budget by 70 percent in the current fiscal year, and to increase it nearly 100 percent in the three-year period ending in June, 1954. Other nations were asked to raise their defense budgets by lesser amounts. Immediately the reply among some of Europe's statesmen was that the United States was seeking to get Europe to pledge itself to fixed sums of expenditure over a period of years, while it would merely have to be assumed that the United States would follow suit. After all, Article I, Section 8 of the Constitution says that no appropriation of money to raise and support armies "shall be made for a longer term than two years."

Jean Monnet, the brilliant author of the Monnet plan for the modernization of French industry, has repeatedly said that there should be a common budget for the financing of the armed effort of the North Atlantic Pact. Such a development seems a long way off, even though common sense might dictate to us its wisdom. But that question may stir up a very heated controversy over whether the Congress would have the constitutional power to authorize such a thing.

These, then, are some of the constitutional problems which have arisen in creating and implementing the North Atlantic Treaty. They should be of considerable interest to a student of our Constitution, and they should help a student of the recent history of western Europe to have a better understanding of the relations of America to the total North Atlantic community.

SELECTION IV–B

From "What Does the Pact Promise?" Copyright 1949 Christian Century Foundation. Reprinted by permission from the June 22, 1949 issue of *The Christian Century*, pp. 758–59. This liberal interdenominational journal was concerned for the future of the United Nations and disturbed over the implications of militarism in the American identification with NATO.

The Senate foreign relations committee celebrated the fifth anniversary of the landing on the Normandy beaches by recommending ratification of the North Atlantic Treaty. As expected, the committee's action was unanimous. It was accompanied by a 28-page report in which the committee declared that ratification would "greatly increase the prospect" of averting another world war, but pointed out that if "war is imposed upon us, the treaty assures us that eleven other nations will stand with us to defend our freedom and our civilization." This report is intended to clear away any uncertainties as to the promises, explicit or implied, in the treaty. It is our belief that it actually increases the ambiguity of a document which is open to misconstruction.

Senator Connally predicts that, when this military alliance comes up for ratification, not more than ten or twelve senators will vote against it. That is quite possible. But if any such overwhelming majority as the chairman of the foreign relations committee expects is cast for ratification, there will be many a member of that majority who will act in deep perplexity of mind, not simply as to the wisdom of his vote but also as to what it really is that he is voting for. Senators, as well as American citizens in general, still cannot be sure what the United States is promising to do for its prospective allies.

I

Within the past week we have seen two striking revelations of this persisting ambiguity. The first is to be found in the report of the Senate committee, giving its reasons for recommending ratification. The second is in an article favoring ratification by Hanson W. Baldwin, military editor of the

New York Times, and published in that newspaper. Let us look at Mr. Baldwin's article first.

Mr. Baldwin has proved himself such a dispassionate, fair-minded and prodigiously informed writer in all fields of military policy and action that his argument for ratification must be given great weight. Nevertheless, that argument seems to us to conclude in a dangerously ambiguous interpretation of the meaning of the North Atlantic alliance. It opens with a statement that congressional slowness in acting is a result of "fears that the Atlantic pact and its arms-aid program might be provocative of war, instead of a deterrent to it." "Those fears," writes Mr. Baldwin, "represent the anxiety of many sincere Americans lest the nation's political and economic and psychological programs for security be subordinated and emasculated by its military program. They represent, too, genuine apprehension lest an alliance (the Atlantic pact), intended primarily as a defensive deterrent, be transformed by changing emphasis and the arms-aid program into an offensive entente."

Like the honest man he is, Mr. Baldwin agrees that there is plenty of historical ground for such fears. "Too great an emphasis upon military strength, too great military influence usually has been provocative of war rather than deterrent to it." German history is adduced to show how Bismarck's "purely defensive" alliances became a source of the European debacle. "Clearly," Mr. Baldwin warns, "the implementation of the Atlantic pact and the arms-aid program must avoid this danger." If it does not, "then we are undone."

But how is this danger to be avoided? At this critical point Mr. Baldwin's article becomes disappointingly vague. All that he has to say is that it can be done. No program for doing it is outlined; Mr. Baldwin is content simply to repeat that "they [pact and arms-aid] must not be provocative; they must not sacrifice economic and political and psychological recovery for military strength alone." Then the article reaches what is supposed to be its constructive climax: "But on the other hand the positive objective of the Atlantic pact-arms-aid program must be the defense of western Europe, not its reconquest once overrun, for invasion of western Europe means the bankruptcy of all our past policies and the mortgaging of the future."

II

Here, we maintain, is an ambiguity that the nation's representatives in the Senate should not ignore. What is Mr. Baldwin actually saying? We believe he is saying that the United States will be committed by this alliance to maintain forces in Europe sufficiently large to defend the western part of that continent against any invasion. If his interpretation of the pact does not involve that, what does he have in mind? In the first part of his article he scorns "the almost hysterical dependence of United States senators and representatives on the atomic bomb," which apparently means that he rejects the idea of protecting western Europe from invasion by long-range bombing from American bases.

Is there any reasonable interpretation to be placed on Mr. Baldwin's words other than an insistence that the proposed pact will obligate the United States to keep armies in being within striking distance of the Russian front lines large enough to pin the Russians down? That, it should be remembered, was also the apparent meaning of the pact as interpreted by General Bradley. If this is *not* what is meant, then the great newspaper for which Mr. Baldwin writes owes it to the American people, and to the people of western Europe, to clear this ambiguity away and to make it plain what *is* meant.

Turn now to the report in support of the treaty sent to the Senate by its foreign relations committee. (We comment on the basis of the condensed text published in the *New York Times* on June 8.) This entire document is full of wordy passages which can be interpreted in many ways. We direct attention, however, to the interpretation of Article 5 of the alliance, which the committee calls "the heart of the treaty." Let us quote a little:

> Obviously Article 5 carries with it an important and far-reaching commitment for the United States; what we may do to carry out that commitment, however, will depend upon our own independent decision in each particular instance reached in accordance with our own constitutional processes.
>
> During the hearings substantially the following questions were repeatedly asked: In view of the provision in Article 5 that an attack against one shall be considered an attack against all, would the United States be obligated to react to an attack on Paris or Copenhagen in the same way it would react to an attack on New York City? In such an event does the treaty give the President the power to take any action, without specific congressional authorization, which he could not take in advance of the treaty?
>
> The answer to both these questions is "No." . . . In the event any party to the treaty were attacked the obligation of the United States government would be to decide upon and take forthwith the measures it deemed necessary to restore and maintain the security of the North Atlantic area. The measures which would be necessary to accomplish that end would depend upon a number of factors, including the location, nature, scale and significance [*sic!*] of the attack.

Now, does this interpretation agree with the Bradley-Baldwin interpretation? Does it mean that the United States is promising to protect western Europe against any invasion, and under the treaty will maintain a military force there that will undertake not simply to drive out the Russians if they invade but to stop them from invading? We do not so read it. We do not see how anyone can so read it—including the peoples of western Europe—especially in view of the direct denial that this nation is assuming any obligations to defend Paris and Copenhagen such as it has to defend New York. In fact, we do not see how anyone can read this passage in the Senate committee's report (and other passages of similar nature) without concluding that what the committee is intimating is that the United States is assuming no greater obligations under the treaty than, in the actual circumstances which will obtain at a time when the treaty may be invoked, Congress is inclined to assume.

III

Here, then, are two interpretations of the treaty's meaning. Each is ambiguous within itself, and one apparently does not accord with the other. One is made by the distinguished military editor of the most influential newspaper in the country, and we think it echoes an interpretation made earlier by the chief of staff of the army. The other is made by Senator Connally and his colleagues on the foreign relations committee. While these two interpretations are put forward, the vital question of the nature of the promises which the United States is making to the eleven other nations involved in this alliance is shrouded in ambiguity. However senators may vote on the pact, they owe it to the people of the United States, and to the people of these other eleven nations as well, to make sure that not a shred of this ambiguity remains by the time the decisive vote is cast.

> *SELECTION IV–C*
>
> An excerpt from Lawrence S. Kaplan's "NATO and the Language of Isolationism," in *South Atlantic Quarterly*, LVIII (Spring, 1958), pp. 207–9; 214–15. Reprinted by permission of the Duke University Press. Kaplan, professor of history at Kent State University, noted the ingenuity of the administration and its supporters in defending the Treaty against attack at the Senate Foreign Relations Committee Hearings in 1949. Anticipating rejection of a forthright avowal of a traditional alliance with Europe, they attempted to disguise it as an extension of the Monroe Doctrine.

In observing the method whereby advocates of the treaty in the Senate and in the Administration blunted criticism and set forth the virtues of the new program, one can uncover a pattern of argument revealing how the North Atlantic Treaty fitted into the isolationist tradition. Instead of avoiding such subjects as Washington's Farewell Address, Jefferson's First Inaugural, and the Monroe Doctrine as a source of potential embarrassment, the treaty's managers appear to have gone out of their way in their testimony and in leading questions posed to witnesses to show that the treaty conformed not only with the spirit but also with the letter of isolationism. Anticipating the strategy of their opponents, they put the emotionally charged words of Washington, Jefferson, and Monroe to the service of a new American foreign policy, thereby upsetting those critics who would have used the same language to damn the treaty.

The first, and in many ways the most powerful, element of isolationism was the projection of the physical separation of Europe from America to a psychological plane through images inspired by such proclamations as the Monroe Doctrine. On the surface it seemed virtually impossible to reconcile a doctrine resting on an eternal cleavage between the Old World and the New with a doctrine that would tie them together again.

The foes of the North Atlantic Treaty were not slow in pointing out the discrepancies between the nature and purposes of the Monroe Doctrine and those of the treaty. An obvious stumbling block was the fact that the countries with which the United States proposed to associate were for the most part the very ones against which the Monroe Doctrine had been directed. Lest their evil deeds be forgotten, one particularly vehement private witness felt it necessary to remind the Senators that one has only to look at the map of Latin America today to find evidence of territories seized by England, France, and the Netherlands before the Monroe Doctrine went into effect. The implication was that these countries would now use the Atlantic Pact to win American support for new depredations. The United States would then be on the side of those who would destroy the Monroe Doctrine, and the stigma of the colonial tradition would be attached to the champion of anti-colonialism.

More moderate was the attack that drew strength from the unilateral character of the Monroe Doctrine. This argument even accepted the necessity of giving American protection to Western Europe, but it precluded action in co-operation with any other country. As presented effectively by Professor Curtis Nettels, the United States acted alone in 1823, not in conjunction with Britain, or even any Latin American nation. Why violate this tradition by engaging in an alliance that might limit American freedom of action, and hence the effectiveness of American power? It would be far better for Europeans themselves, as Taft claimed on the Senate floor, if the United States would throw the protective mantle of the Monroe Doctrine around Western Europe but remain free to interpret this enlarged Monroe Doctrine unfettered by any ties. This move would have a greater deterrent effect upon Soviet expansionism than the ratification of the treaty itself. To emphasize this point, Taft in collaboration with Senator Flanders introduced a resolution extending the Monroe Doctrine to Western Europe as a substitute for the North Atlantic Treaty. Although this resolution never went beyond the Committee on Foreign Relations, it reflected the power possessed by the slogans of isolationism.

The counterattack of the Administration spokesmen and their allies in the Senate was prepared well in advance of the actual inquisition. Defense of the treaty as a fulfillment of the Monroe Doctrine had as its first proposition the fact that the Doctrine itself had stretched the original boundaries of isolation. Secretary Acheson pointedly announced that "For more than a century and a quarter this Government has contributed to the peace of the Americas by making clear that it would regard an attack on any American state as an attack on itself." The elasticity of the borders of isolationism was thereby established.

.   .   .   .

Despite their willingness to play with words, the friends of the pact did not appear to be playing a cynical game with the Senate or with the public. The distinctions between the North Atlantic Treaty and a military alliance had more than a semantic meaning for them, even though many had trouble articulating those distinctions. In effect, the connotations of the term, "military alliance," did violence to their conception of the purpose of the pact, and any such association would be a misstatement of fact a well as an obstacle in the way of public acceptance. To Senator Henry Cabot Lodge, Jr., for example, a military alliance meant quite plainly "an aggressive combination of nations who are going out on the rampage to attack and oppress people . . . in a spirit of cynicism and opportunism, without regard to any common idealistic values." To observers of this mind, terms such as "partnership for peace" or "broad partnership for security" represent not merely euphemisms designed to lull the public but ideals directly in the American tradition of foreign relations.

The North Atlantic Treaty was ultimately accepted on terms laid down by the Government. On July 21, 1949, the Senate approved the treaty 82 to 13, a majority large enough to be hailed as an impressive vote of confidence in a milestone of America's foreign policy. It signified that the Senate Committee on Foreign Relations' report on the treaty convinced isolationists that the pact conformed with the spirit of the Monroe Doctrine and had nothing in common with the old European military alliances. In brief, the Government succeeded in invoking the shibboleths of isolationism to win acceptance of a policy that marked a departure from the isolationist traditions.

While the spokesmen for the treaty obviously recognized the speciousness of some of the claims, it was equally obvious that their arguments were based on something more than political expediency. They interpreted the isolationist symbols to justify a new turn in the foreign policy but not a new policy. Though they spoke for foreign entanglements and accepted the balance-of-power philosophy, they did so in the name of the Founding Fathers and of their concern for American security.

The symbols that they exploited might have destroyed the concept of the North Atlantic Treaty, and possibly America's leadership in world affairs. Instead, the language of an old policy served to open new vistas for the free world. There were dangers in this method. The symbols of isolationism could be used differently at another time, and the frequency of the "Great Debates" in the succeeding years attests to the latent power of isolationism. Furthermore, the future of NATO was to be complicated because of the circumlocutions and ambiguities of the treaty. But whatever the languaged employed in 1949, Europeans at last knew that the vast weight America could yield in international politics had swung behind them.

5

FALL OF CHINA
America's Guilt?

I. EDITORIAL INTRODUCTION

At the very time when the United States appeared to have broken the barrier of isolationism by extending a major commitment to the defense of Europe, China—a traditional area of American concern—fell into communist hands. In 1949, Nationalist China was forced off of the mainland as the territory held by Chiang Kai-shek, America's ally of World War II, became limited to Formosa. There is irony here as well as tragedy. Throughout much of the nineteenth century and the first half of the twentieth century, the United States had maintained an interest in the Far East in general and in China in particular. An interest initiated first by businessmen seeking economic advantage, then expanded upon by missionaries seeking to extend the benefits of American religions, and continued by a public that looked upon itself as a defender of China against European exploitation. The isolationist arguments which had such force in Europe had little meaning in the Far East; the ideology of isolation was based on the dangers of involvement in Europe and with Europeans, not with Asians who could be regarded with Americans as fellow-victims of Europe's intrigues. The "open door" in the Far East coexisted with "no entangling alliances" in Europe.

Considering the history of American involvement with China, it is not surprising that many opponents of the Truman administration—friends of Chiang Kai-shek, Republican politicians, and ardent isolationists—found a plot that linked the China debacle with the new discovery of Europe. The Asia-minded Americans had long suspected that official Washington held Europe in greater esteem than China; the relatively smaller support of the Pacific forces as opposed to the European forces in World War II had fed their suspicions. Instead of seeking an explanation of the catastrophe in the policies of the Nationalist leaders, they turned to the presumed errors and crimes of the United States. They theorized that Communist successes in China must be a product of a world conspiracy, abetted by sympathizers and fellow-travelers in Washington, rather than the product of the failings of the Nationalists or of the shrewdness of Chinese communist tactics.

A convenient focus for anti-administration attackers was the Yalta agreement of 1945 concerning the future of China. In return for the entry of the Soviet Union into World War II, the allies granted to the Russians many of the concessions in Manchuria which they had lost in the Russo-Japanese War of 1905. Having learned of some secret agreements which had been made at this important conference, critics asked how many other unpublished concessions might have been made at Yalta in turn facilitating the accession to power of the Chinese Communists. Such American expectations as are revealed in the "briefing book paper," (Selection II.), memoranda for the use of policymakers—envisaging a strong united and friendly China and discounting fears about the future behavior of the communists—appeared naive or communist-inspired to many enemies of the administration's China policy. America's subsequent attempts to unite the Chinese factions after the war, particularly the Marshall Mission of 1946, followed from the assumption that the Nationalists and Communists could be brought successfully into a coalition government. Another mission by General Albert Wedemeyer in 1947 reported the futility of the task and suggested massive aid to the government of Chiang Kai-shek. When Wedemeyer found his report tabled and his recommendations ignored, he attributed the fall of China to the State Department's inability to respond properly to the communist challenge. (Selection III–A.)

To counter these charges, the Department of State produced in 1949 a White Paper, including detailed records of American attempts (at the cost of $1.5 billion) to shore up, unify, and reform the China of Chiang Kai-shek so that it might realize its potential as a great power in and out of the United Nations. The frustrations of the Marshall and Wedemeyer missions were recounted at great length. Secretary of State Acheson was convinced that the evidence would show the magnitude of American help, its good faith, and Chiang's incredible waste of most of the aid. Acheson made it clear in his letter of transmittal to the President (Selection III–B.), that if China fell it was because of corruption, incompetence, and inability of Nationalist China to implement the reforms that should have accompanied American military and political aid. If Chiang was in exile, the fault was his own.

The White Paper did not convince critics in 1949. Indeed, the rise the demagogue, Senator Joseph R. McCarthy, was built largely upon unproved and sensational charges of Communism in the State Department in which the administration emerged either as dupes of or collaborators with the Chinese communists. The major victim was Secretary of Defense Marshall who had the task of attempting to explain how a million and a half Communists could defeat three million Nationalist troops. He believed that no amount of military aid could have balanced the lack of leadership among the Nationalists. But to McCarthy and his followers the policies of Acheson and Marshall, reflecting the Communist Party line, led directly to the disaster. (Selection III–C.)

In the eyes of many observers the loss of China remained as evidence of the incompetence of the administration's handling of foreign policy—if not necessarily proof of communist influence in the government—long after 1949. Two years later, Freda Utley stressed the administration's folly in misunderstanding the communist threat more than she did the possible influence of communist agents in the State Department. Her major theme was that communist power was indivisible and could not be appeased as the United States appeared to have been attempting. (Selection IV–A.)

More detached in time and in emotion is the selection by Tang Tsou. Writing fifteen years after the event, he shared the administration's criticism of China's incapacity in 1949 and understood why Wedemeyer's recommendation of a trusteeship for Manchuria was impractical and impolitic. Yet, he felt that the government had erred in suppressing Wedemeyer's report and also in failing to inform the public of the magnitude of its problem in China. With so much attention focused on Europe, he felt that Washington had not devoted proper attention to Asia, and had not taken the public into its confidence. McCarthyism was one of the prices of this failure. (Selection IV–B.)

But British historian Sir Denis Brogan raised a question that might be asked of all Americans, both the administration and its critics. Did the United States ever have China to lose? If China was lost or betrayed, was it not possible that the events would have occurred independently of whatever the United States did or did not do? If in the past the United States had contributed to world chaos by the excessive limitations of its power, it was apparent that the swing of the pendulum after the war had led too many Americans to believe that, in accepting leadership of the "free world," it had the power and responsibility to control events everywhere. Much of the debate over China, therefore, was irrelevant; and it was conceivable that China's fate was always beyond America's control. (Selection IV–C.)

II. DOCUMENT

SELECTION II

The following excerpt is taken from "The Conferences at Yalta and Malta 1945" *Foreign Relations of the United States* (Washington, 1955), pp. 353–54. In a background report for the statesman at Yalta, the State Department aides prepared a "Briefing Book Paper" which encompassed many of America's hopes for the future of China.

UNITY OF ANGLO-AMERICAN-SOVIET POLICY
TOWARD CHINA

There exist areas of potential discord between our policies and those of the United Kingdom and the U.S.S.R. toward China. At present, the British recognize that China is a theater of primary concern to us in the prosecution of the war, and the Russians desire to see established in China a government friendly to them. But the progress of events during the war and in the immediate post-war period may develop discords detrimental to the achievement of victory and peace—detrimental to our objective of a united, progressive China capable of contributing to security and prosperity in the Far East.

An unstable, divided, and reactionary China would make stability and progress in the Far East impossible, and would greatly increase the difficult task, which will be largely ours, of maintaining peace in the western Pacific. A strong, friendly China would do much to lighten our task and to promote mutually beneficial cultural and commercial intercourse.

It is not enough that we merely hope for a strong, friendly China or that we simply pursue the negative policies of the pre-war period. We should assume the leadership in the development of the kind of China that will contribute toward peace in the Pacific in cooperation with the United Kingdom and the U.S.S.R. We may reasonably expect that a strong, united China will cooperate with the United States, the United Kingdom and the U.S.S.R. in dealing with post-war Japan.

There is now Kuomintang China, Communist China, and puppet China. Kuomintang China is being weakened by dissident elements and widespread popular discontent. Communist China is growing in material and popular strength. Puppet China is filled with pockets of Communist guerrilla resistance. A partial settlement between the Kuomintang and the Communists would not eliminate the fundamental struggle for power, one aspect of which will be competition to win over the puppet troops as Japan is driven from China. The only hope of preventing civil war and disunity will lie in the creation of a democratic framework within which the opposing groups can reconcile their differences on a political level.

There are reports that elements among the British out of imperial considerations desire a weak and possibly disunited China in the post-war period. The British are undoubtedly less optimistic—more cynical—than we are regarding the future of China but neither the British Government nor the British people will derive benefit from an unstable China in the post-war period.

Some apprehension has been voiced lest the Russians may utilize the Chinese Communists to establish an independent or autonomous area in north China and Manchuria. There is nothing in Russia's present attitude as officially disclosed to us to substantiate those fears. But if Russia comes into the war in the Far East, or if an open break between the Kuomintang and the Communists occurs, Russia may be strongly tempted to abandon its policy declared in 1924 of non-interference in China's internal affairs.

It is our task to bring about British and Russian support of our objective of a united China which will cooperate with them as well as with us. The British attitude is characterized by skepticism and is influenced by a residue of nineteenth century thinking. We hope that the British, given a clear knowledge of our objective and assurance that we mean to work consistently and energetically for that objective, will support our efforts. The Russians primarily want a China friendly to them. We should give Russia definite assurance that we too desire and are working for a united China friendly to all its neighbors.

Our policy toward China is not based on sentiment. It is based on an enlightened national self-interest motivated by considerations of international security and well-being. Unless the United Kingdom and the U.S.S.R. are in substantial agreement with us it is doubtful whether we can accomplish the objective of our policies.

III. VIEWS OF PARTICIPANTS

SELECTION III–A

An excerpt from Albert Wedemeyer, *Wedemeyer Reports!* (New York, 1958), pp. 394–95, 397–98. Copyright © by Albert C. Wedemeyer. Reprinted by permission of Holt, Rinehart and Winston, Inc. General Albert Wedemeyer, a retired Army officer and veteran of the Pacific War, headed a mission to China in 1947, after General Marshall had returned to become Secretary of State. When his recommendations were ignored, he became an articulate critic of the administration.

Although I believed that Chiang Kai-shek was sincere in his desire to establish a democratic form of government, I was not certain that he had sufficient determination to do so if this required "overruling of the political and military cliques surrounding him." The receipt of realistic U.S. aid required that he show evidence of such determination. As I wrote: "Adoption by the United States of a policy motivated solely toward the expansion of Communism without regard to the continued existence of an unpopular, repressive government would render any aid ineffective."

I was in a dilemma. I recognized the weaknesses and the oppressive character of the Nationalist Government and its decreasing popular support, but I was equally aware that Communist totalitarian tyranny would be infinitely worse. Finally I realized that only American military, economic, and political support of the Chinese Nationalist Government against the Communists would establish a climate in which the best, most progressive, and liberal forces in China could win influence and power and an opportunity to reform their country. The real liberals in China had so far been given a choice only between adherence to the Kuomintang, in spite of its degeneration and corruption, and Communism. We ourselves were largely responsible for this tragic fact. We had rendered confusion worse confounded by making our aid and support conditional on the establishment of a Chinese Government deemed to be democratic by both ourselves and the Communists. Since the Communist view of what constitutes democracy is diametrically opposed to that of the free world, we had impaled the Chinese on the horns of an insoluble dilemma. By equating democracy with willingness to collaborate with Communists, and by castigating as reactionaries those who believed that "co-operation by the Chinese Communist party in the government was inconceivable and that only force could settle the issue" General Marshall had positively encouraged the liberals to go over to the Communist side, or at least support it against the Nationalist Government. The tragedy was that, had it not been for the false equation on which U.S.-China policy was based in the Truman-Acheson-Marshall era, we could have strengthened the influence of the real liberals and reformers instead of either driving them to retire from the struggle in despair or go over to the Communists in the hope that the Americans' favorable view of them would be justified.

In 1947 on my mission I believed it was not yet too late to remedy the unfortunate consequences of our former China policy, which had been formulated on the basis of illusions and myths about communism which had already been discarded in our policy toward Greece and Europe in general. I thought that if we gave Chiang Kai-shek military aid and moral support against the Communist menace, but also compelled, or galvanized him into instituting vitally necessary reforms in administration, the best elements in China would once again rally to the Nationalist Government.

.   .   .   .

No doubt I had been naïve. I had had many warnings concerning the negative attitude of the State Department toward giving any military aid to the Nationalist Government or taking any concrete steps to dam the advancing Communist tide in China. It had refused all along to give even the political and moral support to the Chinese Government which might have sustained the morale of its armed forces. I felt more and more frustrated and alarmed. I knew that the delay in implementing my recommendations for immediate moral and material support to the Chinese Nationalist Government was serving the purpose of the Communists. The State Department knew as well as I that the situation was deteriorating rapidly, yet the hands-off attitude prevailed. I asked myself with increasing anxiety why I had been sent to China. Had General Marshall simply wanted me to reinforce his own views by submitting a report completely confirming his existing do-nothing policy? Had he wanted me to join the host of sycophants whom he had despised in the earlier years when he told me that he valued most those who frankly expressed their honest convictions?

When questioned by Congressional committees and the press as to why my report to the President had been suppressed, Secretary of State Marshall indicated that it contained confidential material the publication of which might cause embarrassment to the nations concerned. Of course it was not my function to determine the effect of the information embodied in my report and certainly I did not feel qualified to make such determination. But the conclusions and recommendations were carefully phrased to insure that no offense would be given, and practically all of the ideas had been previously discussed in a most friendly atmosphere with Generalissimo Chiang Kai-shek. I feel positive today that the publication of my report would not have caused embarrassment to my Government or to the Chinese and Koreans. If I am wrong, then it would appear that the subsequent publication of my report in the White Paper in 1949 was a serious mistake in diplomacy.

I visited General Eisenhower and told him I wished to be returned to duty with the Second Army, since I was doing nothing in the State Department. He agreed to ask that I be reassigned, pointing out that I would be readily available for conferences, inasmuch as my headquarters were located in Baltimore, Maryland.

Not that I was ever again consulted, nor my report discussed. It was simply buried until in the course of time it was exhumed by Senate Committee investigators alarmed at the imminent loss of China to the Communists. Long before this, Ambassador Leighton Stuart's dispatches from China (which are to be found buried in the 600 pages of annexes to the unindexed State Department White Paper of 1949, in which my own suppressed Report was eventually published) had begun to echo the recommendations I had made in the spring of 1947, and which he himself had failed to support.

> SELECTION III–B
>
> A portion of Acheson's Letter of Transmittal as printed in *United States Relations with China, with Special Reference to the Period, 1944–1949* (Washington, 1949), pp. xiv-xvii. Secretary of State Acheson blamed Nationalist China for its disaster in his introduction to the State Department's White Paper on the problem.

The reasons for the failures of the Chinese National Government appear in some detail in the attached record. They do not stem from any inadequacy of American aid. Our military observers on the spot have reported that the Nationalist armies did not lose a single battle during the critical year of 1948 through lack of arms or ammunition. The fact was that the decay which our observers had detected in Chungking early in the war had fatally sapped the powers of resistance of the Kuomintang. Its leaders had proved incapable of meeting the crisis confronting them, its troops had lost the will to fight, and its Government had lost popular support. The Communists, on the other hand, through a ruthless discipline and fanatical zeal, attempted to sell themselves as guardians and liberators of the people. The Nationalist armies did not have to be defeated; they disintegrated. History has proved again and again that a regime without faith in itself and an army without morale cannot survive the test of battle.

The record obviously can not set forth in equal detail the inner history and development of the Chinese Communist Party during these years. The principal reason is that, while we had regular diplomatic relations with the National Government and had the benefit of voluminous reports from our representatives in their territories, our direct contact with the Communists was limited in the main to the mediation efforts of General Hurley and General Marshall.

Fully recognizing that the heads of the Chinese Communist Party were ideologically affiliated with Moscow, our Government nevertheless took the view, in the light of the existing balance of forces in China, that peace could be established only if certain conditions were met. The Kuomintang would have to set its own house in order and both sides would have to make concessions so that the Government of China might become, in fact as well as in name, the Government of all China and so that all parties might function within the constitutional system of the Government. Both internal peace and constitutional development required that the progress should be rapid from one party government with a large opposition party in armed rebellion, to the participation of all parties, including the moderate non-communist elements, in a truly national system of government.

None of these conditions has been realized. The distrust of the leaders of both the Nationalist and Communist Parties for each other proved too deepseated to permit final agreement, notwithstanding temporary truces and apparently promising negotiations. The Nationalists, furthermore, embarked in 1946 on an over-ambitious military campaign in the face of warnings by General Marshall that it not only would fail but would plunge China into economic chaos and eventually destroy the National Government. General Marshall pointed out that though Nationalist armies could, for a period, capture Communist-held cities, they could not destroy the Communist armies. Thus every Nationalist advance would expose their communications to attack by Communist guerrillas and compel them to retreat or to surrender their armies together with the munitions which the United States has furnished them. No estimate of a military situation has ever been more completely confirmed by the resulting facts.

The historic policy of the United States of friendship and aid toward the people of China was, however, maintained in both peace and war. Since V–J Day, the United States Government has authorized aid to Nationalist China in the form of grants and credits totaling approximately 2 billion dollars, an amount equivalent in value to more than 50 percent of the monetary expenditures of the Chinese Government and of proportionately greater magnitude in relation to the budget of that Government than the United States has provided to any nation of Western Europe since the end of the war. In addition to these grants and credits, the United States Government has sold the Chinese Government large quantities of military and civilian war surplus property with a total procurement cost of over 1 billion dollars, for which the agreed realization to the United States was 232 million dollars. A large proportion of the military supplies furnished the Chinese armies by the United States since V–J Day has, however, fallen into the hands of the Chinese Communists through the military ineptitude of the Nationalist leaders, their defections and surrenders, and the absence among their forces of the will to fight.

It has been urged that relatively small amounts of additional aid—military and economic—to the National Government would have enabled it to destroy communism in China. The most trustworthy military, economic, and political information available to our Government does not bear out this view.

A realistic appraisal of conditions in China, past and present, leads to the conclusion that the only alternative open to the United States was full-scale intervention in behalf of a Government which had lost the confidence of its own troops and its own people. Such intervention would have required the expenditure of even greater sums than have been fruitlessly spent thus far, the command of Nationalist armies by American officers, and the probable participation of American armed forces—land, sea, and air—in the resulting war. Intervention of such a scope and magnitude would have been resented by the mass of the Chinese people, would have diametrically reversed our historic policy, and would have been condemned by the American people.

It must be admitted frankly that the American policy of assisting the

Chinese people in resisting domination by any foreign power or powers is now confronted with the gravest difficulties. The heart of China is in Communist hands. The Communist leaders have foresworn their Chinese heritage and have publicly announced their subservience to a foreign power, Russia, which during the last 50 years, under czars and Communists alike, has been most assiduous in its efforts to extend its control in the Far East. In the recent past, attempts at foreign domination have appeared quite clearly to the Chinese people as external aggression and as such have been bitterly and in the long run successfully resisted. Our aid and encouragement have helped them to resist. In this case, however, the foreign domination has been masked behind the façade of a vast crusading movement which apparently has seemed to many Chinese to be wholly indigenous and national. Under these circumstances, our aid has been unavailing.

The unfortunate but inescapable fact is that the ominous result of the civil war in China was beyond the control of the government of the United States. Nothing that this country did or could have done within the reasonable limits of its capabilities could have changed that result; nothing that was left undone by this country has contributed to it. It was the product of internal Chinese forces, forces which this country tried to influence but could not. A decision was arrived at within China, if only a decision by default.

And now it is abundantly clear that we must face the situation as it exists in fact. We will not help the Chinese or ourselves by basing our policy on wishful thinking. We continue to believe that, however tragic may be the immediate future of China and however ruthlessly a major portion of this great people may be exploited by a party in the interest of a foreign imperialism, ultimately the profound civilization and the democratic individualism of China will reassert themselves and she will throw off the foreign yoke. I consider that we should encourage all developments in China which now and in the future work toward this end.

In the immediate future, however, the implementation of our historic policy of friendship for China must be profoundly affected by current developments. It will necessarily be influenced by the degree to which the Chinese people come to recognize that the Communist regime serves not their interests but those of Soviet Russia and the manner in which, having become aware of the facts, they react to this foreign domination. One point, however, is clear. Should the Communist regime lend itself to the aims of Soviet Russian imperialism and attempt to engage in aggression against China's neighbors, we and the other members of the United Nations would be confronted by a situation violative of the principles of the United Nations Charter and threatening international peace and security.

Meanwhile our policy will continue to be based upon our own respect for the Charter, our friendship for China, and our traditional support for the Open Door and for China's independence and administrative and territorial integrity.

SELECTON III–C

A passage from Joseph R. McCarthy, McCarthyism: the Fight for America (New York, 1952), pp. 637–38. Copyright © 1952 by Joe McCarthy. Reprinted by permission of the Devin-Adair Co. Senator Joseph R. McCarthy of Wisconsin led Republican charges of communist influence in the Truman administration and centered much of his thesis on Acheson's and Marshall's treatment of China. In his book McCarthy purported to provide a "documented" response to the many cries of slander raised against him as he presented and then answered questions regarding the administration's handling of the situation in China.

Do you think Acheson realized he was following the Communist Party line in Asia?

Either he knew what he was doing or he was incompetent beyond words. As late as November, 1945, William Z. Foster, head of the Communist Party of the United States, notified the world that China was the prime target of the Soviet Union. He said:

On the international scale, the key task . . . is to stop American intervention in China . . . The war in China is the key of all problems on the international front.

Less than a month after this Communist proclamation, Marshall embarked upon the "Marshall Mission to China." The testimony before the Russell Committee was that this mission was an Acheson-Marshall-Vincent project. Before Marshall went to China the Communists occupied a very small portion of China. Their Army numbered less than 300,000 badly equipped troops. When Marshall returned from China to be rewarded by Truman with an appointment as Secretary of State, the Communist-controlled area had greatly increased and the Communist Army had grown from 300,000 badly equipped troops to an Army of over 2,000,000 relatively well-equipped soldiers.

What about the State Department's excuse that we withdrew aid from Chiang Kai-shek because his government was corrupt?

Chiang Kai-shek had been engaged in conflict and warfare since 1927—first with the Communists, then with Japan, then simultaneously with the Communists and Japan, and after Japan's defeat, again with the Communists. During that time, all the disruption of war beset Chiang's Government. Under the circumstances it would be a miracle if there were no corruption or incompetence in his government.

But if corruption and incompetence are grounds for turning an administration over to the Communists, then Earl Browder should be President of the United States, Harry Bridges should be Secretary of Labor, and Alger Hiss should be Secretary of Defense.

What about Acheson's claim that we gave Chiang Kai-chek every help which he could ultize, including $2 billion worth of aid since the end of World War II?

That is untrue. Acheson made this claim in a letter to Senator Pat Mc-Carran on March 14, 1949, in arguing against any further aid to anti-Communist China, which according to Acheson, "would almost surely be catastrophic."

Of the phony $2 billion figure, $335,800,000 was for repatriating Japanese soldiers in China and transporting Chinese Nationalist armed forces to accept the surrender of the Japanese. Even President Truman declared that those expenditures should properly have been charged to World War II. The $2 billion also included UNRRA payments, part of which went to Red China.

Nationalist China was also charged for war materials never received—no one will ever know how much. For example, 120,000 tons of ammunition were dumped in the Bay of Bengal shortly after Japan's surrender, and China's Lend-Lease account was charged at the rate of $1,000 per ton for this ammunition.

China was charged unreasonably high prices for the material we did deliver. Some slight idea of the fantastic prices we charged China can be obtained from the following figures quoted on page 47 of Freda Utley's book, *The China Story*:

	"Surplus" price to other nations	List Price	Price to China
Bazookas	$3.65	$36.25	$162.00
Rifles, .30-caliber	5.10	51.00	51.00
Rifle ammunition (per 1,000 rounds)	4.55	45.55	85.00
Machine-gun ammunition (per 100 rounds)	4.85	45.85	95.00

And so runs the sordid story of the dishonest bookkeeping which is the basis for Acheson's claim that China fell to the Communists despite our "two-billion-dollar" generosity. Left-wing radio commentators and newspaper columnists have parroted this attempted deception.

The year 1949 marked the Communist conquest of China. Will you list a few of the events which might help explain that victory?

Certainly. Following are a series of a few of the events which took place in 1949. They illustrate how Acheson made it impossible for the anti-Communists in China to withstand the determined drive of the Communists.

Event No. 1

Senator Pat McCarran, an intelligently courageous anti-Communist fighter, introduced a bill on February 25, 1949, to provide aid to our anti-Communist friends in China.

Event No. 2

On March 1, 1949, the Communist Party of New York State directed all of its members to write their Congressmen and Senators and demand:

. . . an end to all forms of American intervention in China and of plans to aid elements and remnants of the Kuomintang.

Continued aid to anti-Communists, the Communist directive stated, would cause "frictions and misunderstandings."

Event No. 3

On the same day the Communist directive was issued, Drew Pearson reported that the Secretary of State thought the anti-Communist leaders of China were cheap petty crooks and thieves. Acheson, according to Pearson, said that much of the past aid which America had given the anti-Communists "wasn't used to fight Communism, but went into the pockets of Chiang Kai-shek's lieutenants." The Chinese embassy patiently replied to this attack by saying that they could not believe the Secretary had actually said this because the great bulk of American aid to China had been spent and distributed under direct American supervision.

Event No. 4

On March 13, 1949, Acheson wrote Senator Tom Connally, chairman of the Senate Foreign Relations Committee, that McCarran's Aid to China Bill:

. . . would only prolong hostilities and the suffering of the Chinese people and would arouse in them deep resentment against the United States.

In arguing against aid to the anti-Communists, Acheson said, "the outcome . . . would almost surely be catastrophic."

The anti-Communist government, Acheson wrote, "does not have the military capability of maintaining a foothold in South China against a determined Communist advance."

Acheson then went on to state that aid to China since V-J Day had reached a point "over $2 million."

Event No. 5

After making an analysis of all aid to China since V-J Day, Senator Mc-Carran released a statement to the press on April 17, 1949, declaring that Acheson's letter was both "inaccurate and misleading." McCarran went on to state: "The State Department Division of Far Eastern Affairs is definitely soft to Communist Russia." Senator McCarran pointed out that "unrealistic analysis shows that post V-J Day effective military aid has totaled only $110 million—not the $2 billion implied in the Secretary's letter."

Event No. 6

On May 10, 1949, General Claire Chennault, a military man of many years experience in China, set forth his views in his "Summary of Present Communist Crisis in Asia." They were far different from those of Mr. Acheson's in Washington. While Acheson felt that the anti-Communists did not have the "military capability of maintaining a foothold in South China," General Chennault stated that some 150 million people in southern and western China—described by Chennault as "hardy mountaineers with a tradition of warlike defense of their native provinces against all invaders"— could supply "effective resistance to the Communist advance." Chennault wrote:

Both the people and their leaders are prepared to resist the Communists and will in any case resist whether we help them or not. *But what we give in aid will make the difference between a hopeless and an effective resistance.*

A few months later Acheson was to claim in his letter of transmittal of the *White Paper* that the anti-Communists had lost because "its troops had lost the will to fight, and its government had lost popular support."

Event No. 7

On December 23, 1949, the State Department announced it had refused a permit for a New York firm, the Driggs Engineering Company, to ship 100,000 Springfield rifles "for the defense of Formosa." The company was acting as an agent for the Chinese Nationalists.

This was not a request for money. Chiang had the funds to pay for the rifles. It merely involved the granting of a permit by the State Department so the rifles could be shipped.

Did Acheson and Marshall recommend that we aid the Chinese Communist army?

Yes. This was recommended after the war with Japan had ended.

On June 19, 1946, Acheson appeared before the House Foreign Affairs Committee and requested that the United States Government arm 10 Chinese Communist divisions.

At that time, Acheson reported that General Marshall had agreed to assign 69 U.S. officers and 400 tons of American equipment to train the Chinese Communist armies.

Ten months previously the war with Japan had ended. Acheson did not say who was to be fought by this American-equipped Communist army.

IV. VIEWS OF OBSERVERS

SELECTION IV—A

The following excerpt is taken from Freda Utley, *The China Story* (Chicago, 1951), pp. 220–21, 231–33. Copyright © 1951 by Henry Regnery Company. Reprinted by permission of the publisher. Freda Utley, a free lance journalist and frequent spokesman for anti-communist causes, denounced the administration for its naiveté in China.

TIME FOR RE-EXAMINATION

The White Paper shows beyond doubt that the State Department has all along considered the Chinese Communists either as "not real Communists," or as detachable from Moscow. Whether or not Mao Tse-tung would, or could, relinquish his allegiance to Moscow, in the very different geographical, military, and economic situation of China as compared to Yugoslavia is, to say the least, questionable. The main point, however, is that United States policy seems to be based on the belief that "heretical" Communists are more desirable allies than those who, like Chiang Kai-shek, have tried to uphold the principles of respective government and been uncompromising enemies of Communism.

In China we interfered at every turn to insist that the National Government should institute extensive "democratic reforms" in the midst of war and should make concessions to the Chinese Communists, if it hoped to receive our friendship and aid. But toward Communist governments the Administration's attitude has been conciliatory and based on a strict policy of non-interference in the internal affairs of the countries they rule.

Leniency toward Russia during the war can be ascribed to our preeminent desire to "win the war" whatever the consequences. But this aim cannot explain the partiality shown by the State Department after the war for Communist regimes such as the government of Yugoslavia, as contrasted with its continued denial of aid to the Chinese Nationalists.

.   .   .   .

Believers in *Realpolitik* can argue that the United States should have pursued a foreign policy based solely on considerations of American interests, without regard, one way or another, for the ideologies, or forms of government of other nations. But the attempt of the State Department to represent its policy as based on ethical considerations and "democratic" principles, while giving right of way to the Communists, could not but end in disaster, since General Marshall and Mr. Acheson refused to be consistent. Far from applying the principles of power politics in an unprejudiced fashion, they continually gave aid and comfort to the Communists while weakening the conservative forces, or believeers in free enterprise, whom they should, logically, have considered to be our best friends.

Mr. Acheson seems never to have realized that it was illogical to refuse alliances, or arms aid, to such "people on our side" as the anti-Communist Chinese because he disapproved of their governments, while insisting on aid being given to Communist regimes, such as that of Marshal Tito, provided only that they are not dependable allies of Soviet Russia. His sentiments are echoed by such erudite but ignorant columnists as Mr. Lippmann who, in his column on February 6, 1951, urging aid to Tito, deplored America's "undiscriminating anti-Communism." Nor is it consistent to cold-shoulder Spain while still proffering the hand of friendship to Communist regimes.

It is, in any case, impossible for a government responsible to the will of the people to follow a course based on *Realpolitik*. For most of the voters will always insist on the observance of moral principles.

Consequently, the attempts of the United States Administration to pursue a Far Eastern policy based on a nice judgment of how to win Communists over to our side was doomed to failure from the start. The tug of war between the Administration and its opponents resulted in our getting the worst of both worlds. If there ever was any possibility of "detaching" the Chinese Communists from their allegiance to Moscow, it required an early and complete abandonment of the Nationalists and whole-hearted support of the Communists. But this course was politically impossible for any United States Administration, however large its majority. Consequently, we neither gave sufficient support to Chiang Kai-shek to enable him to defeat the Communists, or transferred our support to the Communists.

Neither the Administration, nor the opposition in Congress was prepared to follow through a consistent policy to its logical conclusion. Those partial to the Chinese Communists hesitated to go all-out to appease them; and those who opposed the Administration's policy dared not face the consequences which a bold stand against Communist aggression might have entailed. The opponents of appeasement were as anxious to avoid the danger of a third world war as the present-day "men of Munich" who want to recognize Communist China and abandon our ally, the Chinese National Government. The consequence has been that neither a principled nor a completely opportunistic policy has been pursued.

A realistic view of the situation would have anticipated Chinese Communist intervention in Korea, once the Korean Communists were defeated. But, prior to November 1950, when the Chinese Communists started killing Americans in Korea, one heard, in all quarters, that Peiping would never send its troops to fight us because it would be against the interests of the Chinese people. And even after the Chinese Communist Army had intervened in Korea, and forced us to retreat, all sorts of excuses were still being offered by those who refused to abandon old illusions. The *Washington Post* and other newspapers argued that the blame must be placed on America, rather than on Russia, because we had failed to reassure Peiping soon enough that we would, under no circumstances, destroy the hydroelectric stations on the Yalu River which supply power to Manchuria; and because we had not finally abandoned the Chinese National Government and admitted Communist China to the United Nations.

Illusions die hard, especially when reputations depend upon their preservation. General Marshall, Mr. Acheson, and the host of journalists, authors, and radio commentators who gave ill-calculated advice, based on false assumptions, to the Administration and the American people, cannot, or dare not, admit that they were wrong. Like the Bourbons, they have learned nothing and forgotten nothing. Just as formerly the majority of Americans were deluded into thinking that Stalin would be driven by Russia's interests to follow a post-war policy friendly to America, so even today, voices are still being raised to persuade us that the Chinese Communists can be induced to follow a policy beneficial to China and to the western world if we stop fighting them.

Not until this great and persistent illusion is destroyed can we hope for the adoption of a sane American policy. Until we understand that *all* Communists are animated by the same ideals, and the same drive for power and expansive urges, our strength and good will will be unavailing to avert disaster, and more and more Americans will die in more and more futile wars.

SELECTION IV–B

An excerpt from Tang Tsou, "Civil Strife and Intervention: Marshall's China Policy." Reprinted by permission from *Orbis* VI (Spring, 1962), pp. 99–101, a quarterly journal of world affairs published by the Foreign Policy Institute of the University of Pennsylvania. A research associate with the Center for the Study of American Foreign and Military Policy at the University of Chicago, Tang Tsou drained the China issue of much of its emotion as he examined the premises of Marshall's foreign policy in the Far East. He found Marshall's major error to be "an error in communication rather than in substance."

THE BASIC ASSUMPTION

When the China debacle was in the making, it became clear that the United States was acting on the assumption that China was unimportant, that she could not possibly be a menace to the United States and that she would be a liability to her ally. In February 1948, Secretary Marshall told the Committees on Foreign Affairs and Foreign Relations:

China does not itself possess the raw material and industrial resources which would enable it to become a first-class power within the foreseeable future. The country is at present in the midst of a social and political revolution. Until this revolution is completed—and it will take a longe time—there is no prospect that sufficient stability and order can be established to permit China's early development into a strong state.

James Reston reported on April 24, 1949: "China, as the Administration sees it, is not a 'strategic springboard' but a 'strategic morass.' . . . It is a vast, unconnected, poorly organized continent of a country, populated by undernourished, highly individualistic people."

This assumption was not publicly affirmed, and thus was not made the subject of a rational debate, at an early date when the basic policy decisions were being arrived at and when American efforts to reverse the military and political trends in China could have reaped proportionate results. As a matter of fact, official pronouncements until 1946 stressed the vital interests of the United States in China, although the crucial term "vital interest" was used in such a way or in such a context that rendered it virtually meaningless. But the actual course of action pursued in China during those years was consistent only with a low estimate of American interests at stake. When American officials and scholars began again seriously to ponder and discuss the basic problem of the importance of China, the collapse of the Nationalist government was drawing near. The political chaos, military disintegration and economic dislocation were more disheartening than similar events in the memory of the present generation. Understandably, most American officials, scholars and men of affairs concluded that China was not important to the United States either as an ally or as a potential enemy. In October 1948, Marshall made a series of negative decisions in which he in effect wrote off not only mainland China but also Formosa.

But most of the analyses made in 1948 and 1949 failed to take adequately into account a political factor: the ability of a tightly organized and rigorously disciplined elite monopolizing all levers of control to manipulate mass attitudes, to reorganize political life, to effect fundamental social changes and to industrialize rapidly a backward country. It is a new dimension which American specialists and officials, trained and immersed in the liberal, democratic environment of a free society, naturally failed to gauge. The trend of the social sciences up to that time, which emphasized the determining effects of social forces on political actions, also left them unprepared to appraise correctly a situation in which the political actors deliberately and methodically sought to manipulate the social environment and to achieve a preconceived purpose. This deterministic bias, which was a measure of the separation of knowledge from practice, led the West at once to overestimate the difficulties confronted by the communists and to underestimate the ability of the Free World to work out its own destiny. This was one of the basic sources of its complacency as well as its lack of vigor in undertaking a bold program to meet the communist challenge.

Ever since Peking's intervention in the Korean War, Marshall's basic assumption has been challenged by the growing power of Communist China and the threat it posed to the United States. It would seem that General Marshall's failure to take decisive action in China was a mistake. But one must not forget that Marshall operated within the framework of his calculations of the reasonable limits of America's capability and of his estimate of what the American people were willing to do for China. In 1947 and 1948 General Marshall's views, regardless of their intrinsic merits, would in all probability have been overwhelmingly endorsed by the American people if he had made his policy a subject of public debate. Unfortunately, the Administration suppressed the Wedemeyer report of September 1947 for almost two years, and failed to bring its case to the American people at the appropriate time. This omission enabled the critics of the Administration to charge it with the sole responsibility for the China debacle. If Marshall's strategic policy is being evaluated as a whole, then against this error in China policy—an error in communication rather than in substance—must be balanced Marshall's statesmanship in planning and promoting the industrial recovery of Western Europe. For immediately after the statement quoted above in which Secretary Marshall disparaged the importance of China, he added:

On the side of American interests, we cannot afford, economically or militarily, to take over the continued failure of the present Chinese povernment to the dissipation of our strength in more vital regions where we now have a reasonable opportunity of successfully meeting or thwarting the Communist threat, in the vital industrial area of Western Europe with is tradition of free institutions.

Any evaluation of General Marshall's policy toward China which fails to see it in global terms and to balance the American defeat in China by Marshall's impressive achievements in Europe is not impartial or reasonable.

> ### SELECTION IV–C
>
> Excerpted from "The Illusion of American Omnipotence" in *American Aspects* (1964) by D. W. Brogan. Copyright 1952 by D. Brogan. Originally appeared in *Harper's Magazine*, and reprinted by permission of Harper & Row, Publishers. Sir Denis Brogan, Professor of Political Science at Cambridge University and a distinguished British interpreter of American society, was at the University of Washington at Seattle when he wrote this article in which he identified the loss of China with an American "illusion of omnipotence."

I am writing this on the Pacific Coast, before the election, but in the conviction that the result of the election will very little affect the problem that I want to discuss. Even if the Republicans should make a clean sweep, even if the State Department is cleaned out, from the Secretary to the doorkeepers, even if the Pentagon is purged from the Joint Chiefs of Staff to the leaders of the rescue teams who find lost visitors, one problem of American policy will remain: the problem of the existence, in the American mind, of what I call the illusion of omnipotence. This is the illusion that any situation which distresses or endangers the United States can only exist because some Americans have been fools or knaves.

Such a situation may exist because of conditions about which the United States has, and will have, little to say. For America, powerful though she is, is not omnipotent. A great many things happen in the world regardless of whether the American people wish them to or not. I deeply regret this state of affairs; like Bertrand Russell, I would gladly settle for an American hegemony; but we are not representative characters, and American hegemony not only does not exist, but is not even universally expected or desired.

I should, perhaps, say that the illusion of omnipotence to which I refer is not shared by all Americans. Nothing could be sillier than to attribute to nearly 160,000,000 people one common attitude, or to assume, as many European intellectuals do, that there is such a thing as "what the American people are thinking." Nevertheless, the idea that I am trying to describe is expressed by Senators and columnists, by candidates, by preachers, by people overheard in taverns and club cars, in drugstores and restaurants— the idea that the whole world, the great globe itself, can be moving in directions annoying or dangerous to the American people only because some elected or non-elected Americans are fools or knaves. When something goes wrong, "I wuz robbed" is the spontaneous comment—the American equivalent of that disastrous French cry, *"Nous sommes trahis."*

.   .   .   .

This illusion of omnipotence is best illustrated by a very common American attitude toward the Chinese Revolution. In this attitude— apparently the dominant one at the moment—there is a curious absence of historical awe and historical curiosity. The Chinese Revolution, an event of immense importance, is often discussed as if it were simply a problem in American foreign and domestic policy and politics. The Communist triumph in China is discussed as if it were simply the result of American action or inaction, the result of the mistakes, and worse than mistakes, of General Marshall, Secretary Acheson, President Roosevelt, and the Institute of Pacific Relations; and as if the Communists or the Russians would not have "captured" China had American policy been represented and controlled by Representative Judd—or even, perhaps, by Senators Cain and Jenner.

Is this not to display the belief in American omnipotence in very striking form? What is going on in China affects the oldest civilization now in existence. It affects about a fifth of the human race. It must have roots, deep roots, in the Chinese problem as seen by the Chinese. This is no matter of a regime imposed by Russia on a helpless small nation like Romania or Hungary. It is a historical phenomenon that may turn out to be more important than the Russian Revolution. It may well turn out, also, to be disastrous for us and for China. But the first thing to notice is the size of the phenomenon; to notice, for example, that there are five Chinese for every two Americans. What inherent necessity is there that the decision in China is, was, or ever will be in American hands?

It is not only a matter of scale. There is distance. China is six thousand miles from the Pacific Coast of America. How was and is American power to be effectively exercised at that distance? I anticipate one answer—that Russian power *is* being exercised, and that it was Russian power (in the absence of American power because of American folly and treason) that "took over" China. This is not demonstrated and in this crude and popular form is not probable. But even if it were true, Russia is not six thousand miles from China. Russia has had a common frontier with China for three hundred years, and as Russia's center of industrial gravity moves eastward, Russian power gets nearer China and can be more readily exercised there. In a straight contest for control of China between the United States and the U.S.S.R., with the Chinese regarded as vile bodies, the U.S.S.R. would hold the trumps. To ignore that is to show the attitude of mind of those who have complained that, at Yalta, F.D.R. "permitted" Russia to become a Pacific power. Russia was a Pacific power before the United States existed. And she was and is an Asiatic power, which the United States is not. Lake Baikal and Lake Superior are on different continents. Vladivostok and Peiping are not.

But the real lack of historical reverence and realism is in the assumption that Russia "took over" China as she took over Poland. Even if we assume that there is as united an opposition to Communist rule in China as I believe there is in Poland, the scale of the taking-over ought to impose reflection. By what miracle was it done? Could General Hurley or General Chennault have prevented it? Would a sounder understanding of what the Communists were have prevented the Communist triumph? If it would have, then China is a more torpid body, more open to mere manipulation, than it is pleasant to think. If so great an event as the Chinese Communist Revolution could have been prevented by a different American policy, China is "a corpse on the dissecting table," as Charles Gavan Duffy said of Ireland after the Famine. In this case, Mao and Stalin may dissect it and make a monster of it like Dr. Moreau in H. G. Well's prophetic story. If it was taken over as easily as all that, it will be kept taken over even more easily.

There is some reason to believe and to hope that it is not quite as simple as this. We are in danger of being obsessed with the important and indisputable fact that world Communism is a real and potent force and that it is controlled from Moscow. We tend, therefore, to see the hand of Moscow everywhere and attribute to it an initiating and dominant role that may not always be justified. The Chinese Revolution, we should remember, has been going on longer than the Russian Revolution. Sun Yat-sen was the successful leader of a revolution when Lenin was an obscure and not too hopeful exile in Switzerland. But, I shall be told, that was a *different* Chinese Revolution; that was the *good* Chinese Revolution, the one that deposed the Manchu dynasty and abolished the pigtail and the binding of feet; that was the revolution which was inspired and encouraged by American missionaries and

American-trained students. But isn't it a truism of history that when you start a revolution, you can't be sure where it is going and how far?

It wasn't Lenin who overthrew the Tsardom or Robespierre who stormed the Bastille. In a long, bloody, and profound revolution, the extreme party has many advantages. It may not win; it may not stay victorious; the Jacobins learned that. But it may destroy the old order, the old ruling classes, the rival revolutionary parties, Social Revolutionists or Girondins. It doesn't need, in a genuine revolutionary situation, outside aid, outside doctrine, though it may get and benefit by both. The Chinese Communists got aid; they got doctrine. They probably benefited by both (though in 1927 they might have done better without either). But to deny that the Chinese Communists are a large, native Chinese party is to fly in the face of all the evidence. Their leaders may be docile tools of Moscow, but that doesn't alter the fact that the Chinese Communist party which survived the Kuomintang war against it, which survived the "long march," is a formidable indigenous party. On the record, it seems to have been the most formidable indigenous party—the one that, had both the U.S.A. and the U.S.S.R. stayed out, might have won anyway.

Could it have been prevented from defeating the Kuomintang by the provision of "massive and controlled" American aid? I have already suggested that the Russians could play that game too, and their aid could have been both more massive and controlled than the American. But even assuming that they did not so react to open American intervention in a civil war against their political allies, in a neighboring country, how was the aid to be made massive and how was it to be controlled?

Does anyone think that a continuation of what arms aid had been given, or even a stepping-up of such aid, would have done the trick? The Washington wit who said that supplying arms to Chiang was simply a roundabout way of Lend-Lease to the Chinese Communists was a jester, possibly frivolous; but he was not altogether wrong. Lend-Lease to Britain, Lend-Lease to Russia was direct and massive aid to coherent, united, and combative governments. It was not aid to a divided party in a country torn and tired by a generation of foreign and domestic war. More aid to Chiang might have prolonged the war; it might have saved the situation south of the Yangtse; but would it have brought conquest of the Communists by Chiang's forces?

And how was American aid to be controlled—except by exercising a degree of American authority which would not only have inflamed the *amour propre* of the Generalissimo, but would have deprived the Kuomintang of its last political asset, its claim to be "nationalist," to represent the independence of China? Could the aid have been effective without active American participation—without keeping the Marines in China, without sending in more troops, without, in fact, involving the United States in a greater Korean war? Does anyone who remembers the temper of the American people in 1945, from the White House and Capitol to churches and bars, believe that such a policy was politically practicable?

I have been in America every year since 1944 with the exception of 1949. I have sometimes been twice in America in one year. I have been in all regions. At no time before the Korean war did I find anything like the resolution to make great sacrifices to save China which alone could have saved China.

6

THE KOREAN CONFLICT
The United States and the United Nations

I. EDITORIAL INTRODUCTION

The warning given the Truman administration by the fall of China was followed quickly by another challenge from the Far East: the North Korean invasion of the Republic of Korea on June 25, 1950. Korea's direction like China's since 1945 had been set by the events of World War II. As early as the Cairo Conference of 1943 the allies, or at least a part of the alliance—the United States, the United Kingdom and China—had agreed that Korea would "in due course" become independent. But the Cairo declaration had not been signed by the Soviet Union which was not yet at war with Japan and in 1945 military expediency dictated a division of authority in Korea. Soviet occupation was limited to the territory north of the 38th parallel. This temporary arrangement, which had been intended to yield ultimately to a united and fully independent Korea, hardened into a permanent division under the impact of the Cold War.

Korea was never a central area of American concern in the postwar conflicts with the Soviet Union, but it remained an obligation and a responsibility which the United States could not ignore permanently. Despairing of the economic or political viability of a free South Korea, the United States pushed the problem of unification onto the United Nations in 1947. The latter created a Temporary Committee on Korea which was to implement a plan of nation-wide elections in 1948. But a boycott of the United Nations plan by Soviet-controlled North Korea confined elections to South Korea where a conservative faction, buoyed by American military support, assumed power.

The new Republic of Korea launched in 1949 under the presidency of a strong-willed patriot, the venerable Syngman Rhee, was accepted by Americans as part of the free world. Particularly since the year 1949 witnessed the collapse of Nationalist China, the administration and critics alike appreciated that at least South Korea had escaped from the Iron Curtain. Economic assistance and some military aid through the Military Assistance Act of 1949 were earmarked for the support of Rhee, although little of either had arrived before the attack from the north in June 1950. In retrospect it was obvious that American support for the Republic of Korea had certain strong qualifications, some military and some political. Certainly the Department of Defense was disturbed by Rhee's talk of using force to reunite Korea and by his opposition to any United Nations efforts at unification that did not agree fully with his own. Not only would President Rhee be an uncomfortable ally in the event of war, but his country was not the place where America's military analysts expected the defense of the free world to be made.

Such was the setting for Secretary of State Acheson's address to the National Press Club of Washintgon on January 12, 1950, in which he identified an American "defense perimeter" in Asia that excluded South Korea. (Selection II–A.) At no point did he suggest America's surrender of its interest in Korea; it was merely that the countries west of the perimeter should either manage their own defenses, with American military help, or look to the United Nations for protection. The government of the Republic of Korea was, after all a product of United Nations' intervention.

But six months later the Republic was invaded, and Acheson's words, or rather his omissions, have been blamed for inciting the communist attack. The results of the conflict might have been abandonment of America's European policy as the country concentrated upon a Far Eastern war; and it might have been the sacrifice of the United Nations through unilateral action by the United States which would have exposed the ineffectuality of that body. Neither action took place. President Truman announced to the world two days after the attack that American response would be through the United Nations. (Selection II–B.)

A year later, after General Douglas MacArthur's triumphs and failures, Secretary of State Acheson could still make an eloquent case for the reaction of the United States to the communist thrust over the 38th parallel. It was to show the world the credibility of the United Nations' and the United States' defense of free nations. He claimed that in repelling invasion the United States had checked communist imperialism in Asia. (Selection III–A.)

But from the beginning of the war opposition to the administration's conduct manifested itself. Inevitably the charge was raised, as stated by Senator Kenneth Wherry, that the President had acted hastily and unconstitutionally, without the approval of Congress. The administration's one virtue, according to Wherry, was that action in the Far East had belatedly recognized the tragic errors of the past years in Asia. But with the operation in the hands of the men responsible for communist aggression, how much confidence could be placed in their leadership? (Selection III–B.)

Much of the Republican criticism was muted in the next few months as it became clear that the leadership would be in the hands of Douglas Mac-Arthur, who cleared South Korea of its invaders in a brilliant campaign, and by November was not only in possession of most of North Korea but almost at the border of Communist China itself.

From the winter of 1950–51 until his recall in April 1951 all that had been apparently won by MacArthur's efforts appeared irreparably lost; the prestige of the United Nations, the victory over North Korea, the authority of the President all were jeopardized when the Chinese entered the war, rolling back American columns from their exposed positions in North Korea. Mac-Arthur, seeking to recover his losses, acted more and more independently of the Commander-in-Chief, arousing the fears of the allies in the United Nations as he risked total war with China, and courted the opportunity for a showdown with the major enemy in Asia. Such was the implication of his impassioned plea to the Congress after his recall from his command. (Selection III–C.)

The passions of 1951 embraced more than the General and the President. Behind the MacArthur position was a deeply felt American emotion that belonged to an isolationist past. It nurtured the belief that Europe's interest in monopolizing American attention compromised America's own basic concerns with the Far East, that Europe would rather appease communism than defeat it. Professor Spanier suggests that the administration shared many of MacArthur's views on China and communism. If Truman rejected MacArthur's plans in 1951 it was because a war at the wrong place and time might bring Soviet power to the service of China. (Selection IV–A.)

To a young Korean nationalist such as Dr. Tae-Ho Yoo, neither Truman nor MacArthur was serving Korea's cause, or the cause of world peace. He could see little difference between Soviet Union's plans for Korea and those of the United States. Each party was acting for its own advantage at the expense of Korea and of the United Nations. The major contribution of the "third world" representing the majority of the United Nations, was to ameliorate the effects of the cold war struggle in Korea. Still, Korea itself was only a pawn in the machinations of the great powers. (Selection IV–B.)

Such an interpretation wounded American sensibilities, particularly their pride in service to the free world. Indeed, as Professor Arnold Wolfers has pointed out, Americans justified the Korean police action as the substitution of collective security for power politics. He doubted the validity of this assertion, since American behavior was motivated less by the needs of the United Nations than by the imperatives of the containment policy. These reservations notwithstanding, the United Nations, and with it the principle of collective security, gained stature by the American led action in the conflict. (Selection IV–C.)

II. DOCUMENTS

SELECTION II–A

An excerpt from the text of Secretary of State Dean Acheson's speech before the National Press Club, on January 12, 1950, as it appeared in the Department of State *Bulletin,* XXII (January 23, 1950), pp. 11. 115–16.

What is the situation in regard to the military security of the Pacific area, and what is our policy in regard to it?

In the first place, the defeat and the disarmament of Japan has placed upon the United States the necessity of assuming the military defense of Japan so long as that is required, both in the interest of our security and in the interests of the security of the entire Pacific area and, in all honor, in the interest of Japanese security. We have American—and there are Australian—troops in Japan. I am not in a position to speak for the Australians, but I can assure you that there is no intention of any sort abandoning or weakening the defenses of Japan and that whatever arrangements are to be made either through permanent settlement or otherwise, that defense must and shall be maintained.

This defensive perimeter runs along the Aleutians to Japan and then goes to the Ryukyus. We hold important defense positions in the Ryukyu Islands, and those we will continue to hold. In the interest of the population of the Ryukyu Islands, we will at an appropriate time offer to hold these islands under trusteeship of the United Nations. But they are essential parts of the defensive perimeter of the Pacific, and they must and will be held.

The defensive perimeter runs from the Ryukyus to the Philippine Islands. Our relations, our defensive relations with the Philippines are contained in agreements between us. Those agreements are being loyally carried out and will be loyally carried out. Both peoples have learned by bitter experience the vital connections between our mutual defense requirements. We are in no doubt about that, and it is hardly necessary for me to say an attack on the Philippines could not and would not be tolerated by the United States. But I hasten to add that no one perceives the imminence of any such attack.

So far as the military security of other areas in the Pacific is concerned, it must be clear that no person can guarantee these areas against military attack. But it must also be clear that such a guarantee is hardly sensible or necessary within the realm of practical relationship.

Should such an attack occur—one hesitates to say where such an armed attack could come from—the initial reliance must be on the people attacked to resist it and then upon the commitments of the entire civilized world under the Charter of the United Nations which so far has not proved a weak reed to lean on by any people who are determined to protect their independence against outside aggression. But it is a mistake, I think, in considering Pacific and Far Eastern problems to become obsessed with military considerations. Important as they are, there are other problems that press, and these other problems are not capable of solution through military means. These other problems arise out of the susceptibility of many areas, and many countries in the Pacific area, to subversion and penetration. That cannot be stopped by military means.

> SELECTION II–B
>
> Text of a statement by President Harry S Truman ordering U.S. Air and Sea Forces into action in support of Korea and the UN (June 27, 1950). Taken from the Department of State *Bulletin*, XXIII (July 3, 1950), p. 5.

In Korea, the Government forces, which were armed to prevent border raids and to preserve internal security, were attacked by invading forces from North Korea. The Security Council of the United Nations called upon the invading troops to cease hostilities and to withdraw to the 38th Parallel. This they have not done but, on the contrary, have pressed the attack. The Security Council called upon all members of the United Nations to render every assistance to the United Nations in the execution of this resolution. In these circumstances, I have ordered United States air and sea forces to give the Korean Government troops cover and support.

The attack upon Korea makes it plain beyond all doubt that communism has passed beyond the use of subversion to conquer independent nations and will now use armed invasion and war. It has defied the orders of the Security Council of the United Nations issued to preserve international peace and security. In these circumstances, the occupation of Formosa by Communist forces would be a direct threat to the security of the Pacific area and to United States forces performing their lawful and necessary functions in that area.

Accordingly, I have ordered the Seventh Fleet to prevent any attack on Formosa. As a corollary of this action, I am calling upon the Chinese Government on Formosa to cease all air and sea operations against the mainland. The Seventh Fleet will see that this is done. The determination of the future status of Formosa must await the restoration of security in the Pacific, a peace settlement with Japan, or consideration by the United Nations.

I have also directed that United States forces in the Philippines be strengthened and that military assistance to the Philippine Government be accelerated.

I have similarly directed acceleration in the furnishing of military assistance to the forces of France and the Associated States in Indochina and the dispatch of a military mission to provide close working relations with those forces.

I know that all members of the United Nations will consider carefully the consequences of this latest aggression in Korea in defiance of the Charter of the United Nations. A return to the rule of force in international affairs would have far-reaching effects. The United States will continue to uphold the rule of law.

I have instructed Ambassador Austin, as the representative of the United States to the Security Council, to report these steps to the Council.

III. VIEWS OF PARTICIPANTS

> *SELECTION III–A*
>
> Excerpted from Dean Acheson's statement on the "Military Situation in the Far East," *Hearings*, 82nd Congress, 1st sess. Part 3, pp. 1714–17. Acheson's explanation of American action in Korea as presented to the Senate Armed Services and Foreign Relations Committee.

PEACE OR WAR

Mr. Chairman and gentlemen, the real issues in the discussion before us are peace or war, and the survival of human freedom.

It is not just a difference as to method which is now under examination. What is challenged is the bedrock purpose of our foreign policy, and of what we have been trying to do. That is the place I would like to start in this brief statement.

The foreign policy of the United States has a central and dominant objective—to protect the Nation and to safeguard the future of its people. We stand ready to defend our future by force of arms if that necessity is forced upon us. But we seek to deter war if we can.

Another world war would be destructive beyond experience; it would not solve problems, but multiply them. Therefore, it is part of our fundamental purpose to prevent, by all honorable means, the outbreak of another general war.

Even before the last World War was over, while our young men were storming the beaches at Normandy and Saipan and dozens of other places now engraved in our memories, the resolution was forming among our people that future wars must be prevented.

IDEAL OF COLLECTIVE SECURITY

Their conviction grew that the best way to protect the security of our Nation and of our people was to prevent war, and that the way to go about it was through an international system of collective security.

The Four Freedoms, the Atlantic Charter, the United Nations—these were not cynical slogans. They represented the idea which our people felt in their hearts was worth fighting for.

It has been the purpose of our foreign policy to keep faith with that idea.

The attempt to build a collective-security system on the basis of the cooperation of all the great powers broke down because of the policies of the Soviet Union. But Soviet ambitions have not been able to obstruct our determined efforts.

Within the framework of the Charter of the United Nations we have been building a collective-security system based on the cooperation of those nations who are dedicated to peace.

The united and determined effort of our people to build effective instruments for keeping the peace is recorded in a series of vigorous and far-sighted actions: the United Nations Charter itself, the Rio Treaty, the Greek-Turkish aid program, the Marshall plan, the North Atlantic Treaty, and the mutual defense assistance program.

We have been building our strength, together with our allies. We must be strong enough to keep the peace.

Side by side with these programs there is another basic element in our foreign policy—to assist the hundreds of millions of people who were acquiring their independence after the war, so that they might be free to develop in their own way, and to join in an international system for preserving the peace.

Our hopes for peace required us to understand the changes which were in motion among vast populations of the Middle East and Asia, and to help peoples who had just gained their independence from losing it again to the new imperialism of the Soviet Union.

Those are the big central ideas that express what we have been trying to do in the world.

CHALLENGE OF KOREA

The attack on Korea was a blow at the foundation of this whole program. It was a challenge to the whole system of collective security, not only in the Far East, but everywhere in the world. It was a threat to all nations newly arrived at independence. This dagger thrust pinned a warning notice to the wall which said: "Give up or be conquered."

This was a test which would decide whether our collective-security system would survive or would crumble. It would determine whether other nations would be intimidated by this show of force.

The decision to meet force with force in Korea was essential. It was the unanimous view of the political and military advisers of the President that this was the right thing to do. This decision had the full support of the American people because it accorded with the principles by which Americans live.

As a people we condemn aggression of any kind. We reject appeasement of any kind. If we stood with our arms folded while Korea was swallowed up, it would have meant abandoning our principles, and it would have meant the defeat of the collective security system on which our own safety ultimately depends.

What I want to stress here is that it was not only a crucial decision whether or not to meet this aggression; it was no less important how this aggression was to be dealt with.

WAYS IN WHICH AGGRESSION WAS MET

In the first place, the attack on Korea has been met by collective action. The United States brought the aggression in Korea before the United Nations, not only because the Charter requires it, but also because the authority and even the survival of that organization was directly involved.

The response of some members of the United Nations, in terms of their capacities and their other security responsibilities, has been generous and wholehearted.

The total action is admittedly an imperfect one, as might be expected of beginning steps in a collective-security system. But the development of this system requires us to take into consideration the dangers and interests of those associated with us, just as we want them to take into consideration our dangers and interests.

In the second place, our response to the aggression against Korea required a careful estimate of the risks involved in the light of the total world situation.

There was the risk that the conflict might spread into a general war in Asia, a risk that the Chinese Communists might intervene, a risk that the Soviet Union might declare itself in.

We take it for granted that risk of some sort is implicit in any positive policy, and that there is also a risk in doing nothing.

The elements of risk and the means of reducing that risk to us and to the rest of the free world quite properly influenced our policy in Korea.

It has been our purpose to turn back this Communist thrust, and to do it in such a way as to prevent a third world war if we can. This is in accord with one of the most fundamental tenets of our policy—to prevent, insofar as we can do so, another world war.

It is against this basic purpose that the operation in Korea, and the plans for carrying it to a conclusion, need to be considered.

WHAT THE DEFENSE OF KOREA HAS ACCOMPLISHED

The operation in Korea has been a success. Both the North Koreans and the Chinese Communists declared it to be their purpose to drive the United Nations forces out of Korea and impose Communist rule throughout the entire peninsula. They have been prevented from accomplishing their objective.

It has been charged that the American and allied forces fighting in Korea are engaged in a pointless and inconclusive struggle.

Nothing could be further from the fact. They have been magnificent. Their gallant, determined, and successful fight has checked the Communist advance and turned it into a retreat. They have administered terrible defeats to the Communist forces. In so doing, they have scored a powerful victory.

Their victory has dealt Communist imperialist aims in Asia a severe set-back.

The alluring prospect for the Communist conspiracy in June 1950—the prospect of a quick and easy success which would not only win Korea for the Kremlin but shake the free nations of Asia and paralyze the defense of Europe—all this has evaporated.

Instead of weakening the rest of the world, they have solidified it. They have given a powerful impetus to the military preparations of this country and its associates in and out of the North Atlantic Treaty Organization.

We have doubled the number of our men under arms, and the production of matériel has been boosted to a point where it can begin to have a profound effect on the maintenance of the peace.

The idea of collective security has been put to the test, and has been sustained. The nations who believe in collective security have shown that they can stick together and fight together.

New urgency has been given to the negotiation of a peace treaty with Japan, and of initial security arrangements to build strength in the Pacific area.

These are some of the results of the attack on Korea, unexpected by—and I am sure most unwelcome to—the Kremlin.

> *SELECTION III–B*
>
> A portion of Senator Kenneth Wherry's attack on Truman's action as it appeared in the *Congressional Record*—Senate, 81st Congress, 2d sess., June 30, 1950, pp. 9537–38. Senator Wherry of Nebraska had been Republican whip in the 80th Congress, and was one of the most articulate isolationist opponents of the Truman administration.

Mr. President, a sigh of relief has swept across the country that, at last, at long last, the President has accepted the suggestion of some of us that he draw a line, that he stop his vacillation in the Pacific.

The President's action is belated, and therefore it will be more difficult to protect countries threatened by the tide of communism.

The administration let China slip into the hands of Moscow-directed Communists, with one excuse or another. How many hundreds of thousands of lives were lost, as a result of this appeasement of Soviet Russia is anyone's guess.

These terrible, ghastly failures by the administration cannot now be swallowed up with a show of flag-waving and cries of emergency, hurry up, and do not question this or that.

It was high time that the President acted, because the breath of the Communist dragon has begun to breathe upon the Philippines, and the entire Pacific was and still is in jeopardy.

President Truman has acted to draw a line. At last, at long last, he says to the Communist hordes, "thus far and no further." But there is a long row to hoe, and much more to be done, very much more. This action by the President is only a beginning.

The American people long ago had lost confidence in Secretary Acheson. His resignation is now definitely in order. His appeasement policies now stand repudiated by the President.

The President having indicated his purpose to take a stand against the Red tide, certainly it would be inconsistent to put the implementation of that new policy in the hands of a man who has swallowed the Owen Lattimore propaganda, hook, line, and sinker.

At the same time, if the "new look" in our Far East policy is to take tangible form, all the remnants of what former Assistant Secretary of State Adolf Berle described as the Acheson-Hiss clique must be removed from the State Department.

Since sons of America are, at this very moment, engaged in combat in Korea, the wisdom of the Senate in directing the Committee on Foreign Relations to comb the Department of State, and other Government agencies, of subversives is indelibly portrayed.

The course that the President now has elected to take is the only honorable course that could be taken.

The courageous thing—and I say this with emphasis—that the President has done is to repudiate the Acheson appeasement policy in the Far East, and place in the hands of General MacArthur and the National Defense Department the responsibility for protecting the security of the United States.

Because of the repudiation of the Acheson policy in the Pacific—and because it should be repudiated in Europe—the time has come for Mr. Acheson, in all decency and fairness to the American people, to step out.

But the President has yet to repudiate Mr. Acheson's misguided policies in western Europe, policies based upon revenge, prejudice, and political partisanship.

In the face of the tremendous developments in the last few days, the utter futility and lack of wisdom shown in Secretary Acheson's attitude toward recognition of the Chinese Communist delegation by the United Nations, is made so clear that it should be obvious to everyone.

Think of it. The Secretary of State, who is supposed to be taking the leadership in winning the cold war, which may conceivably lead to a hot war, has taken a neutral position on seating the Chinese Communists and welcoming these usurpers of control over China into the family of nations.

The President and the State Department should take the leadership in resisting the seating of these delegates by the United Nations, and the United States should never recognize officially the Communist regime in China.

To do either would greatly enhance the prestige of Soviet Russia, and be utterly inconsistent with all of our efforts to resist possible attack with material means.

Recognition of the Moscow-directed Communist government of China would give to the Communists incalculable prestige, and all of our preaching of democracy, fairness, and representative republican way of doing things would be tremendously impaired.

The next step is for the President to call the Congress into a joint session, give the facts and a complete review of what has taken place, and give Congress his recommendations.

The junior Senator from Nebraska voted for the United Nations Charter when it was before the Senate for ratification. The junior Senator from Nebraska was assured on the Senate floor that the constitutional power of Congress to declare war was in no way modified by the Charter. Others have contended on the floor of the Senate that regardless of the provisions of the United Nations Charter the President had full authority to act in the emergency in Korea, and order our troops into action.

This point was argued by the majority leader, who gave precedents for the President's action. But I want to point out that in these precedents all the actions taken were for the protection of American lives and property. This was a very different situation than was brought about by the President's ordering air power and warships to southern Korea.

It seems to the junior Senator from Nebraska in all fairness the President should not have acted under the resolution passed by the United Nations without congressional authorization. Perhaps there was an immediate emergency. Perhaps time did not permit. I am not questioning the President's sincerity at all. However, Congress was in session, and this was a possibility. I refer to it only as a way in which I think it should have been done if it could possibly have been done that way.

But the practical side of this is whether the President acted within the constitutional processes, or whether he acted under the resolution adopted by the United Nations.

One thing he did not do, and that was to call the Congress of the United States, which is now in session, into a joint session, and there reveal to us the facts that he knew and make his recommendations at that time, so that the Congress, the legislative branch, could determine and assume the responsibilities, which the Congress should assume and thereby bring about the unity which must be had all along the line among not only Members of Congress but the American people. No doubt full authority and funds would have been voted by the Congress to prepare for the protection of American interests. At least I would have been one who would have given the President that assurance.

While it is too late now, and nothing would be accomplished by trying to amend what has been done, the junior Senator from Nebraska, calls attention to this as a notice for future conduct, in the event that this present situation develops into something much more serious than it is now.

SELECTION III–C

The following article is an excerpt from MacArthur's speech in the Congressional Record—House, 82nd Congress, 1st sess., v. 97, April 19, 1951, pp. 412–25. General MacArthur's valedictory was presented before a joint meeting of both houses of Congress on April 19, 1951.

With this brief insight into the surrounding areas I now turn to the Korean conflict. While I was not consulted prior to the President's decision to intervene in support of the Republic of Korea, that decision, from a military standpoint, proved a sound one [applause] as we hurled back the invaders and decimated his forces. Our victory was complete and our objectives within reach when Red China intervened with numerically superior ground forces. This created a new war and an entirely new situation—a situation not contemplated when our forces were committed against the North Korean invaders—a situation which called for new decisions in the diplomatic sphere to permit the realistic adjustment of military strategy. Such decisions have not been forthcoming. [Applause.]

While no man in his right mind would advocate sending our ground forces into continental China and such was never given a thought, the new situation did urgently demand a drastic revision of strategic planning if our political aim was to defeat this new enemy as we had defeated the old. [Applause.]

Apart from the military need as I saw it to neutralize the sanctuary protection given the enemy north of the Yalu, I felt that military necessity in the conduct of the war made mandatory:

1. The intensification of our economic blockade against China;

2. The imposition of a naval blockade against the China coast;

3. Removal of restrictions on air reconnaissance of China's coast areas and of Manchuria [applause];

4. Removal of restrictions on the forces of the Republic of China on Formosa with logistical support to contribute to their effective operations against the common enemy. [Applause.]

For entertaining these views, all professionally designed to support our forces committed to Korea and bring hostilities to an end with the least possible delay and at a saving of countless American and Allied lives, I have been severely criticized in lay circles, principally abroad, despite my understanding that from a military standpoint the above views have been fully shared in the past by practically every military leader concerned with the Korean campaign, including our own Joint Chiefs of Staff. [Applause, the Members rising.]

I called for reinforcements, but was informed that reinforcements were not available. I made clear that if not permitted to destroy the build-up bases north of the Yalu; if not permitted to utilize the friendly Chinese force of some 600,000 men on Formosa; if not permitted to blockade the China coast to prevent the Chinese Reds from getting succor from without; and if there were to be no hope of major reinforcements, the position of the command from the military standpoint forbade victory. We could hold in Korea by constant maneuver and at an approximate area where our supply line advantages were in balance with the supply line disadvantages of the enemy, but we could hope at best for only an indecisive campaign, with its terrible and constant attrition upon our forces if the enemy utilized his full military potential. I have constantly called for the new political decisions essential to a solution. Efforts have been made to distort my position. It has been said, in effect, that I am a warmonger. Nothing could be further from the truth. I know war as few other men now living know it, and nothing to me is more revolting. I have long advocated its complete abolition as its very destructiveness on both friend and foe has rendered it useless as a means of settling international disputes. Indeed, on the 2nd of September 1945, just following the surrender of the Japanese Nation on the battleship *Missouri,* I formally cautioned as follows:

"Men since the beginning of time have sought peace. Various methods through the ages have been attempted to devise an international process to prevent or settle disputes between nations. From the very start, workable methods were found insofar as individual citizens were concerned, but the mechanics of an instrumentality of larger international scope have never been successful. Military alliances, balances of power, leagues of nations, all in turn failed, leaving the only path to be by way of the crucible of war. The utter destructiveness of war now blots out this alternative. We have had our last chance. If we will not devise some greater and more equitable system, Armageddon will be at our door. The problem basically is theological and involves a spirit recrudescence and improvement of human character that will synchronize with our almost matchless advances in science, art, literature, and all material and cultural developments of the past 2,000 years. It must be of the spirit if we are to save the flesh." [Applause.]

But once war is forced upon us, there is no other alternative than to apply every available means to bring it to a swift end. War's very object is victory—not prolonged indecision. [Applause.] In war, indeed, there can be no substitute for victory. [Applause.]

There are some who for varying reasons would appease Red China. They are blind to history's clear lesson. For history teaches with unmistakable emphasis that appeasement but begets new and bloodier war. It points to no single instance where the end has justified that means—where appeasement has led to more than a sham peace. Like blackmail, it lays the basis for new and successively greater demands, until, as in blackmail, violence becomes the only other alternative. Why, my soldiers asked of me, surrender military advantages to an enemy in the field? I could not answer. [Applause.] Some may say to avoid spread of the conflict into an all-out war with China; others, to avoid Soviet intervention. Neither explanation seems valid. For China is already engaging with the maximum power it can commit and the Soviet will not neccessarily mesh its actions with our moves. Like a cobra, any new enemy will more likely strike whenever it feels that the relativity in military or other potential is in its favor on a world-wide basis.

The tragedy of Korea is further heightened by the fact that as military action is confined to its territorial limits, it condemns that nation, which it is our purpose to save, to suffer the devastating impact of full naval and air bombardment, while the enemy's sanctuaries are fully protected from such attack and devastation. Of the nations of the world, Korea alone, up to now, is the sole one which has risked its all against communism. The magnificence of the courage and fortitude of the Korean people defies description. [Applause.] They have chosen to risk death rather than slavery. Their last words to me were "Don't scuttle the Pacific." [Applause.]

I have just left your fighting sons in Korea. They have met all tests there and I can report to you without reservation they are splendid in every way. [Applause.] It was my constant effort to preserve them and end this savage conflict honorably and with the least loss of time and a minimum sacrifice of life. Its growing bloodshed has caused me the deepest anguish and anxiety. Those gallant men will remain often in my thoughts and in my prayers always.

I am closing my 52 years of military service. [Applause.] When I joined the Army even before the turn of the century, it was the fulfillment of all my boyish hopes and dreams. The world has turned over many times since I took the oath on the plain at West Point, and the hopes and dreams have long since vanished. But I still remember the refrain of one of the most popular barrack ballads of that day which proclaim most proudly that—

"Old soldiers never die; they just fade away."

And like the old soldier of that ballad, I now close my military career and just fade away—an old soldier who tried to do his duty as God gave him the light to see that duty. Good-by.

IV. VIEWS OF OBSERVERS

SELECTION IV–A

The following material is reprinted by permission of the publishers from John W. Spanier, The Truman-MacArthur Controversy and the Korean War (Cambridge, Mass.: Harvard University Press). Copyright 1959 by the President and Fellows of Harvard College. John Spanier is a professor of political science at the University of Florida and author of American Foreign Policy since World War II.

CHINA'S CONDEMNATION AND MacARTHUR'S DISMISSAL: HARRY TRUMAN, MIDDLEMAN

During December 1950 and January 1951, the United States government found itself caught between the viewpoints and pressures of General

MacArthur and his political supporters on the one hand, and the allies on the other. Moreover, their conflicting attitudes were so far apart that it was impossible to bridge them. MacArthur pointed to Communist China as an inveterate enemy of the West and a great threat to the future of Asia; the remedy was a vigorous military course. The allies were convinced—or, more accurately, hopeful—that Moscow could not control Peking, and that Communist China would develop an independent policy if the Western powers left the door to the free world open; in short, they saw Peking as a potential friend and counterbalance to Russia in Asia. The General saw the failure to liberate all of Korea as a betrayal of a promise made to the Korean people by the United States and the United Nations; the Europeans acknowledged no such pledge. The Commander in Chief, Far East, was convinced that the struggle between the United Nations and Red China would not demand substantially more forces, only the lifting of current restrictions on his air and naval arms and the "unleashing" of Chiang Kai-shek. The allies feared that an extended war in the Far East would divert considerable American strength from Europe and leave the West defenseless. One doubted that Soviet Russia would openly participate in the war, and therefore stigmatized the desire to negotiate an end to the war as a symptom of weakness which would provoke rather than deter Russian intervention; the other thought that the Kremlin would fight and thereby precipitate a total war for which they were not yet prepared.

The two sides shared only one common characteristic: they thought of each other in blackest terms. MacArthur thought the Europeans held an unrealistic picture of the world and condemned them as too prone to "appeasement." The Europeans in their turn, were distrustful of MacArthur: they disliked his impatience for results, his preoccupation with political matters that allegedly were no concern of his, and they were always fearful lest Washington fail to control him.

These contradictory viewpoints and pressures presented the American government with a real dilemma. Whose advice ought it to take? Should it listen to General MacArthur and risk the possibility of a world war and the alienation of its allies? Or should it accept the counsel of its NATO partners and thereby precipitate a cold war at home, particularly between itself and Congress? The choice was not an easy one. For notwithstanding popular mythology, the Administration did not totally reject the argument presented by its field commander; nor did it wholeheartedly welcome the views of its allies. With the former it agreed that no concessions ought to be made to the Chinese Communists; with the latter it agreed that the war must not be expanded.

The Administration's firm opposition to admitting Communist China into the United Nations or granting her a free hand in the Strait of Formosa was not based upon recognition of the facts of domestic political life; its argument against these concessions rested upon their harmful effects upon

America's international status and prestige. An accommodating spirit might encourage the Communists to commit further acts of aggression; it would probably lead them to raise their demands; and even if it did not increase their appetite, a settlement at the price of the United Nations admittance and Formosa would undermine Asian confidence in the United States, particularly in Japan and the Philippines. Rewarding Peking's aggression would be tantamount to admitting that the Communists "had won the game and could now collect the stakes." The American people, Acheson told Attlee during his visit, could not at the same time be expected to support a vigorous foreign policy in Europe and accept aggression in the Far East, or at least the aggression of a large power—"It would be a very confusing thing . . ." Should Communist China's entry into Korea, moreover, foreshadow the possibility of Russia's intervention in Korea or elsewhere, it would be a grievous error to try and buy her off. "My own guess" declared Acheson, "is that it wouldn't work. All we might get would be time, but never enough to do any good. Just enough time to divide our people bitterly. Just enough time to lose our moral strength." It was better to be forced out of Korea than to negotiate at the point of a gun.

Apparently, then, Communist China's intervention had changed the Secretary's views, for the time being at least, on Sino-Soviet relations and the possibility of a Chinese-Russian struggle for power in Northern China. On November 29, in the same speech in which he had said that "no possible shred of evidence could have existed in the minds of the Chinese Communist authorities about the intentions of the United Nations" in North Korea, Acheson denounced Peking's intervention as an "act of brazen aggression . . . the second such action in five months . . . This is not merely another phrase of the Korean campaign. This is a fresh and unprovoked action, even more immoral than the first." And when the British Prime Minister suggested that the Western powers should pursue a policy which would turn Communist China against Russia—a policy which before China's intervention Acheson had himself hoped to implement upon the fall of Formosa—Acheson answered that "we could not buy the friendship of the Chinese Communists . . . and we ought not try to prove that we were more friendly to them than the Russians. After what they had done to us, it seemed to him that the Chinese would have to prove that they were *our* friends."

While the Administration thus agreed with General MacArthur that the acceptance of Communist China's demands would be politically disastrous, it did not share his enthusiasm for more vigorous military action. President Truman and his advisers agreed with the allies that air and naval bombardment of Communist China would probably result in a world war. Red China was the Soviet Union's largest and most powerful ally or satellite. Consequently, Russian self-interest and prestige in the Far East, embodied in the Sino-Soviet treaty, would make it difficult for her to ignore a direct attack upon the Chinese mainland.

Indeed, even without American bombardment of Communist China, the Administration believed that it stood on the brink of war. The imminence with which it expected the Soviets to launch their attack is suggested by a story in Mr. Truman's memoirs. On the morning of December 16, 1950, Under Secretary of Defense Lovett called the White House and reported that radar screens in the Far North were reporting large formations of unidentified planes. Fighter planes were immediately set up to reconnoiter and alert signals flashed to air centers throughout New England. For a time apparently, it was believed that these planes were Soviet bombers on their way to drop their deadly cargo on American cities. Later, Lovett informed the President that the report had been in error, and that the mistake had been due to the effects of some unusual atmospheric disturbance upon the radar equipment.

China's aggression, in short, seems to have given American policy-makers a jolt. The containment policy had been based upon the assumption that the Soviet Union would not accept the risk of a major war until 1952–1954; but North Korea's aggression, and now Communist China's intervention, suggested that the Soviet timetable might be much shorter than had originally been anticipated. The Kremlin, in other words, might not be talking of a world war simply to frighten the Western powers and weaken their powers of resistance; it might actually have decided that the time was ripe for war with the United States and its allies. Soviet military preparations and propaganda indicated the possibility of moves in Berlin, West Germany, Indochina, Yugoslavia, and Iran.

SELECTION IV–B

Excerpted from Tae-Ho Yoo, *The Korean War and the United Nations: A Legal and Diplomatic Historical Study* (Louvain, 1964), pp. 80–81, 179–81. Reprinted by permission of the author and of the Libraries Desbarax (Anc.) Louvain. Published under the auspices of the Collection de l'Institut des Sciences politiques et sociales of the University of Louvain. Dr. Yoo has been an official of the European Economic Community and a research associate at the Institute for Political and Social Sciences at the University of Louvain.

The traditional war diplomacy consisted of dominating one Power by another through the military superiority of the latter. When a local war forced the Big Powers to intervene in that conflict, the latter became necessarily extensive, because all the wars were done in the form of alliance. Such a process appeared again in the Korean Conflict even after the creation of the United Nations.

The United States extended the Korean Conflict despite the opposition of its allies. The U.S. ambition to destroy the *status quo* was certainly contradictory to the Soviet ambition still to maintain the Korean zone of influence under her strict control. The UN's military intervention in North

Korea still rendered stronger the communist alliance and diminished even more the possibility to negotiate. Therefore, the U.S. solution inclined to the military solution. However, we have to note that at that time the Soviet Union never thought that a peaceful coexistence with capitalist countries could be possible and believed that the international movement of communism by force had a real chance to conquer the whole world, particularly the newly independent countries.

As to Communist China, she intervened in the Korean Conflict for the reason of historical and ideological solidarity with North Korea. On the other hand, Communist China thought through this war to reinforce her national revolutionary movement and claim her sovereign right to represent continental China at the United Nations.

The Korean local Conflict became an all-out war of two world blocs. All the decisions of the General Assembly were legally and morally valid, but deprived of real effect, because the United Nations could not override the conflicting ideological movements and nationalistic rivalry going on within itself.

However, the Members States of the "Tiers-Monde," concious of the bipolarization of world powers in this conflict, sought to bring the conflicting Big Powers to a peaceful negotiation. At that time, the Soviet Union and the United States denounced, each in her own way, the immorality of neutralism. Therefore, the role of the non-committed countries was reduced to an advisory or recommendatory effect. However, their role of mediation was very necessary to keep the Big Powers from exceeding their limit of action. The Big Powers ignored, however, this role of mediation with the result of the sacrifice of more than one million people. All the UN intervention which followed later showed that the commitment of the Big Powers in a local conflict brought a negative effect. Apart from maintaining their internal political unity the increasing role of the "Neutrals" in international relations is also necessary to put an end to the ridiculous race of the Big Powers as regards atomic weapons and to balance their power politics in the direction of peaceful coexistence.

Even though that was the case, in face of the conflict of the Big Powers, the Korean people had no chance to discuss their problems in their own way, because the problems of the Big Powers were superposed on the Korean Question.

.   .   .   .

In principle, in the Charter's system of collective security the right of a neutral to discriminate against or to penalize an aggressor has been transformed into a duty. In practice, the existence of neutrals has been justified, and even been necessary, on the ground that they serve for mediation, listening-post and controlling role as did the UN Neutral Commission for the Korean Armistice. Moreover, the notion of neutrality is more of a political character than a legal one. Since the UN system is based on the principle of equal sovereignty and conventional or contractual collaboration between the States, the Charter admits qualified neutrality under Article 47 and the abstention of Members or non-Members in the execution of the Assembly's resolutions. It is a sign of a legal lacuna of the Charter's system of collective security. The UN has to find sooner or later a formula by which the decisions of the General Assembly will be binding. For that purpose we may suggest the "proportional" system of vote in the Assembly so that the vote in the Assembly will represent the real value of each member State. We may also suggest the strengthening of the UN authority by the representation of more Members to the United Nations.

Although there may be different interpretations, the Geneva Convention of 1949 for Prisoners of War will be applicable even in a conflict which involves the enforcement action of the UN. The Korean case shows that forced repatriation is not equivalent to humanely arranged repatriation according to the Geneva Convention. Repatriation on a voluntary basis is within the scope of the Convention and on the basis of the Human Rights universally recognized.

After having studied the Korean Conflict under the rules of the UN Charter, we felt that, the UN Charter being particularly a political treaty, the pure legal analysis of the UN Charter would have brought a subjective judgment to the question, therefore we thought that the law was not an idealistic pattern of actual international society, but a functional or indicative standard of rules of an international society in constant evolution. Consequently, the rules of the UN would function normally when the rulers of the UN law apply laws with an objective understanding of the effectiveness of the social and political contents of law.

Finally, we have some words to say about the unification of Korea. In this regard, we should not forget that the division of Korea is a result of the world-wide Cold War between two power-blocs. The Geneva Conference of 1953 attempted to find a formula for the unification of Korea. The failure of that Conference was due to the fact that at that time both parties were not entirely freed from ideological sectarism and did not stress their common efforts to discuss their problems independently from the influences of the Big Powers. The unification of Korea is essentially a problem of the Korean people. On the one hand, the unification of Korea will depend on the degree of their political independence from the conflicting Big Powers and on their spontaneous approach; on the other hand, it will depend also on the effective guarantee of democratic elections in both areas by the United Nations.

SELECTION IV–C

Portions of Arnold Wolfers' "Collective Security and the War in Korea," as it appeared in *The Yale Review,* XLIII (June, 1954), pp. 481–83, 495–96. Reprinted by permission of the author and of *The Yale Review.* © Yale University Press. Professor Wolfers was Director of the Washington Center of Foreign Policy Research of Johns Hopkins University and formerly professor of international relations at Yale.

The action taken by the United Nations in 1950 to halt the attack on South Korea has been heralded as the first experiment in collective security. The implication is that a radical break with the traditional foreign policy of nations has occurred; power politics, we are told, have been replaced by police action of the world community. It is quite likely that many who suffered in the Korean War on our side have been comforted by the thought that they have served the cause of law enforcement by community action, though others who believed that no vital interests of their country were at stake may have found the ordeal harder to bear. Whatever the emotional reaction, it is necessary to investigate dispassionately whether in fact a turning point in world politics was reached when the United Nations flag was unfurled in Korea. On the answer may depend what future policy we and others are entitled to expect of this country.

It may sound like quibbling to ask whether Korea was an example of "collective security." Obviously, the answer depends on the definition of the term. If one chooses to make it include every collective action undertaken for defensive purposes by a group of nations, then the Korean intervention by the United States and its associates falls under the term. Actually, it has become the habit of official spokesmen of our government to use the term in this way. For instance, they speak of NATO as a means of "collective security," although the treaty was legally justified by reference to Article 51 of the United Nations Charter, which explicitly permits "collective self-defense" in cases where the universal collective security provisions of the United Nations *fail* to protect a victim of aggression. But there is nothing new or revolutionary in nations' aligning themselves for purposes of defense against their common national foes. Except for countries pursuing a "go it alone" policy, such conduct has been traditional among the members of multistate systems.

This is not what exponents of the principle of collective security have in mind when they urge nations to change the customary direction of their defense policy. They call upon nations to go beyond aligning themselves with each other only to meet the threats emanating from common national enemies and to embrace instead a policy of defense directed against aggression in general or, more precisely, against any aggressor anywhere. Coupled with arrangements to name the aggressor by community decision, nations—instead of reserving their power to defend or enforce their national interests

—would be lined up like a police force to strike against any country, friend or foe, that had been declared an aggressor. Such a policy would constitute a radical break with tradition.

Since there are fundamental differences between these two types of collective action, with only one of them constituting a break with traditional national foreign policy, to avoid confusion and misunderstanding the two should be distinguished by the use of different labels. And since "collective security" has become the symbol for a break with power politics, it should be reserved for action that meets this test. It will be used so in this discussion, while other types of multilateral defensive action will be called "collective defense." Aside from semantics then, the problem is whether intervention in Korea represents a radical break with the traditional foreign policy of nation-states and, as a consequence, fulfils the expectations widely held for "collective security."

How serious a break with tradition the policy of collective security would be becomes evident if one considers what risks and sacrifices nations would have to incur in order to make such a policy effective and meaningful. It stands to reason that provisions and commitments for police action would add nothing to the protection that victims of aggression have enjoyed under the old system unless such victims could expect more military assistance than they would have received otherwise. The exponents of collective security have stressed this point. They have assumed that under a system of collective security such as they advocate, overwhelming force would be placed behind the law and at the disposal of a victim of attack. As in municipal affairs, therefore, the power of the police would usually suffice to deter any would-be attacker and thereby serve to maintain the peace rather than merely to punish the offender.

In order that collective security add in this way to the strength of the defense and to the chances of deterrence, it must be assumed that some nations, including one or more of the great powers, will be prepared to resort to force—that is, for all practical purposes, go to war—when, if they had not been devoted to the principle of collective security, they would have remained neutral or fought on the side of the aggressor. Instead of being allowed to reserve their military strength for the exclusive task of balancing the power of countries considered a threat to themselves or their allies, nations committed to a policy of collective security must divert their strength to struggles in remote places or, worse still, take action against friends and allies on whom reliance had been placed for defense against common foes. In extreme cases, a nation might even be called upon to defend and strengthen a foe at the expense of a friend or ally, if the latter were condemned as an aggressor.

． ． ． ． ． ． ． ． ． ． ． ．

It may be objected that if Korea has not opened the way for a universal system of collective security against all aggression, it has merely served to demonstrate once more the tragic hold that "power politics" has on the nations even of the free world. The United Nations as a security organization, it will be said, can have no place in such a world. However, such conclusions are not warranted. The United States and its associates made good on a policy of "collective defense of the free world" carried out under the authority and control of the United Nations. While the control was weak, it nevertheless brought a restraining influence to bear on one of the world's greatest powers engaged in a bitter and costly defensive struggle. The one great contribution to the development of more lawful conditions in the world which this country can claim to have made in Korea consists therefore of its willingness to recognize the authority of the United Nations over actions which required sacrifices mainly from the American people. If some deplore the way in which the majority in the General Assembly exercised this control, believing that it would have been better for this country and the free world to have fought for victory at all costs, they give testimony thereby to the price countries may have to pay for the advantages of having collective defense operate according to the rules and with the approval of an international organization.

As to the United Nations itself, it has gained stature by the fact of having been able to be useful to the free world in its defense against Communist aggression without having to give up its universal character and its mediatory potentialities. Obviously, its role has been a more modest one than that contemplated by the exponents of collective security. Instead of being able to order the bulk of its members to fight aggressors whatever their relations to the aggressor, all the United Nations could do was to name the aggressor, to authorize and recommend action by its members, to lend its name to their action, and to seek to exert influence on the way it was carried out and terminated. This is exactly the role which would fall to the United Nations in cases in which collective self-defense was carried out under Article 51 and preceded action by the Security Council. The similarity is not accidental. If nations will resort to force only against national opponents when it accords with their national defense interests, as was true in Korea, the United Nations must limit itself to functions which are consistent with the needs of collective defense of likeminded countries. This has now been shown to be a practical and beneficial way of using an organization which, it should be added, has many important tasks to perform other than to stop or punish aggression.

7

DIPLOMATIC ISSUES IN
THE 1952 ELECTION
Dulles vs. Acheson

I. EDITORIAL INTRODUCTION

For twenty years after 1932 the Republican Party had been looking at the White House from the outside. First, the bitter years of the Depression not only brought Franklin D. Roosevelt to power but maintained him there as the leader who could treat the ills of society and return America to the prosperity that had disappeared under Hoover. Second, the spectre of war, and then the reality of war itself, gripped America for seven years and permitted Roosevelt to win his unprecedented third and fourth terms. Third, when peace had returned and an apparently vulnerable Harry Truman replaced the invincible Roosevelt a combination of special economic circumstances, overconfidence within the Republican Party, and the public admiration for Truman's fighting spirit in foreign as well as domestic affairs, snatched victory from the surprised Governor Thomas E. Dewey in 1948.

Few thought that the magic of a Roosevelt or the pluck of a Truman would have much bearing in 1952. All the errors, sins and crimes, real and imagined, with which any political party in power for twenty years would be charged weighed too heavily upon the attractive newcomer, Adlai Stevenson, Governor of Illinois, who would have to bear the burden. There was a crisis of confidence in the administration which the Democrats were unable to dispel. Spectacular charges of corruption in high places suggested that the administration was hopelessly unequipped to deal with it; frequent if often unfair and inaccurate accusations of communist influence in government inflamed public opinion and pushed Senator Joseph McCarthy to prominence as the nation's leading foe of communism in the government. But most damaging of all was the continuing drain of the Korean conflict on American manpower, economy, and morale. The Democrats, as the party in power for twenty years, could not escape responsibility for the nation's troubles, while the Republicans had in the person of a popular war hero, General Dwight D. Eisenhower, a candidate who offered hopes for remedies of the nation's ills, particularly, those relating to the involvement in Korea.

Inevitably, the Korean war, still smouldering after two years and without prospects of a clear-cut victory, lay in the background of both party platforms. While campaign oratory has a special rhetoric of its own, the eagerness with which the Republican platform arraigned the administration for the failure in foreign policy that led to war—from its inability to preserve "the peace so dearly earned by World War II" to the lack of foresight that brought on the Korean war—suggested that public opinion was sufficiently aroused by the troubles in the Far East to make them the major issues in the election. (Selection II–A.) There was a defensive note in the Democratic party platform which reflected sensitivity to criticism. The United Nations and collective security were understandably emphasized; the reverses in Asia understandably muted. (Selection II–B.)

Behind the words of the Republican platform, many of them phrased by the shadow Secretary of State John Foster Dulles, was the spirit of American isolationism exemplified in the leadership of Senator Taft. A year before in a book designed to show a knowledge of world as well as of domestic affairs, Taft made clear his own belief that a communist conspiracy lay behind America's problems and summoned the nation to meet the challenge. (Selection III–A.)

It was this kind of analysis that tried the patience of Secretary of State Dean Acheson. He emphasized instead the need to match America's strength with the interests to be defended. The mobilization of public opinion, the winning of men's minds, either as Taft or Eisenhower conceived it, would not be sufficient; only by assuming the responsibilities of leadership of an alliance of free nations could the communist world be forced into a situation in which disputes will be settled by negotiation. (Selection III–B.)

For the future secretary of state, however, the policy advocated by Acheson and by the Democrats in general was too passive. Unlike Senator Taft, he paid tribute to America's identification with NATO and the defense of Korea. But he felt the administration did not go far enough in its action against communism. It only reacted. What Dulles advocated was a dynamic, aggressive policy that went beyond containment but which used bold statecraft rather than war to achieve its goal. Such was the promise of Dulles to the American people six months before election day. (Selection III–C.)

Years later, after Dulles had an opportunity to give meaning to his alternative to containment, most contemporary critics of the Dulles foreign policy gave a negative verdict. Many of his expectations were not fulfilled; many of his successes appeared to have been won by continuing the Truman-Acheson policies. Even worse, his posture of moralism exposed him to ridicule and accusations of hypocrisy. In a bitter attack upon Dulles's moralistic posturing in foreign policy William Lee Miller of the Yale Divinity School made a point of the immorality of the "liberation" theme used by Dulles in his address to Polish-American audiences when the Secretary knew both the limitations of the Truman administration's responsibility for communist Poland and the limitations of the Eisenhower administration's help in freeing Poland from Soviet domination. (Selection IV–A.)

Professor O. William Perlmutter in a scholarly examination of the "neo-realism" of Dean Acheson suggests that Dulles' "idealism" was expressed in his ideological struggle with communism as a religious movement, while Acheson was more willing to accept the realities of power politics in the outside world. Acheson upheld his religious values in his personal political affairs; Dulles was willing to compromise his principles in his relations with Congress so that the greater struggle with the external enemy would not have to be compromised. (Selection IV–B.)

But as Coblentz and Drummond make clear, in the year 1952 Dulles was the man who could be acceptable to both Taft and to Eisenhower, who appeared able to maintain the accomplishments of the Truman administration with which he had been identified without unleashing the kind of opposition then facing Truman and Acheson. (Selection IV–C.) Whether his "policy of boldness" was indeed a positive step beyond "containment" is another matter.

II. DOCUMENTS

SELECTION II–A

An excerpt from the Republican Party platform of 1952. Reprinted from Kirk H. Porter and Donald Bruce Johnson, ed. *National Party Platforms,* 1840–1956 (Urbana, 1956), pp. 497–98. Copyright © 1956 by the Board of Trustees of the University of Illinois. Reprinted by permission of the University of Illinois Press.

FOREIGN POLICY

The present Administration, in seven years, has squandered the unprecedented power and prestige which were ours at the close of World War II.

In that time, more than 500 million non-Russian people of fifteen different countries have been absorbed into the power sphere of Communist Russia, which proceeds confidently with its plan for world conquest.

We charge that the leaders of the Administration in power lost the peace so dearly earned by World War II.

The moral incentives and hopes for a better world which sustained us through World War II were betrayed, and this has given Communist Russia a military and propaganda initiative which, if unstayed, will destroy us.

They abandoned friendly nations such as Latvia, Lithuania, Estonia, Poland and Czechoslovakia to fend for themselves against the Communist aggression which soon swallowed them.

They required the National Government of China to surrender Manchuria with its strategic ports and railroads to the control of Communist Russia. They urged that Communists be taken into the Chinese Government and its military forces. And finally they denied the military aid that had been authorized by Congress and which was crucially needed if China were to be saved. Thus they substituted on our Pacific flank a murderous enemy for an ally and friend.

In all these respects they flouted our peace-assuring pledges such as the Atlantic Charter, and did so in favor of despots, who, it was well-known, consider that murder, terror, slavery, concentration camps and the ruthless and brutal denial of human rights are legitimate means to their desired ends.

Tehran, Yalta and Potsdam were the scenes of those tragic blunders with others to follow. The leaders of the Administration in power acted without the knowledge or consent of Congress or of the American people. They traded our overwhelming victory for a new enemy and for new oppressions and new wars which were quick to come.

In South Korea, they withdrew our occupation troops in the face of the aggressive, poised for action, Communist military strength on its northern border. They publicly announced that Korea was of no concern to us. Then when the Communist forces acted to take what seemed to have been invited, they committed this nation to fight back under the most unfavorable conditions. Already the tragic cost is over 110,000 American casualties.

With foresight, the Korean War would never have happened.

In going back into Korea, they evoked the patriotic and sacrificial support of the American people. But by their hampering orders they produced stalemates and ignominious bartering with our enemies, and they offer no hope of victory.

They have effectively ignored many vital areas in the face of a global threat requiring balanced handling.

The people of the other American Republics are resentful of our neglect of their legitimate aspirations and cooperative friendship.

The Middle East and much of Africa seethe with anti-American sentiment.

The peoples of the Far East who are not under Communist control find it difficult to sustain their morale as they contrast Russia's "Asia First" policy with the "Asia Last" policy of those in control of the Administration now in power.

Here at home they have exhibited corruption, incompetence, and disloyalty in public office to such an extent that the very concept of free representative government has been tarnished and has lost its idealistic appeal to those elsewhere who are confronted with the propaganda of Communism.

They profess to be following a defensive policy of "containment" of Russian Communism which has not contained it.

Those in control of the Party in power have, in reality, no foreign policy. They swing erratically from timid appeasement to reckless bluster.

The good in our foreign policies has been accomplished with Republican cooperation, such as the organization of the United Nations, the establishment of the trusteeship principle for dependent peoples, the making of peace with Japan and Germany, and the building of more solid security in Europe. But in the main the Republican Party has been ignored and its participation has not been invited.

The American people must now decide whether to continue in office the party which has presided over this disastrous reversal of our fortunes and the loss of our hopes for a peaceful world.

The Republican Party offers, in contrast to the performances of those now running our foreign affairs, policies and actions based on enlightened self-interest and animated by courage, self-respect, steadfastness, vision, purpose, competence and spiritual faith.

The supreme goal of our foreign policy will be an honorable and just peace. We dedicate ourselves to wage peace and to win it.

We shall eliminate from the State Department and from every Federal office, all, wherever they may be found, who share responsibility for the needless predicaments and perils in which we find ourselves. We shall also sever from the public payroll the hordes of loafers, incompetents and unnecessary employees who clutter the administration of our foreign affairs. The confusions, overlappings, and extravagance of our agencies abroad hold us up to the ridicule of peoples whose friendship we seek.

We shall substitute a compact and efficient organization where men of proven loyalty and ability shall have responsibility for reaching our objectives. They will reflect a dynamic initiative. Thus we can win the support and confidence which go only to those who demonstrate a capacity to define and get results.

We shall have positive peace-building objectives wherever this will serve the enlightened self-interest of our Nation and help to frustrate the enemy's designs against us.

SELECTION II–B

An excerpt from the Democratic Party platform of 1952 reprinted from Kirk H. Porter and Donald Bruce Johnson, eds., *National Party Platforms, 1840–1956* (Urbana, 1956). pp. 475–77. Copyright © 1956 by the Board of Trustees of the University of Illinois. Reprinted by permission of the University of Illinois Press.

THE DEMOCRATIC PROGRAM FOR PEACE AND NATIONAL SECURITY

SUPPORTING THE UNITED NATIONS

Under Democratic leadership, this country sponsored and helped create the United Nations and became a charter member and staunchly supports its aims.

We will continue our efforts to strengthen the United Nations, improve its institutions as experience requires, and foster its growth and development.

The Communist aggressor has been hurled back from South Korea. Thus, Korea has proved, once and for all, that the United Nations will resist aggression. We urge continued effort, by every honorable means, to bring about a fair and effective peace settlement in Korea in accordance with the principles of the United Nations' charter.

STRONG NATIONAL DEFENSE

Our Nation has strengthened its national defense against the menace of Soviet aggression.

The Democratic Party will continue to stand unequivocally for the strong, balanced defense forces for this country—land, sea and air. We will continue to support the expansion and maintenance of the military and civil defense forces required for our national security. We reject the defeatist view of those who say we cannot afford the expense and effort necessary to defend ourselves. We express our full confidence in the Joint Chiefs of Staff. We voice complete faith in the ability and valor of our armed forces, and pride in their accomplishments.

COLLECTIVE STRENGTH FOR THE FREE WORLD

We reject the ridiculous notions of those who would have the United States face the aggressors alone. That would be the most expensive—and the most dangerous—method of seeking security. This nation needs strong allies, around the world, making their maximum contribution to the common defense. They add their strength to ours in the defense of freedom.

The Truman Doctrine in 1947, the organization of hemisphere defense at Rio de Janeiro that same year, the Marshall Plan in 1948, the North Atlantic Treaty in 1949, the Point IV program, the resistance to Communist aggression in Korea, the Pacific Security pacts in 1951, and the Mutual Security programs now under way—all stand as landmarks of America's progress in mobilizing the strength of the free world to keep the peace.

III. VIEWS OF PARTICIPANTS

> *SELECTION III–A*
>
> "The Battle against Communist Ideology Throughout the World," from *A Foreign Policy for Americans* by Robert A. Taft. Copyright © 1951 by Robert A. Taft. Reprinted by permission of Doubleday & Company, Inc., pp. 114–15, 151. Taft, Republican Senator from Ohio, a leading contender for the Republican nomination in 1952, was also the leading Congressional spokesman for isolationism, as this passage reveals.

The threat of communism against liberty is not by any means a purely military threat—in fact, if we had only to face the military strength of Soviet Russia I think there would not be any such concern as we see today. Communism is strong because it has developed a fanatical support and missionary ardor, which have spread throughout the world and appealed everywhere to some of those who are dissatisfied with their present condition. It is a threat because it has developed methods of infiltration and propaganda well-fitted to this missionary ardor and has succeeding in building up, even in the most free countries, at least a strong minority of people who form, in effect, a fifth column behind our lines. In France the 1951 elections showed 26 per cent of the voters to be Communists, in Italy more.

Whether we have to meet the forces of communism on the battlefield is open to question. The Russian leaders may be wholly unwilling to trust the entire future of communism to a war, in which Russia, and the Communist leaders, and perhaps communism itself, may be destroyed. They have always felt that communism has in it such elements of strength that it is bound to prevail over the system of capitalism which they denounce. They feel that capitalism has within it the seeds of its own destruction, that depression will follow depression, until the people turn to the Communist leaders for improvement in their economic conditions. They feel that the steady progress of socialism brings many countries closer and cloaser to the general ideals of communism. They know that socialism in the long run cannot be imposed upon a people, except by dictatorial power, and that socialism imposed by a dictatorship of a small group of enthusiasts is almost exactly the same as communism.

And so we have to consider the methods by which we can battle against the spread of communism and so weaken its spirit that its missionary ardor is destroyed. I believe that can only be done by a positive campaign in behalf of liberty. Liberty has always appealed to the minds of men and today is a far more appealing ideal than communism or material welfare can ever be. Even today I believe that a great majority of the people in the iron-curtain countries yearn for liberty against the Communistic dictatorship imposed upon them by a small minority of their own people backed by Soviet troops. In America we have clear evidence of the fact that liberty can produce the highest standard of living and the greatest happiness of any system that has ever been devised.

And when I say liberty I do not simply mean what is referred to as "free enterprise." I mean liberty of the individual to think his own thoughts and live his own life as he desires to think and to live; the liberty of the family to decide how they wish to live, what they want to eat for breakfast and for dinner, and how they wish to spend their time; liberty of a man to develop his ideas and get other people to teach those ideas, if he can convince them that they have some value to the world; liberty of every local community to decide how its children shall be educated, how its local services shall be run, and who its local leaders shall be; liberty of a man to choose his own occupation; and liberty of a man to run his own business as he thinks it ought to be run, as long as he does not interfere with the right of other people to do the same thing.

.   .   .   .

In short, a war against communism in the world must finally be won in the minds of men. The hope for ultimate peace lies far more in the full exploitation of the methods I have suggested than in a third world war, which may destroy civilization itself. Far from establishing liberty throughout the world, war has actually encouraged and built up the development of dictatorships and has only restored liberty in limited areas at the cost of untold hardship, of human suffering, of death and destruction beyond the conception of our fathers. We may be able to achieve real peace in the world without passing through the fire of a third world war if we have wise leadership. Communism can be defeated by an affirmative philosophy of individual liberty, and by an even more sincere belief in liberty than the Communists have in communism. In the United States we see the product of liberty to be the greatest and most powerful nation the world has ever seen, with the happiest people. If we rise to the power of our strength, there has never been a stronger case to present to the world, or a better opportunity to dissolve its darkness into light.

SELECTION III–B

Taken from Dean Acheson's off-the-record remarks to a group of magazine and book publishers, June 29, 1951 as printed in Department of
State *Bulletin*, XXV (July 23, 1951), pp. 127–28. Secretary of State Acheson's defense of his record a year before the presidential elections.

NO SUBSTITUTE FOR CENTRAL STRENGTH

We must also recognize that there is no substitute for strength at the center. Alliances are important. It is of vital importance to us that our allies in the North Atlantic Treaty and in the Rio treaty be strong and that the bonds between them and us be strong. But it is equally important, if not more important, that there be strength at the center of these groups—the strength of the United States, its economic strength, its military strength, which will, in itself, breed strength at the periphery of our associations. The same applies in the United Nations. In that union of nations there is no substitute for the strength of the United States at the heart of the great group of powers which share our determination to uphold the principles of the Charter.

In building that strength it is very important that we should not underestimate ourselves. We have to meet and face limitations and difficulties. But if every time a difficulty comes along somebody says, "Oh, to do that will wreck the economy of the United States," that is underestimating ourselves. I have no doubt that there is a point beyond which the United States cannot go, but I am equally sure that we are not anywhere near that point. Therefore the thing to do is not to be timid about ourselves but to realize that our great strength is there to be used, and to use it wisely and economically and sensibly to create the defenses which we need.

May I say right here in connection with this business of creating strength at the center, we must not for one second allow any development which may occur in Korea to lull us into a belief that now we have turned the corner, and now things are going to get better, and therefore we do not need to make the effort which we have been making. I think we need to make it even more than we made it before. If it is possible to bring about an end of the fighting in Korea, it will be because of the efforts which we have already made and the sacrifices of the men in Korea. The success of our policy will mean only one thing, and that is that we have held off this conspiracy against us and that we have some time now which, if used wisely, will give us the power and give us the union with powerful allies which can deter World War III. If we do not do that, if we allow ourselves to be lulled by Korea, I can assure you that, just as certainly as you are sitting here, we will be hit within the next 6 months to a year with a much tougher blow somewhere else. If we do not make the efforts now, we will be unprepared for that blow. We may completely deter it if we now all bend together every effort we can to going forward with the program.

Another point is that we must believe that time is on our side. I concede to you that in saying this there is an element of faith. There is an element of faith because I believe that we are people who act. Time is not on our side if we merely sit in the shade and fan ourselves. Time is on our side if we go to work. We can do much in time. We can strengthen ourselves, we can strengthen our allies. We have a vast productive power which is now not harnessed, much greater than those opposed to us. We can harness it. There is much we can do and, if we will do it, time is on our side. If we don't do it, it is not.

Therefore, we come to the matter of will. We have a strong geographical position. We have people who are skilled in industry, who have courage, who make fine soldiers and producers. We have natural resources. We have the productive plant. All of those things are no good at all unless they are cemented together and thrown into action by will. I believe that the American people have that will and that they can put that will strongly behind everything of a material nature that they have so that they, along with their allies, will secure for the future the things they value.

Another attitude of the utmost importance is that we must keep constantly before us the goal toward which we are working. What we are working toward is a situation in which the normal course of settling disputes will be negotiation. We are enthusiastic people, and occasionally we get so enthusiastic about what we are doing that we believe that is the end instead of the means. We must never get ourselves into the state of mind where we say that we are building this strength in order to use it. We are building this strength in order that we may never have to use it, in order that we may get to the point where the normal way to settle things is to sit down, to argue about them, to negotiate about them, and to find a solution with which all parties concerned can live, even though it is not ideal for any of us.

That is not really a hopeless ambition. It seems a long way off—and it is a long way off when you are dealing with the Soviet Union under the present imbalance of power—but we have reached a situation in the Western Hemisphere where negotiation is the normal way of settling disputes. The normal way for the American republics to settle all their differences—and there are very grave and serious difficulties—is by negotiation and reasonable settlement. That has taken nearly 60 years to work out. It has taken all of that time to build up the trust of the American republics among themselves and between them and us. For years we were called the "Colossus of the North," and we took actions from time to time which made the other American republics apprehensive of us, but I think that no longer exists. I do not believe there ever took place in the world a more harmonious or constructive meeting than the recent meeting between the Foreign Ministers of the American republics, in which all sorts of questions, vitally affecting all our countries, were taken up and discussed. Sometimes points of view were very far apart. On one very tough economic question it took staying up all night for three nights to get people to realize that there was a good deal in common between them! But we solved that question and we will solve other differences in this Hemisphere in that way.

PATTERN OF RESPONSIBILITY FOR LEADERSHIP

There is one last attitude which I should like to stress, and that is that we must always keep in mind that we must deal with these problems within a pattern of responsibility. I should like to talk a little bit about what I mean by a pattern of responsibility. I mean that we must act with the consciousness that our responsibility is to interests which are broader than our own immediate American interests. Great empires have risen in this world and have collapsed because they took too narrow a view. There is no divine command which spares the United States from the seeds of destruction which have operated in other great states. There is no instruction to that one of the Fates who holds the shears that she shall withhold them from the thread of life of the United States. We must operate in a pattern of responsibility which is greater than our own interests. We cannot yield to the temptation, because we are virile and enthusiastic, of thinking that, because we believe a thing, it just must be right. We must not confuse our own opinions with the will of God.

That is essential for leadership. It is not merely a moral dissertation which I am making. It is essential to leadership among the free nations if we are going to maintain the sort of coalition which we have. We cannot take the attitude that we will coerce nations, that we are so right that if they do not do exactly what we want them to do we will withhold economic aid, or we will withhold military aid, we will do this, we will do that. If we take that attitude, then we are creating a relationship indistinguishable from that which exists between the Soviet Union and countries associated with it. That must never be our attitude. We are the leader. We are accepted as the leader. But we will continue to be accepted as the leader only if the other countries believe that the pattern of responsibility within which we operate is a responsibility to interests which are broader than our own—that we know today what Thomas Jefferson was talking about when he spoke of the need of paying a decent respect to the opinions of mankind.

How can we institutionalize that sense of responsibility? The means are at hand, have been used, and must continue to be used. The means lie in the United Nations. There is much talk these days that the United Nations has proved itself ineffective—it does not do this, it does not do that, we must scrap it in favor of some other kind of coercive machinery. I do not agree with any of those views.

I don't think anyone is more conscious than I am, unless it be General Bradley, of the difficulties of working within a coalition as large as the group in the United Nations who are associated together in Korea. There are a thousand problems in working with so many nations, considering their points of view, and modifying your own so that you may maintain a true friend. But I assure you that it is worth it a million times. Whatever loss there is in efficiency of operation is gained a million times by the strength which comes from the group's believing that the leader is paying attention to other people's points of view. We should be forever grateful to the United Nations for furnishing a forum where the United States of America, to maintain its leadership, must enter and must explain itself to the rest of the world, and do so in terms which are so persuasive that countries will be convinced, do so under circumstances where the United States and its representatives listen to the representative of the smallest country in the world who has a point of view which he wishes to express, do so under circumstances where we make every effort to harmonize the views, adjust views, and may not force views down other people's throats. If we do that, then I believe the United States will avoid that narrow view which has led to the destruction of great powers and great empires in the past. The United States will lead into a new course in which the free nations will continue to be free nations, freely associated, freely, willingly, and eagerly accepting leadership which they believe considers their interests as deeply as it does its own.

> ### SELECTION III–C
>
> Excerpts from John Foster Dulles, "A Policy of Boldness," *Life* XXXII (May 19, 1952), p. 146 ff. Reprinted by permission of Allen W. Dulles. Dulles, foreign affairs specialist for the Republican Party and future secretary of state, outlined proposed departures in foreign policy under new management.

Soviet Communism confronts our nation with its gravest peril. To meet its long-term strategy of encirclement and strangulation, we have adopted a series of emergency measures which are fantastically costly not only in money but in their warping of our American way of life.

No one would begrudge the cost of what we are doing if, in fact, it was adequate and was ending the peril, and if there was no better way. Actually, our policies are *inadequate* in scope. They are *not* ending the peril. There *is* a better way.

.   .   .   .

Once the free world has established a military defense, it can undertake what has been too long delayed—a political offense.

It is ironic and wrong that we who believe in the boundless power of human freedom should so long have accepted a static political role. It is also ironic and wrong that we who so proudly profess regard for the spiritual should rely so utterly on material defenses while the avowed materialists have been waging a winning war with social ideas, stirring humanity everywhere.

There are three truths which we need to recall in these times:

1) The dynamic prevails over the static; the active over the passive. We were from the beginning a vigorous, confident people, born with a sense of destiny and of mission. That is why we have grown from a small and feeble nation to our present stature in the world.

2) Nonmaterial forces are more powerful than those that are merely material. Our dynamism has always been moral and intellectual rather than military or material. During most of our national life we had only a small military establishment and during the last century we had to borrow money abroad to develop our expanding economy. But we always generated political, social and industrial ideas and projected them abroad where they were more explosive than dynamite.

3) There is a moral or natural law not made by man which determines right and wrong and in the long run only those who conform to that law will escape disaster. This law has been trampled by the Soviet rulers, and for that violation they can and should be made to pay. This will happen when we ourselves keep faith with that law in our practical decisions of policy.

We should let these truths work in and through us. We should be *dynamic*, we should use *ideas* as weapons; and these ideas should conform to *moral principles*. That we do this is right, for it is the inevitable expression of a faith—and I am confident that we still do have a faith. But it is also expedient in defending ourselves against an aggressive, imperialistic despotism. For even the present lines will not hold unless our purpose goes beyond confining Soviet Communism within its present orbit.

Consider the situation of the 20-odd non-Western nations which are next door to the Soviet world. These exposed nations feel that they have been put in the "expendable" class, condemned in perpetuity to be the ramparts against which the angry waves of Soviet Communism will constantly hurl themselves. They are expected to live precariously, permanently barred from areas with which they normally should have trade, commerce and cultural relations. They cannot be enthusiastic about policies which would merely perpetuate so hazardous and uncomfortable a position. Today they live close to despair because the United States, the historic leader of the forces of freedom, seems dedicated to the negative policy of "containment" and "stalemate."

As a matter of fact, some highly competent work is being done, at one place or another, to promote liberation. Obviously such activities do not lend themselves to public exposition. But liberation from the yoke of Moscow will not occur for a very long time, and courage in neighboring lands will not be sustained, *unless the United States makes it publicly known that it wants and expects liberation to occur*. The mere statement of that wish and expectation would change, in an electrifying way, the mood of the captive peoples. It would put heavy new burdens on the jailers and create new opportunities for liberation.

Here are some specific acts which we could take:

1) We could make it clear, on the highest authority of the President and the Congress, that U.S. policy seeks as one of its peaceful goals the eventual restoration of genuine independence in the nations of Europe and Asia now dominated by Moscow, and that we will not be a party to any "deal" confirming the rule of Soviet despotism over the alien peoples which it now dominates.

2) We could welcome the creation in the free world of political "task forces" to develop a freedom program for each of the captive nations. Each group would be made up of those who are proved patriots, who have practical resourcefulness and who command confidence and respect at home and abroad.

3) We could stimulate the escape from behind the Iron Curtain of those who can help to develop these programs.

4) The activities of the Voice of America and such private committees as those for Free Europe and Free Asia could be coordinated with these freedom programs. The agencies would be far more effective if given concrete jobs to do.

5) We could coordinate our economic, commercial and cultural relations with the freedom programs, cutting off or licensing intercourse as seemed most effective from time to time.

6) We could end diplomatic relations with present governments which are in fact only puppets of Moscow, if and when that would promote the freedom programs.

7) We could seek to bring other free nations to unite with us in proclaiming, in a great new Declaration of Independence, our policies toward the captive nations.

We do not want a series of bloody uprisings and reprisals. There can be peaceful separation from Moscow, as Tito showed, and enslavement can be made so unprofitable that the master will let go his grip. Such results will not come to pass overnight. But we can know, for history proves, that the spirit of patriotism burns unquenched in Poles, Czechs, Hungarians, Romanians, Bulgarians, Chinese and others, and we can be confident that within two, five or 10 years substantial parts of the present captive world can peacefully regain national independence. That will mark the beginning of the end of Soviet despotism's attempt at world conquest.

IV. VIEWS OF OBSERVERS

> SELECTION IV–A
>
> William Lee Miller, "The 'Moral Force' behind Dulles's Diplomacy," *The Reporter* (August 9, 1956), pp. 17–20. Copyright 1956 by The Reporter Magazine Co. Reprinted by permission of the author and The Reporter. Professor Miller, a member of the faculty of Yale Divinity School, charged that the morality of Dulles's positions and claims was both false of itself and harmful to the interests of the country.

An editorial in Henry Luce's *Life* magazine once asked, "Should U.S. Policy Be Moral?" The answer turned out to be "Yes." How was U.S. policy to be made moral? By supporting John Foster Dulles. "His policies have a religious motivation. . . . He is trying to put U.S. foreign policy back on an explicitly moral basis. . . ."

But putting U.S. policy *back* on a moral basis, presumably after the long years of Democratic immorality, has proved to be a little more difficult than it seemed at first. Take the recent Administration brouhaha over "neutralism." When Dulles spoke at Iowa State College on June 9 he seemed to contradict the genial words the President had spoken at a press conference three days earlier and to lay down a strict moral line about neutrality. At any rate, Mr. Luce's *Time* magazine seemed to think so. It was not an easy case, for *Time* had to choose between two kindred spirits, both usually on the moral side: Eisenhower and Dulles. But the Luce publications do not hesitate in the strife of Truth with Falsehood: Ike had strayed.

In the gentle words he spoke for neutralism, said *Time,* the President of the United States "got in over his head . . ." In his claim that we ourselves had long been a neutral, he made a "disconserting misstatement of U.S. history." Luckily, "the slip" was not allowed to stand unchallenged. ". . . At week's end," intoned *Time,* "Secretary of State Dulles tried to repair the damage . . ." In one paragraph of Dulles's speech the word "neutrality" was pretty clearly linked with the word "immoral."

But then, after Richard Nixon, another prominent Administration moralist, had twice entered the discussion (once on each side); and after considerable boiling around among foreign diplomats about U.S. views on neutralism; and after Dulles, under questioning at a press conference, had avoided explaining his views and simply claimed there was no conflict between them and the President's; and after Prime Minister Nehru had kidded the United States for its apparently contradictory views and chided Dulles and Nixon for wanting everybody to think as they did, there came at last on July 11 a further amplification from Dulles about the immorality of neutralism.

Recalling the complicated language of his original statement, Mr. Dulles explained that what he really meant was "immoral" was not necessarily "neutrality" but "being indifferent to the fate of others." U.N. membership shows concern for other nations, and even for countries like Switzerland that haven't joined the U.N., Mr. Dulles was able to point out an escape clause about "exceptional circumstances" in his Iowa State speech. The Secretary admitted that there were "very few, if any" countries that actually fitted his definition of immoral neutrality. Having, in the New York *Times's* words, "vexed" some and "puzzled" all of Washington's diplomatic corps and having given Nehru a chance to lead the Commonwealth Prime Ministers in a laugh and a growl at the United States, the "moral" statement was at last harmlessly retired to the shelf of abstract principle, inapplicable to any discernible nation. One wonders if it should have been taken down from there in the first place.

'ABSOLUTE RIGHT AND WRONG'

Secretary Dulles is a more complicated man than most of those with whom he is associated. For the President, the Vice-President, or the Secretary of Defense, for example, there is a standard set of adjectives, an expected position, a relatively clear political image. But not for Mr. Dulles. He is a complex man in a simple Administration.

On reading his speeches one is struck by the quality of many of them. His thought is clearer and more sophisticated, his language more varied and precise than that of most of his colleagues—certainly than that of his chief. But President Eisenhower manages, despite his trouble with language, to make his larger meaning come through; Mr. Dulles manages, despite his greater facility with language, to keep his larger meaning obscure. With Mr. Eisenhower the words are fuzzy but the real intention clear; with Mr. Dulles the words are clear but the real intention fuzzy.

This complexity may be the result of a curious kind of overtraining. We have all heard about his Grandfather Foster and Uncle Lansing, both Secretaries of State, and about those long years of yearning and studying to follow them. Perhaps he knows the job too well to learn it.

As a college boy he was taken by his uncle, later Wilson's Secretary of State, to the 1907 Hague Peace Conference, and he has lived among the virtuosos of high-level negotiation ever since. He entered diplomacy at the top, and never had to learn the arts of keeping quiet and listening, of reporting and co-ordinating, from the bottom.

His image of a Secretary seems to be drawn from a romantic version of the past, when the personal diplomat appeared as an individual performer on the international stage. Leaving the State Department to mind its own business, whatever that might be, Dulles flies to London, Paris, Manila, Denver, Duck Island, New Delhi, Cairo, and Geneva as his own ambassador and his own negotiator. Nonvisitation becomes a diplomatic weapon, as when, after the European Defense Community was beaten in 1954, he pointedly did not stop in to see Mendès-France. Personal visitation becomes a normal channel of policy. "It is silly," the Secretary said on television, "to go at it the old-fashioned way of exchanging notes, which take a month perhaps before you get a good understanding," when "by overnight flight" and "talking a few minutes face to face" the good understanding can be reached at once. But, as Walter Lippmann pointed out: "Mr. Dulles has traveled 310,000 miles, and can it be said that the globe is studded with good understandings?"

Mr. Dulles goes at his job with the assurance of a skilled lawyer, able to develop all the elements of each side of the case, to make multiple and varying readings, and to remember the small print when it's necessary. His pronouncements—on neutralism, liberation, positive loyalty, massive retaliation, brinks of wars—are usually surrounded by a haze of qualifications and provisos, of interpretations, misinterpretations, and reinterpretations. He also seems well supplied with the lawyer's trust in formulas and pacts, in written words and formal agreements.

Another of Mr. Dulles's excesses shows up in his partisanship. Having been a prominent representative of bipartisan foreign policy, he seems eager to take the curse off that by heaping blame on the "Democrat" Party and paying strictest attention to Republican needs.

But behind these well-known aspects of the man, as the overtrained diplomat, the oversubtle lawyer, the over-Republican campaigner, may be a still more important aspect, the one Mr. Luce's publications unwittingly portray: the overconfident moralist. This may be the core of it, both the cause and the explanation of his lack of restraint in the other roles. "Into the counsels of his workaday diplomacy," the Luce people have explained, "he is admitting a criterion of absolute right and wrong."

. . . .

Just as Mr. Dulles's unique training in diplomacy means that he can carry on without consulting his staff, so his unique position in "moral leadership" means that he can speak on his own authority in that field. Maybe it would be better, in both, not to be quite so well qualified—and to realize that others may have something to contribute.

In a commencement speech he gave in 1946, Mr. Dulles said: "We laugh about the puritanism and austerity of the past. But that is the way our forebears trained their moral muscles for the struggle for freedom. Today these muscles are flabby. . . ." One sometimes has the impression that Mr. Dulles, far from flabby after all those years of weight lifting in the specialized gymnasium of professional moral leadership, has become somewhat morally muscle-bound.

This overdeveloped ethical confidence may help to account for the other dominant element of his public personality, his toughness. The Presbyterian elder, when he ran for the Senate in 1949, turned out to be a surprisingly rough campaigner. He challenged his opponent, Herbert Lehman, to prove that "if elected he would not unwittingly be a carrier of danger into high places." And he warned the voters that "it is up to you in this election to decide whether or not you will do what the Russian Communists want." And when this spokesman for moral force became Secretary of State he showed a startling ability to adapt himself to the hard requirements of Republican politics in the era of McCarthy. The student of a Just and Durable Peace became the stiffest talker on the team, not only toward the Communists but toward neutrals and allies as well, and also turned up as the advocate of "massive retaliatory power." One is also impressed by the revelations of his swashbuckling derring-do on the brink of war.

All of this may reflect that compensatory worldliness which is often adopted by those who are formally connected with goodness. The preacher says a cuss word or tells a joke to make it plain he's a real guy after all. A man who has known Mr. Dulles says he overdoes the part of the rugged realist just because he is eager to avoid any accusation of sentimentality that might be brought forth by his churchly doings.

But the Calvinist-Puritan-Presbyterian tradition Dulles comes from isn't as sentimental as some strands of American Protestantism anyway. In that Presbyterian Church back in Watertown there wouldn't have been as much talk of love and harmony and brotherhood as one would get later, farther west and in more liberal churches. There would probably be more talk of Holy Law and righteousness and the solid, sober Calvinistic virtues.

Mr. Dulles represents characteristic virtues of that tradition: an unfrivolous sense of responsibility, an untiring pursuit of duty, an unbending opposition to what he regards as evil. He may also represent some characteristic vices of that tradition, including an undue confidence that one has identified evil once and for all and that it's on the other fellow's side. When you've got it arranged that way, you can talk tough and be moral at the same time.

.   .   .   .

What is worse, the language may not mean a thing. There is a habit, among those for whom preaching is a central activity, to delight in the mere sound of stern, demanding words and then, like Channing's father, to go whistling home to a warm house and big dinner. Sometimes one feels that what admirers of Mr. Dulles want most is just for somebody to say, and to keep on saying, that we are good and the Communists are not.

The typical Protestant is unhappy with the cool and rational practitioners of the diplomatic art because there is nothing in their counsel about restraint, limited wars, and the modest pursuit of the national interest to which one can respond with *zeal*. And yet issues of world politics, of whether humanity will go over the brink, are dramatic and moving; they should be dealt with in a way that a man can respond to with a revivalist enthusiasm.

Mr. Dulles can do it. To the National Council of Presbyterian Men, for example, he told the story of the Japanese Peace Treaty, of which he himself had been the chief artisan:

"Four years ago, speaking here, I said that moral power was the greatest power in the world. . . . Now here is a new exhibit: the Japanese Peace Treaty.

"There were two possible powers to invoke, the power of evil or the power of good. . . . We had to go all out in one direction or another. Half measures would not avail. . . ." Mr. Dulles explained which of the two powers he had invoked, all the way, in drawing up the Treaty. Now that's the kind of foreign policy the evangelistic heritage really can respond to. Of course, others gave a slightly different picture of the treaty, particularly of Mr. Dulles's own pressure, despite a promise to the British, to make Japan recognize Nationalist China. But details like that would have spoiled the dramatic simplicity.

The emphasis on zeal, boldness, and dynamism recurs continually, and usually in conjunction with morality. Mr. Dulles always puts the best fact on everything, finding diplomatic gains for us even in the Geneva Foreign Ministers' Conference, avoiding any admission of weakness or loss, claiming that our system of alliances is better than ever, asserting that changes in Russia since Stalin's death are the result of our own dynamic policies. Talk strong.

'LIBERATION'—BEFORE AND AFTER

The "liberation" theme, set over against the "negative" and "sterile" doctrine of "containment," is an example. Mr. Dulles, its chief proponent, said that since it would be immoral and undynamic to leave the satellites under Soviet control, the United States should proclaim its intention to "liberate" them. This energetic declaration of intent, however, was all that could be done. On taking office the Administration made a few lame gestures against the Yalta agreements, but then the dynamic Eisenhower-Dulles policy more or less forgot about "liberation." For one thing, it scared the daylights out of our European Allies; for another, it seemed to encourage our friends behind the Iron Curtain to rise, and maybe get killed, when we had no real intention of going to war to rescue them. Elmer Davis once described it as a policy of "You throw off your chains, and we'll give three cheers." The favorable response of Polish voters in Hamtramck and Buffalo to the "liberation" theme gave to its no doubt sincere proponents a mixture of motives; it is always helpful when ethical convictions turn out handily to serve one's more earthbound interests. But in the end these splendid sounds may prove to be neither dynamic nor even, after all, particularly moral.

Perhaps American foreign policy should try to *be* moral—and not spend so much time labeling itself. Perhaps it should try to present programs that evoke zeal—instead of trying to drum up zeal by talking about it. The words may mean nothing; they may rouse passions where thought would serve better. Worse, they may forge a divine ratification of one group's preferences.

The diplomatic moralizer has a weapon that those who argue policies on more rational grounds do not have; he can simply draw a line that excludes some possibilities as immoral. Maybe the policies Mr. Dulles doesn't like can be proved mistaken, but it ought to be necessary to *prove* it—instead of simply ruling them out from the unassailable pinnacle of "absolute right and wrong."

.   .   .   .

Mr. Dulles said on coming into office that his would be a policy of "openness, simplicity, and righteousness." That "righteousness" may be a cause of the increased isolation of the United States from neutral and allies that some see as the great danger of the present day.

> ### SELECTION IV–B
>
> Taken from O. William Perlmutter's "The 'Neo-Realism' of Dean Acheson," *The Review of Politics*, XXVI (January, 1964), pp. 107, 121–23. Reprinted by permission of *The Review of Politics*. Professor Perlmutter, currently Dean of the College of Arts and Sciences at the State University of New York in Albany and professor of political science contrasts and compares the personal qualities and professional positions of Dean Acheson and John Foster Dulles.

It was as a realist that he served as Undersecretary of State, and as a confirmed realist, as Secretary of State from 1949 to 1953. However, Acheson applied the principles of power politics to the foreign policies of the United States only and not to his personal political affairs. These remained under the sway of a somewhat orthodox Christian moral philosophy and theology. He is an interesting contrast to John Foster Dulles in this respect. Dulles and Acheson have many philosophical ideals in common but, unlike Acheson, Dulles was prepared to accommodate himself to the McCarthy influences and to accept office upon conditions that would have been utterly repugnant to Acheson. On the other hand, Acheson was much better prepared to accept the ideological differences between the United States and the Soviet Union (and China) than was Dulles. Both men represent attempts to bring Christian principles into the working life of the statesman. While Dulles was willing to accept the realities of power politics in domestic and internal affairs, Acheson was not. On the other hand, Dulles was more confused in his attempt to apply Christian principles to foreign policy. Acheson made an uneasy peace with secular principles of power politics. The formulation, in more final form, of his new philosophy is contained in his book which is significantly titled, *Power and Diplomacy*.

.   .   .   .

Applying Acheson's general conceptions to the power politics of the world, and more specifically, to the problem of forming and maintaining a coalition of powers under American leadership, he maintained that it was necessary to regard the nations that are geographically closest as most important—that is, Canada, Latin America, and the nations of Europe. Here, he said, was the source of power for the noncommunist world system. "To say this is not to minimize the importance of Asia and Africa; but if the center is not solid, relations with the periphery will not supply strength." Since, in his time, Canada and Latin America presented no overwhelming or novel problems, the major diplomatic effort of the United States had to be concentrated on Europe. Without America, Europe would have become a series of Soviet Peoples Republics. "Of Soviet capacity to bring this about —absent the American alliance—there can be no doubt." At any rate, the Russians, he said, made it clear that they would act to the limit of their capacity to determine the alignment of Europe. The United States and Western Europe must stand together in an alliance or else Europe will fall to the Russians.

A second phase in this approach to diplomacy was to make Africa, the Middle East, South and Southeast Asia, and Japan part of the "open world system." This approach might at least serve to prevent them from being absorbed into the Soviet system. The problems in these areas were of a different order from those of Europe. In the first place, nationalism and genuine revolutionary sentiments were much more potent factors here than in Europe, said Acheson. Furthermore, these peoples are suspicious of the West. They cannot be swayed by political and philosophical ideas alone. The political leaders of these countries face a special problem. They cannot remain in power unless they make economic progress, and in order to do so, Acheson asserted, they must turn to the possible sources of aid. They face a dilemma. If they do not get aid from the Free World system, then they must turn to the communists. It is essential to American diplomacy, he added, to hasten the emancipation of these countries from their agrarian conditions and facilitate their transition to industrialism.

The basic difficulty, as Acheson saw it, was not to reach an agreement in American politics upon the ends of foreign policy but on the means. We may be agreed, he said, that we ought to "create in the non-Communist world the power, unity, and will capable of balancing and checking the Sino-Soviet system, preserving civilization, and preventing atomic war." But how can this be best accomplished? There are two approaches, and he over-simplified the political aspects of the questions: one of which is to spend in order to achieve these ends, and the other is to stress a balanced budget. "Some of the hardest-fought issues of party politics arise from these two approaches."

Another difficulty, according to Acheson, is the tendency for politicians to become entangled in a fixed and rigid policy. Certain pressure groups have a way of maneuvering American leaders into the adoption of rigid policies. He criticized both the Democrats and the Republicans for giving in to narrow domestic political pressures—the former in the case of Palestine and the latter in the case of China.

One of the most noteworthy aspects of Acheson's stewardship of American foreign policy was his radical revision of the conception of the fundamental nature of foreign policy. He was not, as he claimed, simply quarreling over the means with his opponents. He was firmly, and quite candidly, committed to realistic participation in the balance of power struggle in world politics and he undertook to bring this about in the face of strong isolationist and neo-isolationist sentiment still prevalent among conservative groups in both parties. He firmly believed that the national interest is the dominant guideline to policy and parted company with both isolationists and crusading ideologists of democracy. He clearly distinguished moral and ideological aims from the operating principles of power politics. However, this point of view created serious difficulties for him in American politics. Alienating conservative and liberal groups within both parties, he was forced into a lonely position, a position he accepted courageously. Although he suffered much personal abuse because of his approach to foreign affairs, his policies were widely supported in Congress. A poor pleader for himself, he was a master in dressing up the new doctrine in rhetorical terms that were sufficiently acceptable to a coalition drawn from both parties, and was able to realize the major part of his program.

SELECTION IV–C

Excerpted from *Duel at the Brink: John Foster Dulles' Command of American Power* by Roscoe Drummond and Gaston Coblentz, pp. 30–34. Copyright © 1960 by the authors. Reprinted by permission of Doubleday & Company, Inc. Roscoe Drummond and Gaston Coblentz are Washington journalists who viewed the scene of the 1950's with some sympathy for Dulles' problems.

Dulles did not passively wait for Eisenhower to appoint him Secretary of State. He actively promoted himself for the post while Eisenhower was still Supreme Allied Commander of NATO in Paris.

In May 1952, after Eisenhower had become a declared candidate for the Republican nomination, Dulles called on him at his Paris headquarters. He paid the visit at the suggestion of General Lucius D. Clay. He had accepted an invitation to address the French National Political Science Institute, which helped to make the call appear casual. His prime purpose was to explore Eisenhower's thinking on foreign policy. It was already clear that Dulles was going to have a major hand in drafting his party's foreign policy platform.

One visit grew into two. Eisenhower and Dulles found themselves comfortable in each other's company. It was quickly evident that there was a wide-ranging identity in their views—on unyielding opposition to Communist expansion, on strengthening the Atlantic alliance, on promoting Jean Monnet's grandiose scheme for a United States of Europe.

In the end, Dulles told Eisenhower that he hoped to see him nominated for the Presidency. He also frankly informed Senator Robert A. Taft of his pro-Eisenhower position, before starting to work with the chairman of the Republican platform committee, Senator Eugene Millikin of Colorado. However, he refrained from identifying himself with the Eisenhower camp until the late hours of the Chicago convention, although it hardly mattered, as his political influence at the convention was insignificant.

As one of his friends put it, Dulles was "a very long-lead planner." He sought to anticipate the circumstances which would enable him to perform most effectively if he became Secretary of State. He believed that it would be vital for him not to have alienated, if he could avoid it, the political forces in the Republican party which favored Senator Taft—and this was the majority of the party in Congress. This was his controlling reason for not openly supporting Eisenhower until his nomination was a foregone conclusion. He looked upon himself as a bridge between the Taft and Eisenhower camps and felt that, in achieving the maximum area of agreement between them on foreign policy, he was both devising a platform on which Eisenhower could conscientiously run and reducing the danger of irreconcilable party divisions.

Dulles was the only candidate for Secretary of State whom Eisenhower seriously and continuously considered. From the time he began to ponder his most important Cabinet appointment, there appeared to be no doubt he intended to name Dulles. Although he weighed many factors in the total equation and although other names went through his mind and appeared on various lists of suggested appointees—particularly Henry Cabot Lodge and John J. McCloy—Dulles was the man from the start.

However, Eisenhower displayed an initial reserve toward Dulles after appointing him. It was illustrated by his selection of General Walter Bedell Smith, a long-time Eisenhower military intimate, as Undersecretary of State. He wanted someone he knew and trusted without reservation working closely with Dulles at the start. Moreover, in no way to Dulles' liking at the outset, the President invited Lodge, whom he had chosen as chief delegate to the United Nations, to become a regular participant at Cabinet meetings. This gave Lodge a quasi-independent status in the foreign policy field and enabled him to exercise greater latitude of judgment, particularly in dealing with the Communists at the UN. Dulles-Lodge relations were strained for some time. Dulles later came to feel that Lodge used his latitude to good effect and that he was performing valuable service.

Within the first six months of the administration, three factors enabled Dulles to win the President's unlimited confidence.

One was his grasp of historic and current fact on nearly every phase and nuance of foreign policy. These facts were at his finger tips, available on call. Eisenhower was enormously impressed. He showed respect for Dulles' knowledge. Dulles renewed and increased this respect almost every time they talked. "I find him to have encyclopaedic knowledge," the President remarked to friends. "I have never seen anyone with so many facts at his command." Dulles had a good memory, but his fount of ready information derived from a prodigious capacity to do his homework. He never entered negotiations, Cabinet meetings, or his private sessions with the President without briefing himself thoroughly. Nothing annoyed him more than to deal with associates who expounded their views to him with only 90 per cent of the pertinent information.

The second factor which consolidated his relationship with the President was that Dulles never just "took a problem" to the White House. He invariably had thought it through to the end. He always took a proposed solution to the President. In fact, he took more than one; he took several alternative solutions to be examined side by side. However, he inevitably came prepared to advance the proposal which he favored. Eisenhower never liked "bull sessions" just to mull problems over. Neither did Dulles.

The third factor was Dulles' detachment and candor in presenting a problem to the President. He was careful to give him every argument for different courses of action. In presenting his own suggestions, he would never argue a purely "parochial" State Department view. He would stress the implications and consequences of any proposed action on other government policies and departments. He never made slick debating points with the President; he never sought to win his approval by rhetoric rather than by presentation of the facts as he saw them.

Before either had completed their first year together, these qualifications and qualities—detailed knowledge, decisiveness, and objective discussion—evoked from Eisenhower a trust and ultimately a deep affection for Dulles which was never to diminish. It constantly broadened and deepened.

At no time did either Eisenhower or Dulles have the least whispering wish to dissolve their partnership.

At the beginning of the second Eisenhower term, when rumors circulated of impending major changes in the Cabinet, including the Secretaryship of State, one of these authors wrote a column stating unqualifiedly that the Cabinet's two most controversial members—Foster Dulles and Secretary of Agriculture Ezra Taft Benson—would not resign, would not be asked to resign, would not be allowed to resign. On the morning it appeared in the New York *Herald Tribune,* Dulles asked the new Undersecretary of State, Christian Herter, to remain a minute after the staff conference. "Have you read Drummond's column this morning?" Dulles asked. Herter allowed that he had. With a wisp of a smile on his face, Dulles remarked solicitously: "I hope you are not disappointed."

Eisenhower, deeming Dulles pre-eminently qualified, never wanted him to leave. The idea never entered the President's mind. Moreover, he had no justification, with rare exceptions, to criticize Dulles' policies and actions. He had himself shared in every decision of substance.

Other than Presidential aide Sherman Adams, no official of the government had Dulles' instant and frequent access to Eisenhower. Adams, whose delegated authority permitted him to inform many Cabinet members when they could and when they could not see the President, never assumed to stand between Eisenhower and Dulles. The Secretary did not tiptoe timidly into Eisenhower's presence. The White House staff could recognize Dulles' firm gait as he strode down the corridor.

After his death, Eisenhower repeatedly, nostalgically, told intimates how much he missed both Dulles' counsel and the camaraderie which had developed between them. He often recalled "how much fun we had together."

"I just can't believe," he said to a high-ranking diplomat, "that I won't be seeing Foster coming through that door with that almost puckish smile on his face."

8

DULLES AND BRINKMANSHIP

Formosa in the 1950's

I. EDITORIAL INTRODUCTION

The Far East was the most logical place for Republicans to act on charges they made against Democratic foreign policies during the presidential campaign of 1952. The supposed errors in the statecraft of Truman and Acheson which led to the fall of China and to the invasion of the Republic of Korea required immediate Republican response. Not only had the Democrats failed in Asia to help liberate captive peoples from communism, but they had been unable to maintain a position of containment as in Europe, insufficient as that position was there. It was obvious that the new administration's freedom of action was limited. In Korea the most that could be expected was the continued restraint of the Chinese at the 38th parallel, and even that only after protracted negotiations which hardly seemed to implement the promises of 1952. Direct action against the mainland of China was even more difficult, given the thorough routing of Chiang Kai-shek and the obvious strength as well as confidence exhibited by the Chinese intervention in Korea.

There was one response to this problem that could be made immediately. President Eisenhower could announce dramatically and forcefully the removal of the United States Seventh Fleet from its mission of preventing either a communist attack on Formosa or a nationalist attack on the mainland of China. The fleet had been dispatched to the Formosa straits as one American reaction to the North Korean attack when, in the confusion following the communist invasion, the administration had feared that Formosa as well as the Republic of Korea was an immediate communist objective. The fear proved to be unwarranted at that moment in 1950, but the fleet re-

166

mained. Two and a half years later the new President announced to the world in his first State of the Union address that the United States would no longer serve as a "shield" to protect Chinese communists from invasion by the forces of Chiang Kai-shek. (Selection II–A.) The explicit assumption was that the former administration had sent the fleet to Formosa to save world peace, and indirectly Chinese communists, from the fury of the nationalist leader. Since the communists had shown no gratitude for this service they deserved no such consideration; Chiang would be "unleashed" to use Formosa as a base of operations against the mainland if he so chose.

While this statement might be dismissed as mere verbiage, and ridiculous verbiage at that, in light of the power realities in the Far East, it did serve the purpose of heartening the American public at a moment of crisis by underlining the more positive, if not aggressive, posture of the new administration. At the same time, it gave critics an opportunity to condemn the Dulles strategy as one of dangerous rhetoric that could have serious consequences for the United States and Chiang Kai-shek in the future. The danger was not in stimulating the nationalist appetite for war, but in provoking the mainland to implement its own threats of conquering Formosa, a major goal of Communist China's foreign policy.

Secretary of State Dulles reacted with promises of military assistance to potential allies and ultimately with binding alliances as deterrents to attack. When the Chinese, emboldened by the defeat of the French in Indochina, threatened invasion in 1954, the United States formed the Southeast Asia Treaty Organization and a bilateral mutual defense with Formosa that limited Formosa's freedom of action on the matter of invasion. The key factor was the position the United States would take toward Quemoy and Matsu, two islands off the China shore and exceedingly vulnerable to communist seizure. The administration asked for and received a joint resolution of the Congress authorizing the President to employ armed forces to defend Formosa and the Pescadores. But the offshore islands were mentioned only indirectly and whether or not they were included in the United States promise was purposely left vague. (Selection II–B.) If the communists wanted to know American intentions, they could learn them by an act of aggression involving Quemoy or Matsu, and that could lead to war. Such was the essence of brinkmanship over Formosa under the Dulles administration of the Department of State.

What was the meaning of American policy toward China? Did the United States continue to consider Formosa as a base for Chiang's return to the mainland? Or did the treaty of 1954 "releash" Chiang when the Nationalists promised not to attack the mainland without American approval? Were the offshore islands, less than ten miles from the mainland, essential to the defense of Formosa, and would the United States risk World War III to defend them? Was the inviolability of Formosa itself the best solution to the China problem?

To Secretary of State Dulles the answers were not difficult; they merely could not be fully spelled out lest the advantage of keeping the enemy off balance be lost. Dulles had gone beyond containment with a new policy of deterrence based on American willingness to risk war, to get to the brink of war if necessary to win the objective. Surrender of the offshore islands could lead to the fall of Formosa itself. In 1955 and again in 1958 the communists retreated on the Formosan issue because they believed the United States would stand fast; and Dulles, speaking through James Shepley of *Life,* claimed credit for the success. (Selection III–A.) But Sherman Adams, the President's principal assistant, doubted if the country was ever at the brink over Formosa, or that Eisenhower himself ever regarded Quemoy or Matsu as guaranteed under the Formosan resolution. (Selection III–B.)

Whether or not the President intended a crisis over the offshore islands, they developed into centers of friction between Communist China and America. According to Adlai Stevenson, not only were the islands unimportant to the defense of Formosa, but by unilaterally and incautiously risking war over them we could lose friends in Asia and allies in Europe whose importance in the defense of Formosa was too great to jeopardize. Even more dangerous was Dulles's dealing with words rather than deeds. The bold words of brinkmanship over Formosa would be no more convincing than the "unleashing" of Chiang had been in 1953. (Selection III–C.)

David Rowe, a Far Eastern specialist at Yale, reflected the feelings of those who feared that any diminution of support for defense of the offshore islands, as well as Formosa, would destroy free China. They could see signs of this danger notwithstanding the Eisenhower administration's apparently firm support of Chiang's hold on Formosa. Dulles himself was not above suspicion. (Selection IV–A.) Equally indignant and suspicious was D. F. Fleming, who saw the American position in Formosa as nothing more than appeasement of right wing Republicanism at the expense of the national interest and against the interest of world peace. Given the indefensibility of the notion that the defense of Formosa was vital to the United States, Fleming saw its defense as vital only to an American "war party." (Selection IV–B.)

With considerably less passion, former Foreign Service Officer O. Edmund Clubb, writing in 1965, offered a new view of the Formosa problem. Instead of looking forward to "two Chinas" as an escape from the American dilemma in the Far East, he believed that the close relation of the offshore islands to Formosa in the Eisenhower period damaged the prospect of a permanent acceptance of the status quo. He suspected that the next generation in Formosa and in mainland China might find a community of interests independent of those of the United States. (Selection IV–C.) Indeed, the continuing rigidity of the American position suggests that there were few differences between the Dulles policies and the Acheson policy of containment which had been criticized by his successor. Dulles' brinkmanship succeeded in maintaining the status quo but not in going beyond it.

II. DOCUMENTS

> *SELECTION II–A*
>
> An excerpt from President Eisenhower's State of the Union message, February 2, 1953, Department of State *Bulletin*, XXVIII (February 9, 1953), p. 209, in which he specifically noted that the Seventh Fleet would "no longer be employed to shield Communist China."

In June 1950, following the aggressive attack on the Republic of Korea, the United States Fleet was instructed both to prevent attack upon Formosa and also to insure that Formosa should not be used as a base of operations against the Chinese Communist mainland.

This has meant, in effect, that the United States Navy was required to serve as a defensive arm of Communist China. Regardless of the situation in 1950, since the date of that order the Chinese Communists have invaded Korea to attack the United Nations forces there. They have consistently rejected the proposals of the United Nations Command for an armistice. They recently joined with Soviet Russia in rejecting the armistice proposal sponsored in the United Nations by the Government of India. This proposal had been accepted by the United States and 53 other nations.

Consequently there is no longer any logic or sense in a condition that required the United States Navy to assume defensive responsibilities on behalf of the Chinese Communists. This permitted those Communists, with greater impunity, to kill our soldiers and those of our United Nations allies in Korea.

I am, therefore, issuing instructions that the Seventh Fleet no longer be employed to shield Communist China. Permit me to make crystal clear, this order implies no aggressive intent on our part. But we certainly have no obligation to protect a nation fighting us in Korea.

> *SELECTION II–B*
>
> Text of the Joint Resolution on Defense of Formosa (H. J. Res. 159, 84th Congress, 1st sess.) as it appeared in the Department of State *Bulletin*, XXXII (February 7, 1955), p. 213. It was adopted by the House of Representatives on January 25, 1955 by a vote of 400 to 3 and by the Senate on January 28 by a vote of 85 to 3.

Whereas the primary purpose of the United States, in its relations with all other nations, is to develop and sustain a just and enduring peace for all; and

Whereas certain territories in the West Pacific under the jurisdiction of the Republic of China are now under armed attack, and threats and declarations have been and are being made by the Chinese Communists that such armed attack is in aid of and in preparation for armed attack on Formosa and the Pescadores,

Whereas such armed attack if continued would gravely endanger the peace and security of the West Pacific Area and particularly of Formosa and the Pescadores; and

Whereas the secure possession by friendly governments of the Western Pacific Island chain, of which Formosa is a part, is essential to the vital interests of the United States and all friendly nations in or bordering upon the Pacific Ocean; and

Whereas the President of the United States on January 6, 1955, submitted to the Senate for its advice and consent to ratification a Mutual Defense Treaty between the United States of America and the Republic of China, which recognizes that an armed attack in the West Pacific area directed against territories, therein described, in the region of Formosa and the Pescadores, would be dangerous to the peace and safety of the parties to the treaty: Therefore be it

Resolved by the Senate and House of Representatives of the United States of America in Congress assembled, That the President of the United States be and he hereby is authorized to employ the Armed Forces of the United States as he deems necessary for the specific purpose of securing and protecting Formosa and the Pescadores against armed attack, this authority to include the securing and protection of such related positions and territories of that area now in friendly hands and the taking of such other measures as he judges to be required or appropriate in assuring the defense of Formosa and the Pescadores.

This resolution shall expire when the President shall determine that the peace and security of the area is reasonably assured by international conditions created by action of the United Nations or otherwise, and shall so report to the Congress.

III. VIEWS OF PARTICIPANTS

SELECTION III–A

Excerpts from the article, "How Dulles Averted War," by James Shepley, in *Life*, XL (January 16, 1956), pp. 70 ff. Reprinted by permission of James Shepley, *Life* Magazine, January 16. © 1956 Time, Inc. Shepley, presently publisher of *Fortune*, was chief Washington correspondent of *Time* and *Life* in 1956.

At 2 a.m. on June 18, 1953, Secretary of State John Foster Dulles was awakened by the ringing of the telephone in the bedroom of his home in Washington. It was the officer of the dog watch at the State Department with an urgent radio message from Korea. President Syngman Rhee had ordered his troops guarding the prisoners of war compounds to release all captured North Koreans and Red Chinese. The handful of American officers and noncoms at the camps were powerless to prevent the action and the prisoners were streaming away from the compounds by the thousands.

Dulles listened quietly, grunting an occasional "Yow" to acknowledge. Then he reached over to switch on the light. And at that moment, as his fully aroused mind shook off the fog of sleep, Dulles saw himself and the nation standing on the brink of a new war. It was the first of three times during the Eisenhower administration when the U.S. was brought perilously close to war—and when the new policy of deterrence instituted by Dulles preserved peace.

.　　.　　.　　.　　.　　.　　.　　.　　.　　.　　.　.　　.

The third time Dulles faced war came in those weeks in late 1954 and early 1955, when menacing Communist maneuvers were made against Quemoy and the Matsus—the time now identified as the Formosan crisis. Here war was avoided mainly by a resolution drafted by Dulles and passed by an overwhelming bipartisan vote in Congress which authorized the President to use U.S. military forces should the Chinese Communists attack Formosa. Thus the Chinese were publicly put on notice that Eisenhower was ready and authorized to retaliate . . .

.　　.　　.　　.　　.　　.　　.　　.　　.　　.　　.　　.

The two cardinal principles which Dulles substituted for the containment doctrine of his predecessor are the "long haul concept" and "deterrence." Dulles explained the long haul concept on his first appearance before the NATO foreign ministers on April 23, 1953. He said, ". . . The Soviet menace . . . is [one] which . . . may persist for a long time, through periods of retreat as well as of advance. . . . We must be prepared to be strong . . . for an entire historical era."

The policy of deterrence is based on Dulles' belief that wars are caused by miscalculation. His first public declaration on deterrence came in his speech to the Council on Foreign Relations on Jan. 12, 1954: "Local defense," he said, "must be reinforced by the further deterrent of massive retaliatory power. A potential aggressor must know that he cannot always prescribe battle conditions that suit him. . . . The way to deter aggresssion is for the free community to be willing and able to respond vigorously at places and with means of its own choosing."

Dulles' ever-alert critics jumped on the phrase "massive retaliation" as 1) too tough, and 2) ineffectual. It implied, they argued, that every time a squad of infantry crossed a frontier somewhere, Dulles would drop atomic bombs on Moscow. It was argued that we would never do it, and because the Communists knew we would not, it was nothing more than a dangerous bluff.

Actually Dulles did not mean what some critics have put in his mouth. In an article written for the April 1954 issue of *Foreign Affairs* he explained that by "massive retaliation" he was thinking not of an attack on Moscow but of such retaliation as would make a Communist military adventure of any size unprofitable. He said in effect that it was his intention to make the punishment fit the crime.

The best example of what he meant is the retaliation planned, if necessary, against the Chinese Communists, either in connection with Korea or Indochina. "They were specific targets reasonably related to the area," he recalls. "They did not involve massive destruction of great population centers like Shanghai, Peking or Canton. Retaliation must be on a selective basis. The important thing is that the aggressor know in advance that he is going to lose more than he can win. He doesn't have to lose *much* more. It just has to be *something* more. If the equation is such that the outcome is clearly going to be against him, he won't go in."

.   .   .   .

In those situations, all of them peripheral, where the Communists have tried force—Korea, Indochina, Formosa—the policy of deterrence has worked. Deterrence, as practiced by Dulles, has not only prevented the "big" hydrogen war but the littler wars as well.

Always, of course, there has been and continues to be risk. Says Dulles, "You have to take chances for peace, just as you must take chances in war. Some say that we were brought to the verge of war. Of course we were brought to the verge of war. The ability to get to the verge without getting into the war is the necessary art. If you cannot master it, you inevitably get into war. If you try to run away from it, if you are scared to go to the brink, you are lost. We've had to look it square in the face—on the question of enlarging the Korean war, on the question of getting into the Indochina war, on the question of Formosa. We walked to the brink and we looked it in the face. We took strong action.

SELECTION III–B

Taken from pp. 117–20 *First Hand Report: The Story of the Eisenhower Administration* by Sherman Adams. Copyright © by Sherman Adams. Reprinted by permission of Harper & Row, Publishers. Sherman Adams, a former Governor of New Hampshire, was chief assistant of President Eisenhower until 1958.

TROUBLE IN THE FAR EAST

Two years later Dulles said that the Indo-China situation of 1954, along with the Korean War truce crisis of 1953 and Red China's threatened invasion of Formosa in late 1954 and early 1955, had forced the United States to the brink of total war. The Secretary of State cited these three instances as crucial tests of his so-called policy of "deterrence" in an interview with James Shepley, chief of the Washington bureau of *Time* and *Life* magazines.

The statement stirred up one of the major controversial storms of the whole Eisenhower administration. The Dulles policy of deterrence, as Shepley explained it in his article, was based on the Secretary's conviction that no national leader would start a war unless he thought he could get away with it. The Korean War, for example, would not have been started by the Communists, in Dulles' opinion, if Moscow had known that the United States would be willing to fight for the protection of South Korea. Dulles believed that the Reds invaded that area because his predecessor, Dean Acheson, had suggested six months earlier that South Korea was outside of the "vital perimeter" of the United States defenses. If you are ready to stand up against a potential aggressor with an impressive deterrent of "massive retaliatory power," the Dulles theory contended, the aggression was not likely to occur. This was indeed an accurate summation of the basic theory of the Dulles strategy as it opposed the containment defense policy of the Truman-Acheson regime. But whether the Dulles policy was actually put to three crucial tests, as the Secretary believed it was, is a matter that is open to question.

"You have to take chances for peace, just as you must take chances in war," Dulles was quoted as saying in Shepley's article.

Some say that we were brought to the verge of war. Of course, we were brought to the verge of war. The ability to get to the verge without getting into the war is the necessary art. If you cannot master it, you inevitably get into war. If you try to run away from it, if you are scared to go to the brink, you are lost. We've had to look it square in the face—on the question of enlarging the Korean War, on the question of getting into the Indo-China war, on the question of Formosa. We walked to the brink and we looked it in the face. We took strong action. It took a lot more courage for the President than for me. His was the ultimate decision. I did not have to make the decision myself, only to recommend it. The President never flinched for a minute on any of these situations. He came up taut.

I doubt that Eisenhower was as close to the brink of war in any of those three crises as Dulles made him out to be. Although the President revealed that a threat of an atomic bombing and total war was made to the Chinese Communists in order to persuade them into the Korean truce negotiations, he has never suggested that the threat was as specific and as near to being carried out as Dulles intimated it was in his interview with Shepley. Moreover, there is no clear evidence that we were teetering on the brink at Geneva in the bold front that Dulles contended saved half of Indo-China from the Communists. The President knew that the American people had no appetite for another prolonged war in Southeast Asia. He was determined not to become involved without the approval of Congress and without the participation of the British, and neither Congress nor the British wanted to fight in Indo-China.

The issue at stake in the Formosa crisis of the late fall of 1954 was the same one that developed into a hot argument between Nixon and Kennedy in the presidential campaign of 1960, the question of whether the United States should defend the islands of Quemoy and Matsu from a threatened invasion by the Chinese Reds. A strong body of opinion, headed by Admiral Radford and Senator Knowland, held that these islands close to the shore of the Chinese mainland, occupied by Chiang Kai-shek's Nationalist forces, should be protected by the United States from any kind of attack. Eisenhower had no desire to provoke a war with China unless Formosa itself was in jeopardy. The ultimatum from Eisenhower to the Chinese Communists, that Dulles subsequently referred to as a step to the brink of war, was an unprecedented resolution passed by Congress in January, 1955, giving the President his requested authority to use United States armed forces to safeguard Formosa and the Pescadores Islands. But Eisenhower carefully worded the resolution so that it did not specifically guarantee a defense of Quemoy and Matsu along with protection of Formosa and the Pescadores. He inserted a wait-and-see clause that gave him the privilege of deciding in the event of an attack on Quemoy and Matsu whether the safety of Formosa and the Pescadores was actually threatened before committing himself to a fight over the smaller islands near the Chinese mainland. The Formosa Resolution was not quite the belligerent challenge that Dulles said it was in his interview with Shepley. Eisenhower did not draw a definite line across the Strait of Formosa and warn the Communists that if they crossed it there would be war.

During the furor that followed the publication of Shepley's article there was naturally some speculation and concern among us on his staff about how Eisenhower would handle the inevitable questions that would be put to him about it. Eisenhower never wasted any time talking to me about newspaper stories and articles. Had he not been asked about it in his press conference he would not have taken any public notice of the Shepley article. In the briefing session with the President before the press conference, Hagerty began a discussion about how the expected questions from the reporters on the Shepley article could be handled. Eisenhower told us abruptly and with a little irritation that he had already decided how he would reply to such questions and quickly changed the subject. Sometimes when Eisenhower disagreed with a public statement made by somebody in the administration his displeasure crept into his replies to questions at a press conference. In this case, Eisenhower was very careful about what he said. He observed that Dulles was the best Secretary of State he ever knew and he reminded the reporters that the tactics used in stopping Communist aggression in the Far East involved decisions of the National Security Council that a President could not discuss with propriety in public. But he did make one remark that revealed what he felt under the surface. He did not know, he said, whether unfortunate expressions had been used by Mr. Dulles or by the author of the article. But Eisenhower was saying they had been used by someone, and in his carefully guarded way of speaking he was taking exception to the wisdom of what Dulles had been credited with saying. Incidentally, after the President's press conference, Dulles took full responsibility for the interview by confirming the substance of what Shepley had reported.

> SELECTION III–C
>
> The following excerpts are from pp. 215, 220–23 "The Formosa Crisis: A Peaceful Solution" in *What I Think* by Adlai Stevenson. Copyright © 1956 by R. Keith Kane. Reprinted by permission of Harper & Row, Publishers. Stevenson, the Democratic presidential candidate in 1952 and 1956, was a vigorous opponent of brinkmanship.

I have not spoken to you for more than four months. And I do so tonight only because I have been deeply disturbed by the recent course of events in the Far East and because many of you have asked me for my views. I have waited until the first excitement about the islands, Quemoy and Matsu, has subsided and we can more calmly examine our situation in the Straits of Formosa and in Asia. In matters of national security emotion is no substitute for intelligence, nor rigidity for prudence. To act coolly, intelligently, and prudently in perilous circumstances is the test of a man—and also a nation.

.   .   .   .

One of the weaknesses of our position is that we have been making Formosa policy as we thought best regardless of others. We have not made it clear that we are helping to hold Formosa not as an offensive but as a purely defensive measure. We have not made it clear because the administration has not been clear itself. But we can't expect other nations to support policies they disagree with, let alone ambiguous and dangerous policies.

.   .   .   .

To profit from this unhappy experience we might ask ourselves how we ever got in this position, how the prestige and honor of the great United States, not to mention the peace of the world, could be staked on some little islands within the very shadow of the China coast in which we have no claim or interest.

The answer, of course, lies partly in the fact that domestic political considerations have influenced our Formosa policy lately. Domestic politics should not enter our foreign affairs, least of all factional conflict between the two wings of the President's party, but they have, and too often our hot and cold, vacillating behavior has reflected efforts to please both of the views that divide our government and the Republican party, especially on Far Eastern policy.

And, while I do not belittle some recent achievements in the foreign field, for the same reasons too much of our foreign policy of late has disclosed a yawning gap between what we say and what we do—between our words and deeds.

For example, you recall that just a year ago as the Communist pressure rose in Indo-China, so did our warlike, menacing words. The Vice-President of the United States even talked of sending American soldiers to fight on the mainland of Asia. But what happened? Nothing.

Likewise all the bold, brave talk about liberation that raised such vain hopes among the peoples behind the iron curtain has long since evaporated, with the loss of half of Vietnam and much of our prestige and influence.

So also we hear no more of last year's dire threats of instantaneous and massive atomic retaliation. Instead, the President has spoken lately of pinpoint retaliation with tactical weapons. I fear, however, that the psychological effect of the use of atomic weapons, large or small, will be most unfortunate.

But there has been plenty of massive verbal retaliation, and the administration's policy of extravagant words has alarmed our friends a good deal more than it has deterred the aggressors. For our allies assumed that the great United States meant what it said.

Now let me be clear. I am not criticizing the administration for abandoning these extravagant positions; I am criticizing it for taking such positions, for making threats which it is not prepared to back up, and thereby undermining faith in the United States. Theodore Roosevelt said: "Never draw unless you intend to shoot," and I fear this wordy warfare has made more friends in Asia for China than for us.

Another example of these winged words, as we have seen, was President Eisenhower's dramatic announcement two years ago that he was unleashing Chiang Kai-shek, taking the wraps off him, presumably for an attack on the mainland to reconquer China. However, it was apparent to everyone else, if not to us, that such an invasion across a hundred miles of water by a small, overage, underequipped army against perhaps the largest army and the largest nation on earth could not possibly succeed without all-out support from the United States.

Since it seemed incredible to sober, thoughtful people that the government of the United States could be bluffing on such a matter, the President's unleashing policy has caused widespread anxiety that we planned to support a major war with China which might involve the Soviet Union. Hence we find ourselves where we are today—on Quemoy and Matsu—alone.

What, then, are the lessons to be drawn from the past two years?

In the first place, I think we should abandon, once and for all, the policy of wishful thinking and wishful talking, the policy of big words and little deeds.

We must renounce go-it-aloneism.

We shall have to face the fact that General Chiang's army cannot invade the mainland unless we are prepared to accept enormous burdens and risks —alone.

The world will respect us for recognizing mistakes and correcting them. But if our present posture in the offshore islands, for example, is a wrong one, who will respect us for stubbornly persisting in it? If we cease to deceive ourselves over the hard realities of power in the Formosa situation, we shall have taken the first step toward our first essential—the restoration of unity of purpose and action between ourselves and our allies in the free world. But our friends have made it clear that so long as fantasy, rigidity, and domestic politics seem to stand in the way of peaceful Formosa settlement, they will not support us if, in spite of our endeavors, a conflict should break out.

So, finally, let us face the fact that keeping friends these days calls for more statesmanship than challenging enemies, and the cause of world peace transcends any domestic political considerations.

But, preoccupied as we all are these days with the immediate problem of these islands, we must try to keep things in perspective somehow, and not lose sight of our main objectives. For beyond Quemoy and Matsu, and even Formosa, lie the urgent and larger problems of Asia—the growing attraction of enormous, reawakened China, the struggle of the underdeveloped countries to improve their condition and keep their independence, and the grave misgivings about America.

If the best hope for today's world is a kind of atomic balance, the decisive battle in the struggle against aggression may be fought not on battlefields but in the minds of men, and the area of decision may well be out there among the uncommitted peoples of Asia and Africa who look and listen and who must, in the main, judge us by what we say and do.

It is not only over the offshore islands crisis that we need a new sense of direction and to mend our fences. Too often of late we have turned to the world a face of stern military power. Too often the sound they hear from Washington is the call to arms, the rattling of the saber. Too often our constructive, helpful economic programs have been obscured, our good done by stealth. Thus have we Americans, the most peaceful and generous people on earth been made to appear hard, belligerent, and careless of those very qualities of humanity which, in fact, we value most. The picture of America—the kindly, generous, deeply pacific people who are really America—has been clouded in the world, to the comfort of the aggressors and the dismay of our friends.

IV. VIEWS OF OBSERVERS

SELECTION IV–A

Taken from "Will We Sacrifice Free China?" by David Nelson Rowe, in the *National Review* (April 27, 1957), pp. 397–99. Reprinted by permission of *National Review*, 150 East 35th Street, New York, N.Y. 10016. David N. Rowe is professor of political science at Yale and a strong supporter of the Nationalist cause.

At first glance, the question here asked would seem to have only one possible answer—a negative one. There is, of course, the Mutual Defense Treaty between the U.S. and Nationalist China which specifically pledges this country to use force to resist any attack against Taiwan and the Pescadores Islands. Further, Congress has voted overwhelmingly to give the President discretionary power to employ force for that purpose without prior consent of Congress.

In addition, both party platforms of 1956 pledged continued support of the Republic of China (on Taiwan) and continued opposition to either recognition or admission to the UN of Red China. Finally, the retention of Mr. Walter Robertson as Assistant Secretary of State for Far Eastern Affairs would seem to indicate the continuity of our China policy along these lines.

There is no doubt that the vast majority of the American public supports the Free Chinese against the Chinese Communists. But popular sentiment can be changed, and the initial efforts in this direction are already under way.

The recent statement by "someone who might well know," to the effect that President Eisenhower is by no means finally committed to non-recognition of Communist China, was probably a trial balloon. The same may also be true of the statement by Senator Green, Chairman of the Senate Foreign Relations Committee, who recently said that he believed the U.S. "should recognize Red China sooner or later." He then qualified this statement by saying that he was not advocating immediate recognition of Red China, but that "the President eventually would have to face the recognition issue." This statement by the Senator who is most directly concerned with our foreign policy doubtless evoked Secretary Dulles' statement the next day to the effect that recognition was not contemplated *at present*.

.　　.　　.　　.　　.　　.　　.　　.　　.　　.　　.　　.

The danger of such an inadequately informed opinion is clear. If our China policy remains rooted more in fear of Communist China than in support of Free China, we are far more likely to be susceptible to Communist blackmail and intimidation than to be aware of the vital need for cooperation with our allies, the Free Chinese.

This is the real issue: Can and will freedom survive in China? And this issue is the outcome of thirty years of continuous civil war. During those thirty years, the struggle has sometimes gone one way, sometimes another. But it has not yet ended in final victory for either side. Each side is still resolved to exterminate the other.

To many it seems nonsensical today to consider the Chinese Nationalists as a real threat to the Chinese Communists. But it should be remembered that twenty years ago (a short time-span in the Chinese way of thinking) the Communists were within an inch of being exterminated by the Nationalists. The relative strength of the two groups, then, was far more in favor of the Nationalists than it is today in favor of the Communists. It was the pressure of the Japanese armies on the Chinese Government which forced it to call off its war against the Communists.

Such external factors still largely control the fate of freedom in China. Had it not been for the fear that Russian support of the Chinese Communists would bring another general war if we crushed the Chinese Reds in Korea, their rash aggression there would have ended, in all probability, in their total destruction. And if it were not for the support of the U.S. to the Free Chinese today, they could hardly survive at all.

This places in the hands of the Communists an "ultimate weapon" of diplomacy—namely, the threat that non-compliance with their demand for the liquidation of Free China will lead, however slowly and indirectly, to general (*i.e.,* atomic) war. Yes, our diplomacy tends to lead us, however slowly and indirectly, into sacrificing Free China.

What evidence is there of this? We need the correct answer to only this main question: In the course of U.S. negotiations with the two Chinas, which one of them is being asked to make, and is making, the major concessions? The Chinese Nationalists not only have been *asked* to make major concessions (in the interest of keeping the U.S. out of war in the area) but *have made* some major concessions that affect their territorial sovereignty.

For example, at Geneva we are still negotiating with the Red Chinese regime which we do not recognize; and this alone is a great concession to that regime. We have, at Geneva, asked the Chinese Communists for two things: the release of American prisoners still held by them, and an agreement by them not to use force in the solution (!) of the Taiwan problem. On the first, they have promised to comply, but have not kept their promise fully. The second demand is patently impossible for them to grant without compromising their entire case in respect to Taiwan.

This case rests on the basic premise, which they must maintain, that Taiwan is legally theirs and thus, therefore, they have the right to take possession of it by force. They cannot abandon this position without undercutting their assertion that they are legal owners of China, of which everyone recognizes Taiwan to be a part. Furthermore, if they agreed to abjure the use of force against Taiwan they would, at our request, be giving up their main weapon of intimidation against us.

In addition, when we talk to the Chinese Communists in terms of a peaceful "solution" to the Taiwan question we aid and abet their constant efforts at subversion in Taiwan. Why should the Chinese in Taiwan wait for a "solution" to be worked out by *others?* Why not negotiate *directly* with the Chinese Communists? That our allies have resisted such a temptation is not to be credited to U.S. diplomacy, but rather to their solid conviction that there is no possible basis for a real agreement with Communists on anything.

CONCESSIONS BY NATIONALISTS

Now, by contrast to our position towards the Chinese Communists today, we have in the past demanded and obtained some major concessions from the Chinese Nationalists. Most important among them was the evacuation, in 1955, of the Tachen Islands. These islands, located near the China mainland and considerably north of Taiwan, had been held by the Chinese National Government and had been fortified with American assistance. When the Communists began to attack them from the air in 1954 and 1955, the United States urged their evacuation. Thus we convinced many of our supporters in the Far East that initial military support by the U.S. in any given area will not stand firm when the actual attack comes.

Subsequently, pressure has been brought on the Chinese Nationalists to withdraw from the remaining offshore islands of Kinmen (Quemoy) and Matsu. Again, the U.S. has helped in setting up the defenses of these islands, and in the past has urged the National Government to remain there (at a time when its inclination was to leave the islands to the Communists). The Chinese Government states that it will not withdraw from these islands under any circumstances. And it has increasingly committed its military resources to their defense—so much so that for the Communists to take them now would call for a major military effort. They would have to cut all communications between the offshore islands and Taiwan itself, and destroy the airpower based on Taiwan only a few minutes flight away. This would clearly extend the attack beyond the confines of the offshore islands themselves. Under these circumstances, if only for the safety of Taiwan and the Pescadores themselves, our military guarantees would be brought into effect. Thus our announced policy of keeping the Communists guessing as to whether or not we would join in a defense of the offshore islands would seem entirely irrelevant.

Accordingly, the Chinese Communists have abandoned hope of intimidating the U.S. on the basis of small-scale military preparation. In fact, their preparations in the Taiwan area now reach back a long distance into the China mainland. They include rail and road communications and a network of airfields from central China to the north and northwest of Fukien (the mainland province opposite Taiwan). Since the Nationalist Chinese forces on Taiwan could hardly carry the war into the interior of China, it is clear that the Chinese Communists are preparing against the likelihood that the U.S. would become involved in a conflict arising from an attack on the offshore islands.

In the light of this situation it is not surprising to find some of our civil and military officials coming around to the view that Free China will be liquidated—and as soon as decently possible. Any plan for this would include the following steps:

1) the U.S. would threaten withdrawal of aid to Taiwan unless the off-shore islands are evacuated;

2) the U.S. would agree to a demilitarized zone in the Taiwan strait;

3) the U.S. would recognize Communist China and accede to its admission to the United Nations;

4) in order to "relieve tensions" in the minds of the Chinese Reds, we would secure the demilitarization and neutralization of Taiwan.

Such a plan would doubtless be pursued under the spurious label of a scheme for the preservation of "two Chinas"—a scheme which both the Chinese Communists and the Government on Taiwan have repeatedly rejected. And the label is spurious simply because any such plan would surely result in liquidating Free China.

In view of the open commitment of the Administration to the contrary such ideas are not much aired in public. But it is not possible to keep them completely hidden from view. And at every opportunity the pro-Communist-China Lobby seeks to strengthen such tendencies of thought among policy-makers. (It would be interesting to know, for instance, what intelligence estimates lie behind the recent public statements on the "inevitability of the recognition of Red China.")

What is it we are committed to defend in Free China? The issue is nothing less than the defense of freedom against slavery, and those who are blind to this issue are blind, indeed, to everything. They would rather express the matter in terms of bits of "real estate," and argue the tenability of certain pieces of property against possible invasion. Those who would impose a "temporary" solution in the Taiwan area by drawing a line down the Taiwan strait will have no better success in contesting the real issue, or preventing the eventual resolution one way or the other, than did our statesmen of the pre-Civil War era. The Chinese Communists, like all Communists, already know this. It is time we faced it ourselves.

SELECTION IV–B

An excerpt from *The Cold War and Its Origins, 1917–1960,* II by D. F. Fleming, pp. 732–35. Copyright © 1961. Reprinted by permission of Doubleday & Company, Inc. Fleming was a professor of political science at Vanderbilt University and an opponent of containment, both in Europe and in Asia.

Nor was it strange that Eisenhower should be persuaded that Formosa was really essential to our defense. The most remarkable feature of the entire crisis was the near-unanimity with which all Americans agreed that of course Formosa and the Pescadores must be held. Virtually all of the liberal Senators who tried to oppose the Formosa resolution united in saying that Formosa must be defended. The liberal Americans for Democratic Action said the same. There was at first muted and then rising protest against the absurdity of fighting for Quemoy and Matsu, and doubtless many Americans privately held the same opinion about war for Formosa, but only a very few private citizens ventured to question the national dogma that Formosa must be retained.

By this time the MacArthur dictum that if Formosa were lost everything back to the California coast would be lost had become national policy. Yet obviously such an oceanic Red sweep was most unlikely. Island stepping is not a one-way street. There are many islands in the Pacific and the burdens of logistics would not all fall on the defending Americans. It would be strange indeed if with our tremendous naval and air power we could not hold our share of the islands in the Pacific in any foreseeable war.

This was not really feared. What was desired was to perpetuate American control of the entire Pacific Ocean, even into the mouths of Chinese harbors. It was a very comfortable situation for us to have the world's greatest ocean an American lake, but it was also an unrealistic one. As Russia and China grew in strength, and Japan in independence, they would inevitably assert their fair share in the control of the Pacific, from their side of the ocean.

This is apparent when our strategic claims to Formosa are examined more closely. It is said that it is a very important island, that it controls passage up and down East Asia, and that the Philippines were attacked from it in 1940 and could be again. That China would exercise some control over her own coastal waters from Formosa is evident, a control which would injure no one in time of peace. If war came, Formosa in Chinese hands would be a "threat" to the Philippines, 230 miles away, just as the great American air base at Clark Field, near Manila, with its new town of 7000 is now the main defense of Formosa, and would be a threat to it in Chinese hands. Yet Formosa was by-passed by us in winning World War II and the Philippines could be attacked from the China mainland as well as from Formosa. Nor would the seizure of the Philippines be a practical proposition for China for decades, even if she could amass the great naval strength essential for an island hopping war.

After his months of observation in the Far East, Joseph Alsop came to the conclusion that "it may be heresy to say so, but this country and the free world could well afford to lose Formosa if we could be sure of losing nothing further." Earlier, at the start of the crisis, Hanson W. Baldwin had concluded that "in a military sense the island is important but not vital to the United States and to our position in the Western Pacific and Eastern Asia." Its real importance was political and psychological.

Any other conclusion about the essentiality of Formosa to our defense would seem untenable. If it were essential to our defense then Cuba would be essential to the defense of the Soviet Union, and Catalina Island, off Los Angeles, to the defense of China.

DID THE UNITED STATES HAVE IMPORTANT AND LEGITIMATE INTERESTS IN FORMOSA?

Our emotional interest is obvious. We went to war with Japan to prevent her domination of China. We sought all during the war to build up China into a great friendly power. We backed Chiang against the Chinese Communists. They humiliated us deeply in the Korean war and in backing Ho Chi Minh to victory in North Indo-China.

Legally and morally we had a right to a voice in the disposition of Formosa. It was our military power which freed it from Japan. She had renounced title to it in the Japanese peace treaty. We had no right to use it as a springboard for the reconquest of China for Chiang, but we did have a right to insist that, after our war with China in Korea the island should not at once fall into her hostile hands. The temporary neutralization of Formosa was justifiable.

On the practical side, about a million upper class refugees from Red China and a half million mainland troops were on Formosa. In the climate of the time it was easy for us to believe that they would be massacred if the Reds took the island, though it was more probable that only a small part of the leaders would be dealt with drastically. In any event no country was prepared to evacuate and receive any considerable part of this great body of refugees. After unleashing Chiang to bait China, under our protection, honor would hardly permit his forcible suppression.

There was also the usual fear of galloping Communism, the fear that if Formosa fell to Communism the Chinese in South East Asia would go over to Peking, carrying that region with them. Then India, the Middle East, Africa and Europe—all would go. There is also some danger in any increase in Communist held territory. The older generations of the overseas Chinese were already rich, having no love for Communism, but their sons were already flocking through Hong Kong to Red China for education and jobs.

The idea that a second China could be maintained was an illusion. Joseph Alsop saw the drift when he wrote: "Two Chinas, one small and in the process of withering away, the other vast and growing stronger month by month, are thus to be recognized."

There is only one China and since most of the world believed Formosa to be a part of it there was no built-in disaster involved in recognizing the inevitable and standing aside from the Chinese civil war, as Truman did steadfastly in the first half of 1950, until the Korean war led him to neutralize Formosa.

After the rash and abortive "unleashing" of Chiang, this could not be done again. After the Communist victory in North Indo-China, which we were powerless to prevent, the problem became one of disengagement, a process which would have to proceed gradually.

As it proceeds it is well to remember that the interests of China in Formosa are far deeper than ours. Its people are unquestionably Chinese. To all

Chinese—on both sides of the civil war—it is a part of China. It is also essential to the "defense" of China, if she is to have any independence in her home waters. In 1955 and thereafter its bombing and blockading of the mother country was an intolerable humiliation such as no people could accept permanently. But, above all, Formosa was also the fortress of counter-revolution, bent on the destruction of a great and proud revolution, and backed by the world's strongest foreign power.

These interests make it impossible for China to cease striving to recover Formosa. No amount of "no-force" argument will seem valid to the Chinese, and no cease-fire can be accepted unless it provides for the return of Formosa to China within a reasonable time. Otherwise China will industrialize and arm until she is surely capable of overwhelming the island. She might have to wait a considerable period, but she could not continue to grow in strength as a great power and fail to assert her sovereignty over Formosa.

Since China had all the advantages of geography, and also the basic sympathy of the vast bulk of the Asians, the American position on Formosa was untenable from the close of the war for North Indo-China. This was so clear that the war party was fully justified, from the standpoint of its deep frustrations, in seeking to bring about the crushing of China in 1955 or 1956, while there was still time.

That effort failed, leaving the problem of disengagement from Formosa more acute than ever.

SELECTION IV–C

An excerpt from "Sino-American Relations and the Future of Formosa," by O. Edmund Clubb. Reprinted with permission from *The Political Science Quarterly*, March 1965, Vol. LXXX, No. 1, pp. 17–21. O. Edmund Clubb, now a lecturer in government at Columbia University, was a foreign service officer with experience in the Far East.

In law, there patently cannot be two Chinas; at most, there could only have been one China and a Formosa. But when the Taipei and Peking strategists in 1958 welded the offshore islands to Formosa and the Pescadores they interposed a strong roadblock to any shift in American policy; for they thus barred an approach to the two-Chinas solution. The aforementioned *Wen Wei Pao* editorial dwelt again on the theme, in opposition; and Chiang Kai-shek, in a speech the following October, said that Formosa and the mainland China provinces were "like blood in the same vein and [with?] their fate inextricably linked." The American acceptance of the Quemoy-Formosa tie in 1958 served Chiang Kai-shek's ends—but it served Mao Tse-tung's too.

A shift in Peking's foreign policy line tends to facilitate China's progress in the field of foreign relations. Mao Tse-tung in 1949 announced his doctrine of "leaning to one side"—the side of the Soviet Union. In January of last year, coincident with the French recognition, the Peking regime proposed that China should lean in another direction, not indeed toward the United States, but toward "the intermediate zone" comprising not only the newly independent and aspiring nations of Asia, Africa, and Latin America, but Western Europe, Canada, Australia, "and other capitalist countries." By this new doctrine, Peking proposed in effect to form a united front with all countries against the United States; in other words, Mao Tse-tung and his captains now sanction political coexistence with all except the United States —and, perhaps, the Soviet Union.

In practical immediate terms, China's urgent purpose is to obtain from that intermediate zone some replacement for the economic support it lost by reason of its estrangement from the Soviet Union. Since it obviously cannot obtain such material things as passenger planes, machinery, steel cable, and tin plate from Communist parties (however sympathetic) in the intermediate zone, it must approach bourgeois—and capitalistic—governments of such countries as Japan, France, Britain, and West Germany. To be successful in the intermediate zone, China must adopt the manners of the company it would keep. Where it was unable to get Moscow to adopt its behavior patterns, it will hardly be successful with Japan, Canada—or, be it acknowledged, President de Gaulle's France. In the field of foreign trade, business considerations will govern. But regardless of its revolutionary pronunciamentos, China will be able to buy and sell if it *acts* in a manner acceptable to the respectable bourgeois bankers and traders of the world. China has a better chance than before to make friends—or at least acquire new trading partners.

This shift in Peking's foreign policy has a direct significance for the future of Formosa. The world is swinging over to the belief that occupancy of China's seat in the United Nations would perhaps calm Peking, and would surely facilitate the application of international curbs to the more violent (even nuclear) Chinese urges. The big trading countries, noting Peking's new willingness to "coexist" with them, and remarking further China's shift away from trade with the Communist bloc, envisage the clear possibility that they may benefit from the reorientation. The countries now exploring the commercial possibilities offered by China will doubtless give due regard to China's limited capacity to pay, but they will give much less heed to American lectures on the wickedness of trading with "aggressor" China. And as they come closer politically and economically to China, remaining ties to and sympathy with the Nationalists on Formosa will tend progressively to lapse.

Given particularly the critical developments of 1964, then, the U.S. government is now confronted by a categorical imperative to find a way out of the cul-de-sac it entered by allying itself with one Chinese faction against another in 1954. Since that date, it has supported not only the Nationalist military and economic establishments, but the Nationalist dream of returning to power over the Chinese people. From 1958 onward, it has been abundantly clear that the China and Formosa problems can only be solved together; but in the past six years Washington has failed to take one bold firm step in the direction of a solution.

Time is now rapidly running out. The formulation of a new integral China-Formosa policy is patently a formidable political task. Former Ambassador George F. Kennan, in a recent article, took note of the attendant difficulties, but held that one approach to the men at Peking is "being careful to hold open to them and their people the possibility of negotiation and accommodation if their ambitions are moderated and their methods change." Mr. Hilsman (now retired from the State Department), in a speech about the same time, said bluntly that the "time has come to increase communications with the Chinese Communists, specifically to increase communications on the subject of arms control." And the New York *Times* has come out editorially to support action *now* aimed at winning a seat for Formosa in the UN General Assembly while ceding the China seats in both the General Assembly and the Security Council to Peking.

A recent limited survey of American public opinion disclosed that twenty-eight per cent of those queried did not know that Communists ruled mainland China, but that of those aware of the existence of the Chinese Communist government a majority favored our discussion of mutual problems with that regime. The new administration at Washington comes to authority with a mandate from the American people adequate to permit its seizing the "China Problem." But the administration is saddled with the legacy of the past, and it must be regarded as at least doubtful whether, even with the most strenuous efforts, it could extricate itself from the tangled web of our China-Formosa policy before being overtaken by events.

It is hardly to be anticipated in existing political circumstances that, without an American initiative, Formosa will alone be able to attain to a state of independence. United States policy-makers a few years back were firmly convinced that there was no possibility of a falling-out between Communist China and the Communist U.S.S.R. Mao Tse-tung now, even as Chiang Kai-shek, has assumed an anti-Soviet stance. Washington today is equally certain that the rulers in Taipei are staunch anti-Communists, even to the extent of being anti-Chinese. In that final ratiocination lies the crux of an error; the Nationalists are Chinese, too. If events are simply permitted to take their course, it is entirely possible that at some not distant date the United States will see the successors to Chiang Kai-shek on Formosa reach an agreement with their brother Chinese in Peking. For both the Chinese Communists and the Nationalists are determined that Formosa's future shall be linked to that of the mainland—regardless of Washington's wishes.

9

THE SUEZ CRISIS OF 1956

Role of American Statecraft

I. EDITORIAL INTRODUCTION

On July 19, 1956, the United States abruptly withdrew its support for the construction of the Aswan Dam which Egypt under the leadership of its dynamic young president, Gamal Abdel Nasser, had hoped would increase arable land by one-third. (Selection II–A.) This action set in motion events leading to Egypt's nationalization of the Suez Canal, presumably to raise revenue to finance the dam, which in turn led to the abortive attempt by Britain and France (and Israel for different reasons) to seize the canal in October 1956.

World war might have been sparked by this action; the Atlantic Alliance might have been permanently broken by the division of the United States from its principal allies; communism might have engulfed the Middle East. None of these nightmares materialized but the United States was sufficiently shaken by the events to put forth the Eisenhower Doctrine a little more than two months after the Suez crisis, whereby the United States promised military support to any Middle Eastern country threatened by "armed aggression from any nation controlled by International Communism." (Selection II–B.) It appeared then that Secretary Dulles had inadvertently initiated a sequence of events that facilitated the very action his Aswan announcement had been intended to avert—the elimination of a communist threat from the Middle East. With England's influence shattered by the Suez crisis, the United States was forced to intervene more directly in the area than it had ever attempted before.

Given the sudden violence with all its attending dangers to world peace, the Suez crisis has been a source of bitter contention among participants and commentators alike. Was there a fatal element of unrealism in American policy toward the Middle East that induced Secretary Dulles to believe he could support the principle of anticolonialism and at the same time be responsible for the interests of America's colonialist allies? Certainly America's prior encouragement of Britain's evacuation of the Canal and her reluctance to offer firm guarantees of Israel's survival sapped the confidence of those two states without convincing the Arab nations that the United States was not the heir of colonialism and imperialism in the Middle East. Was there an error in judgment in believing communism to be a major threat to the Middle East? If communism was spoken of as a danger in the Middle East, it was to give comfort to America's obsession with the subject; to most Arabs the enemies were Israel and Western imperialism, while the Soviet Union was to be useful as a counterweight to both. Did the United States misjudge the role and character of Nasser? Initially, there was a temptation to see in him the charisma of an Ataturk, the man who might unite and westernize the Arab world. This image gave way to the spectre of an Arab Hitler, with a will to power built on a cynical pitting of the United States against the Soviet Union, which would lead to communist control of the Middle East.

Inevitably, John Foster Dulles emerges as the central scapegoat. It was the Secretary of State who had advanced the United States position among the Arabs beyond that of a secondary partner to England, to a major participant as the Soviet Union moved its influence into the area. If NATO had rebuffed Soviet expansionism in Europe, a Middle Eastern equivalent, the aborted MEDO, should do as much for the southern border of Russia. He was unable to understand why Nasser did not accept the American evaluation of the Soviet danger and America's own self-estimate as a friend of emerging nations. Instead of appreciating American support, which in Dulles' view was significantly different from the behavior of the Truman administration, the Egyptian leader attempted to blackmail the United States with threats of turning to the Soviet Union for aid in constructing the Aswan Dam, and thereby invited American punishment. Among other advantages Dulles calculated that the rebuke over the dam would expose the promise of Soviet aid for the fraud that it was.

When Nasser used American action as an occasion for nationalizing the Suez Canal, Dulles was genuinely shocked not only by the action but also by the accompanying bitter denunciation of the United States. For Egypt the American note proved that the United States was no different from Britain and France, and that the time had come to dramatize the Canal issue as a symbol of Arab independence of the West, whether or not the Soviet Union honored its commitments. Little of this sentiment was apparent to Secretary Dulles. Speaking to the nation over television, he only accepted the seizure of the canal as "an angry act of retaliation against fancied grievances." But has was also confident that world opinion would dictate an equitable solution to the problem without recourse to force. (Selection III–A.)

Not only was Dulles's optimism unjustified by Egypt's subsequent behavior but he was unable to understand the resentments he had fostered
among America's British and French allies. They had not forgotten that
Dulles's anticolonial action had expedited Egypt's removal of British troops
from the Canal zone and strengthened Algeria's demands for independence
from France. They distrusted his sudden reversal withdrawing support of the
Aswan Dam in the summer of 1956. How far would he go in bringing Nasser
into line over the use of the Canal? Anthony Eden, prime minister of the
United Kingdom in 1956 but writing after retirement, a few years later,
expressed his bitterness toward Dulles and implied that the Anglo-French
operation against Egypt was a consequence of a lack of faith in the United
States understanding of their plight and of a lack of cooperation in efforts to
win redress from Nasser. This suspicion of bad faith as well as of the wisdom
of American leadership accounted for the decision to recapture the Canal
without consulting the United States. The result was the Suez debacle in
which France and England not only failed to retrieve the canal but linked
the United States and the Soviet Union in opposition to their action. (Selection III–B.)

The Suez invasion took place on the eve of the presidential election and
hence it is hardly surprising that the Suez issue became a subject of partisan
debate. Adlai Stevenson, reviewing America's role in the Middle East since
1953, noted that Dulles's errors of judgment had encouraged the Soviet
Union to enter the area. If Nasser was a menace in 1956 it was because the
United States first promoted his ambitions, and then rudely insulted him,
opening the way for the confiscation of the Canal. (Selection III–C.)

Political scientist Herman Finer was even more scathing than Stevenson
in his denunciation of Dulles for the split among the allies. Although Dulles
was responsible for the creation of the Suez Canal Users Association and
talked of making the Egyptians disgorge the Canal, his actions did little to
divert Egypt from its course of action. When England and France, in conjunction with Israel, employed force his fear of Soviet intervention, his
moralism and his indignation, all served to drive him, and the United States
policy, toward a potentially suicidal break with the nation's allies. If the
European allies' actions were not sensible, they were at least understandable.
(Selection IV–A.)

British observer Ian Gilmour, however, was much less inclined to heap
the blame for Britain's disaster solely upon the American secretary of state.
Commenting on Eden's memories of his relations with Dulles, he could not
find Dulles' errors sufficient to justify the Anglo-French deception of the
Americans, let alone the poorly planned, badly executed invasion of Egypt
which followed. (Selection IV–B.)

Looking at the Suez crisis in light of American foreign policy since the
World War II, Professor M. A. Fitzsimons saw the American action in the
Middle East as an affirmation and extension of the containment policy that

was almost a decade old in 1956. Until the humiliating failure of the British and French to seize the Canal in 1956, the United States had been able to play a subsidiary role in the region and even to assume the posture of mediator with the Arabs. The departure of Britain and the imminence of a Soviet replacement forced the United States to assume a primary role in maintaining the status quo in Middle East, and the Eisenhower Doctrine with its promise of aid was the earnest of America's intentions. (Selection IV–C.) As an instrument of containment the Doctrine symbolically has had a limited success, which suggests that the misadventures over the Aswan Dam produced, if not a stabilized Middle East, a clearer picture of America's responsibility in that area.

II. DOCUMENTS

> ### SELECTION II–A
>
> In a press release dated July 19, 1956, Secretary of State Dulles made a statement on the Aswan High Dam which appears here as it was subsequently printed in the Department of State *Bulletin,* XXXV (July 30, 1956), p. 188.

At the request of the Government of Egypt, the United States joined in December 1955 with the United Kingdom and with the World Bank in an offer to assist Egypt in the construction of a high dam on the Nile at Aswan. This project is one of great magnitude. It would require an estimated 12 to 16 years to complete at a total cost estimated at some $1,300,000,000, of which over $900,000,000 represents local currency requirements. It involves not merely the rights and interests of Egypt but of other states whose waters are contributory, including Sudan, Ethiopia, and Uganda.

The December offer contemplated an extension by the United States and United Kingdom of grant aid to help finance certain early phases of the work, the effects of which would be confined solely to Egypt, with the understanding that accomplishment of the project as a whole would require a satisfactory resolution of the question of Nile water rights. Another important consideration bearing upon the feasibility of the undertaking, and thus the practicability of American aid, was Egyptian readiness and ability to concentrate its economic resources upon this vast construction program.

Developments within the succeeding 7 months have not been favorable to the success of the project, and the U.S. Government has concluded that it is not feasible in present circumstances to participate in the project. Agreement by the riparian states has not been achieved, and the ability of Egypt to devote adequate resources to assure the project's success has become more uncertain than at the time the offer was made.

This decision in no way reflects or involves any alteration in the friendly relations of the Government and people of the United States toward the Government and people of Egypt.

The United States remains deeply interested in the welfare of the Egyptian people and in the development of the Nile. It is prepared to consider at an appropriate time and at the request of the riparian states what steps might be taken toward a more effective utilization of the water resources of the Nile for the benefit of the peoples of the region. Furthermore, the United States remains ready to assist Egypt in its effort to improve the economic condition of its people and is prepared, through its appropriate agencies, to discuss these matters within the context of funds appropriated by the Congress.

> SELECTION II–B
>
> The "Eisenhower Doctrine," as it came to be known, was first presented in a "Message of the President on the Middle East" on January 5, 1957. The following reading represents part six of that message as it was published in the Department of State *Bulletin*, XXXVI (January 21, 1957), p. 86.

It is nothing new for the President and the Congress to join to recognize that the national integrity of other free nations is directly related to our own security.

We have joined to create and support the security system of the United Nations. We have reinforced the collective security system of the United Nations by a series of collective defense arrangements. Today we have security treaties with 42 other nations which recognize that their, and our, peace and security are intertwined. We have joined to take decisive action in relation to Greece and Turkey and in relation to Taiwan.

Thus, the United States through the joint action of the President and the Congress, or, in the case of treaties, the Senate, has manifested in many endangered areas its purpose to support free and independent governments —and peace—against external menace, notably the menace of International Communism. Thereby we have helped to maintain peace and security during a period of great danger. It is now essential that the United States should manifest through joint action of the President and the Congress our determination to assist those nations of the Mid East area which desire that assistance.

The action which I propose would have the following features.

It would, first of all, authorize the United States to cooperate with and assist any nation or group of nations in the general area of the Middle East in the development of economic strength dedicated to the maintenance of national independence.

It would, in the second place, authorize the Executive to undertake in the same region programs of military assistance and cooperation with any nation or group of nations which desires such aid.

It would, in the third place, authorize such assistance and cooperation to include the employment of the armed forces of the United States to secure and protect the territorial integrity and political independence of such nations, requesting such aid, against overt armed aggression from any nation controlled by International Communism.

These measures would have to be consonant with the treaty obligations of the United States, including the Charter of the United Nations and with any action or recommendations of the United Nations. They would also, if armed attack occurs, be subject to the overriding authority of the United Nations Security Council in accordance with the Charter.

The present proposal would, in the fourth place, authorize the President to employ, for economic and defensive military purposes, sums available under the Mutual Security Act of 1954, as amended, without regard to existing limitations.

The legislation now requested should not include the authorization or appropriation of funds because I believe that, under the conditions I suggest, presently appropriated funds will be adequate for the balance of the present fiscal year ending June 30. I shall, however, seek in subsequent legislation the authorization of $200,000,000 to be available during each of the fiscal years 1958 and 1959 for discretionary use in the area, in addition to the other mutual security programs for the area hereafter provided for by the Congress.

III. VIEWS OF PARTICIPANTS

> *SELECTION III–A*
>
> Portions of a Radio-Television Address on the crisis of the Middle East given by the Secretary of State, August 3, 1956, are here reprinted as they appeared in the Department of State *Bulletin,* XXXV (August 13, 1956), pp. 260–61.

Now, why did President Nasser suddenly decide to take over this operation of the Suez Canal? Now, he has told us about that in a long speech that he made. And in that speech he didn't for a moment suggest that Egypt would be able to operate the canal better than it was being operated so as to assure better the rights that were granted under the 1888 treaty. The basic reason he gave was that if he took over this canal it would enhance the prestige of Egypt.

He said that Egypt was determined "to score one triumph after another" in order to enhance what he called the "grandeur" of Egypt. And he coupled his action with statements about his ambition to extend his influence from the Atlantic to the Persian Gulf.

And also he said that by seizing the Suez Canal he would strike a blow at what he called "Western imperialism." And he thought also that he could exploit the canal so as to produce bigger revenues for Egypt and so retaliate for the failure of the United States and Britain to give Egypt the money to enable it to get started on this $1 billion-plus Aswan Dam.

Now President Nasser's speech made it absolutely clear that his seizure of the canal company was an angry act of retaliation against fancied grievances. No one reading that speech can doubt for a moment that the canal, under the Egyptian operation, would be used not to carry out the 1888 treaty better but to promote the political and economic ambitions of Egypt and what, as I say, President Nasser calls the "grandeur" of Egypt.

Now, of course, the government of a free and independent country— which Egypt is, and we want to have it always that—should seek to promote by all proper means the welfare of its people. And President Nasser has done much that is good in that respect.

But it is inadmissible that a waterway internationalized by treaty, which is required for the livelihood of a score or more of nations, should be exploited by one country for purely selfish purposes. And that the operating agency which has done so well in handling the Suez Canal in accordance with the 1888 treaty should be struck down by a national act of vengefulness.

To permit this to go unchallenged would be to encourage a breakdown of the international fabric upon which the security and the well-being of all peoples depend.

And the question, Mr. President, as we've agreed, is not *whether* something should be done about this Egyptian act—but *what* should be done about it.

Now, there were some people who counseled immediate forcible action by the governments which felt themselves most directly affected. This, however, would have been contrary to the principles of the United Nations Charter and would undoubtedly have led to widespread violence endangering the peace of the world.

At London we decided upon a different approach. We decided to call together in conference the nations most directly involved with a view to seeing whether agreement could not be reached upon an adequate and dependable international administration of the canal on terms which would respect, and generously respect, all of the legitimate rights of Egypt.

SELECTION III–B

Anthony Eden, prime minister of Britain at the time of the Suez Crisis, vigorously denied his blame for the debacle. He reports Dulles' responses to Nasser's nationalization of the Canal and suggests that America's equivocal support of plans to counter Nasser's actions explains the Anglo-French action three months later. From Lord Avon, *The Memoirs of Anthony Eden: Full Circle* (New York, 1960), pp. 486–89; 538–40. Copyright © 1960 by The Times Publishing Company, Ltd. Reprinted by permission of Houghton Mifflin Company.

Mr. Dulles brought with him a message from the President, who was emphatic upon the importance of negotiation. The President did not rule out the use of force. He recognized the transcendent worth of the canal to the free world and the possibility that the eventual use of force might become necessary in order to protect international rights. But he felt that every possibility of peaceful settlement must be exhausted before this was done.

At his first meeting with the other Foreign Secretaries on August 1 Mr. Dulles summed up his views as follows:

1. It was intolerable that the canal should be under the domination of any single country without any international control;

2. We should use the 1888 Convention as a basis for discussion in order to avoid complications with the Panama Canal;

3. Force was the last method to be tried, but the United States did not exclude the use of force if all other methods failed;

4. We should mobilize world opinion in favour of international operation of the canal;

5. We should attempt to get our tripartite views accepted by at least a two-thirds majority of the conference that was to be called.

In further discussion at this meeting on the 1st, Mr. Dulles said:

A way had to be found to make Nasser disgorge what he was attempting to swallow. . . . We must make a genuine effort to bring world opinion to favour the international operation of the canal. . . . It should be possible to create a world opinion so adverse to Nasser that he would be isolated. Then if a military operation had to be undertaken it would be more apt to succeed and have less grave repercussions than if it had been undertaken precipitately.

Dulles had several conversations with the Foreign Secretary, and one at Downing Street with both of us, in addition to the three-power meetings. We were encouraged by his statements. He agreed emphatically that the seizure of a great international waterway was intolerable. This was still more so when the single nation that set out to dominate the canal was Egypt. Nasser must be made, as Mr. Dulles put it to me, "to disgorge." These were forthright words. They rang in my ears for months.

I did not wish to conceal anything from Mr. Dulles and I told him that the United States Naval Attaché had been asking for information about our military preparations. I said that we were quite ready to give this, but that I wanted first to make sure that the United States Government really wished to have it. Mr. Dulles replied that the United States Government perfectly well understood the purpose of our preparations and he thought that they had had a good effect. It was preferable that the United States Government should not seek detailed information.

I felt a great sense of relief that evening. Every allowance had to be made for a different approach between us and the Americans, and for a differing sense of urgency. But if Nasser had in the end "to disgorge," the result would be plain for all to see. Theft would not have paid off, a breach of agreement would not have been endured, a wholesome lesson would have been taught in respect for the sanctity of agreements. The United States, we were told by Mr. Dulles, did not exclude the use of force if all other methods failed, but there must be genuine efforts first to reach a settlement by negotiation. Mr. Eisenhower believed that our countries could marshal world opinion in support of a conciliatory but firm position, and that an international conference of canal users would have, at the least, a profound educational effect throughout the world. Such was also my hope. But I did not wish to lose momentum, or to allow discussions to drag on from conference to conference.

The three Governments were now committed to summon an international conference. Britain and France would have preferred it to meet as soon as possible; Dulles favoured several weeks of preparation. In the end we compromised and August 16 was the date fixed. We also compromised on membership. We accepted the American request that invitations should be sent to the eight signatories of the Constantinople Convention, Russia included. The Americans agreed that invitations should likewise be sent to the sixteen principal users of the canal, selected in terms of tonnage and trade. These twenty-four countries were listed in the statement issued at the close of the consultations on the evening of August 2.

One further difficult question aroused much discussion at these three-power meetings. It concerned the payment of canal dues in the weeks ahead. Most British shipowners paid their dues into the account of the Suez Canal Company in London; the French paid in Paris. A number of other countries, including the United States, were in the habit of paying in Egypt. Normally 55 per cent of the dues were annually collected in London, 35 per cent in Egypt and 10 per cent in Paris. We wished British shipowners to continue to pay the legitimate Canal Company in London until such time as a new international authority was established. If the new Egyptian authority attempted to exact payments, we might have to instruct British shipowners to reroute their ships by the Cape. The French and ourselves intended that as little money as possible from ships passing through the canal should find its way into Egyptian hands. On this we found it hard to secure American co-operation. Mr. Dulles could not say how the United States shipowners would react to any advice given them. Moreover, the American Government had no power to give instructions to the numerous American-owned ships, registered in Panama, Liberia and elsewhere, and flying the flags of those countries. Our talks on this point were inconclusive and the problems of dues remained to perplex us for many a long day and night.

·   ·   ·   ·   ·   ·   ·   ·   ·   ·   ·   ·   ·

I told the House that we had informed the President of the Security Council of the situation and we certainly did not exclude referring the dispute to the United Nations, if it became necessary. But we were setting up immediately a Suez Canal Users' Assocation, which I then described, concluding in the exact words agreed upon with the United States and French Governments:

> I must make it clear that if the Egyptian Government should seek to interfere with the operations of the association, or refuse to extend to it the essential minimum of co-operation, then that Government will once more be in breach of the Convention of 1888. In that event, Her Majesty's Government and others concerned will be free to take such further steps as seem to be required either through the United Nations, or by other means for the assertion of their rights.

I was at once interrupted with a request to explain the meaning of these words. This I declined to do, the words having been deliberately chosen by the three powers.

Sir Robert Boothby wound up the debate on that evening in words which expressed my own thoughts. He said:

> We went through all this in the nineteen-thirties, and it was not much fun. Shameless appeasement does not really pay. . . .
> As I listened to the Prime Minister this afternoon, I thought of what Nasser had been saying about what he was going to do to establish an Arab Empire from Morocco to the Persian Gulf, and how he was going to eliminate Israel altogether. That is all in his speeches, and in a horrible little book called *A Philosophy of Revolution,* which is like a potted edition of *Mein Kampf.* As I heard the Prime Minister speaking, I said to myself, "Well, thank goodness, at any rate we shall not have to go through all that again," and we shall not.

Though there were some difficult moments on the first day of the debate and some encouraging shouts of "provocation" and "resign," all went reasonably well. On the morning of the following day, M. Mollet made his parallel statement in Paris in the agreed terms. This aroused no critical comment. Mr. Dulles did the same in Washington, but in answer to questions afterwards, he made a remark which caught world-wide attention and entirely submerged the identity of our original statements. "We do not intend," he said, "to shoot our way through. It may be that we have the right to do it but we don't intend to do it as far as the United States is concerned." The alternative for the United States, he admitted, was to "send our vessels around the Cape." On being asked whether there was a conflict between British and American views on this point, Mr. Dulles replied:

I think that each nation has to decide for itself what action it will have to take to defend and if possible realize its rights which it believes it has as a matter of treaty. I do not recall just exactly what Sir Anthony Eden said on this point. I did not get the impression that there was any undertaking or pledge given by him to shoot their way through the canal.

It would be hard to imagine a statement more likely to cause the maximum allied disunity and disarray. The Americans having themselves volunteered that the new arrangements would be less acceptable to the Egyptians than the eighteen-power proposals, Mr. Dulles proceeded to make plain at this juncture that the United States did not intend to use force, even though it had the right to do so. The words were an advertisement to Nasser that he could reject the project with impunity. We had never been told that a statement of this kind was to accompany the announcement of the Users' Club. Had we known that they were to be used as an accompaniment to the American announcement, we would never have endorsed it. To us, the emphasis had been that the Egyptians, having rejected reasonable eighteen-power proposals, could not expect to do as well. To the public, the emphasis now was that, whatever happened, the Egyptians had nothing to fear. The Users' Club was an American project to which we had conformed. We were all three in agreement, even to the actual words of the announcement. Yet here was the spokesman of the United States saying that each nation must decide for itself and expressing himself as unable to recall what the spokesman of a principal ally had said. Such cynicism towards allies destroys true partnership. It leaves only the choice of parting, or a master and vassal relationship in foreign policy.

> SELECTION III–C
>
> An excerpt from a televised speech at Buffalo on November 1, 1956, by Adlai Stevenson, the Democratic nominee for President, in which he made the NATO split over the Suez a campaign issue. Taken from pp. 34–36 *The New America* by Adlai E. Stevenson. Copyright © 1957 by Adlai Ewing Stevenson. Reprinted by permission of Harper & Row, Publishers.

The President spoke to you about the Middle East crisis last night. The networks have been good enough to accord me time to speak tonight, and I want to tell you how this crisis came about, this crisis which is so threatening to peace and to our interests in this strategic area.

This matter should be above politics—if anything can be a few days before election—because all Americans suffer from any failure of our foreign policy, and from war anywhere in the world; for in this hydrogen age war is contagious.

I have only a few moments, so let me hastily sum up the central facts of the situation. I can find no better way to do this than to read you a sentence from a special dispatch from Washington in today's *New York Times:* "The United States has lost control of events in areas vital to its security. This is the main conclusion of serious and well-informed men here tonight concerning the United States' role in the Middle East crisis."

The condition which confronts us is stark and simple—our Middle-Eastern policy is at absolute dead end. And the hostilities going on tonight in which Israel, Egypt, Britain and France are involved reflect the bankruptcy of our policy; and they have given the Soviet Union two great victories.

The first Communist victory is the establishment in the Middle East of Russian influence.

The second Communist victory is the breakdown of the Western alliance. This has been a supreme objective of Soviet policy since the end of the Second World War.

As the climax, the United States finds itself arrayed in the United Nations with Soviet Russia and the dictator of Egypt against the democracies of Britain, France and Israel.

A foreign policy which has brought about these results—which has benefited Communism and has cut our own country off from our democratic friends—is a foreign policy which has failed.

And, at a time when the uprisings in Poland and Hungary are opening the Soviet world to freedom, the strategic Middle East is opening to Communist penetration.

I have three points to make tonight.

The first is that this series of failures could have been averted—that they were in great part the result of ill-considered and mistaken policies of this administration.

The second is that this administration not only made mistake after mistake in its Middle Eastern policy, but has withheld the consequences from the American people.

The third is that there are many things which might have been done in the past year to avert war in the Middle East.

The Middle East is one of the most important strategic areas in the world. It has three-quarters of the world's known oil reserves, and it controls the land, sea and air communications linking three continents. All nations which have sought world domination have wanted to control the Middle East.

When President Eisenhower came to office in January, 1953, Communist influence in the Middle East was at a low ebb, and the area was more free of violence than it had been in years.

Things changed.

Secretary of State Dulles began by giving General Naguib—Colonel

Nasser's predecessor—a pistol as a personal gift from President Eisenhower. The fateful symbolism of this gift was not lost upon Israel or the Arab states. It was the token of a new policy called "impartiality" between the Arab states, on the one hand, and, on the other, the new democracy of Israel whom they had vowed to destroy and whom we and the United Nations were pledged to defend.

Following this, and pursuing the new policy of trying to build up Nasser as a bulwark of stability in the Middle East, the United States pressured the British to evacuate their great military base along the Suez Canal without making any provision for international control of the canal.

Then Mr. Dulles fanned the flames of ambition, nationalism and rivalry in the Middle East with the so-called Baghdad Pact as a defense against Russia. But its military advantages were far outweighed by its political disadvantages. And it was particularly offensive to Nasser—the very man whom we had been trying to build up.

Then in 1955 Colonel Nasser's negotiations for some arms from the United States bogged down in everlasting haggling. And so he negotiated an arms deal with the Communists.

We not only failed to stop the introduction of Communist arms into the Middle East, but we refused to assist Israel with arms too. We also refused to give Israel a guarantee of her integrity, although we had given such guarantees to others.

And in the meantime we dangled before Colonel Nasser the prospect of financial aid for building a great dam on the Nile.

In time, the bankruptcy of the Eisenhower administration's policy began to become evident even to Mr. Dulles. It became clear that Colonel Nasser was not a bulwark of stability, but a threat to peace in the Middle East. Thereupon President Eisenhower abruptly and publicly withdrew the aid he had led Colonel Nasser to expect.

As anyone could have foreseen, Colonel Nasser promptly retaliated by seizing the Suez Canal.

Driven by our policy into isolation and desperation, Israel evidently became convinced that the only hope remaining was to attack Egypt before Egypt attacked her. So she took her tragic decision.

Here we stand today. We have alienated our chief European allies. We have alienated Israel. We have alienated Egypt and the Arab countries. And in the UN our main associate in Middle Eastern matters now appears to be Communist Russia—in the very week when the Red Army has been shooting down the brave people of Hungary and Poland. We have lost every point in the game. I doubt if ever before in our diplomatic history has any policy been such an abysmal, such a complete and such a catastrophic failure.

IV. VIEWS OF OBSERVERS

SELECTION IV–A

Herman Finer is professor of political science at the University of Chicago
and a vigorous critic of Dulles' Middle Eastern policies. This excerpt is
from his book, *Dulles over Suez* (Chicago, 1964), pp. 491–95. Copyright
© 1964 by Herman Finer. Reprinted by permission of Quadrangle Books,
Inc.

Dulles's Suez diplomacy must now be appraised by the standards of
America's national interests and of the moral obligation which she, like
every person or nation, owes to civilization.

At the very outset, it must be emphasized that it was not Dulles who
waged war in Suez and Sinai, but Britain, France, and Israel. The losses in
world power and economic well-being suffered by Britain and France as a
result of their military action were not Dulles's direct fault. But that does not
by any means end the lesson. For their action was from the beginning, to a
very substantial extent, demonstrably impelled and shaped by Dulles's foreign policy and diplomatic methods. His allies trusted him to work for their
reasonable benefit. Considerable blame for the injurious results of the Suez
affair is clearly imputable to Dulles, because, from July 19, 1956, he was
of his own will a principal, even *the* principal, decision-making person in the
train of events leading to war.

Dulles is entitled to credit for certain of his announced purposes, even if
they were failures in practice. He persevered for weeks to find a just and
viable solution to the specific conflict over the Suez Canal seizure. His ingenuity, forensic gifts, diplomatic eloquence, and tenacious moral character
almost succeeded, but Nasser's despotic ambitions and aggressive imperi-
ousness defeated his efforts. He sought to fortify the Rule of Law in world
politics (or in "world opinion"), and therefore employed his talents in up-
holding the U.N. Charter. Some applaud Dulles for having avoided an
atomic war with the Soviet Union, one that might have begun with a mere
clash of ground forces and then have been "escalated." Others laud him for
his befriending of the anticolonial forces, so, it is suggested, attracting to
the U.S.A. the gratitude and good will of the Afro-Asian peoples. Finally, it
is claimed, he compelled the British and French to realize their position of
subordinacy in world politics—as interpreted by the United States, which
must be the principal, even the dominating, power throughout the world.

THE DEFICIENCIES OF DULLES'S SUEZ POLICY

If, for the sake of argument, we accept the wisdom and nobility of Dulles's
purposes, the question arises how serious he and President Eisenhower were

in espousing them and what they were sincerely prepared to pay to secure their fulfillment. Another consideration is the weight they attached to each purpose in relation to the others. Dulles's actual policy and personal conduct largely contributed to his allies' desperation and political and military defeat and to the magnification of Nasser's power.

Dulles first erred in not protesting with adequate vigor against the Egypto-Soviet arms deal of 1955. Without a single stern word, he indulgently allowed Nasser to open to Russia a foothold in the world of the Arab and African nations, when he well knew that one of the motives for Britain's wish to remain in the Suez base was precisely to block an enemy's road into Africa.

Then, if Dulles had not offered the Aswan loan, would Nasser have had occasion to seize the Canal? It would have been better to signal the displeasure the Administration felt at Nasser's dangerous ambitions. Dulles again erred in revoking the offer of a loan in so brusque and insulting a manner. He lacked the foresight—the sovereign talent of the statesman—to apprehend an act of violence by Nasser, well known to be a desperado. The ignorance or, perhaps, want of concern certainly demonstrated insensitivity to the dangers that threatened his allies. He gave Nasser an excuse to seize the Canal in hot blood.

The Canal seized, Dulles was without a policy to follow through and make Nasser "disgorge." When he rather belatedly realized that Nasser had contemptuously dragged him, through his allies, to the "brink of war" (supposed to be a favorite location of Dulles's), Dulles acted swiftly to avert a possible military retort by Britain and France. These nations were the victims who bore the brunt of Dulles's myopia and Nasser's radical violence. They could, Dulles knew, invoke the right of self-defense to make war against Nasser's kind of delict. He exaggerated the imminence of military action, to indulge his own conceit as a potent maestro of world political savoir-faire, and to secure leverage over the American public and Congress and President Eisenhower. He tried to defer the approaching First London Conference, but Eden and Mollet insisted on an early session: they, not Dulles, had invented the idea of such a conference, although he tried to claim sole credit for it.

Thenceforward, Dulles did not tell his allies, precisely, candidly, or comprehensively, what America's Suez policy was, above all, whether it absolutely excluded their use of force. He and Eisenhower, in public and private utterances, left open the corollary that if all the peace-seeking conferences failed, force could not be excluded, indeed, would be justified. At the end of July, Dulles became what he had been denouncing as immoral in June, a neutral. He avoided the exertion of any available nonviolent pressures on Nasser to enforce just restitution on him, and he was terrified by the destructive possibilities of any act of war. War outraged his moralism on this occasion, if not when he had proposed it over Indo-China in 1954. War threatened him and the President with a loss of reputation as the vindicators of the United Nations and as men of peace. These pacific feelings were acutely intensified because the President was a candidate for a second term in the election of November 6, 1956. While Dulles in public paraded the idea of the economic attrition of Egypt, he was acknowledging in private that it could not possibly be effective in view of the primitiveness of the Egyptian economy. At any rate, he did not even try it.

From the instant Britain and France showed fight, Dulles was fear-stricken by two factors in the situation: the military power of the Soviet Union, and the impact that internationalizing Suez might have on America's status in the Panama Canal. About the first, he was misled by his own prejudices regarding Soviet politics in the world arena; he was overterrified. About the second, Panama, he preferred to deflect to his allies the anger of "colonial" nations by pampering these so that they temporarily forgot Panama. However, his allies were bitterly antagonized by his sermons against their "colonialism." For they knew quite as well as Dulles what he was hiding about Panama, and the Suez issue was not colonialism, even if it suited Dulles to pretend that it was while he was abandoning them. The Suez conflict was due to the rapacious violation of treaties for reasons of Egyptian national grandeur, as Dulles himself repeatedly asserted. But, taken to the brink of war, Dulles puffed out an iridescent smoke screen, false and irrelevant, about "anticolonialism." It was good for votes in the U.N.; it outbid the Soviet Union; it obscured Panama; it depressed his allies. But Panamanians were absorbing his arguments.

His diplomatic virtuosity was at its brightest at the First London Conference. But his triumph, the eighteen-power proposal, was brought by public, specific, and clear official American commitments to uphold British and French legal and political rights in Suez against Nasser. His allies were entitled to believe he intended to honor these commitments. He then made the critical mistake of refusing to lead the mission to Cairo which was to present the proposal to Nasser.

When the British and French, and especially Sir Anthony Eden, sincerely and urgently proposed to appeal to the United Nations, while there was still some fluidity in Nasser's *fait accompli,* Dulles obstructed the move. Instead, he constrained them (because he had *force majeure*) to accept a kind of stopgap, the Suez Canal Users' Association. He was fully conscious of the fact that the plan was unworkable, because it contained no means of compelling Nasser to accept it. Dulles promised it would make a "dry ditch" of the Canal. He knew quite well that to boycott the Canal was the only "teeth" the Association might have, but when Nasser threatened war if the Association tried to have its ships pass through the Canal, Dulles, in panic, dropped the "teeth." He had no genuine plans to help his allies economically on his avowed road to peace and justice. The allies concluded that Dulles had beguiled them by prevaricating persuasions into the morass of SCUA to win time and deflate their expectations of justice, and so they further lost faith in his sincerity, friendship, and clarity of mind.

Dulles had never entirely excluded the use of force by his allies; but neither had he clearly explained to them the actions the U.S.A. would be compelled to undertake to carry out the Tripartite Declaration or the stand it would take in the United Nations, if they did use force. Nor did he ever suggest that the Administration would arraign them or impose direct American economic punishment on them. He and the President negligently left them guessing with far too much room for miscalculation. This is not a wise practice for the strongest party in an alliance.

Dulles more and more came to look like a friend of Nasser's and an enemy of his allies. His Ambassador to Cairo advised and encouraged Nasser to keep the Canal operating smoothly. Dulles repeatedly refused to stop American-owned ships from paying tolls to Nasser, though he simultaneously made lusty announcements that Nasser must be made to feel the economic pinch. He did not prevent American citizens from taking jobs as pilots for the Egyptian Suez Canal Authority, the legality of which he had denied.

When the delays and detours used by Dulles to edge his allies into renunciation of their just claims had made them unbearably heartsick, they appealed to the United Nations. He still tried to obstruct their appeal, rather than bring discipline to bear on Nasser. Desperation forced them to override his objections. He could hardly do other than support their Six Principles regarding the future status of the Canal, for they were substantially his very own, pronounced by him in public for weeks. But he almost simultaneously subverted the moral strength of his allies by denouncing "colonialism" and linking the smear to the Suez dispute! He then pretended that his inimical slur was only a "blunder" of the tongue, but they suspected and very soon after verified that his hostility was deliberate. He was buying prestige and an easy life at their expense.

Dulles still pretended optimism when the Soviet Union vetoed the Six Principles and their administrative-political implementation. His oft-proclaimed injunction that without justice there could be no peace was derisively flouted before his very nose, by Nasser and Nasser's friends.

During all these weeks, and in the preceding years he had held office, Dulles neglected to cope firmly with the imperialistic mischief perpetrated by Nasser's agents in Jordan, Syria, Iraq, and Israel. He pretended reliance on the United Nations, while knowing it was unjust and powerless. He failed to concert, with Eden, planned prophylactic measures, before a hot-war crisis should occur, to implement the Tripartite Pact.

Whatever one may think of the wisdom and expediency of making war on Egypt, there was hardly left to Britain, France, and Israel any alternative to such a course except surrender to Nasser, once Dulles's timid and tortuous diplomacy had delayed, confused, and weakened them. He underestimated their tenacity and under-valued their national interests and their concern for their national dignity, while overindulging Nasser's corresponding interests and concern. The Suez war having broken out, because his own proposals had been flouted by Nasser (with Moscow and Belgrade in support), Dulles allowed his personal indignation and his personal moral proctorship to govern the foreign policy of America. He totally abandoned a feasible insistence on a constructive settlement of the issues that had caused the outbreak of war. He was abjectly intimidated by the seething passions of the Afro-Asian nations, transmitted to him by Henry Cabot Lodge, whose own personal susceptibilities amplified their hysteria. Dulles's intellectual and spiritual pride and colossal self-righteousness drove him into a morally indefensible role, for he evoked the Rule of Law as the world's hope while he and the President (the latter soon with some reluctance) clandestinely subdued Britain, France, and Israel with mortal economic sanctions. Behind his public appeals for "a decent respect for the opinions of mankind," Dulles was motivated by overt and covert panic before Russian power. He seems, also, to have been intimidated by Dag Hammarskjold's even more powerfully pious personality, as though he, too, was Dulles's confessor.

SELECTION IV–B

In this excerpt from "Eden, Dulles and Collusion," the British journalist Ian Gilmour responds to the charges against Dulles made by Eden in his memoirs. He blames the former prime minister for the division of the allies in 1960. Reprinted by permission of *The Spectator*, 204 (February 5, 1960), pp. 167–68.

"Had the Americans considered," Sir Anthony asked Admiral Radford, "the effect [of using force] on world opinion?" Sir Anthony was refering to the Dulles policy over Indo-China in 1954; Mr. Dulles might easily have asked Sir Anthony the same question two years later, over Suez (possibly he did). There is, in fact, an obvious similarity between the two crises; and it has been strikingly illustrated in the Eden memoirs which have been appearing as a serial in *The Times*.

Eden was against war over Indo-China. Dulles was against war over Suez. Over Indo-China Eden was solidly backed by British opinion and by a large segment of American opinion; over Suez Dulles was solidly backed by American opinion and by a large segment of British opinion—in both crises, in other words, the man working for a peaceful solution led a coalition composed of his own country and a substantial part of the other country. On both occasions the "falling domino" argument was used in favour of military action—i.e., if the Chinese (Egyptians) got away with it over Indo-China (Suez) then the whole Far East (Middle East) would fall to the Chinese (Egyptians). The language and arguments used by Dulles over Indo-China were similar to those used by Eden over Suez; and the arguments Eden used over Indo-China refute those he was later to use over Suez.

    .   .   .   .

One obvious difference between Indo-China and Suez is that whereas Eden was in no way responsible for the first crisis, Dulles bears a heavy responsibility for the second. Sir Anthony says that the British Government had, like the American Government, decided not to proceed with its offer of help to finance the Aswan Dam, but that he was not consulted on either the timing or the terms of Dulles's announcement of the American refusal. There is little doubt that Dulles's action rankled, and was an important factor in Anglo-American friction throughout the crisis. Dulles, for his part—to judge from the fact that he continued his South American visit after he heard about the nationalisation of the Canal Company, and only abandoned it after receiving a message from his envoy in London—was less alarmed by what President Nasser had done than by what Britain and France proposed to do in reply.

Sir Anthony says that, to begin with, Dulles and Eisenhower "did not rule out the use of force . . . but felt that every possibility of peaceful settlement must be exhausted before this was done." This sort of sentiment could be expressed about almost any international dispute; whether Eisenhower and Dulles seriously meant that in the absence of direct provocation by Egypt force might be used is doubtful. Dulles was certainly going through an anti-Nasser phase or he would not have dealt with the Aswan question in the way he did, but it is probable that in August, as in September and October, he thought force was not a suitable way of resolving the crisis, and that in talking about the use of force he was merely being conciliatory to his allies, never seriously envisaging military action.

Dulles also fell in with his allies' wishes over international control of the Canal, and presented their proposals at the first London Conference. This was probably his only big mistake in the crisis (apart, of course, from having caused it in the first place). There was never more than the thinnest chance that Nasser would accept these proposals. And if he did not, what then? Either Britain and France would use force, to which Dulles was opposed, or they would have to retreat into a possible negotiating position. But by that time Eden had converted the crisis into a prestige contest between himself and Nasser, so that retreat would not be easy. Dulles would have been better advised to have refused to commit himself to the Western proposals, and to have attempted to persuade the British and French to agree to the Indian plan, which was almost certainly acceptable to Egypt. He made a mistake, therefore; but it lay less in failure to co-operate with his allies than in an excess of co-operation with them.

Once Egypt had turned down the London proposals Dulles, who wanted a peaceful settlement, had to think of some other expedient to avoid force being used. But to Eden, who did not want a peaceful settlement except on his own terms, any such expedient was useless unless it would provide an excuse for war. For Dulles, negotiations in the UN and elsewhere were an alternative to force; for Eden they were an obstacle to it.

From as early as September 3, when President Eisenhower told him that American opinion was dead against force, Eden had the choice between working for a peaceful settlement in conjunction with America and of going to war without her. Faced with a similar situation over Indo-China Dulles decided to respect the wishes of his ally. Eden decided differently.

．　　　　．　　　　．　　　　．　　　　．　　　　．　　　　．　　　　．　　　　．　　　　．

The essential difference, then, between the two crises is that in the first Eden succeeded in restraining Dulles; in the second Dulles failed to restrain Eden. Like Eden two years before, Dulles "was determined that [he] should not endorse a bad policy for the sake of unity." His tactics were probably mistaken. He tried to gain time by humouring Eden and Mollet, and only suceeded in exasperating them. A firm refusal from the start to countenance the Anglo-French idea of using force would have been more effective. Nevertheless, even from Sir Anthony's account, Dulles, for all his deviousness, emerges as much the more responsible statesman of the two. In the last resort he was prepared to draw back, to contain his frustrations, and to pay attention to the views of his weaker ally. Eden two years later was not prepared to draw back, he allowed his frustrations full rein, and not only did he not heed his much more powerful ally, he double-crossed her. Yet it is Eden, with an exact reversal of the true roles reminiscent of Ahab's accusation of Elijah, who now says of Dulles "such cynicism between allies destroys true partnership."

SELECTION IV–C

M. A. Fitzsimons, professor of history at the University of Notre Dame, and editor of *The Review of Politics* is the author of "The Suez Crisis and the Containment Policy." This portion of that article is reprinted by permission from *The Review of Politics*, XIX (October, 1957), pp. 419–21; 444–45.

Since 1947 the major foreign policy of the United States government has been containment. This policy of creating situations of strength which would prevent the extension of Communist power and influence in the world was first proclaimed in the Truman Doctrine (March 12, 1947). The policy had been anticipated in 1946 when the battleship *Missouri* visited Turkey and some forty Mediterranean ports. In the course of this display the *Missouri* was joined by two aircraft carriers, seven cruisers, and eighteen destroyers. The early sensitivity to Soviet threats to the Middle East and its approaches, revealed in the Doctrine and that naval demonstration, was not consistently maintained at this time or later. Perhaps, indeed, American foreign policy only operates with fullest energy, when directly confronted with a serious Soviet threat. At any rate, it may be argued that for the period 1946–1955, when the Soviet Union was neither conspicuously active nor influential in the Middle East, United States policy contributed little to the solution or easing of the area's all but intractable problems. So to describe the problems is to propose a good excuse, but they were the problems, and, unfortunately, they did not wither from neglect or incantations.

The containment policy, which eventually took many forms, including recovery and technical assistance programs, and treaties and pacts, was often criticized for being negative, for unduly emphasizing military considerations, for a constricting obsession with Communism, for concentrating on the periphery rather than the core of Communist strength, and for encouraging heavy commitments to unsatisfactory regimes. It has engendered many debates, and evoked promises of a new liberation policy. But, so far, these debates and promises have ended in nothing more substantial than the affirmation and extension of the containment policy.

The relative consistency with which the policy has been maintained by the Eisenhower administration is all the more remarkable because of the greatly quickened pace of internationally significant events since the death of Stalin in March 1953. The Korean Armistice, Soviet explosion of a thermonuclear bomb, two major Geneva Conferences, the grim extension of the North African challenge to France, the Austrian Peace Treaty crowd the ensuing thirty months. But 1956 is the year of change intruding upon change. Khrushchev's famous speech on the crimes of the Stalin era and the ensuing play of change and reversals in the Communist world mark one current. Another current swelled in the Middle East culminating in the Anglo-French-Israeli attack on Egypt. The two currents converged briefly in the last weeks of October and the first weeks of November. From those hectic days and the joining of issues came an exegesis of the liberation policy, which in effect equated it with containment. In the Middle East the consequence was much the same, the Eisenhower Doctrine, a serious but limited adaptation of the containment policy to the conditions and temper of the Middle Eastern states. This reiteration of the containment policy and the history of our recent policies in the Middle East suggest two conclusions: the first is that the containment policy in a minimum way corresponds to the realities of our interests and the range of our means to protect them in the present world; and the second is that the containment policy, as originally drawn up with its emphasis on adroitness, flexibility, and vigilance, has not been consistently maintained. The policy requires continuity, if it is to be effective; it cannot simply be used sporadically and only for the acute manifestations of crisis. The containment policy was drawn up for what was correctly diagnosed as a long-term crisis.

The enunciation of the Eisenhower Doctrine marked the debut of the United States as the Western power with major responsibility for the Middle East. When the British and French forces failed to seize the Suez Canal quickly in early November and complying with a United Nations resolution ceased their military action, the Middle East became a major American foreign policy problem. The United States faced a sobering and inescapable responsibility. Earlier, the presence of Britain had permitted the United States on occasion to lurk in the wings or even to appear as the good, mediating friend of the Arabs. The crash of Eden's and Mollet's charade of strength denied such opportunities to future American policy. The Middle Eastern problems, hitherto apparently insoluble and now made more dangerous by Soviet influence, became a primary American concern.

.   .   .   .

American policy has been based on action in the United Nations and on the approach made in the Eisenhower Doctrine. The first aspect appears in President Eisenhower's letter to the Israeli Foreign Minister, Mrs. Golda Meir, written after she had informed the United Nations General Assembly that Israel would withdraw its troops from Gaza and the Gulf of Aqaba, if the United Nations Emergency Force took over there; "I believe, however, that Israel will have no cause to regret having thus conformed to the strong sentiment of the world community as expressed in the various United Nations resolutions relating to withdrawal." When this Presidential trust, and the large American commitments it vaguely implies, are confronted with the record of the past, the judgment of *The Times* was more plausible: "Events have moved back nearer to the old and familiar dangers and uncertainties, with only a few hundred U.N. soldiers as a screen—for how long?"

The Eisenhower Doctrine, presented as a resolution for Congressional approval, expressed the determination of the United States to use its armed forces in behalf of any Middle Eastern state which requested "such aid against overt armed aggression from any nation controlled by international communism." Such employment of United States forces would have to be in accord with the treaty obligations of the United States, and, as a consequence of recent American policy more important, with the Charter of the United Nations and its recommendations. Moreover, such employment would have to be reported to the Security Council, whose authority and responsibility to take action in behalf of international peace and security were recognized. This military measure was accompanied by plans for a crash program of economic assistance to the Middle Eastern states, a program designed to make the Doctrine more persuasive to them.

This was a seriously limited version of the containment policy. The limits were imposed by the temper of the Middle Eastern states and recent American policy. Here, the legalism of American policy coincided, at least temporarily, with the views of the anti-colonial states. Perhaps, in the future, this containment policy will be developed with the continuity, vigilance, adroitness, and flexibility that it requires. Perhaps, too, after the Hungarian Revolution starkly revealed liberation as a meaningless but dangerous alternative, the containment policy will be recognized not as a negative policy but as a responsible attempt in a long-term crisis to erode the Iron Curtain and ultimately to revise the grim territorial outlines of the Cold War.

The new Eisenhower policy has had initial success in Jordan. Indeed, the new Eisenhower policy is likely to appeal to the heads of such states as Saudi Arabia, Libya, Lebanon, and Iraq. Apart from the special case of Lebanon, this means that the policy is likely to be an obstacle to Arab revolutionary nationalism. That force, then, is likely for some time to continue to be hostile to the West, and responsive to Soviet foreign policies. But the policy, limited as it is, is an indication of serious intent, and with the accompanying economic aid has momentarily stiffened the anti-Communist forces in the Middle East. This point about the necessity of a serious gesture was made by the former American Ambassador to Egypt, Jefferson Caffrey, in his testimony before the joint Senate Committee hearing on the Eisenhower Doctrine—an interesting reflection on American policy in the preceding year.

For the future, the United States has gambled heavily on the United Nations and placed a burden on that organization which may yet put its very existence at stake. In spite of the professions of American policy and the very grave dangers in the use of force, is it likely that the United States, if faced by a dire threat to its vital interests, will refrain from the use of force, and trust its interests to the dictates of the conscience of the United Nations?

10

SPUTNIK DIPLOMACY

Disengagement in Europe 1955–60

I. EDITORIAL INTRODUCTION

The panic over the future of Europe aroused in NATO circles by the crisis in Korea had subsided with the vigorous rebuilding of a NATO military structure in the early 1950's. NATO's reorganization had begun effectively with the appointment of General Eisenhower in 1951 as Supreme Commander of forces in Europe and culminated in the accession of a partially rearmed Germany to NATO in 1955. Even though the fifty divisions promised at the Lisbon Conference of the NATO Council in 1952 never fully materialized the United States and its allies had assembled a sophisticated military machine by the middle of the decade which appeared able to cope with Soviet attack on any member of the alliance. If the deterrent of the allies' conventional weapons was not sufficient as a deterrent, the implied threat of American nuclear weapons employing massive retaliation reinforced it. In any event, Soviet responses to NATO's power in Europe were limited to the establishment of a counter-NATO in the Warsaw Pact as major communist attention turned to other parts of the world in this period. However, success did not bring the sense of security the allies had hoped for. First, the entry of Germany into the alliance, even as a limited partner, awakened old fears in eastern and western Europe which the Soviet Union skillfully exploited. By the same token, admission of Germany into NATO hardened the division of the Germanies despite Adenauer's promise to West Germans that NATO's strength would bring unification to Germany. Second, the rapid development of Soviet nuclear weaponry, signalized by the Russian explosion of the nuclear bomb in 1949, came to a dramatic climax with the 1957 success of the Soviet Sputnik, an earth satellite that America feared would dominate the world from outer space. Accompanied by the development of rocket artillery, it was expected that the ICBM (Intercontinental Ballistic Missile) would make the United States as vulnerable to Soviet attack as the Soviet Union was to American strikes with the installation of medium-range missile bases in western Europe. Thus a "balance of terror," to use Churchill's term, might negate an atomic war, but it might also undermine the American atomic deterrent underpinning NATO and thus expose Europe to the still real dangers of conventional warfare. Third, the leadership of the Soviet Union had changed with the death of Stalin in 1953, and once the struggle for succession had been completed the new leadership under Khrushchev appeared more flexible and to some observers more reasonable in the exercise of power. But the new reasonableness posed dangers of its own. Where Stalin's rigidity at least had cemented the NATO allies, the flexibility of Khrushchev permitted the latter to exploit the schisms within the alliance of conciliatory talk of banning atomic weapons and by threats over the future of Berlin.

The changed situation in Europe and the increased dangers of nuclear warfare produced new debates over American policy. The willingness of President Eisenhower to attend summit conferences from Geneva, to Camp David, to Paris between 1955 and 1960 suggests American hopes of an accommodation based on a nuclear stalemate. But American initiative was not matched by a clear Soviet response. While the Russians undoubtedly recognized the possibilities of mutual suicide in the event of war, their genuine or pretended fear of Germany induced them to exact too high a price for a detente. Their price was simply the demilitarization of Germany which—they announced to the world—was a modest proposal to end the division of the country, forestall German revanchism feared by all Europeans, and remove the most likely arena of nuclear warfare in which the western world and Soviet world directly confronted each other.

The major Soviet diplomatic offensive based on fear of nuclear war was the Rapacki Plan of 1958, proposed to the United States by the Polish foreign minister, Adam Rapacki, centering on the establishment of a denuclearized zone in Central Europe. The plan called for the removal of American and Soviet forces from positions of contact, but on terms highly favorable to the communist bloc. (Selection II–A.) The American response, while appropriately diplomatic in attributing the highest motives to the Polish proposal rejected the Rapacki Plan. The Plan omitted too much that was essential to genuine denuclearization, such as a system of inspection of existing nuclear stocks and a plan for discontinuing production of nuclear weapons. Less directly, but with equal clarity, the United States criticized the plan for its implicit removal of America's presence from Europe while the Soviet Union remained a menacing neighbor in the East to a Germany still divided. (Selection II–B.)

A major propaganda advantage of the Rapacki Plan, not matched by

Eisenhower's "Open Skies" plan of aerial reconnaissance, was its ability to exploit a debate that had been begun in the West. In the fall of 1957 influential Western voices were raised to promote the aims if not the spirit of the Rapacki Plan: namely, the need for the world to recognize that nuclear warfare would mean world disaster, that there would be no winners in such a contest. The most influential of all the spokesman was George Kennan, the retired American ambassador and father of the containment philosophy, who asserted in a widely publicized series of radio addresses from London in the fall of 1957 that the Soviet challenge had changed its form, and that the nuclear escalation of forces in Europe was not only unnecessary but suicidal. If there was any hope in the future, it lay in "separating geographically the forces of the great nuclear powers." NATO would continue to offer guarantees, but the primary dangers would be from internal communist elements, not from an external Soviet attack. (Selection III–A.)

From a former partner in the translation of containment from theory to fact came a strong rebuttal of Kennan's recommendations which reflected the views of official Washington. Dean Acheson warned America against relaxation of the Cold War with the Soviet Union, and pointed in particular to the exposed position of Germany. Withdrawal of American forces would lead to the removal of other troops and to the demise of NATO. The consequences would be the sacrifice of West Berlin and the neutralization of Germany, to the point where it would be a satellite in the Soviet system. (Selection III–B.)

The perplexities arising from NATO's problems were well illustrated in the collapse of the summit conference of 1960, when Khrushchev attempted to use the U–2 aerial reconnaissance of Soviet territories from European and Asian bases to humiliate the United States and to advance the Soviet claims of being the true supporter of world peace. To President Eisenhower, Russian behavior was the reason for "spy planes." If the Soviet Union genuinely feared a nuclear holocaust, why did it not accept the inspection system which would have made the U–2 unnecessary? Why did it attempt to raise tensions by threats over the status of Berlin? In his report to the nation after the failure in Paris in 1960, he exposed the instability in Soviet behavior which continued to make it a threat to peace, but at the same time repeated the American belief that underlay the appeal of the disengagement idea: namely, that "in a nuclear war there can be no victors—only losers. Even despots understand this." (Selection III–C.)

Outside government circles, but not very far outside, were observers from academic life, many of whom had been enlisted by various branches of government into advisory and occasionally policymaking roles in foreign affairs. Henry A. Kissinger of Harvard was one of this group. He was an articulate critic of both massive nuclear retaliation and of disengagement as answers to NATO's problems. Disengagement would be a moral as well as military failure if it should stimulate the Soviet Union to the very actions it intended to avert, while strategic nuclear warfare increasingly lacked credibility because of its destructive potential. The way out of the dilemma in his view was to proceed with negotiations but to maintain force, preparing for a limited war in which nuclear weapons could serve tactical purposes. The deterrent would thereby be restored. (Selection IV–A.)

Lincoln Gordon, another Harvard scholar with a distinguished record of government service, agreed in general with Kissinger's diagnosis that NATO was not properly geared to the realities of a nuclear age. But he wondered if the NATO nuclear shield as Kissinger conceived it would do much to avert disaster. It could be only a partial deterrent. Gordon was convinced that the imperatives of the late 1950's demanded closer, more convincing efforts of cooperation from NATO partners on every level to maintain the status quo in Europe. (Selection IV–B.)

Four years after the initial crisis over "disengagement," Chicago political scientist Robert E. Osgood concluded that disengagement would have compromised an essential condition of the security of the NATO allies: namely, the belief in the Soviet mind created by NATO that an attack on one member would engage every ally. "The neutralization of Germany and the withdrawal of American and other NATO troops could not help but weaken this belief." The chief dangers to NATO would be psychological rather than military, a situation that could be averted only if the nations in the zone of withdrawal had the "political capacity and internal stability to withstand Soviet blackmail." (Selection IV–C.)

It is worth noting that the issue of disengagement received more attention than almost any other problem in the late 1950's as the inadequacy of both disengagement and exclusive reliance on nuclear weapons became apparent. It is also worth noting that Eisenhower's administration ended without resolution of this dilemma.

II. DOCUMENTS

SELECTION II–A

The Rapacki Plan is outlined in this excerpt from the note of February 14, 1958 from the Polish Foreign Minister to U. S. Ambassador Jacob Beam (Rapacki Plan). Department of State *Bulletin*, XXXVIII (May 19, 1958), pp. 822–23.

MEMORANDUM

On October 2, 1957, the Government of the Polish People's Republic presented to the General Assembly of the United Nations a proposal concerning the establishment of a denuclearized zone in Central Europe. The governments of Czechoslovakia and of the German Democratic Republic declared their readiness to accede to that zone.

The Government of the Polish People's Republic proceeded with the conviction that the establishment of the proposed denuclearized zone could lead to an improvement in the international atmosphere and facilitate broader discussions on disarmament as well as the solution of other controversial internal issues, while the continuation of nuclear armaments and making them universal could only lead to a further solidifying of the division of Europe into opposing blocks and to a further complication of this situation, especially in Central Europe.

In December 1957 the Government of the Polish People's Republic renewed its proposal through diplomatic channels.

Considering the wide repercussions which the Polish initiative has evoked and taking into account the propositions emerging from the discussion which has developed on this proposal, the Government of the Polish People's Republic hereby presents a more detailed elaboration of its proposal, which may facilitate the opening of negotiations and reaching of an agreement on this subject.

I. The proposed zones should include the territory of: Poland, Czechoslovakia, German Democratic Republic and German Federal Republic. In this territory nuclear weapons will neither be manufactured nor stockpiled, the equipment and installations designed for their servicing would not be located there; the use of nuclear weapons against the territory of this zone would be prohibited.

II. The contents of the obligations arising from the establishment of the denuclearized zone would be based upon the following premises:

1. The states included in this zone would undertake the obligation not to manufacture, maintain nor import for their own use and not to permit the location on their territories of nuclear weapons of any type, as well as not to install nor to admit to their territories of installations and equipment designed for servicing nuclear weapons, including missiles' launching equipment.

2. The four powers (France, United States, Great Britain, and U.S.S.R.) would undertake the following obligations:

(A) Not to maintain nuclear weapons in the armaments of their forces stationed on the territories of states included in this zone; neither to maintain nor to install on the territories of these states any installations or equipment designed for servicing nuclear weapons, including missiles' launching equipment.

(B) Not to transfer in any manner and under any reason whatsoever, nuclear weapons nor installations and equipment designed for servicing nuclear weapons—to governments or other organs in this area.

3. The powers which have at their disposal nuclear weapons should

undertake the obligation not to use these weapons against the territory of the zone or against any targets situated in this zone.

Thus the powers would undertake the obligation to respect the status of the zone as an area in which there should be no nuclear weapons and against which nuclear weapons should not be used.

4. Other states, whose forces are stationed on the territory of any state included in the zone, would also undertake the obligation not to maintain nuclear weapons in the armaments of these forces and not to transfer such weapons to governments or to other organs in this area. Neither will they install equipment or installations designed for the servicing of nuclear weapons, including missiles' launching equipment, on the territories of states in the zone nor will they transfer them to governments or other organs in this area.

The manner and procedure for the implementation of these obligations could be the subject of detailed mutual stipulations.

> SELECTION II–B
>
> On May 3, 1958 the Ambassador to Poland, Jacob D. Beam, delivered the U.S. reply to the Rapacki plan. Ambassador Beam handed the U.S. note to Polish Deputy Foreign Minister Jozef Winiewicz. A portion of this note has been reprinted from the Department of State *Bulletin*, XXXVIII (May 19, 1958), pp. 821–22.

EXCELLENCY: I have the honor to acknowledge the receipt of Mr. Rapacki's note of February 14, 1958, enclosing a memorandum elaborating on the Polish Government's proposals concerning the establishment of a denuclearized zone in Central Europe.

Recognizing that the initiative of the Polish Government stems from a desire to contribute to the attainment of a stable and durable peace, my Government has given these proposals serious and careful consideration. On the basis of this study it has concluded that they are too limited in scope to reduce the danger of nuclear war or provide a dependable basis for the security of Europe. They neither deal with the essential question of the continued production of nuclear weapons by the present nuclear powers nor take into account the fact that present scientific techniques are not adequate to detect existing nuclear weapons. The proposed plan does not affect the central sources of power capable of launching a nuclear attack, and thus its effectiveness would be dependent on the good intentions of countries outside the area. The proposals overlook the central problems of European security because they provide no method for balanced and equitable limitations of military capabilities and would perpetuate the basic cause of tension in Europe by accepting the continuation of the division of Germany.

An agreement limited to the exclusion of nuclear weapons from the territory indicated by your Government without other types of limitation would, even if it were capable of being inspected, endanger the security of the Western European countries in view of the large and widely deployed military forces of the Soviet Union. Unless equipped with nuclear weapons, Western forces in Germany would find themselves under present circumstances at a great disadvantage to the numerically greater mass of Soviet troops stationed within easy distance of Western Europe which are, as the Soviet leaders made clear, being equipped with the most modern and destructive weapons, including missiles of all kinds.

The considerations outlined above have caused the United States in association with other Western Powers to propose that nations stop producing material for nuclear weapons, cease testing such weapons and begin to reduce present stockpiles. The United States has further proposed broader areas of inspection against surprise attack, including an area in Europe, roughly from the United Kingdom to the Ural mountains. We remain willing to do this. You will recall, moreover, that the Western nations offered at the London disarmament negotiations to discuss a more limited zone in Europe. With regard to missiles you will recall that over a year and a half ago the United States proposed that we begin to study the inspection and control needed to assure the exclusive peaceful use of outer space now threatened by the development of such devices as intercontinental and intermediate range ballistic missiles.

The United States, in association with other Western Powers, has also proposed that a comprehensive and effective European security arrangement be established in conjunction with the reunification of Germany. The proposed arrangements would provide for limitations on both forces and armaments, measures for the prevention of surprise attack in the area, and assurances of reaction in the event of aggression.

Your note speaks of the existence of opposing military groupings in Central Europe as being responsible for tensions in the area. It should not be necessary for me to recall that the present division of Europe stems primarily from the decision of the Soviet Union not to permit Eastern European nations to participate in the European Recovery Plan. Nor need I repeat the many assurances given as to the defensive character of the North Atlantic Treaty Organization which is reflected in its entire organizational and command structure. The entire history of its creation and development testify to this, though persistent efforts are made in some quarters to portray it otherwise.

III. VIEWS OF PARTICIPANTS

SELECTION III—A

George Kennan who had formerly served as Director of the Policy Planning Staff of the Department of State and also as Ambassador to Moscow, was a member of the Institute for Advanced Studies at Princeton in 1957. His series of Reith lectures presented over the BBC at this time were incorporated in his book.

The following selection is taken from pp. 60—65, *Russia, the Atom and the West* (New York: 1958) by George F. Kennan. © 1958 by George F. Kennan. Reprinted by permission of Harper & Row, publishers.

I am aware that similar warnings against the introduction of the atomic weapon into the armaments of the continental countries have also recently been part of the stock-in-trade of Soviet diplomacy. I cannot know what the motives of the Soviet Government have been in taking this position. I certainly cannot say that they have all been ones we could respect. But I think we must beware of rejecting ideas just because they happen to coincide with ones put forward on the other side. Moscow says many harmful and foolish things; but it would be wrong to assume that its utterances never happen to accord with the dictates of sobriety and good sense. The Russians are not always wrong, any more than we are always right. Our task, in any case, is to make up our minds independently.

Is there, then, any reasonably hopeful alternative to the unpromising path along which we are now advancing? I must confess that I see only one. This is precisely the opposite of the attempt to incorporate the tactical atomic weapon into the defense of Western Europe. It is, again, the possibility of separating geographically the forces of the great nuclear powers, of excluding them as direct factors in the future development of political relationships on the Continent, and of inducing the continental peoples, by the same token, to accept a higher level of responsibility for the defense of the Continent than they have recently borne. This is still a possibility. Close as we are to it, we have not yet taken the fatal step. The continental countries have not yet prejudiced their usefulness for the solution of continental problems, as we have ours, by building their defense establishments around the atomic weapon. If they could be induced to refrain from doing this, and if there could be a general withdrawal of American, British and Russian armed power from the heart of the Continent, there would be at least a chance that Europe's fortunes might be worked out, and the competition between two political philosophies carried forward, in a manner disastrous neither to the respective peoples themselves nor to the cause of world peace. I would not know where else this chance is to be looked for.

I am aware that many people will greet this suggestion with skepticism. On the Continent, in particular, people have become so accustomed to the thought that their danger is a purely military one, and that their salvation can be assured only by others, that they rise in alarm at every suggestion that they should find the necessary powers of resistance within themselves. There is a habitual underestimation among these peoples of the native resources of Europe. The Western Europe of 1957 reminds me of the man who has grown accustomed to swimming with water wings and cannot realize that he is capable of swimming without them.

It is plain that in the event of a mutual withdrawal of forces, the continental NATO countries would still require, in addition to the guarantees embodied in the NATO Pact, some sort of continuing local arrangements for their own defense. I am free to admit that for this purpose their existing conventional forces, based on the World War II pattern, would be generally inadequate. These conventional forces are designed to meet only the least likely of the possible dangers: that of an outright Soviet military attack in Europe, and then to meet it in the most unpromising manner, which is by attempting to hold it along some specific territorial line. All of this is obviously futile. If this were the problem, then of course foreign assistance would be needed, although it is questionable whether it could ever be enough.

But this is not the problem. We must get over this obsession that the Russians are yearning to attack and occupy Western Europe, and that this is the principal danger. The Soviet threat, as I have had occasion to say before, is a combined military and political threat, with the accent on the political. If the armed forces of the United States and Britain were not present on the Continent, the problem of defense for the continental nations would be primarily one of the internal health and discipline of the respective national societies, and of the manner in which they were organized to prevent the conquest and subjugation of their national life by unscrupulous and foreign-inspired minorities in their midst. What they need is a strategic doctrine addressed to this reality. Under such a doctrine, armed forces would indeed be needed; but I would suggest that as a general rule these forces might better be paramilitary ones, of a territorial-militia type, somewhat on the Swiss example, rather than regular military units on the World War II pattern. Their function should be primarily internal rather than external. It is on the front of police realities, not on regular military battlefields, that the threat of Russian Communism must primarily be met. The training of such forces ought to be such as to prepare them not only to offer whatever overt resistance might be possible to a foreign invader but also to constitute the core of a civil resistance movement on any territory that might be overrun by the enemy; and every forethought should be exercised to facilitate their assumption and execution of this role in the case of necessity. For this reason they need not, and should not, be burdened with heavy equipment or elaborate supply requirements, and this means—and it is no small advantage—that they could be maintained at a fraction of the cost per unit of the present conventional establishments. I am inclined to wonder whether this concept could not well find application even as things are today, and in the absence of any Great Power withdrawal.

I would not wish to make a fetish of this or to suggest any sweeping uniform changes. The situations of no two NATO countries are alike. There are some that will continue to require, for various reasons, other kinds of armed forces as well. I mean merely to suggest that if there could be a more realistic concept of the problem and the evolution of a strategic doctrine more directly addressed to the Soviet threat as it really is and not as we have imagined it, the continental countries would not be as lacking in the resources or means for their own defense as is commonly assumed.

Let me reiterate that the primary purpose of the dispositions would be not the defense of the country at the frontier, though naturally one would aim to do whatever could be done in this respect, but rather its defense at every village crossroads. The purpose would be to place the country in a position where it could face the Kremlin and say to it: "Look here, you may be able to overrun us, if you are unwise enough to attempt it, but you will have a small profit from it; we are in a position to assure that not a single Communist or other person likely to perform your political business will be available to you for this purpose; you will find here no adequate nucleus of a puppet regime; on the contrary, you will be faced with the united and organized hostility of an entire nation; your stay among us will not be a happy one; we will make you pay bitterly for every day of it; and it will be without favorable long-term political prospects." I think I can give personal assurance that any country which is in a position to say this to Moscow, not in so many words, but in that language of military posture and political behavior which the Russian Communists understand best of all, we have little need of foreign garrisons to assure its immunity from Soviet attack.

SELECTION III–B

The following article is from "The Illusion of Disengagement," excerpted by special permission from *Foreign Affairs,* XXXVI (April, 1958). Copyright by the Council on Foreign Relations, Inc., New York.

Dean Acheson, a private citizen in 1958, reacted sharply to George Kennan's plea for disengagement as expressed in the latter's Reith lectures over the radio in the fall of 1957. He feared the combination of Kennan's prestige and message would dangerously weaken NATO morale. It should be emphasized, however, that Kennan proposed the disengagement of Soviet as well as American forces from the heart of Europe.

The evils of a timid and defeatist policy of retreat are far deeper than its ineptness as a move in the propaganda battle. It would abandon the efforts of a decade, which are bringing closer to realization the hopes of Western

Europe, of Germany, and of Eastern Europe as well. From the low point
of 1946–1947 the economic, social and political health and strength of
Western Europe—of which West Germany has become an integral and vital
part—have grown greatly. Their pull on Eastern Europe continues to mount.
To continue this the American connection is essential. The success of the
movement toward unity in the west of Europe is no longer in doubt. Only
the rate of progress is undecided. The Coal and Steel Community, Euratom,
the Common Market have been accepted. A common currency and political
community are on the way.

All of this is threatened by the call to retreat. It will not do to say that a
united Germany, made militarily impotent and neutralized, can play an
effective part in bringing to fruition a united and vigorous European community. The slightest puff of reality blows this wishful fancy away. The
jockeyings and tensions of the two parts of Germany, the unopposable
threat of Russian power, the bribes which can be dangled before Germany
by the Soviet Union in the form of boundary rectifications and economic
opportunities—these alone are enough to put an end to hope of a united and
strong Europe, invigorated by Germany.

For those who believe that Eastern Europe would welcome American and
Russian troop withdrawals as the beginning of liberation, I suggest a quiet
sampling of candid Polish opinion. I venture to predict that what they
would find is a horror at being abandoned by the West and left between the
Soviet Union and a Germany similarly abandoned, to which the offer of
another partition of Poland might be irresistible.

But, if one looks at the other side of the medal, what a different face it
bears! A strong, united Europe could have the men and the resources—
along with British and United States contingents—to deal by conventional
forces with invasion by conventional forces, particularly as the Eastern
European satellites are becoming a danger, and not an asset, to Soviet military power. This, if pressed, gives real mutuality of benefit to a negotiated
reduction in forces. It makes possible, too, a time when nuclear forces would
no longer have to be relied on as a substitute for conventional forces, and
with it a real opportunity to negotiate this threat further and further into
the background.

Finally, a thriving Western Europe would continue its irresistible pull
upon East Germany and Eastern Europe. This would, in turn, have its effect
upon the demands of the Russian people on their government. With a rise
in the standards of living in the Soviet Union, and as some broader participation in the direction of affairs was made essential by their very magnitude
and complexity, the Russian need for the forced communization and iron
control of Eastern Europe would diminish. Then negotiations looking toward
a united Germany, under honorable and healing conditions, and toward the
return of real national identity to the countries of Eastern Europe, while
preserving also the interests of the Russian people in their own security

and welfare, could for the first time be meaningful and show the buds of hope. This has been the goal of Western policy for the past decade.

It would be self-delusion to close our eyes to the difficulties which lie before us along this road. Some we have created ourselves. Our military strategy, with its sole reliance on massive retaliation, and a budgetary policy which has neglected even that, have caused us a lot of relative military power and of prestige. Some of our political policies have weakened our alliances. Our allies, too, are having their troubles. In what are perhaps the two closest of them, we could wish (as they undoubtedly do, too) that both the present and the immediate future held greater promise for the development of strength and popular attitudes more attuned to reality. We all share together the common problem of devising a military policy for NATO which will avoid making the proposed defense seem as fearsome as the potential enemy's threat, and which will be a real deterrent because it is a credible one.

I have suggested elsewhere that this is possible. Briefly, the way is to create a situation in fact which equals the political purpose of the North Atlantic Treaty—that is, a situation where in order for the Soviet Union to attack, or coerce, Europe it would have to attack, or coerce, the United States as well. This, if we all use a fair degree of intelligence about our defenses, the Soviet Union could be deterred from doing. What is required is a short-range effort which does not preclude a sustained effort toward a wiser long-range goal. The short-range effort would be to provide NATO with such effective nuclear power that the Soviet Union could not have its way without destroying that power; and an attempt to destroy it would be impractical apart from a simultaneous attempt to disable the United States, which could be made too dangerous. The longer-range purpose would be to develop adequate conventional forces in Europe, with British and American participation, to make mutually desirable a real reduction and equalization of both Soviet and NATO forces and a controlled elimination of nuclear material for military use.

I quite understand that all of this is difficult. But I believe also that "the mode by which the inevitable comes to pass is effort."

> SELECTION III–C
>
> This excerpt, taken from the Department of State *Bulletin,* XLII (June 6, 1960), pp. 900–902, is a portion of the address on the collapse of the summit conference in Paris on May 25, 1960 as it was presented by President Eisenhower in his report to the nation on television and radio.

Aerial photography has been one of many methods we have used to keep ourselves and the free world abreast of major Soviet military developments. The usefulness of this work has been well established through 4 years of effort. The Soviets were well aware of it. Chairman Khrushchev has stated that he became aware of these flights several years ago. Only last week, in his Paris press conference, Chairman Khrushchev confirmed that he knew of these flights when he visited the United States last September.

Incidentally, this raises the natural question—why all the furor concerning one particular flight? He did not, when in America last September, charge that these flights were any threat to Soviet safety. He did not then see any reason to refuse to confer with American representatives.

This he did only about the flight that unfortunately failed, on May 1, far inside Russia.

Now, two questions have been raised about this particular flight: first, as to its timing, considering the imminence of the summit meeting; second, our initial statements when we learned the flight had failed.

As to the timing, the question was really whether to halt the program and thus forgo the gathering of important information that was essential and that was likely to be unavailable at a later date. The decision was that the program should not be halted.

The plain truth is this: When a nation needs intelligence activity, there is no time when vigilance can be relaxed. Incidentally, from Pearl Harbor we learned that even negotiation itself can be used to conceal preparations for a surprise attack.

Next, as to our Government's initial statement about the flight, this was issued to protect the pilot, his mission, and our intelligence processes, at a time when the true facts were still undetermined.

Our first information about the failure of this mission did not disclose whether the pilot was still alive, was trying to escape, was avoiding interrogation, or whether both plane and pilot had been destroyed. Protection of our intelligence system and the pilot, and concealment of the plane's mission, seemed imperative. It must be remembered that over a long period these flights had given us information of the greatest importance to the Nation's security. In fact, their success has been nothing short of remarkable.

For these reasons, what is known in intelligence circles as a "covering statement" was issued. It was issued on assumptions that were later proved incorrect. Consequently, when later the status of the pilot was definitely established and there was no further possibility of avoiding exposure of the project, the factual details were set forth.

I then made two facts clear to the public: First, our program of aerial reconnaissance had been undertaken with my approval; second, this Government is compelled to keep abreast, by one means or another, of military activities of the Soviets, just as their Government has for years engaged in espionage activities in our country and throughout the world. Our necessity to proceed with such activities was also asserted by our Secretary of State, who, however, had been careful—as was I—not to say that these particular flights would be continued.

.   .   .   .

And now, most importantly, what about the future?

All of us know that, whether started deliberately or accidentally, global war would leave civilization in a shambles. This is as true of the Soviet system as of all others. In a nuclear war there can be no victors—only losers. Even despots understand this. Mr. Khrushchev stated last week that he well realizes that general nuclear war would bring catastrophe for both sides. Recognition of this mutual destructive capability is the basic reality of our present relations. Most assuredly, however, this does not mean that we shall ever give up trying to build a more sane and hopeful reality—a better foundation for our common relations.

To do this, here are the policies we must follow, and to these I am confident the great majority of our people, regardless of party, give their support:

First. We must keep up our strength, and hold it steady for the long pull —a strength not neglected in complacency nor overbuilt in hysteria. So doing, we can make it clear to everyone that there can be no gain in the use of pressure tactics or aggression against us and our allies.

Second. We must continue businesslike dealings with the Soviet leaders on outstanding issues, and improve the contacts between our own and the Soviet peoples, making clear that the path of reason and common sense is still open if the Soviets will but use it.

Third. To improve world conditions in which human freedom can flourish, we must continue to move ahead with positive programs at home and abroad, in collaboration with free nations everywhere. In doing so, we shall continue to give our strong support to the United Nations and the great principles for which it stands.

Now as to the first of these purposes—our defenses are sound. They are tailored to the situation confronting us.

Their adequacy has been my primary concern for these past 7 years— indeed throughout my adult life.

In no respect have the composition and size of our forces based on or affected by any Soviet blandishment. Nor will they be. We will continue to carry forward the great improvements already planned in these forces. They will be kept ready—and under constant review.

Any changes made necessary by technological advances or world events will be recommended at once.

This strength—by far the most potent on earth—is, I emphasize, for deterrent, defensive, and retaliatory purposes only, without threat or aggressive intent toward anyone.

IV. VIEWS OF OBSERVERS

> *SELECTION IV–A*
>
> From Henry A. Kissinger, "Missiles and the Western Alliance." Excerpted by special permission from *Foreign Affairs*, XXXVI (April, 1958), pp. 392–96. Copyright by the Council on Foreign Relations, Inc., New York. Kissinger, professor of government at Harvard and Director of Harvard's Defense Studies Program, was a leading critic of both massive retaliation and disengagement. His concern was in large measure with the tactical employment of missiles and atomic weapons.

The real argument about missile installations in Europe thus turns less on the nature of the weapon than on the strategy which underlies it. Before any real progress can be made in NATO strategy, *all* allies will have to realize that their increasing vulnerability causes the threat of all-out war to become an increasing obstacle to decisive action. The chief bar to the development of an effective NATO strategy has been reluctance to accept the fact that some of the most likely challenges in Europe, if not dealt with locally, are not likely to be dealt with at all. Our European allies have been unwilling to face the prospect of a local defense because they have been unwilling to make the effort it requires and because they feared that, once they admitted the possibility of less than all-out American participation, we might withdraw altogether. We in turn have been prevented from pressing the issue of local defense party by the absolutism of our own military doctrine and partly by the fear that to do so would weaken the confidence of our allies.

But this evasion of reality can become demoralizing. A mere commitment to all-out defense will only create an impasse if no partner is prepared to face the consequences. Our allies have a right to insist on American participation in their defense; they should not be permitted to prescribe a course of action which involves the most catastrophic risks, the more so if this strategy reduces their willingness to resist the most likely challenges. A local deterrent in Europe is required to increase the range of our options, and to bring the deterrent policy of NATO into line with the strategy it is prepared to implement. A strategy of local defense is essential not as a device to save the alliance—though it will serve this purpose; rather, the alliance alone offers the possibility of a strategy which does not inevitably involve catastrophe.

If European missile forces are to be designed primarily for local deterrence, they should not be under United States but under NATO control, and they should fit the requirements of local defense. The retaliatory force for all-out war must be able to inflict the greatest amount of devastation in a minimum of time. Accuracy here is less important than power and range. A deterrent force for local defense, on the other hand, should be able to apply its power with discrimination and in such a manner that a settlement can be reached before the situation gets out of hand. And, above all, it should seek maximum mobility.

It is possible to launch a retaliatory force of manned planes at the first warning of an attack; planes can always be called back if the alarm turns out to be false. The decision to launch a missile, however, is irrevocable. Therefore it is essential that a strategy based on missiles shall find some way of understating the response. The more invulnerable missile installations are made, the more possible it becomes to reduce the danger of misinterpretation. If missile installations cannot be destroyed, the side which is on the defensive can delay its counterblow until the enemy has struck and thus avoid acting on a surmise which may prove false.

This is particularly important in the case of missiles for local defense, which must minimize by all means available the danger that local resistance will produce an all-out war by miscalculation. Accuracy and mobility are therefore prime requisites for such a missile system. Accuracy is necessary to permit a discriminating application of power; mobility is needed to reduce the vulnerability to surprise attack. NATO should therefore strive to create a missile system which can be moved by motor, a major part of which is constantly shifting position. Submarines, and to a lesser extent surface ships, provide another form of ideal mobile launching site. Both destructiveness and range should be sacrificed to accuracy and mobility, for the purpose of NATO missiles is not primarily to destroy the Soviet homeland but to pose risks out of proportion to any gains Soviet forces might make in Europe. Even an 800-mile or 1,000-mile missile would prove highly useful in posing such a threat, even though it could not be decisive in an all-out war—and perhaps because of it. The very fact that missile installations in Europe could not destroy Soviet retaliatory power would be a guarantee of their defensive intent.

Thus the proposed missile installations and nuclear weapons will add to European security, provided they are accompanied by a meaningful European effort and provided we do not gear our own military establishment exclusively to an all-out strategy. The prime issue in NATO is not missile sites, much less the degree to which the United States is dependent upon them. The basic problem is to elaborate an effective NATO strategy. The worrisome aspect of the current United States defense budget is that strategic power is once more purchased at the expense of the capability for local defense. The disquieting aspect of much of European comment about NATO is the refusal to accept the reality that maximum security can no longer be purchased at minimum cost. If NATO cannot develop a real capability for local defense, disengagement may become inevitable. But this should not cause rejoicing among our critics, for under present conditions it would mean the end of Europe's influence on world affairs.

What, then, of the theory of disengagement? How about the proposals for a neutral belt or a zone free of nuclear weapons?

It is easy to sympathize with the motives behind the "disengagement theory." As long as two large military establishments face each other in the center of Europe, so the argument goes, the danger of an incident that might spark a conflagration is ever present. Another argument maintains that the establishment of a neutral belt is the quid pro quo which might bring about a withdrawal of Soviet forces from the satellite states and thus permit a more normal evolution of the Communist régimes there. Disengagement is desirable, according to this theory, because NATO as now constituted is not capable of stopping a full-scale Soviet attack, and thus increases tensions without providing security. Finally, disengagement is said to be essential as a means of reassuring the Soviet Union about the sincerity of Western intentions.

The immediate difficulty with these arguments is that they run counter to the entire experience of the postwar period. Where Western and Communist forces face each other directly incidents have been rare and the few that have occurred (such as the Berlin blockade) have not benefited the Soviet Union; the risks are so enormous that both sides generally go to great lengths to forestall clashes wherever they can control events. By contrast, Soviet encroachments have almost always occurred where resistance seemed feeble or impossible. The only case of overt Communist aggression, after all, followed an American attempt to "disengage" itself in Korea and would probably not have occurred otherwise. And the arguments that NATO is both dispensable and a threat to Soviet security are clearly inconsistent with each other. No level of NATO military strength now in prospect will be able to fight an offensive war against the Soviet Union.

We must also take account of the possibility that the Soviet Union is more interested in negotiating about disengagement than in achieving it. Once negotiations were entered upon, it is more than likely that the expectation of disengagement would effectively demoralize NATO planning and undermine any military effort on the Continent. And we can be virtually certain that there will be endless evasions and delays so that the Soviet Union might well achieve one of its prime objectives by default—the dismantling of NATO without any concessions on its part.

That the Soviet Union is more concerned with achieving strategic preponderance than in reducing tensions is shown by the only proposal for disengagement that the Soviet Union has put forward—the Rapacki plan for a zone in Central Europe from which nuclear weapons would be banned. Acceptance of the Rapacki plan would not remove the Soviet nuclear threat from Central Europe, for even short-range Soviet missiles can reach much of Western Europe from Soviet territory. Because our whole strategy is dependent on nuclear weapons, it *would* lead to the withdrawal of *all* American forces from Central Europe. And the precedent having once been established, tremendous pressures would be mounted to exclude nuclear weapons from all of Europe including Great Britain. Since there is no prospect of arresting a Soviet advance without nuclear weapons, a non-nuclear zone in Central Europe would not only create a vacuum in which Soviet conventional strength would predominate but would destroy the balance of forces on which Western Europe's security depends. For ultimately NATO would be so weakened that withdrawal of the American military establishment from the Continent would be almost certain.

This situation would not be changed fundamentally by a simultaneous withdrawal of American and Soviet forces from the center of Europe and the creation of a "neutral belt." Soviet forces would withdraw only 600 miles, within easy missile range of Central Europe, while American forces, for the reasons outlined above, would cross the Atlantic. And would the Soviet Union feel less menaced by a neutral armed Germany than a Germany integrated in the Western Alliance and restrained by the collective interests of the NATO countries? Germany unaligned may be forced by domestic pressures to push its claims to the Eastern territories to the limit. Alternatively, an *un*armed neutral Germany would increase tensions by creating a vacuum at the very point at which the great Powers are competing most bitterly.

Instead of adding to stability, the consequences of a neutral belt may thus make a tense situation even more explosive. A major purpose of the neutral belt is declared to be to permit a more favorable evolution within the satellite orbit. A withdrawal of Soviet forces may, however, turn a long-smoldering resentment into open revolution. Yet Khrushchev has declared repeatedly that the "socialist achievements" in the satellite orbit are sacrosanct, that the Soviet Union would always lend "timely assistance to a fraternal socialist state"—in short, that the U.S.S.R. stands prepared to suppress any upheaval that threatens local Communist régimes. Indeed, neutralization may actually present liberalization in the satellite countries, for only with Russian troops can the Soviet rulers feel confident of controlling the situation. The presence of Soviet forces provides assurance that change will not go beyond tolerable limits. If Russian troops are withdrawn, on the other hand, the Soviet leaders may calculate that they must resist *any* change however small, lest it set in motion a series of events they are no longer able to control.

Thus disengagement invites a variety of new dangers while reducing the forces to meet them. It is not a safe but a daring policy, and it makes sense only if we are ready to prevent the crushing of satellite revolutions. Otherwise it will assure only a temporary withdrawal of Soviet forces from Central Europe, with every likelihood of their return after the American military establishment on the Continent has been dismantled and Europe has been rendered defenseless. A policy of disengagement which has no answer, political or military, to the problem of upheavals in the Soviet satellite orbit, or to the return of Soviet forces under another pretext, is likely to bring about the very conditions it seeks to avoid. Its results will be either a demonstration of Western impotence and irresolution or all-out war.

This is not to say that the withdrawal of American forces from the center of the Continent can never be considered. But the proper context will be European strength not weakness, one in which NATO possesses the capability to pose a significant deterrent to Soviet aggression within Europe. The flexibility so frequently demanded requires a much greater and more sustained effort throughout the Western Alliance. The cause of much of NATO's rigidity is not, as so often alleged, too great concern with military factors, but unwillingness to face the full implications of these factors.

SELECTION IV-B

An excerpt from Lincoln Gordon's "NATO in the Nuclear Age," *The Yale Review*, XLVIII (March, 1959), pp. 333–35. Copyright 1959 by Yale University. Reprinted by permission of *The Yale Review*. Lincoln Gordon, now president of Johns Hopkins University, had been a member of Harvard's faculty and had been United States Ambassador to Brazil.

For the United States, the basic issue which permeates all these discussions is whether our military association with Europe is a mere temporary aberration, arising from the combination of European economic weakness in the late 1940's with a passing need for overseas bases for medium-range aircraft, or whether that association reflects a real and lasting community of interests as durable as the Soviet (or Sino-Soviet) threat which called NATO into being. Kennan's instinct is clearly to look for a withdrawal of American power from Europe on the ground that the United States is "not a European power." Moore likewise argues in effect that a better integrated Europe should come to take care of its own defense, coupled in a very loose partnership with its trans-Atlantic Allies. To my mind, these attitudes are profoundly mistaken. The increase in Soviet capabilities and self-confidence, the continuing shrinkage of distances, the political and economic revival of Europe, and the growing complexity of weapons technology should all serve to reinforce the Atlantic community of interest and the case for even closer military integration within NATO as a whole.

In specific terms, this question bears on the continuance of military assistance to Europe and the continued stationing of American forces there. Why, it is often asked, does American military assistance to Europe continue in the face of Europe's spectacular economic recovery? The answer is simple. The fact is that such assistance has been substantially reduced, and its proportion to Europe's own defense efforts has become progressively smaller.

Britain and Germany for some years have been paying cash for any arms supplied from this country, and when the Algerian problem is somehow resolved, France should be able to do likewise. This leaves the main dollar cost of continuing military assistance directed to the poorer countries, Greece, Turkey, Italy, and Portugal, whose economic base will be inadequate for a long while to come, and to the Scandinavian countries, where small populations are responsible for large areas of great strategic importance. Beyond this, military assistance is not so much a one-way flow as an American contribution to joint projects of infra-structure, production, or research and development—mutual security endeavors in the literal sense. The continuing need for economy of effort among the NATO partners suggests that this type of endeavor should be permanent. There is no reason why it should not involve European supplies of certain specialized weapons to American forces as well as the reverse.

As to the stationing of forces, so long as adequate strategic reserves are maintained in this country for unpredictable brush-fire outbreaks in any part of the world, it should be regarded as an advantage, rather than an aberration, that the NATO Alliance permits us to have a portion of our ready forces constantly at the front line in by far the most significant region of the world bordering on the Sino-Soviet bloc. This does not suggest for a moment that we should be doing Europe's defensive job for it, and it is a heartening sign after many years of frustration and delay to see a substantial German contribution to NATO defense finally coming into being. The challenge, which poses no mean task of leadership and negotiation, is to make the Allied efforts complementary and additive rather than alternative. Apart from their strictly military role, the political and psychological value of these American forces in serving as a daily reaffirmation of the cohesion of the Alliance is a Western defensive asset of enormous value.

Is there any end in sight to the costly prescriptions for strategy suggested above or to a European *status quo* which gives great cause for satisfaction west of the Iron Curtain but is painfully unsatisfactory on the eastern side and which certainly contains some precarious elements of instability? In the short run, the simple answer would appear to be "no." Why should we look for favorable change in a period when Soviet power, economic, military, and technical, has been advancing far more rapidly than that of the West and when Soviet political influence has been penetrating hitherto untouched areas? These are scarcely conditions conducive to an open Soviet recognition of their abysmal political failure in Eastern Europe.

We in the West must hope for an ultimate recognition of this failure as a consequence of domestic strains and changes, increasing comprehension by the Kremlin of the genuinely nonaggressive intentions of the West, and appreciation of the fact that non-Communist regimes on the Soviet borders are not necessarily a threat to the Soviet regime itself. If this takes as long as for "shrimps to learn to whistle," we had best simply reconcile ourselves to that fact. But if there is any hope of advancing that day, it surely lies in the calm and resolute pursuit of a collective strategy which is well within our means, which is less costly than any visible alternative, and which is far less dangerous.

SELECTION IV–C

The following passage is excerpted from Robert E. Osgood, *NATO: The Entangling Alliance* (Chicago, 1962), 316–20, 346. Reprinted by permission of The University of Chicago Press. Robert E. Osgood, formerly a Research Associate of the Center for the Study of American Foreign and Military Policy, is presently a member of the staff of the Washington Center of Foreign Policy Research.

In our preoccupation with the military requirements of containment, reinforced by the oversimple analogy we tend to draw between the problem of containing the Soviet Union and containing Hitler's Germany, we tend to forget that countervailing military power projected abroad by formal commitments to protect territorial boundary lines is only one factor among a variety of non-military factors that may account for the deterrence of aggression. The image of the Soviet Union being restrained from occupying every piece of territory near its borders that is not already under the domination of the Red Army solely by the fear of military resistance or nuclear reprisals is a great oversimplification of the complex motives that actually guide the policy of a regime which by ideology and experience is acutely sensitive to the political and psychological conditions of national power.

Nevertheless, it would be foolhardy for nations who have a choice to intrust their security entirely to non-military deterrents or to ignore the political and psychological conditions of security that depend upon the mere existence of a certain balance of military strength and upon expectations about when and how armed force might be used. In this respect, it is apparent that a withdrawal of foreign troops from the center of Europe would directly contravene the conditions of allied security that previous chapters have discussed.

One essential condition of allied security is the belief which NATO creates in the Soviet mind that one member cannot be attacked without involving the Soviet Union in a war with all members and, especially, with the United States. The neutralization of Germany and the withdrawal of American and other NATO troops could not help but weaken this belief. The withdrawal of foreign forces from the forward line would render Germany more dependent upon the deterrent effect of the West's strategic nuclear power while reducing the credibility of that deterrent in both Soviet and non-Soviet eyes. The Eastern European states, which the United States has clearly considered beyond the sphere of interest that she would protect at the risk of war, would be far more isolated and vulnerable than the Western European states were before the establishment of NATO.

The corrosive impact of disengagement upon the credibility of the American commitment to defend Western Europe, let alone Eastern Europe, would be especially severe if American forces withdrew from the Continent altogether. Perhaps this complete withdrawal would not be inevitable. The insistence of General Norstad and other American military authorities that withdrawal from the Continent would be necessary because of the great expense and difficulty of relocation and the lack of space for realistic training and maneuvers may, as Michael Howard suggests, be due to "the very natural reluctance of men who have spent nine years in creating a complex and expensive organization to contemplate dismantling their creation and going through the whole business again," rather than to insurmountable obstacles. The presence of a few American divisions in France and the Lowlands, although foreign troops are never completely welcome anywhere for long, should not prove politically unacceptable, if the host countries regarded them as the price of securing the overriding advantages of the withdrawal of Soviet troops. Nevertheless, at best, even partial withdrawal would tend to undermine the deterrent and resistance functions that NATO's shield is supposed to perform. Certainly, it would put Germany in an intolerably exposed position unless Soviet forces were withdrawn beyond the Polish-German frontier to the borders of Russia.

Mr. Kennan contended that even if American and British troops were withdrawn from the Continent, Europe would not be less secure militarily:

> We must get over this obsession that the Russians are yearning to attack and occupy Western Europe, and this is the principal danger. The Soviet threat . . . is a combined military and political threat, with the accent on the political. If the armed forces of the United States and Britain were not present on the Continent, the problem of defense for the continental nations would be primarily one of the internal health and discipline of the respective national societies, and of the manner in which they were organized to prevent the conquest and subjugation of their national life by unscrupulous and foreign-inspired minorities in their midst.

These words describe a conception of the requirements of cohesion and security which Kennan and many others considered adequate when the alliance was established, but many things have happened since then to enlarge and complicate those requirements. Most important, the growth of Soviet nuclear striking power has made more urgent the need for ground forces capable of an "intermediate response," and this is not a function which could be performed by the "paramilitary" and civil resistance forces which Kennan originally proposed to substitute for "foreign garrisons." Kennan himself eloquently expressed the reason for this need:

> The beginning of understanding rests, in this appalling problem, with the recognition that the weapon of mass destruction is a sterile and hopeless weapon which may for a time serve as an answer of sorts to itself and as an uncertain sort of shield against utter cataclysm, but which cannot in any way serve the purposes of a constructive and hopeful foreign policy. . . . The suicidal nature of this

weapon renders it unsuitable both as a sanction of diplomacy and as the basis of an alliance. Such a weapon is simply not one with which one readily springs to the defense of one's friends. There can be no coherent relations between such a weapon and the normal objects of national policy. A defense posture built around a weapon suicidal in its implications can serve in the long run only to paralyze national policy, to undermine alliances, and to drive everyone deeper and deeper into the hopeless exertions of the weapons race.

Nevertheless, if the allies remain unwilling to increase the capacity of NATO's shield for conventional resistance, and thereby adopt a suicidal defense posture by default, there is merit in Kennan's judgment that it is more desirable to get the Soviet forces out of Central and Eastern Europe than to retain foreign garrisons in Germany and cultivate a German contribution to NATO for the purpose of opposing them while they remain there. Would Western Europe be any less secure from Soviet aggression than at present if Soviet forces were five hundred miles eastward? Surely Western forces on the Continent could return to their former position in the center of Europe before Soviet forces. Suppose, as Mr. Gaitskell and Mr. Healey proposed, that Germany and the other nations in the zone of withdrawal were armed with substantial conventional forces of their own. Could they not perform the functions of NATO's present shield? Assuming the internal stability of these states and their willingness to combine militarily, their conventional forces could at least prevent infiltration, stop the Russians from making a territorial grab without a major effort, and delay a massive invasion. In fact, such a conventionally armed buffer zone might come closer to providing the kind of intermediate response General Norstad has called for than NATO's present forward line, which seems unable to assume any role between that of a conventional police force and that of a tactical nuclear trip-wire. Militarily, at least, the extra space provided by the buffer zone might compensate for the absence of the integration and joint planning with Western forces that NATO's present forward line enjoys.

However, the crucial consequences of a new military balance under disengagement would be its political and psychological effects. Would the nations in the buffer zone, deprived of their formal connections and the ties of collaboration with Western forces, be able to muster the will and common purpose to withstand Soviet pressure backed by an overwhelming military machine designed to isolate and intimidate them? Even within NATO the security and cohesion of the alliance have come to require more than a mere political guaranty. No political guaranty given by NATO to the states in the zone of withdrawal could compensate for the absence of tangible ties of military collaboration. As Michael Howard has observed, "It is one thing to go to the help of a powerful and integrated alliance capable itself of considerable resistance; it is quite another to help effectively a small power whose neighbors have been bribed or intimidated into neutrality and which would probably be overrun in a few hours." Therefore, again, it would appear that disengagement would be compatible with European security only if the nations in the zone of withdrawal had adequate internal stability and the political capacity to present a common front to Soviet blackmail. But these conditions are not likely to exist, especially during the period of transition from engagement to disengagement.

.　　.　　.　　.　　.　　.　　.　　.　　.　　.　　.　　.　　.

Only if the Soviet Union, pressed by rising unrest in the satellites and thwarted in her ambitions to consolidate Germany under Communist rule, felt compelled to retrench and stabilize her western front in order to contain a threat from Communist China—a contingency that seemed quite remote in 1961—would she be likely to regard the reunification of Germany under comprehensive disengagement as a profitable bargain. But, short of an improbable diplomatic revolution resulting from some such major reversal in Russia's power position, any mutually acceptable disengagement in the center of Europe is virtually precluded.

Yet even if a diplomatic revolution should lead to comprehensive disengagement, this would not eliminate the Communist threat to Europe or the need for NATO to contain it, as long as the Soviet government continued to be moved by a compulsive image of inevitable Western hostility and by a dynamic drive to destroy the centers of Western power. After all, the West's wartime alliance with the Soviet Union did not eliminate that threat. Disengagement would alter—and, in some ways, aggravate—the conditions of tension and conflict in the center of Europe; it would not terminate the cold war. Therefore, insofar as any kind of disengagement is desirable or feasible, it should be viewed as a complement, not as an alternative, to the strategic requirements of allied security and cohesion. In effect, that means that the external and internal strength of NATO is the prerequisite of acceptable disengagement in a general European settlement, just as it is the prerequisite of acceptable engagement in a divided Europe.

11

THE UNITED STATES AND COLONIALISM

The Congo Example

I. EDITORIAL INTRODUCTION

On July 13, 1960, the United States joined with the Soviet Union at the Security Council to call upon Belgium to withdraw its troops from the Congo. (Selection II–A.) The occasion was the mutiny of the Congolese army against its Belgian officers and the consequent return of Belgian troops to protect European lives, all within two weeks of the formal independence of the Congo. At the same time that the United States appeared to support the Congolese charges against Belgium, the Department of State issued a carefully-worded caveat to alert the world that its vote did not imply a condemnation of Belgium's behavior in the Congo. (Selection II–B.) Thus, the Congo crisis of 1960 became a classic example of a dilemma in American foreign policy: the desire to support the worldwide anticolonial movement and the need to placate colonial powers allied with the United States in NATO.

Successive presidential administrations have wrestled with the problem of winning support of the anticolonial world without antagonizing or weakening the present allies in Europe. In older days of isolation and lack of responsibility the United States had been accustomed to identifying itself with various causes of independence and would freely express these sentiments as long as they did not expand into commitments to defend the sovereignty of the oppressed nationalities. Hence, the periodic expressions of sympathy for Greece, Ireland, and Hungary in the nineteenth century, and the Wilsonian principle of national self-determination in the twentieth century.

After World War II America's interests in the newly emerging nations of Asia and Africa became even more important as former colonies became prey to communist influences. This concern accompanied the forging of strong links with western Europe, regrettably the very countries identified with the sins of colonialism and imperialism. If the United States should speak too boldly of its opposition to colonialism, it would have to document its charges and risk offending the sensibilities of its allies and endangering the unity of NATO. Even more serious was the risk the United States took of supporting causes which were communist controlled, or supporting nationalist movements whose weaknesses would make them susceptible to communist influences. Yet, if the United States displayed too much caution, it would lose the friendship of the emerging peoples whose power in the United Nations was increasing throughout the 1950's as new nations were admitted to the world organization. A major element in Soviet propaganda was the identification of the United States, the leader of NATO, as heir of Europe's colonialist tradition. Efforts in the 1950's by Secretary of State Dulles to remind Asians and Africans of America's revolutionary tradition were generally ineffective rebuttals to communist charges.

The most that the United States could achieve were the insulation of Asia or Africa from the Cold War, and a position for itself as an honest broker in the contests between England and India, France and Tunisia, or Belgium and the Congo. It was the latter issue that engaged American energies more than any other in postwar Africa and Asia. Hoping to satisfy both Belgians and Congolese, President Eisenhower pointed to the United Nations as the arena in which the cases of both sides could be fairly heard without bringing Africa into the Cold War. Noninterference in the internal affairs of the Congo could go hand-in-hand with a variety of economic assistance programs for the establishment of a viable society. (Selection III–A.) But noninterference ultimately became massive intervention by United Nations forces as the various schismatic elements in the huge amorphous territory of the Congo asserted themselves. The most successful of them all was Katanga, the wealthiest province, whose Premier, Moise Tshombe, received the covert backing of many Belgians and the overt aid of the powerful Brussels company, the Union Minière du Katanga. As a consequence, the United States was forced to choose between an acceptance of the Tshombe regime, which would have found favor with France and England as well as Belgium, and the continuation of assistance to the United Nations in the hope of creating a central government strong enough to resist communism and to express gratitude to the United States. Under President Kennedy, who as Senator had expressed himself vigorously in favor of American alignment with the emerging nations, the United States chose the cause of the central government. Although the policy risked antagonism with NATO allies and gave unprecedented power to the United Nations, the administration saw only chaos and civil war—and communism—as the alternatives to unification. Assistant Secretary of State for African Affairs G. Mennen Williams drew from American experience with the states of the Confederation to suggest that the United Nations action would do for the Congo what the Constitution did for the United States in 1787. (Selection III–B.)

The result of these efforts was inevitably the left-wing charge of neo-colonialism in which the United States was accused of designs to replace Belgian imperialism with its own influence, using the United Nations as its tool. The same charge was hurled by right-wing critics, and particularly by friends of Belgium concerned about the disregard for the interests of the ally implicit in America's behavior. This view was well expressed by Senator Thomas Dodd of Connecticut who had visited the fighting areas in Katanga. He was convinced that the United States was not only feeding communist-inspired chaos by supporting the incompetent central government but was also committing a crime against Tshombe, the premier of secessionist Katanga, the one true friend of the West in the Congo. (Selection III–C.)

One of the sharpest attacks upon the American support of the United Nations' action against Katanga was that of Arthur Krock of *The New York Times,* writing in 1964 at a time when Tshombe, the exiled rebel, had been called back to form a central government at Leopoldville. Krock regarded the Congo as only an administrative name made to order for chaos while Katanga had been the only province fit for self-government. But American insistence had made the premier a fugitive, and had served to open central Africa to communism. To Krock the sudden State Department acceptance of Tshombe was a cruel irony. (Selection IV–A.)

President Kennedy was dead by the summer of 1964 when Tshombe returned to the Congo, but according to Arthur Schlesinger's account of Kennedy's abbreviated administration, the Congo policy was logical and consistent. True, there were some doubts in the State Department and in the circle of the President's intimates. Schlesinger himself, as a Presidential aide at the time, admitted that he inclined toward the view that "Every nation has a right to its own War of the Roses." It was always possible that the United States had tied itself too closely to a problem that could never be resolved. Yet Kennedy was convinced that the United Nations was the only instrument that could promote unity, and that only unity could stave off disaster. There was even a place for Tshombe once he had withdrawn from his secessionist activities. (Selection IV–B.)

In the problem of the Congo, obviously the Cold War played a vital role in modifying American support of the Belgian ally. Yet, as Lawrence Kaplan pointed out in a review of Belgian-American friction over the Congo the policy of restraining Soviet intervention was not inconsistent with assistance to Belgium's position. Belgium had genuinely surrendered its political control over the Congo before the case went to the United Nations. It shared with the United States a desire for stability in Africa which would ensure an economic relationship that would benefit both the Congo and Belgium. But the Belgian government was unable to allay the world's suspicions that its intervention was part of a neocolonial plot, and the Belgian-owned Union Minière did not help the government by its behavior in the Congo. Where the United States erred was in failing to communicate to the Belgians that it understood their problems and was not courting African good will at their expense. (Selection IV–C.)

II. DOCUMENTS

> ### SELECTION II–A
>
> The following is the text of the Security Council Resolution of July 13, 1960 (U.N. Doc. S/4387)—the Tunisian resolution asking Belgium to withdraw its troops from the Congo. It is taken from the Department of State *Bulletin*, XLIII (August 1, 1960), p. 161.

The Security Council,

Considering the report of the Secretary-General on a request for United Nations action in relation to the Republic of the Congo,

Considering the request for military assistance addressed to the Secretary-General by the President and the Prime Minister of the Republic of the Congo (document S/4382),

1. *Calls upon* the Government of Belgium to withdraw their troops from the territory of the Republic of the Congo;

2. *Decides* to authorize the Secretary-General to take the necessary steps, in consultation with the Government of the Republic of the Congo, to provide the Government with such military assistance, as may be necessary, until, through the efforts of the Congolese Government with the technical assistance of the United Nations, the national security forces may be able, in the opinion of the Government, to meet fully their tasks;

3. *Requests* the Secretary-General to report to the Security Council as appropriate.

> ### SELECTION II–B
>
> On July 14, 1960, the State Department released a statement explaining the American vote at the Security Council in favor of the Tunisian resolution. It is reprinted here as it appeared in the Department of State *Bulletin*, XLIII (August 1, 1960), p. 161.

The United States voted for the Tunisian resolution in spite of its doubts about the wisdom of the first operative paragraph, and we did so because of the vital urgency which we attach to prompt United Nations action to meet the tragic and highly dangerous situation in the Congo.

In voting for this resolution the United States expressly interprets the first paragraph calling upon the Government of Belgium to withdraw its troops as being contingent upon the successful carrying out by the United Nations of the second paragraph, that is, in providing the Government of the Republic of the Congo with the military assistance necessary until national security forces are able to fulfill their task.

The situation we face in the Congo is unique. At the outset of its independence, as power was being passed from the Government of Belgium to the Government of the Republic of the Congo, public law and order collapsed. In these circumstances the United Nations must not contribute to the perpetuation of public disorder by insisting upon the withdrawal of military units capable of assisting in the protection of life and property without establishment of alternate methods to accomplish the task.

The resolution can only be read as a whole in this sense, and it is with this understanding that the United States has supported it.

The United States has confidence that the Government of Belgium will cooperate wholeheartedly with the United Nations along these lines, in accordance with the long tradition which it has of loyal membership in support of the Organization. May I say to the representative of Belgium [Walter Loridan] that he has in fact just this evening made a statement expressing his Government's willingness to withdraw its troops upon introduction of United Nations forces, a statement of Belgium's full cooperation with the United Nations for which the Belgian Government should be congratulated and which reflects credit on the Belgian representative here.

III. VIEWS OF PARTICIPANTS

SELECTION III–A

The following excerpt represents a portion of President Eisenhower's address before the 15th session of the UN General Assembly, September 22, 1960, as it appeared in the Department of State *Bulletin,* XLII (October 10, 1960), p. 551–53.

Mr. President, Mr. Secretary-General, members of the General Assembly, and guests:

The people of the United States join me in saluting those countries which, at this session of the General Assembly, are represented here for the first time. With the admission of new members, mainly from the giant continent of Africa, almost 100 nations will be joined in a common effort to construct permanent peace, with justice, in a sorely troubled world.

The drive of self-determination and of rising human aspirations is creating a new world of independent nations in Africa, even as it is producing a new world of both ferment and of promise in all developing areas. An awakening humanity in these regions demands as never before that we make a renewed attack on poverty, illiteracy, and disease.

Side by side with these startling changes, technology is also in revolution. It has brought forth terrifying weapons of destruction which, for the future of civilization, must be brought under control through a workable system of disarmament. And it has also opened up a new world of outer space—a celestial world filled with both bewildering problems and dazzling promise.

This is, indeed, a moment for honest appraisal and historic decision.

We can strive to master these problems for narrow national advantage, or we can begin at once to undertake a period of constructive action which will subordinate selfish interest to the general well-being of the international community. The choice is truly a momentous one.

Today I come before you because our human commonwealth is once again in a state of anxiety and turmoil. Urgent issues confront us.

A PROGRAM FOR AFRICA

The first proposition I place before you is that only through the United Nations Organization and its truly democratic processes can humanity make real and universal progress toward the goal of peace with justice. Therefore I believe that to support the United Nations Organization and its properly constituted mechanisms and its selected officers is the road of greatest promise in peaceful progress. To attempt to hinder or stultify the United Nations or to deprecate its importance is to contribute to world unrest and, indeed, to incite the crises that from time to time so disturb all men. The United States stands squarely and unequivocally in support of the United Nations and those acting under its mandate in the interest of peace.

Nowhere is the challenge to the international community and to peace and orderly progress more evident than in Africa, rich in human and natural resources and bright with promise. Recent events there have brought into being what is, in effect, a vast continent of newly independent nations.

Outside interference with these newly emerging nations, all eager to undertake the tasks of modernization, has created a serious challenge to the authority of the United Nations.

That authority has grown steadily during the 15 years since the United Nations pledged, in the words of its own charter, "to bring about by peaceful means, and in conformity with the principles of justice and international law, adjustment or settlement of international disputes or situations which might lead to a breach of the peace." And during those years the United Nations successfully supported Iran's efforts to obtain the withdrawal of foreign military forces; played a significant role in preserving the independence of Greece; rallied world resistance to aggression against the Republic of Korea; helped to settle the Suez crisis; countered the threat to Lebanon's integrity; and, most recently, has taken on an even more important task.

In response to the call of the Republic of the Congo, the United Nations, under its outstanding Secretary-General, has recently mounted a large-scale effort to provide that new republic with help. That effort has been flagrantly attacked by a few nations which wish to prolong strife in the Congo for their own purposes. The criticism directed by these nations against the Secretary-General, who has honorably and effectively fulfilled the mandate which he received from the United Nations, is nothing less than a direct attack upon the United Nations itself. In my opinion, he, the Secretary-General, has earned the support and gratitude of every peace-loving nation.

The people of the Congo are entitled to build up their country in peace and freedom. Intervention by other nations in their internal affairs would deny them that right and create a focus of conflict in the heart of Africa.

The issue thus posed in the Congo could well arise elsewhere in Africa. The resolution of this issue will determine whether the United Nations is able to protect not only the new nations of Africa but also other countries against outside pressures.

It is the smaller nations that have the greatest stake in the effective functioning of the United Nations. If the United Nations system is successfully subverted in Africa, the world will be on its way back to the traditional exercise of power politics, in which small countries will be used as pawns by aggressive major powers. Any nation, seduced by glittering promises into becoming a cat's-paw for an imperialistic power, thereby undermines the United Nations and places in jeopardy the independence of itself and all others. It is imperative that the international community protect the newly emerging nations of Africa from outside pressures that threaten their independence and their sovereign rights.

To this end I propose a program which contains five major elements:

First: A pledge by all countries represented at this Assembly to respect the African peoples' right to choose their own way of life and to determine for themselves the course they choose to follow. And this pledge would involve three specific commitments:

To refrain from intervening in these new nations' internal affairs—by subversion, force, propaganda, or any other means;

To refrain from generating disputes between the states of this area or from encouraging them to wasteful and dangerous competition in armaments;

And to refrain from any action to intensify or exploit present unsettled conditions in the Congo—by sending arms or forces into that troubled area, or by inciting its leaders and peoples to violence against each other.

These actions my country—and many others—are now avoiding. I hope this Assembly will call upon all its members to do likewise and that each speaker who follows me to this platform will solemnly pledge his country to honor this call.

Second: The United Nations should be prepared to help the African countries maintain their security without wasteful and dangerous competition in armaments.

United Nations experts are being asked to train the Congo's security forces. If the Secretary-General should find it useful to undertake increased activity in order to meet requests of this nature elsewhere, my country would be glad to join other member states in making essential contributions to such United Nations activity.

More importantly, I hope that the African states will use existing or establish new regional machinery in order to avert an arms race race in this area. In so doing they would help to spare their continent the ravages which the excesses of chauvinism have elsewhere inflicted in the past. If, through concerted effort, these nations can choke off competition in armaments, they can give the whole world a welcome lesson in international relations.

The speed and success of the United Nations in dispatching substantial forces to the Congo should give these states assurance that they can rely on the United Nations to organize an effective response if their security is threatened. This should reduce any pressures on them to raise larger forces than are required to maintain internal security. Thus they would help to free their resources for more constructive purposes.

Third: We should all support the United Nations response to emergency needs in the Republic of the Congo which the Secretary-General has shown such skill in organizing. I hope that states represented here will pledge substantial resources to this international program and agree that it should be the preferred means of meeting the Congo's emergency needs. The United States supports the establishment of a United Nations fund for the Congo. We are prepared to join other countries by contributing substantially for immediate emergency needs to the $100-million program that the Secretary-General is proposing.

Fourth: The United Nations should help newly developing African countries shape their long-term modernization programs. To this end:

The United Nations Special Fund and Expanded Technical Assistance Program should be increased so that in combination they can reach their annual $100-million goal in 1961. The Special Fund's functions should be expanded so that it can assist countries in planning economic development.

The United Nations operational and executive personnel program for making available trained administrators to newly developing countries should be expanded and placed on a permanent basis. The United States is prepared to join other countries in contributing increased funds for this program, and for the Special Fund, and for the United Nations Technical Assistance Program.

The World Bank and International Monetary Fund should be encouraged increasingly to provide counsel to the developing countries of Africa through missions and resident advisers. We should also look forward to appropriate and timely financial assistance from these two multilateral financial sources as the emerging countries qualify for their aid.

Of course, many forms of aid will be needed: both public and private, and on a bilateral and multilateral basis. For this assistance to be most effective it must be related to the basic problems and changing needs of the African countries themselves.

Fifth: As the final element of this program I propose an all-out United

Nations effort to help African countries launch such educational activities as they may wish to undertake.

It is not enough that loudspeakers in the public square exhort people to freedom. It is also essential that the people should be furnished with the mental tools to preserve and develop their freedom.

The United States is ready to contribute to an expanded program of educational assistance to Africa by the family of United Nations organizations, carried out as the Secretary-General may deem appropriate and according to the ideas of the African nations themselves.

One of the first purposes of this assistance, after consultation and approval by the governments involved, might be to establish, staff, and maintain—until these governments or private agencies could take over—institutes for health education, for vocational training, for public administration and statistics, and perhaps other purposes. Each institute could be appropriately located and specifically dedicated to training the young men and women of that vast region, who are now called upon to assume the incredibly complex and important responsibilities inherent in an explosive emergence into nationhood.

If the African states should wish to send large numbers of their citizens for training abroad under this program, my country would be glad to set up a special commission to cooperate with the United Nations in arranging to accommodate many more of these students in our institutions of learning.

These then are the five ingredients of the program I propose for Africa:

Noninterference in the African countries' internal affairs;

Help in assuring their security without wasteful and dangerous competition in armaments;

Emergency aid to the Congo;

International assistance in shaping long-term African development programs;

United Nations aid for education.

SELECTION III–B

G. Mennen Williams, former governor of Michigan, was Assistant Secretary of State for African Affairs in the Kennedy administration. This selection, entitled "The United Nations Plan for the Congo," is taken from the Department of State *Bulletin*, XLV (September 17, 1962), pp. 418–21. It represents the press release of a speech presented by Williams before the Jewish War Veterans national convention at Detroit, August 3, 1962.

Fellow veterans, I am pleased to address a veterans' group today because I want to speak about a country balanced between strife and progress—the Republic of the Congo. I can think of no more timely or more important topic to discuss with you who have experienced past failures to find peaceful solutions.

A United Nations plan for Congo unity was announced on August 20 by Acting Secretary-General U Thant, and its early accepance was indicated by Congolese Prime Minister Cyrille Adoula. Last Friday Robert Gardiner, Chief of the U.N. Operation in the Congo, presented the United Nations plan for uniting that unfortunately divided country to representatives of Katanga Province.

Since its presentation to the Katangese provincial government of Mr. Moise Tshombe, Mr. Adoula announced that his government had studied the Secretary-General's plan and had given its agreement to it. He noted that his government's only criterian for judging the Congo problem was in the context of 14 million human beings aspiring for a better life, and added:

We hope all countries will adopt this view and support in all phases the Secretary-General's plan, which takes into account our observations and is in accord with the Government of the Congo's point of view. If all of these conditions are realized, we do not doubt an era of peace and prosperity would begin for the Congo, which could, in fruitful cooperation with all nations, make its contributions to the international community.

U.S. SUPPORT OF PLAN

Over this past weekend the United States Government also announced its support of the Acting Secretary-General's efforts to reach a settlement in the Congo.

The U.S. announcement pointed out that the U.N. plan offers a reasonable basis upon which Congolese leaders can settle their differences. Our Government said that the plan offers compelling reasons for other nations to lend their support and that statesmanship in the Congo can put that nation on the road to federal unity and progress.

Such progress, the United States concluded, will enable the United Nations and countries like the United States to devote greater resources to economic and technical assistance in the Congo.

It is gratifying to be able to say today that many interested nations have indicated their firm support for the U.N. plan. For example, last weekend, Britain announced its support of the plan, and on Tuesday the Belgian Government issued a statement of support.

While there has not yet been time for an official acceptance of the United Nations plan from the provincial government of Katanga, provision for a federal system of government for the Congo enhances the possibility of its acceptance by Katanga. Evariste Kamba, who handles foreign affairs for Mr. Tshombe, said in a letter to Secretary-General U Thant following his announcement of the plan on August 20 that the plan "contains a number of positive elements." There is considerable reason to hope that Mr. Tshombe will support the plan. On August 1 and August 21 he stated his belief that Katanga was ready to join a Congolese federation.

On the initial evidence, then, we are hopeful that the U.N. plan is the basis for Congolese unity and can put an end to Katanga's secession.

The resolution of this problem is naturally one which the Congolese themselves much achieve. You will recall the United Nations was invited into the Congo by the Congolese Government to assist that new nation in overcoming postindependence disorders, in safeguarding Congolese unity, and in rebuilding the nation's administrative and economic health. The United Nations prevented unilateral Soviet intervention and succeeded to a large extent in keeping order. It has helped maintain Congolese administrative services and assisted in the reestablishment of parliamentary government.

The principal block to Congolese unity and economic progress today is this Katangan problem. Prime Minister Adoula's government was established under orders from Parliament to end this secession, and no Congolese government can long hope to remain in office without demonstrating progress toward this goal. Until this is achieved, Congolese resources, both human and material, will be diverted from the essential long-range task of nation building and economic progress. Until unity is achieved, the threats of chaos and renewed Soviet intervention are ever-present dangers.

We welcome the plan put forth by Acting Secretary-General U Thant because it offers a reasonable way to achieve these goals and head off these dangers.

SEVEN PRINCIPAL POINTS

Because this U.N. plan was not widely publicized at the time of its announcement, I would like to take a few minutes this morning to point out its salient features. There are seven principal points in the U.N. plan:

1. The National Government, after consultation with the provincial governments and interested political groups, will present a federal constitution to the Parliament in September. The United Nations is providing legal experts to assist in drafting this document. Under present law this constitution cannot become law without a two-thirds vote of the Parliament, in which all provinces and parties are represented, plus approval by the provincial assemblies. Under the proposed federal constitution certain powers will be delegated to the National Government. These include:

    a. Foreign affairs.

    b. National defense (other than local police functions).

    c. Customs.

    d. Currency, exchange control, and fiscal policy.

    e. Interstate and foreign commerce.

    f. Taxing powers sufficient for National Government needs.

    g. Nationality and immigration.

    h. Post and telecommunications.

Powers not delegated to the National Government will be reserved to the provincial governments.

2. The National Government, after consultation with the provincial governments and interested political groups, will present to the Parliament a new law to establish definitive arrangements for division of revenues between the National and provincial governments, and regulations and procedures for the use of foreign exchange. U.N. experts also will assist in the preparation of this law.

Until that process is completed, the National Government and Katanga should agree to share revenues, duties, and royalties equally, and all foreign exchange earned by any part of the Congo will be paid to the Monetary Council of the National Government or an agreed-upon institution.

The Monetary Council should control use of all foreign exchange and make available for essential needs in Katanga at least 50 percent of the foreign exchange generated in that province. This provision is of particular importance because upon Congolese independence Katanga generated 50 percent of the Congo's foreign exchange earnings.

3. The National Government will ask the International Monetary Fund to help with a plan for national currency unification, which will be implemented within the shortest possible time.

4. Rapid integration and unification of all military units must be accomplished. A commission composed of representatives from the National Government, Katanga, and the United Nations should prepare a plan within 30 days to go into effect within the following 60 days. Provision is made, however, for the provinces to retain control of their local police forces.

5. There should be a general amnesty.

6. All Congolese authorities—national, state, and local—should cooperate fully with the United Nations in carrying out U.N. resolutions.

7. The National Government should be reconstituted to provide a suitable representation for all political and provincial groups.

The United States Government believes that this program is eminently reasonable and necessary. It provides for full consultation and hearing of interested groups, and the plan provides for democratic approval of the constitution and other laws. We believe that, if prompt action is taken on this plan by all Congolese authorities, it will get the Congo back on the road to a peaceful and viable future.

PEACEFUL REUNIFICATION ESSENTIAL FOR PROGRESS

This, then, is the Congo situation as it stands at this moment. It is delicate; it is difficult; but it is by no means devoid of hope.

In some respects, the current Congo situation is reminiscent of the young, radical America of 1783, when the Dean of Gloucester said:

As to the future grandeur of America and its being a rising Empire under one head . . . it is one of the idlest and most visionary notions that was ever conceived. . . . The mutual antipathies and clashing interests of the Americans, their difference of governments, habitudes and manners, indicate that they will have no center of union and common interest. They never can be united into one compact empire under any species of government whatever. . . .

However, as our Constitution led us to unity and an integrated nation, so the U.N. plan offers a path to peaceful reconciliation of differences in the Congo. And this country has pledged its full support to that plan.

Today I want to call on you and all other Americans to back your country's support of the United Nations on this important issue. I know you share our hope and our desire that reason will prevail over ruin in the Congo. And there really is no alternative to Congolese unification except chaos and civil war.

If the United Nations is unable to achieve unity in the Congo, there is a strong possibility that that country will be plunged into a destructive civil war as the rest of the Congo seeks to reintegrate Katanga by whatever means available or necessary. These conditions, in turn, would breed external subversion and loss of true independence.

This is the principal reason why the United States is so concerned with the Congo situation. This is why our policy continues to be to help establish a unified and stable Congo—a Congo on good terms with the West and able to resist extremist and Communist influence and penetration. This is why we continue to welcome all steps toward political reconciliation of the Congo.

Since the beginning of the crisis, both the United States and the United Nations have looked on reconciliation as one of their major tasks. This is why we look so favorably on the plan drawn up by Secretary-General U Thant.

Once a peaceful reunification of the Congo is achieved, then all parties involved can turn to the really important job of helping the Congo build itself into a strong, viable nation. The U.N. plan offers real promise for a settlement under which the United Nations can work itself out of the expensive job of peacekeeping and policing the country and into the constructive job of economic and technical assistance.

Once this transition is accomplished, we will have made a major contribution toward lasting peace and security, not only in Africa but throughout the world.

This is what we hope will be achieved through the United Nations Congo Plan of Reconciliation. And this is why we are giving our full support and best efforts toward making this plan succeed.

We hope you will join us in support of this endeavor.

SELECTION III—C

The excerpts here reprinted are from the *Congressional Record*—Senate, 87th Congress, 2d sess., January 25, 1962, pp. 894–97, and represent the text of an address "Prospects for Peace in the Congo," delivered to the Congress on that date by Senator Thomas Dodd. The Connecticut senator was a strong supporter of Tshombe's Katanga.

Mr. President, before Congress adjourned last September, I took the floor several times to express misgivings about the course of events in the Congo and about our policy or lack of policy in this critically important area of the world.

I was troubled over the dangerous degree of leftist influence in the coalition government which was established at the so-called Louvanium Conference in early August of last year.

I was troubled by the evidence that, while we were footing the bill for the lion's share of the U.N. operation in the Congo, we had very little to say about U.N. policy in the Congo; that this policy was in fact controlled by the Afro-Asian bloc and, in particular, by Nehru's unspeakable Minister of Defense, Krishna Menon, a man who has justly come to be regarded as the personification of cryptocommunism.

I was disturbed, above all, by the U.N. military action of last September, and by the grave implications of this action for the future of the U.N. and for the future of the Western alliance.

Toward the end of last November, as my colleagues know, I visited the Congo, where I had extensive conversations with Prime Minister Adoula, President Tshombe, and members of their respective governments. Since there has been a good deal of misinformation about the purpose of my visit and about what transpired during the course of my visit, I think it might be useful, first of all, to set the record straight.

There have been some reports in the press to the effect that I had gone to the Congo against the opposition of the Department of State; that I had encouraged President Tshombe to hold out for complete independence; and that I had told him that American policy in the Congo was misdirected because there were Communists in the Department of State.

The real truth is that a major part of my purpose in going to the Congo was to try to explore the possibilities of a Tshombe-Adoula agreement in informal discussions with the two leaders.

I left for the Congo on November 21. On Monday morning, November 20, President Kennedy asked me to come to his office. We talked about the Congo situation for almost an hour. The President expressed the hope that I could help to arrange a meeting between Tshombe and Adoula.

.   .   .   .

At a later date, I plan to report to my colleagues in greater detail on what I saw and learned in the Congo. As of this moment, I feel that a frank and detailed presentation may have an adverse effect on the delicately poised political situation in the Congo and on the critical discussions which are still going on between the central government in Léopoldville and the Government of Katanga.

It is because of this that I have taken the stand that the hearings now proceeding under the separate auspices of the Senate Subcommittee on Internal Security and of the Subcommittee on Africa of the Foreign Relations Committee, should be held in executive sessions.

But I believe there are certain aspects of the situation in the Congo which cry out for immediate consideration and understanding. It is to these aspects that I plan to address myself briefly today.

.   .   .   .

If the Katanga intervention is accepted as a precedent, it will sanctify the abdication of our foreign policy to the United Nations; it will open the way to U.N. intervention in the internal affairs of member nations; and it may commit us to supporting a whole series of wars that are favored by the Afro-Asian bloc and the Soviets.

If we had the virtue of consistency, the stand we have taken on Katanga would have led us to propose that the United Nations should be authorized to intervene militarily, upon the request of any central government, to prevent the secession of any national minority or grouping. Had such a principle been incorporated into the U.N. Charter or adopted as a general resolution, the U.N. would have been involved in half a dozen wars in recent years. It would have intervened to prevent the separation of Pakistan from India, of Sudan from Egypt, of Syria from the United Arab Republic, of Senegal from the Mali Federation, and of Mauritania from Morocco.

How preposterous our position in Katanga really is becomes apparent the moment you attempt to convert this position into a general principle. And, if our position in Katanga does not flow from any general principle, then it remains to be explained why we have decided to make an exception in the case of Katanga.

Morally, Katanga had every right to secede, given the deep-rooted ethnic and cultural differences between the tribes of Katanga and those of the northern Congo, and given the incredible chaos and the serious Communist infiltration which exists in the north. From the standpoint of political realism, however, Katangese secession would certainly be inadvisable because it is true that a completely independent Katanga could not survive if the rest of the Congo went Communist. On this point I am in basic agreement with the State Department.

For that matter, Tshombe himself has never held out for complete secession. He has instead advocated a loose confederation, with the central government controlling currency, customs, foreign affairs, the army and other essential instruments of national policy, but with a very large measure of autonomy in other fields reserved to the member governments.

But, as desirable as Congolese unity may be, I remain opposed to the

U.N. military action against the so-called Katanga secession. The mere fact that a political solution may be desirable does not lead, ipso facto, as some of our State Department logicians have argued, to the conclusion that the U.N. must be authorized to use military force to achieve such a solution.

I am opposed to the socially and morally unjust discrimination against American Negroes which still exists in most of our States. But I would resist with all my powers any effort on the part of the U.N. to terminate this state of affairs by sending Ghurka and Ethiopian troops into Little Rock or Washington or Hartford. This is the internal business of the United States; and any attempt to give the U.N. authority over the internal affairs of this Nation or other nations would, as I see it, spell its doom.

That is why I am so concerned over the U.N. action in the Congo. Because, despite all the pious statements to the contrary, it unquestionably did constitute intervention in the affairs of the Congo in an attempt to impose by military force a political solution advocated by the Afro-Asian nations, the Communist bloc, regrettably, by the United States.

There are those who regard the U.N.'s action in Katanga with joy, hailing it as proof that the U.N. is at last beginning to function in its proper role as a "parliament of man." I wonder if they have ever thought through the implications of this position.

If we permit the Katanga action to be regarded as a precedent, we may soon find ourselves supplying and footing the bill for U.N. military actions all over the world that have been duly authorized by a Communist bloc-Afro-Asian coalition in the General Assembly.

Mr. President, in the interest of the Congo, in the interest of the United Nations, the U.N. operation in the Congo must return to the path of legality and propriety. It must return to its primary functions, which are the maintenance of public order, the maintenance of social services, the safeguarding of human life, and the conciliation of disputes.

IV. VIEWS OF OBSERVERS

> *SELECTION IV–A*
>
> Arthur Krock, former head of the Washington bureau of *The New York Times,* was a bitter critic of the American policy toward the Congo. The following item, datelined Washington, July 1, appeared under the heading "The Ruins of a Vindictive Policy" in the July 2, 1964 edition of the *Times.* © 1964 by The New York Times Company. Reprinted by permission.

All the officials of the central Government of the Congo were too occupied with other matters to attend the leave-taking of the "peace-keeping" troops of the United Nations. Foremost among these other matters was preparation for the triumphant homecoming of Moise Tshombe, whom the U.N., with the indispensable military, financial and economic aid of the Administration in Washington, forcibly deposed as President of the separatist state of Katanga.

Today, the pro-Western fugitive, who was the victim of a vendetta jointly pursued by the State Department and U.N. Secretary General Thant, was asked by the President of the Congo to form a new government. Never did any political action more nearly match the events recorded in *Psalms, cxviii, 22:* "The stone which the builders refused is become the head stone of the corner." And seldom has a policy of the United States Government been more thoroughly discredited.

There is a full enough measure of irony in the proposal to Tshombe. But the crowning irony would be his decision to assume the conduct of foreign affairs instead of the office of Premier. In that case he would deal directly with Thant and Secretary of State Rusk, a situation prompting a great roar of cosmic laughter around a world where there is so little to laugh about nowadays.

A brief history of the U.N.-U.S. Congo policy, which now has collapsed, sufficiently explains why it has been so widely criticized from the outset:

KATANGA ALONE WAS READY

When Belgium, under pressure from this Government in association with the Afro-Asian members of the U.N. General Assembly, granted independence to the feuding tribes of the Congo, Katanga was the only region prepared for orderly self-government. Tshombe, therefore, promoted a meeting at Coquihatville of all the Congolese post-independence leaders except pro-Communist Antoine Gizenga. The conference agreed on a loose federation in which all provinces would have a large measure of autonomy.

For Katanga this meant that the revenues from the processing of its rich concentration of raw materials would not be subject to confiscation by a wasteful, corrupt and incompetent central regime at Leopoldville. For the other states it meant a fair share of Katanga's revenues, with which a viable local and national governing system could be established.

At a subsequent meeting, where Tshombe joined the other Coquihatville conferees for the purpose of incorporating their agreement in a national constitution, he was arrested by officers of the central Government, without protest by Washington or the United Nations. And under this duress, he was forced to sign an agreement with his jailers that required him unreservedly to subscribe to a constitution he had not seen, for the excellent reason that it hadn't yet been written.

This he promptly repudiated when he returned to Katanga and proclaimed an independent nation. There followed the U.N. "peace keeping" operation which developed into three separate military expeditions into Katanga— mounted, financed and transported by the United States—a full-scale war against Tshombe terminable only on his unconditional surrender.

Throughout the operation, which culminated in the surrender and flight of the only strongly pro-Western leader in the Congo, whose States was alone in maintaining law and order and in the possession of a viable economy, the U.N. and the State Department emitted a deluge of propaganda in which factual distortions, downright untruths, denunciation of all critics however qualified, and the spirit of vendetta against Tshombe were dominant. In a speech at Philadelphia, December 1961, Assistant Secretary of State Carl Rowan employing the "guilt-by-association" technique, lumped all critics with "arch conservatives, people who oppose the income tax, avowed defenders of racial segregation, opponents of fluoridation, those who want to destroy the Supreme Court," etc.

Today, however, Tshombe got a wry welcome home from Secretary Rusk. In essence this suggested the reply of the tavern keeper when asked whether Casey was good for a drink: "Has he had it? Then he is."

SELECTION IV–B

Arthur M. Schlesinger, Jr., professor of humanities at the City University of New York, had been an assistant to President Kennedy and an advisor on foreign policy. He reports on the Congo question in this excerpt from his book, *A Thousand Days: John F. Kennedy in the White House* (Boston, 1965), pp. 574–75, 578–79. Copyright © 1965 by Arthur M. Schlesinger, Jr. Reprinted by permission of the Houghton Mifflin Co.

Of the African problems, the one that most commanded the President's attention was the Congo. Independence had descended like a hurricane on the unprepared country in July 1960. In a few days the new state was in chaos: the Force Publique had mutinied; Katanga and other provinces were proclaiming their independence; Belgian paratroopers were coming back to restore order. In desperation Prime Minister Lumumba appealed to the United Nations. On July 14 the Security Council voted to provide the central government with enough military assistance to pacify the country.

Lumumba also cabled N. S. Khrushchev "to watch hourly over the situation"; and Khrushchev responded in his own way. By September several hundred Soviet 'technicians' were in Leopoldville, Russian military equipment was going to Lumumba's army, and communist sympathizers were moving into the central government. Lumumba obviously preferred this to assistance from the United Nations; and in consequence President Joseph Kasavubu dismissed him early in September. In another week Kasavubu, closing the Soviet and Czech embassies, placed his main reliance on the UN peace-keeping force. The Russians, having just missed establishing a powerful military and political presence in this rich, large and strategic land, now turned savagely against the UN. Khrushchev, still watching hourly over the situation, vetoed subsequent Security Council action, launched violent attacks against Hammarskjöld and soon advanced the *troika* proposal. He accompanied this barrage by vigorous support for Lumumba and, after Lumumba's arrest and murder, for his heir, Antoine Gizenga.

In January 1961 Kennedy inherited a Congo still in chaos, divided among the Kasavubu government in Leopoldville, the Gizenga group in Stanleyville and the pro-Belgian secessionist regime of Moise Tshombe in Elisabethville. Overshadowing everything was the prospect that Soviet meddling in the chaos might lead to a Russian base in the heart of Africa. From the start the new President had a simple and constant view: that, unless the United Nations filled the vacuum in the Congo, there would be no alternative but a direct Soviet-American confrontation. As one crisis after another flared up in the months to come, he used to say that, if we didn't have the UN operation, the only way to block Soviet domination of the Congo would be to go in with our own forces. The UN could not bring the great powers together in the Congo, but at least it could keep them apart.

This policy would not work, however, unless the central government in Leopoldville possessed authority. It was here that the secession of Katanga assumed its significance. Katanga, containing the bulk of the country's mineral wealth, produced nearly half the tax revenues and foreign exchange earnings of the Congo. In Elisabethville, Tshombe, a shrewd, humorous and cynical politician, backed by the Belgian Union Minière du Haut Katanga, was using the revenue from the copper mines to hire white mercenaries and mount propaganda campaigns in America and Europe. Moreover, the example of Katanga was stimulating secessionist dreams elsewhere in the Congo.

A unified Congo therefore seemed the condition for the success of the UN policy. Moreover, the question of Katanga was becoming a crucial test of American intentions throughout Africa. Every new state was meticulously scrutinizing our actions to detect evidences of support for Tshombe, whom the rest of Africa regarded as the white colonists' black man. "If we don't have a Congo policy," as Wayne Fredericks remarked, "we don't have an African policy."

. . . .

The Katanga secession thus came to an end. There remained the problems of reconstruction and these were overwhelming. During 1963 Kennedy kept up his interest both in economic assistance to the Congo and in the extension of the UN military presence; he secured the latter from a U Thant highly dubious about the continued financial drain on the UN. But, in time, the Adoula government fell, and in another year Tshombe, who had fled the country in June 1963, renounced his secessionism and returned as Prime Minister of the unified Congo. With impressive agility, Tshombe, having lost his principle, at least recovered what he evidently valued a good deal more —his power. It was an ironic denouement—as if, after having been beaten in the Civil War, Jefferson Davis had returned as president of the triumphant American Union.

The Congo policy did more, however, than simply settle a constitutional argument and preserve the Congo as a nation. It gave the United Nations its greatest success in peace-keeping and its greatest effort in technical assistance (though at a cost, for the expense of the Congo operations led to a UN financial crisis, relieved for a moment by the UN bond issue of 1963 but at a later moment threatening the very existence of the organization). More than that, it averted a possible Soviet-American clash in the heart of Africa. Above all, it consolidated the growing confidence of the new African states in the American President.

> ### SELECTION IV–C
>
> Lawrence S. Kaplan, professor of history at Kent State University, had been Fulbright Lecturer in American History at the University of Louvain in 1964–65. The following is a portion of his article, "The United States, Belgium, and the Congo Crisis of 1960," as it appeared in the *Review of Politics*, XXIX (April, 1967), pp. 252–56. Reprinted by permission.

From the beginning American action was designed to restrain Soviet impulses to profit from Belgium's difficulties in the Congo. If the Soviet Union initially joined the United States in accepting United Nations' help in the Congo it was for purposes of its own, and lasted only as long as those purposes were being served. Failing to control events in Africa, the Soviet turned violently against the United Nations which after August, 1960, was bracketed with Belgium as a lackey of American imperialism. Against the threats from the communist world, both immediate and potential, the continued affirmation of the United Nations' actions in the Congo was more than a quixotic gesture of anticolonialism, and certainly not an unwilling surrender to communist intrigue. All the policy asked for was a genuinely neutral Africa. Without the presence of the United Nations the Soviet Union might have succeeded in a unilateral intervention, which would have led to the counter-intervention of the West and the conversion of equatorial Africa into a battlefield of the Cold War.

The Soviet attack against the United States was mounted on the very first day of the special Security Council session in July, 1960, and there is little doubt that the American delegates were fully aware of Soviet intentions. Soviet Ambassador to the United Nations Arkady Sobolev asserted immediately that Belgian troops in the Congo were serving under a NATO command. Citing the Lebanon operation of 1957, he claimed that the Katangese secession was made with the cooperation of the United States whose 24th division in Germany was poised to intervene in the Congo much as American troops had intervened in Lebanon in 1957. In demanding United Nations' condemnation of Belgian aggression the Soviet Union made it clear that it was also denouncing the United States. The American response was to defend itself vigorously and at the same time to clear Belgium of any imputation of improper behavior while welcoming United Nations' actions on humanitarian grounds. When the Soviet representative attempted to modify the Tunisian-Ceylonese resolution which would bring the United Nations into the Congo, it was American influence that defeated the Russian amendment to condemn Belgium for the mutiny by a vote of 7 to 2. Ambassador Henry Cabot Lodge later made a special point in the August meeting of the Council of congratulating Belgium for its speed in executing its withdrawal from the Congo. In its own eyes certainly the United States played the role of a stanch ally of Belgium.

The argument that the United States acted with greater vigor against Katanga than against Soviet-influenced Orientale province appealed to few in America outside the special group of Tshombe's friends. On the one hand, communist power throughout the period seemed limited to the peripheries whereas the danger in Katanga's secession lay in the dependence of the Congo's economy upon the vast resources of that province. On the other, it was widely assumed in the United States that Belgium itself shared America's support of a centralized united Congo. Although it was obvious that Belgian public opinion was favorably affected by Tshombe's friendliness and that Belgium's financial community wanted to save what it could in Katanga, Belgium itself never recognized the legitimacy of the seceded Katanga province. Aside from the general indifference of the average Belgian—Fleming and Walloon— the difficulties of the Walloon financiers of the Congo, the Socialists repeatedly scored the Tshombe pressure group in Brussels even when they shared the government's resentment of the United Nations. This sentiment was more fully translated into government policy after Socialist Paul-Henri Spaak became foreign minister in a new coalition in 1961. The country gave at least nominal support to the United Nations' campaigns that ended in Tshombe's temporary exile in 1963.

The substance, then, of Belgium's resentment came from America's attitudes rather than actions. In their eagerness to anticipate and to combat Soviet taunts during the Congo crisis, Americans frequently slighted the feelings of their allies. For example, the nature of Ambassador Lodge's responses to Soviet charges against Belgium at the Security Council suggests that the desire to make debater's points against the Russian opponent ranked as high as the defense of the Belgian position. Could Belgians feel suitably grateful for gracious congratulations for their cooperation with the United Nations' resolutions when in the same speech the American representative assailed the Soviet Union for identifying the United States and Belgium as allies in NATO? The explanation that the two countries were allies only in event of Soviet attack in Europe could have afforded Belgians scant comfort at that moment, no matter how innocently the American commentary might have been intended.

There was something missing in the American support of its ally. Perhaps it was an unacknowledged annoyance with Belgium for unnecessarily complicating the delicate relations of the United States and the Soviet Union in their Cold War. Had Belgium trained elite governing cadres in the manner of France or of England, or had Belgium not acted so hastily in its granting of independence, or had Belgium only shared the American opinion on colonies, the crisis of 1960 might not have arisen. Certainly, the attitudes of American newspapers at that time indicate that if the communist factor had been absent in 1960, the United States would not have been even a reluctant champion of the Belgian cause.

Sensitive to this undercurrent of opinion in America, Belgians understandably looked with suspicion upon the initial American statement on the mutiny which said that "what is required is an instantaneous response to the urgent requests of the Congo government rather than ill-advised or malicious attempts to make political capital out of the serious difficulties of the Congolese people." It was the Congolese people, not the Belgian people in the Congo, for whom Americans showed concern; it was the "malicious" Soviet and "ill-advised" African or Asian efforts to exploit Belgium's difficulties, not the injustice of the accusations against Belgium that agitated the United States. Behind the guise of fairness to both sides, Belgians could see prejudice against their position.

By contrast, the British and particularly the French representatives at the Security Council were far more sensitive to Belgian interests. Both the United Kingdom and France had abstained from voting on the July 14 resolution on the grounds that Paragraph 1 of the resolution calling "upon the Government of Belgium to withdraw their troops from the territory of the Republic of the Congo" could be twisted, as the communists immediately attempted, into a condemnation of Belgium. Besides, lack of a plan to mesh Belgian evacuation with the assumption of control by the United Nations' forces would leave civilians—Belgians and Congolese alike—at the mercy of the mutinous army. President De Gaulle was so concerned that he called upon United States' Ambassador to France Amory Houghton to complain of the American vote.

In light of this criticism, although prior to President De Gaulle's complaint, the United States was obliged to explain the reasons for its vote in more detail than would otherwise have been necessary. Ambassador Lodge admitted American doubts about the wisdom of the first paragraph, and wanted the world to understand that Belgium's withdrawal would be contingent upon the successful execution of the second paragraph, which provided military and technical help to the Congolese Government. In other words, restoration of order in the Congo was the prerequisite of Belgium's departure. The Department of State *Bulletin* repeated this *caveat* on August 1 in a special statement to the effect that the United States had voted for the Tunisian resolution only because of the urgency of the Congo's trials. But would such protestations have been made without French and British reproaches? Nowhere did the United States challenge the Soviet Union or

Tunisia with the spirited language used by the French delegate, Armand Berard, who labelled Belgian aggression a myth and its actions merely a life-saving operation in conformity with the Belgian-Congolese Treaty of Friendship of June 29 (a claim even Belgium was hesitant to make).

It was the insensitivity of the United States toward Belgian pride that lay at the base of Belgium's grievances. In retrospect, this is one compelling case against the United States.

Beyond this there is little to add. Belgium's interests as well as those of the United States had been served by the handling of the Congo crisis along American lines, as Belgium's government had consistently announced and had almost as consistently observed. The United States offended in the course of implementing its policy. But even if it had not done so, its position as senior member of the Atlantic alliance would have made it a natural target of its partners whenever troubles arose. Unfair through charges may be, they will emerge periodically in any relationship in which the distribution of power and responsibility is unequal. Where unreserved support for some ally conflicts with American interests outside of Europe, the United States has the right to ask for understanding of its position. In turn, it should grant as much to its allies.

12

THE MONROE DOCTRINE AND
THE GOOD NEIGHBOR
The Cuban Problem

I. EDITORIAL INTRODUCTION

While the United States wrestled with unaccustomed problems in remote parts of the world after 1945, it assumed that an old problem in a familiar part of the world, Latin America, had been solved by the multilateralization of the Monroe Doctrine. Close collaboration with Latin Americans had been a favored program of Franklin D. Roosevelt. The spirit of his Good Neighbor policy animated Latin America's role in the United Nations and, subsequently, in the pact of mutual defense at Rio de Janeiro in 1947 and in the Organization of American States at Bogota in 1948. Into this harmony intruded the rise of a communist-dominated, Soviet-oriented revolution in Cuba under the auspices of its charismatic leader, Fidel Castro. What had gone wrong? Was the communism of the Cuban experience an aberration, or was it a threat that could endanger the entire hemisphere?

The challenge of Castro forced the United States to recognize at least that it had problems with Latin America, a recognition that had been delayed by the priorities given to Europe or to Asia by the State Department. Indeed, one of the factors in the Latin American resentment of the United States was the feeling of neglect produced by the favor NATO enjoyed over the OAS in American foreign policymaking. But if a Castro could arise in the Americas, there had to be better answers for the phenomenon. Americans were perplexed. If they had supported popular revolutions against dictatorships as they had Perón's in Argentina in 1946, the charge of Yankee interference might strengthen the hand of the dictator, even as Perón had been strengthened. On the other hand, if the United States accepted the dictators on a *de facto* basis, such acceptance was considered proof of America's indifference to freedom and of its interest in exploiting its relations with the dictators for its own financial advantage. In either circumstance, communist agents had opportunities to arouse anti-American sentiments. The fact of inequality in power and responsibility, the heritage of past wrongs, real or imagined, all exacted prices to be paid by the United States.

The Cuban Revolution provided Khrushchev an opportunity to choose the presidential election summer of 1960 as a propitious moment to exacerbate American as well as Latin emotions. This he did by announcing at a press conference that the Monroe Doctrine was dead and should be decently buried. (Selection II–A.) In making this pronouncement the Soviet premier found an instrument that could still divide. For Latin Americans Khrushchev's statement revived memories of the unilateral use of the Monroe Doctrine, apparent only six years before in America's action against communism in Guatamala, and soon to be demonstrated in the Bay of Pags and missile crisis of 1961 and 1962. Their concerns were confirmed by Senate Resolution 388 of September 17, 1962, at the height of the missile crisis which clearly invoked the Monroe Doctrine as the basis for supporting the President's authority to intervene in Castro's Cuba. (Selection II–B.)

The Cuban problem, more than any other in Latin America, inspired a major if not a "great" debate among Americans on the proper way of coping with communism in the Americas. Earl E. T. Smith, former Ambassador to Batista's Cuba, had few doubts on the issue. If communists took Cuba, it was the fault of the middle-echelon officials on the "fourth floor" of the State Department who should have known that the so-called revolutionary democracy was controlled by communists. They were carried away by the notion that a leftist dictator was automatically better than a rightist dictator, no matter what their respective attitudes toward the United States might be. If the Batista regime had to be removed—and Smith had some questions here—American influence should have been exercised, even at the risk of charges of intervention, to support a regime other than Castro's. (Selection III–A.)

Whether the United States government was ever as enthusiastic in its welcome to Castro as Smith suggested in 1962 is open to question. Certainly, the Department of State had become disillusioned with Batista in the late 1950's and briefly had looked upon Castro as a friend as well as democrat during his visit to the United States in 1959, as it admitted in the 1961 White Paper on Cuba. But much of the sentiment Smith had attributed to State Department officials more properly belonged to such Congressmen as Charles Porter of Oregon who had rhapsodized over the virtues of Castro and the vices of Batista in 1959, shortly after Castro's seizure of power. Speaking from Cuba he noted the common tradition of "democratic idealism" that linked the United States with Castro's movèment, and welcomed Cuba's support to free the Organization of American States from the tyrannies of dictators such as Trujillo, Somoza, and Duvalier. (Selection III–B.)

Within little more than a year disillusionment had overcome most Americans' enthusiasm for the new regime in Cuba. The barbaric execution of Castro's enemies, the brash expropriation of American properties, the increasing power of communism, and Cuban subversive activities against neighboring Latin American nations frightened and disturbed the United States. The Castro line branding the United States as the villain and enemy of the Cuban Revolution and casting the Soviet Union as a fraternal ally stimulated cries for action against the new menace to the hemisphere.

In some respects, the immediate future of Cuban-American relations proved to be even worse than the events of 1960 would have suggested. Castro revealed himself to be a Marxist; the United States had broken relations with Cuba, and encouraged an abortive invasion at the Bay of Pigs; and, the Soviet Union was in a position of prominence in Cuba that rivalled its role in Eastern Europe. The situation was to grow worse before it could improve. When Khrushchev was tempted in 1962 to establish missile bases on Cuba, it appeared that World War III might begin over Cuba. It did not —as both major powers recognized their limitations: the Soviet Union in intruding into a traditional American sphere of influence, and the United States in adjusting itself to the continuance of the Castro regime. The United States did not succeed in convincing Latin America that the O.A.S. should be the vehicle for the new Monroe Doctrine, or that the Cuban menace was indeed greater than the Yankee menace. In a speech to the Senate in 1964 entitled "Old Myths and New Realities," Senator J. William Fulbright of Arkansas attempted to strip the Cuban question of the emotions raised by the Castro movement and place it in a more objective perspective. His conclusion was that the United States could live with communist Cuba as an unpleasant neighbor without having to fear consequent destruction of the Republic or the Hemisphere. He suggested that the United States had unwittingly contributed to the menace of Castroism by exaggerating his importance, and warned that the United States would alienate Latin America if it permitted the Cuban experience to stifle help to future social revolutions in the Americas. (Selection III–C.)

The emotions over Cuba aroused in the Congress and in the Administration were matched by observations of scholars and journalists attempting to explain reasons for Castro's success. Herbert Matthews of *The New York Times*, often credited with bringing Castro to the favorable attention of the American public through a series of interviews in the mountains of Cuba in 1957, admitted that the communists had assumed control over the Revolution. But he asserted in 1961 that the revolution itself was a genuine one, that it was not communist in its early stages, but was pushed in that direction by the behavior of the United States government and press. (Selection IV–A.) In making this claim, he disputed the findings of Nathaniel Weyl. The latter claimed that the refusal of the State Department to recognize the communist control of the Castro movement led to America's withdrawal of support from Batista and the consequent triumph of communism. (Selection IV–B.)

Informed scholars or public servants relatively detached from the passions of the Castro movement have recognized the fact that a social revolution independent of communism has been taking place in Cuba. Given the history of their relations with the United States, the fear of American intervention could indeed outweigh the fear of communism among many Latin American countries. The United States must not hide behind a doctrine of non-intervention, but should promote forces of democracy that could have canalized the Cuban revolution along the path of liberal democracy without invoking the emotions of the Monroe Doctrine. But as historian Maury Baker pointed out, no matter what position the United States takes, its enormous power and its past experiences in Latin America inevitably make it a focus for frustrations—political, economic, and social. The country must learn to live with them, and to modify them, as the Alliance for Progress is attempting. (Selection IV–C.) Such is the price of power.

II. DOCUMENTS

> SELECTION II–A
>
> The text of Premier Khrushchev's statement at a news conference in the Kremlin on July 12, 1960 and a transcript of questions and answers following it made available in English by Tass, the official Soviet press agency, appeared July 13, 1960 in *The New York Times.*

Various American bourgeois press organs contend that the development of friendly relations between the Soviet Union and Cuba represents open disregard for the so-called Monroe Doctrine. Our readers would like to know your opinion on this question.

MR. KHRUSHCHEV—Our historians paid tribute once to the positive role of the United States foreign policy principles enunciated by President Monroe 137 years ago which came to be known as the Monroe Doctrine. This was directed against the designs of European colonialists on the countries of Latin America, and at the same time proclaimed the principle of noninterference by the United States of America in the internal affairs of the European countries. The United States of America was then still acting as a democratic nation which had the sympathies of many.

But then everything changed abruptly. Now the United States is using the Monroe Doctrine to substantiate a right to rule all the Latin-American countries, meddle in their domestic affairs, keep them under its tutelage and, of course, exploit them.

The Latin-American countries have very rich natural resources. Yet, most of the population of those countries is living under gruelling conditions. What is that due to? It cannot be explained by saying that the peoples of Latin America are averse to hard work. Not at all. They are very hard-working people and they show concern for their countries. The reason is quite different. It is that the ones who rule the roost there are the imperialists of the United States of America, the colonialists, who, like vultures, snatch the last crumb out of the mouths of the dying children and old folk just to wax fat and rich. And it is through the Monroe Doctrine that they want to assure themselves the right to go with this robbery forever.

But the Monroe Doctrine is known to date far back to a remote past. The human race lives under different conditions today. It is Marxism-Leninism, the most progressive teaching, that is flourishing more and more in our time. It triumphs not only in the domain of theory but also in that of practice.

And the peoples see that a country's independence is the road to its liberation. The people are increasingly realizing that to enjoy the fruits of their labor and the natural resources of their land they must have independence above all else.

It goes without saying that, as a Communist, I believe that the Communist way is the best way society can develop. But this is every people's own affair and we do not impose our ideas and our forms of government upon anyone.

Life moves forward, it sweeps away everything that does not correspond to the spirit of the time; it asserts the new, the progressive. We consider that the Monroe Doctrine has outlived its time, has outlived itself, has died, so to say, a natural death. Now the remains of this doctrine should best be buried as every dead body is so that it should not poison the air by its decay. That would be the correct thing to do and this is what will happen apparently.

It is noteworthy, for instance, that the treaty on a military base, which speaks about the right of the United States of America to maintain a military base on Cuba, does not even specify a time limit for its operation. This fact speaks eloquently about the nature of the treaty, about the time and the status of the sides at the moment when it was being signed. A man cannot, can he, sign a treaty without safeguarding his rights by setting some time limit for this treaty. A treaty without a time limit on terms enslaving to a small nation—this is sheer iniquity.

> SELECTION II–B
>
> The Senate supported Presidents Kennedy's authority "to prevent by whatever means necessary" the conversion of Cuba into a Soviet base at the time of the missile crisis of 1962 by passing SR 388, 87th Congress, 2d sess., September 17, 1962, the text of which follows.

Whereas President James Monroe, announcing the Monroe Doctrine in 1823, declared to the Congress that we should consider any attempt on the part of European powers "to extend their system to any portion of this hemisphere as dangerous to our peace and safety."

Whereas in the Rio Treaty of 1947, the parties agreed that "an armed attack by any state against an American state shall be considered as an attack against all the American states, and, consequently, each one of the said contracting parties undertakes to assist in meeting in the exercise of the inherent right of individual or collective self-defense recognized by article 51 of the Charter of the United Nations."

Whereas the Foreign Ministers of the Organization of American States at Punta del Este in January 1962 unanimously declared: "The present Government of Cuba has identified itself with the principles of Marxist-Leninist ideology, has established a political, economic, and social system based on that doctrine, and accepts military assistance from extracontinental Communist powers, including even the threat of military intervention in America on the part of the Soviet Union";

Whereas since 1958 the international Communist movement has increasingly extended into Cuba its political, economic, and military sphere of influence: Now, therefore, be it

Resolved, That it is the sense of the Senate that the President of the United States is supported in his determination and possesses all necessary authority—

(a) to prevent by whatever means may be necessary, including the use of arms, the Castro regime from exporting its aggressive purposes to any part of this hemisphere by force or the threat of force;

(b) to prevent in Cuba the creation or use of an externally supported offensive military base capable of endangering the United States naval base at Guantanamo, free passage to the Panama Canal, United States missile and space preparations, or the security of this Nation and its citizens; and

(c) to work with other free citizens of this hemisphere and with freedom-loving Cuban refugees to support the legitimate aspirations of the people of Cuba for a return to self-determination.

III. VIEWS OF PARTICIPANTS

> *SELECTION III—A*
>
> Earl E. T. Smith, Ambassador to Cuba during the Batista period, defended his own record in blaming the Castro situation and its accompanying problems on the Department of State. The following is an excerpt from his book, *The Fourth Floor* (New York, 1962), pp. 224–30. Copyright © by Earl E. T. Smith. Reprinted by permission of Random House, Inc.

No matter what coloration is put on it, the fact remains that international Communism has established a base ninety miles from our shores, from which it is organizing against the United States throughout Latin America.

It does not matter at all that we have allies close to the Russian border; what does matter is that the Russians had not established a base on the Western hemisphere until Castro appeared in Cuba.

From my experience in Cuba I have concluded that this need not have happened. That it did happen was, to a surprising degree, due to the policy of many in critical positions in the State Department that a Leftist dictator was better than a Rightist dictator, even though the Rightist dictator may be friendly to the United States and the Leftist dictator our enemy. The test with them is not what is beneficial to the United States but what fits their doctrinaire views of the future world.

It is very difficult to understand this policy from an American point of view. I found, as Ambassador to Cuba, that I could not understand this policy as it applied to Cuba. Granted that Batista had outlived his usefulness, the alternative certainly need not have been Castro, our enemy. And it must be noted that Castro would not have been in the position to attain power and could not have created the agency to seize power without the good will of the Fourth Floor.

It cannot be maintained that the government of the United States was unaware that Raúl Castro and Che Guevara, the top men of the 26th of July Movement are Communists, affiliated with international Communism. There are ample evidence to that effect. I have shown in this book that it was impossible for Assistant Secretary of State Roy Rubottom, his associate William Wieland, and the Fourth Floor not to be aware of Fidel Castro's Communist affiliations. It is beyond possibility that the CIA did not know. Roy Rubottom was in Bogotá when Fidel Castro, at the age of twenty-two, was an active organizer of Communist insurrection.

But I am sure that the Secretary of State and the Under-Secretary of State, and the President were not adequately and correctly informed on this subject, until it was too late. It is essential to understand this because while the Cuban situation may have to run its course, it ought not to be possible for the top officials of the United States to be kept in the dark on a matter of policy.

This then raises these questions:

What is really our policy? Who makes it? How is it established? Why did we intervene in Castro's favor in Cuba, when we might have supported able, knowledgeable pro-American men?

If dictatorship *versus* democracy were the only question that faced us, it would not be difficult to make a decision. However, as we are in the midst of a struggle for survival, other considerations are pertinent. Furthermore, to remove one dictator for another does not produce democracy.

If the policy of the United States is to bring about the overthrow of dictators in the hope that democracy will follow, then I believe that the United States must be prepared to take whatever steps are necessary to preserve law and order and prevent chaos during that interim period of transition which may last a long time. If free and open elections are to be held in these nations when a dictator is overthrown, a provisional government must be formed and such government needs outside support to maintain law and order. To do otherwise leaves a vacuum in which the Communists gain control. Such a vacuum did occur in Cuba. A group was ready to seize power, a Communist group, and we aided them to seize power.

We state that our policy is non-intervention, and through our actions imply that the Monroe Doctrine is dead. But we intervene positively or negatively or by innuendo every day. We intervene when we contract to sell armored cars or training planes or whatever, and then withhold what we have agreed to sell even after payment has been advanced. This is intervention to place the existing government in an embarrassing position, unable adequately to defend itself against bandit and Communist-supported forces. The psychological effect of the withdrawal of American support was devastating. That is negative intervention. We permit the Leftist dictator to establish a base for operations in the United States, in violation of our neutrality laws, and the State Department deals with his emissaries. That is positive intervention. We influence other governments not to sell arms to the government of Cuba. That is intervention by innuendo.

If we are to intervene sufficiently to bring about the overthrow of dictatorships then we should intervene to whatever extent is required to fulfill our purpose. Otherwise, in my opinion, we must wait for the normal self-development of a people and not assist revolution of any kind. And we must be prepared to receive the criticism of supporting friendly governments recognized by the United States, although they have been labeled dictatorships.

To make my point clear, let me say that we helped to overthrow the Batista dictatorship, which was pro-American and anti-Communist, only to install the Castro dictatorship which was Communist and anti-American. Because democracy is successful in the United States, influential persons on the Fourth Floor believe that we must transplant and implant our ideas and our form of democracy to all other nations, many of whom are not yet prepared for, and are not suited to our form of government and do not like it. After all, a people has a right to its own form of government and its own way of life.

I testified to the Senate that I had learned from experience and observation that our policies are determined by influential individuals in the lower echelon of the State Department in their day-by-day actions. By the time the higher officials receive them policies have already been made and they have to live by them. In this book I have quoted from testimony of four other Ambassadors who testified under oath to the same effect. It comes too late to correct the errors of the desk-men, who often become so devoted to the countries to which they are assigned that they forget that their business is the United States. The Fourth Floor consists of desk-men, as they are called. They are career Foreign Service Officers who frequently look upon political appointees as here today and gone tomorrow.

.   .   .   .

It is a criticism of the structure of the State Department where the attitude of the United States toward a friendly government may be determined through the day-by-day actions of those in the lower echelon. I am convinced, I repeat, that the alternative to Batista need not have been Castro, the Communist. The United States could have been instrumental in forming a broadly-based government in Cuba without Batista and without Castro. In my judgment, it would have been possible to have established such a government up until the summer of 1958. As the months passed after that, it would have been more and more difficult to exclude Castro. Fidel Castro was not the only alternative for Cuba, nor did Castro singlehandedly conquer the island of Cuba.

We undermined Batista but failed to encourage a peaceful solution. The Fourth Floor said we hoped for acceptable elections. But we would not support the Church, the political opposition and civic groups to make an all-out effort to create an atmosphere which was conducive to holding honest elections, so that the people of Cuba could select their own government. We would not support a broadly based national unity government, which would have acted only as a provisional government and would have remained in office only long enough to hold general elections.

I have shown in this book that on various occasions, when the timing was propitious and opportunities were available for a solution without Batista or Castro, our Department of State refused to lend its support. The refusal was based on the grounds that the United States would be accused of intervening in the internal affairs of Cuba. Yet, eventually, the State Department did advise Batista that the time had come for him to absent himself from his country. That was positive intervention on behalf of Castro.

No formula for a successful solution without Castro or Batista could succeed without the support of the United States. The United States held a dominant position in Cuba. The prestige and influence of the United States in Cuba until January 1, 1959, was all important. Only the United States could have implemented a viable solution. No group, except the Church, was bold enough to incur the enmity of both Castro and Batista by trying to put into effect a solution without the active endorsement of the United States. The Church consistently made attempts for a peaceful solution and consistently hoped, without avail, for United States support.

Yet the composite of United States government agencies, the press and members of Congress, through their unsympathetic actions, did so very much to help bring about the overthrow of the Batista dictatorship. Many influential individuals in the State Department were in sympathy with what they believed was a mass revolution taking place in Cuba. These influential individuals were prepared to gamble on a Leftist dictator in order to bring about the downfall of a Rightist dictator. Such a policy cannot be beneficial to the United States.

> ## SELECTION III–B
>
> In a speech, "Castro's Cuba: A Challenge for Cubans and Americans," delivered at Santiago de Cuba on February 7, 1959—shortly after the Castro revolution had succeeded—Congressman Charles O. Porter reflected the optimism of that time. Portions of the text of that speech are presented here as taken from the *Congressional Record*—House, 86th Congress, 1st sess., February 9, 1959, pp. 2174–76.

I am sure that a year ago, I could not have addressed you as I am today. In the first place, I am sure Fulgencio Batista would not have permitted an invitation to be extended. In the second place, I am told that your organization, as a demonstration of protest against Batista's tyrannical regime, had refused to convene any meeting or hold elections until civil liberties were restored. Your distinguished President informs me that this is your first meeting of 1959 in free Cuba. Let me say, therefore, that all of us owe a debt of gratitude to Fidel Castro.

Cuba is called the Pearl of the Antilles; she is described as one of the most beautiful islands in the Americas, but how much more beautiful she is now that freedom is restored. Yet, what Castro has won for the Cuban people is but a promise of what great expectations lie ahead.

It is customary in speeches by visiting politicians from one foreign country to another to stress traditional ties. Sometimes this is done as nothing more than a gesture, a courtesy extended as a matter of form. With me, I assure you, it is not merely a formality when I say that Fidel Castro has done more than perhaps any other Cuban to stir the consciences and emotions of the American people and to remind your friends to the north of the deep-rooted historic ties of friendship that bind Cuba and the United States. Ours is a relationship born in a common tradition. It is a tradition of democratic idealism, of revolution. Castro has captured the spirit of that tradition of democratic idealism and has elevated it to a new level of prominence not only throughout the Western Hemisphere but also throughout the world.

More than anything else the spirit of democratic idealism, it seems to me, was one of the primary motivating forces underlying Castro's 26th of July movement. There is something remarkably attractive about the drive, the dedication, the sense of nationality of all these men. A year ago they were regarded in some countries as a group of dreamy idealists caught up in a hopeless cause, adventurers of a sort guided more by self-delusion than by any serious, genuine compulsion. Yet, against apparent overwhelming odds the men of this movement have succeeded with almost miraculous speed in sweeping away a regime of terror, violence, and corruption. Press reports in the United States have stressed the totality of Cuban support behind the Castro forces. This was, indeed, a national revolution; of dimensions like that of the Mexican revolution. Perhaps, this fact coupled with the democratic idealism that is at the heart of the 26th of July movement and the leadership of a young Oriente lawyer, driven by an inner compulsion to bring democracy to his people, were more responsible than anything else for the success of democracy in Cuba and the overthrow of the Batista regime.

At first, many persons in my country were shocked by what seemed to be the excesses of the Castro forces. The belief became widespread that a virtual reign of terror was being directed against the Batista followers. It was difficult for them to comprehend the reality of the situation. They had had insufficient evidence of Batista's oppression. It was difficult to grasp the seeming contradiction of a democratic leader governing in apparent irresponsibility, and, as it seemed to them, governing ruthlessly. Americans neither understood the implications of this crisis nor the complications engendered by a nation caught up in violent revolution. Nor did they understand that the pent up indignation of a morally sensitive, oppressed people had to have some outlet, and that the public trial of known murderers was in fact a safety valve for a nation that demanded retribution against its oppressors.

Now, I believe, the American people realize the magnitude and the high morality of the 26th of July movement. Gradually the knowledge is becoming more widespread in the United States that these revolutionaries are not a rabble in arms but are a restrained, disciplined, and dedicated group of patriots who have the overwhelming support of the Cuban people and who are trying under great difficulties to bring to Cuba genuine democracy. The norteamericanos are becoming more and more conscious of the great problems facing your young lawyer and as a consequence a genuine feeling of sympathy and understanding seems to be taking shape.

Certainly, Cubans do not have to be reminded of the great political and economic problems besetting their new Government. In any revolution there always follows a difficult period of adjustment once the fighting has stopped and the tyrant has been overthrown. The legacy of the old regime is always a tremendous burden for the new Government. The general problem of firmly establishing the legitimacy of the new Government in a period of transition is fraught with grave dangers. The problem of reconciling the broadening of democracy with the necessity of maintaining a steady, centralized authority to insure public order and national progress, all in a revolutionary atmosphere, is a tremendous task for any new government. In our own national history it took almost a decade to establish a viable constitutional order after our war of liberation.

Nor are the economic problems facing Fidel Castro and the Cuban people any less burdensome. The economic legacy of the Batista regime would certainly be sufficiently oppressive to crush the enthusiasm of a far less devoted and energetic leader. Corruption and waste had completely enveloped the Batista regime. It is said that many Batista officials deposited millions of dollars in United States and Swiss banks. I hasten to add, money that was taken from the Cuban people. It is also reported that Batista himself has set aside upward of $200 million to $600 million for himself, for the most part no doubt in Swiss numbered accounts, before his flight to the Dominican Republic—again, money that belongs to the Cuban people, and which, by the way, I am encouraging our Government to locate and return if at all possible.

The war for Cuban liberation has also added to the great economic burden. Destruction by the revolution has been estimated at an insured cost of about $15 million. Damage and destruction to railroad bridges, and other means of transport and communication has been extensive. In all, the Government faces a staggering national debt of some $1,500 million.

The political and economic problems facing the Castro government are great, but they are not impossible. From abroad one gets the impression that political stability and orderly government prevails in Cuba. This is a happy beginning because out of political stability economic and social progress will emerge and flourish. Unless he removed himself entirely from politics for a while, Fidel Castro was right to assume the premiership and to participate actively in the management of governmental affairs. Political responsibility, it seems to me, cannot be disassociated from political authority. To govern effectively, and efficiently, responsibility and authority must be indivisible. He now has both the actual and the legal authority.

.   .   .   .

In conclusion, and in all humility, I want to make three suggestions for your consideration, as you go ahead to build a free, honest, and prosperous Cuba.

First, realize that you have the sympathy and support of my country. Call on us for assistance, whether it be more food and clothing for impoverished victims of the revolution, advice on how to attract and hold new industries, or ideas from our experiences how best to solve various social problems. We don't pretend to have all the resources or answers but please realize, as many of you do, our wish to help you establish yourselves in freedom and prosperity.

Second, don't expect too much too soon from the revolution. Insist on civil liberties, yes, and preparations for free elections, but do not expect increased profits and higher wages for everyone immediately. It is one thing to topple a dictatorship, another to build a democracy. Freedom means the right, indeed often the duty, to criticize. It means being able to disagree without being disagreeable. Sometimes it looks awfully sloppy and disorganized, but no better method has been devised for human happiness and governmental strength.

Here I want to leave Cuba a moment and talk about proposals by Cuban and Venezuelan leaders to kick the tyrannies out of the Organization of

American States. Certainly this is something to discuss at Quito next year when the OAS convenes there. For my part I believe in universal membership in international organizations, but of course with constant reminders of and obedience to the governing charters. Article 5, part (d), of the OAS charter reads as follows:

"The solidarity of the American States and the high aims which are sought through it require the political organization of those States on the basis of the effective exercise of representative democracy."

I am reliably informed that the OAS at Quito will have an opportunity to consider a concrete, specific definition of "the effective exercise of representative democracy," a yardstick which would disclose at once the respective shortcomings of Trujillo, Stroesner, Somoza, and Duvalier.

It can't all be done in a day—but it will be done if Cubans exercise self-control, tolerance, a sense of humor, and faith in democracy.

Finally, and this injunction is also not needed by most of you, beware of Communists who would try to make you believe they speak as Cubans, Cubans devoted to Cuba and speedy social and economic changes. Communists, of course, thrive on disorganization and are trained to take advantage of it. Their social justice anti-U.S.A. and pro-Cuba themes should fool no one, certainly not any Cuban who hated Batista and would fight against the resurgence of his counterpart in Cuban politics. Cuba's destiny is not that of Hungary today, Hungary where a local revolt cannot win because of the Soviet Union's intercession from outside its borders.

In Oregon, my home State, last week I heard Vice President Nixon—with whom I often do not agree—say something we all might ponder: "We should be more concerned about the meaning of the American Revolution," he said, "and less afraid of the Russian revolution." High officials in our Department of State would do well to heed the Vice President's timely advice.

In the final analysis, therefore, the greatest burden seems to rest upon Fidel Castro and his associates. In a very real sense he is a man of destiny; for if he fulfills the promise of his revolution and succeeds in imparting throughout all Cuba the zeal, the energy, the dedication to duty, and the democratic idealism that is so much part of his personality, there can be no doubt that Cuba and her people will emerge in a new age of progress and prosperity. But, we must all be patient with this man; as he himself recently said: "I am a man, not a god. We cannot do everything in 1 day." Indeed he can't do everything in 1 day. Nor can he do what is to be done without the support of the Cuban people and his friends in the Western Hemisphere. I do not doubt for 1 minute that Fidel Castro has the overwhelming support of the Cuban people. Nor do I doubt that there are millions of my own countrymen who feel as I do that this man deserves the sympathy and support of our Nation.

Fidel Castro has advanced the trend toward total hemispheric democracy one more significant step. Neither we in the United States, nor you in Cuba can permit him to fail, for, after all, he is the symbol of what all of us desire most: a world of freemen.

SELECTION III–C

"Old Myths and New Realities," delivered on March 25, 1964, was perhaps the most influential speech in Senator William J. Fulbright's distinguished career as Chairman of the Senate Foreign Relations Committee. One of the leading "myths" covered was the menace of Castro's Cuba. The portions here presented are excerpted from the *Congressional Record, Senate,* 88th Congress, 2d sess., March 25, 1964, p. 6231.

In recent years we have become transfixed with Cuba, making it far more important in both our foreign relations and in our domestic life than its size and influence warrant. We have flattered a noisy but minor demagog by treating him as if he were a Napoleonic menace. Cummunist Cuba has been a disruptive and subversive influence in Venezuela and other countries of the hemisphere, and there is no doubt that both we and our Latin American partners would be better off if the Castro regime did not exist. But it is important to bear in mind that, despite their best efforts, the Cuban Communists have not succeeded in subverting the hemisphere and that in Venezuela, for example, where communism has made a major effort to gain power through terrorism, it has been repudiated by a people who in a free election have committed themselves to the course of liberal democracy. It is necessary to weigh the desirability of an objective against the feasibility of its attainment, and when we do this with respect to Cuba, I think we are bound to conclude that Castro is a nuisance but not a grave threat to the United States and that he cannot be gotten rid of except by means that are wholly disproportionate to the objective. Cuban communism does pose a grave threat to other Latin American countries, but this threat can be dealt with by prompt and vigorous use of the established procedures of the inter-American system against any act of aggression.

I think that we must abandon the myth that Cuban communism is a transitory menace that is going to collapse or disappear in the immediate future and face up to two basic realities about Cuba: first, that the Castro regime is not on the verge of collapse and is not likely to be overthrown by any policies which we are now pursuing or can reasonably undertake; and second, that the continued existence of the Castro regime, though inimical to our interests and policies, is not an insuperable obstacle to the attainment of our objectives, unless we make it so by permitting it to poison our politics at home and to divert us from more important tasks in the hemisphere.

The policy of the United States with respect to Latin America as a whole is predicated on the assumption that social revolution can be accomplished without violent upheaval. This is the guiding principle of the Alliance for Progress and it may in time be vindicated. We are entitled to hope so and it is wise and necessary for us to do all that we can to advance the prospects of peaceful and orderly reform.

At the same time, we must be under no illusions as to the extreme difficulty of uprooting long-established ruling oligarchies without disruptions involving lesser or greater degrees of violence. The historical odds are probably against the prospects of peaceful social revolution. There are places, of course, where it has occurred and others where it seems likely to occur. In Latin America, the chances for such basic change by peaceful means seem bright in Colombia and Venezuela and certain other countries; in Mexico, many basic changes have been made by peaceful means, but these came in the wake of a violent revolution. In other Latin American countries, the power of ruling oligarchies is so solidly established and their ignorance so great that there seems little prospect of accomplishing economic growth or social reform by means short of the forcible overthrow of established authorities.

I am not predicting violent revolutions in Latin America or elsewhere. Still less am I advocating them. I wish only to suggest that violent social revolutions are a possibility in countries where feudal oligarchies resist all meaningful change by peaceful means. We must not, in our preference for the democratic procedures envisioned by the Charter of Punta del Este, close our minds to the possibility that democratic procedures may fail in certain countries and that where democracy does fail violent social convulsions may occur.

We would do well, while continuing our efforts to promote peaceful change through the Alliance for Progress, to consider what our reactions might be in the event of the outbreak of genuine social revolution in one or more Latin American countries. Such a revolution did occur in Bolivia, and we accepted it calmly and sensibly. But what if a violent social revolution were to break out in one of the larger Latin American countries? Would we feel certain that it was Cuban or Soviet inspired? Would we wish to intervene on the side of established authority? Or would we be willing to tolerate or even support a revolution if it was seen to be not Communist but similar in nature to the Mexican revolution or the Nasser revolution in Egypt?

These are hypothetical questions and there is no readily available set of answers to them. But they are questions which we should be thinking about because they have to do with problems that could become real and urgent with great suddenness. We should be considering, for example, what groups in particular countries might conceivably lead revolutionary movements, and if we can identify them, we should be considering how we might communicate with them and influence them in such a way that their movements, if successful, will not pursue courses detrimental to our security and our interests.

IV. VIEWS OF OBSERVERS

SELECTION IV—A

Herbert Matthews, who is currently a member of the editorial board of *The New York Times,* was formerly its leading Latin American specialist. His interviews with Castro in 1957 gave the rebel leader a favorable press in the United States. This selection which is taken from his book *The Cuban Story* (New York, 1961), pp. 115–22, is reprinted with the permission of the publisher, George Braziller, Inc. © 1961 by Herbert Matthews.

The problem that future historians will have to face lies in the fact that the Castro regime was not communistic in its early stages but gradually moved deeper and deeper into the Communist camp, and if this trend continues we will have a Cuban variety of communism.

I do not believe myself that there will be any problem for these historians on the question of whether Fidel Castro, Che Guevara, Raul Castro and some other top leaders were, themselves, Communists. They always denied that they were and there is no evidence to date that the top three—Fidel, Che and Raul—ever were Communists in the sense of being members of any Communist party. Not even the United States White Paper was able to claim this. It surely should be obvious (although apparently it is not) that if the CIA or the FBI or the American Embassy in Havana or the State Department was ever able to unearth proof that any of these men were Communists, they would have proclaimed it triumphantly to the world. The argument that they might just as well be Communists is another matter, but this is quite different from saying that they were, or are, Communists.

New evidence may change the picture, but on the evidence available and on my personal knowledge of Fidel Castro, I have always said and I still say that he was not and is not a Communist.

The Publisher of *The New York Times,* Arthur Hays Sulzberger, was, like many others, puzzled by my insistence and asked me for an explanation after a trip I made to Cuba in August, 1960. This was my reply:

I have your note asking what my definition of a Communist is. I have a very simple and straightforward one—and I consider it the only exact one.

A Communist is a man—or woman—who 1) either belongs openly to the Communist party or 2) is a crypto-Communist. In either case the person takes his orders from his party or movement, is responsible to it and is an agent of Moscow.

In my opinion it is most important to make this distinction. Take the Cubans. It may make no difference whatever *today* and in practice for the time being, whether they are Reds or simply doing as the Reds do. In the long run it can make all the difference in the world, because, if they are not under Communist discipline, taking orders from the party and Moscow, they can change. They can even turn on the Reds and destroy them.

The terms communism and Communist are much too loosely used in the American press and by Americans generally. I believe that the precise definition I have given above is the only one we should use in *The Times*—and as a matter of fact, I think it is.

The problem, from the beginning, was that Fidel Castro was making a radical, Leftist, nationalistic revolution that inevitably brought conflict with the United States. The old cry: "Our enemy is on the Right! No enemies to the Left!" heard in the West since the French Revolution was now being heard in Cuba.

The Batista dictatorship had laid the foundation for the Communists. In Cuba all the old-line political parties had been thoroughly discredited or broken up into fragments. The 26th of July Movement was a congeries of men, parties and classes, split down the middle by a dividing line between the Sierra Maestra group, who were out for a very radical social revolution, and the civic resistance, which wanted to make social reforms but in a democratic, evolutionary way.

This left only the Cuban Communists, trained, organized and ready. Their party kept on functioning from the Batista era. It was—and is—called the *Partido Socialista Popular* (Popular Socialist Party). It had not helped Fidel Castro—on the contrary—but it was naturally ready to help now and, being tolerated, became the only political party operating in Cuba. This did not mean that it even remotely had the sort of power Communist parties have in Communist countries, especially for the first year and a half, but American thinking with regard to communism is over-simplified and blinded by emotions, and this simple and obvious distinction was not made.

As a result, the Cuban Communists were given an importance all out of proportion to the reality. Some of us kept warning from the beginning that this played right into their hands. It was exactly what they needed to build them up and to attract adherents. The psychology of Fidel Castro and the other young revolutionaries was such that the more they were attacked for being Communists, or the dupes of Communists, the more difficult it became to oppose communism if they wanted to. For Fidel, especially, to turn against the Reds would have seemed like truckling to the United States, yielding to American attacks, and he would rather have his throat cut than do that.

In Cuba, nothing was more helpful to the Reds than the fact that the American press, radio and television, Congress and many American diplomats and businessmen conceded victory to the Communists long before they had won it. We surrendered before we had begun to lose.

The first, and probably most damaging, major attack in this field came from Stuart Novins of the Columbia Broadcasting System on May 3, 1959. The material had been gathered in March and April. The theme was that "this Cuban island is today a totalitarian dictatorship and is rapidly becoming a Communist beachhead in the Caribbean."

It was nothing of the sort at that time. Because it became more or less that, one gets the appearance of accuracy and prescience. Yet, anyone studying the text of the telecast then and now, knowing the facts or even using common sense, will see that the arguments Novins was using to "prove" his thesis were feeble to the point of ludicrousness. This was true of all the commentators and correspondents who harped on this theme from the beginning and who now say: "We told you so."

The historian will not have such an easy time of it and there is no validity, today, in saying: "What's the difference?" It might have made a lot of difference if there had been more understanding in the formative stages of the Cuban Revolution. This is aside from the desirability of keeping the record straight.

As I remarked earlier, it will never be possible to figure out the extent to which the young Cuban leaders wanted Communism and the extent to which they were forced into reliance on Communism. Those who were closest to Fidel Castro in 1959 could feel assured that neither he certainly, nor, with some doubts, any of the men in positions of control were Communists, and that they had a Cuban revolution, not a Communist revolution. This will surely be the verdict of history.

However, it was always obvious that there were many Communists at secondary and lower levels. They naturally supported the revolutionary government from the beginning. Fidel, on his part, was making a revolution in which he had to attack the conservative, propertied, business classes on the Right. He asked why he should gratuitously attack the Communists on his Left when they were supporting him and when, as he confidently believed, they were weak and unimportant? He wanted to unite all the forces of the Left.

This was the position for many months, until he and his top advisers became convinced that the answer to their revolutionary problems lay in the methods of totalitarian communism. I would place the final decision on this, so far as Fidel was concerned, in the late summer or early autumn of 1960. So far as Che Guevara and Raul Castro were concerned, it would have come sooner and they undoubtedly influenced Fidel.

His early calculations were logical and understandable. He did not want a Communist revolution and I know what a low opinion he had of the Cuban Reds. He was not underestimating them personally, with the possible exception of Rafael Rodríguez, but he was underestimating the efficiency, skill and experience that lay in the Communist technique.

I suppose I was one of the first to warn him and all the young leaders of that danger, for I began in January, 1959, and was hard at it the last time I saw Fidel, which was in August, 1960. The most effective argument, I thought, was to impress upon them all that they could have a Cuban revolution, or a Communist revolution, but not both. I pointed out that the Reds were not working for Cuba or for Fidel and that their revolution was not his revolution. I was myself underestimating the danger, because I believed that the young revolutionaries recognized these threats and would fight against them in the showdown. I now think it is possible that they can have a communistic type of revolution that is also Cuban and Latin American.

The argument that the Cuban Reds had helped Batista, not the 26th of July Movement, was beside the point, in the same way that there was no use pointing out how the trade-union leaders had supported Batista. Fidel needed the urban workers and he thought he needed the Reds. The Communists really were useful to him in 1959. That was safe so long as he did not become dependent on them.

Fidel and I always spoke frankly to each other and he took criticism from me that no one else would have dared to utter. He knew that I was sympathetic, understanding and a friend, and since I was old enough to be his father, he respected my age. He is a normally poor listener, but he used to listen to me—and to my wife when we were both in Havana.

I mention this simply to bolster my argument that Fidel Castro had no desire or intention to go the Communist way until events, pressures, perhaps necessity, drove him that way. It was not a previously calculated or an inevitable development.

Historians will have to ask themselves how much the American attitude and policies helped to force Fidel Castro in this direction. If this was what he wanted all along, there was nothing the United States could have done to prevent it. If he did not, as many of us believe, then the position taken almost from the beginning by the American press, radio, television, Congress, Pentagon, State Department, the business world and so forth, helped to build up communism and drive Cuba irresistibly into the Communist corner.

> SELECTION IV–B
>
> The article which follows is taken from *Red Star Over Cuba* (New York, 1960), pp. 208–15, by Nathaniel Weyl. Reprinted by permission of the Devin-Adair Company. A journalist and writer on politics, Weyl was a frequent critic of communist influences in the United States.

THE CUBAN CASE

Specific suggestions for dealing with the Cuban crisis would probably be out of date by the time this book went through the presses in view of the extreme fluidity of that situation. It would seem evident that the United States has enormous economic power which it can exert in this area, that the propinquity of Cuba offers unrivalled opportunities for blanketing the

Cuban air waves with freedom stations located on U.S. soil and that the security problem presented by Soviet agents on Cuban passports must be a matter of hemispheric concern.

A revolution by the Cuban people against their Communist oppressors must be predicated on mass discontent and mass hatred. This is not automatically created by economic disasters and political injustice. It must be crystallized, channelized against the regime and directed from resentment to specific militant actions by a widely disseminated propaganda which is organized in terms of planned stages of revolutionary discontent. Thus, the radio is of key importance in the Cuban case. American-financed Cuban freedom stations can compete effectively with Castro's radio for the minds of the Cuban people. Should the Castro regime resort to jamming, counterjamming would break the main nexus between the charisma of the Communist dictator and the masses who support him.

When it ceased apologizing for Castro, the State Department embraced the general line of "the revolution betrayed." This presupposed that the Castro movement originally had decent and constructive purposes, but that at some late stage it was taken over by Communist agents.

There are two major weaknesses to the "revolution betrayed" line in addition to its patent falsity. First, it implicitly accepts the Castro position that Cuban soldiers who refused to betray their government are "war criminals" and that Cubans who had enough prescience to oppose Castro from the outset as a Communist are reactionaries. It serves to limit the potential anti-Castro coalition to leftwingers.

In the second place, this approach reflects a much broader political fallacy—the doctrine that the United States in its foreign policy should seek to compete with Soviet-controlled groups in "liberalism," "progressivism," "leftism," or whatever it is to be called. In such a competition, the United States is condemned to defeat. The reason for this is that our advocacy of radical measures must be limited by our desire to preserve the existing social order and reform it by peaceful and evolutionary processes. The Soviets, by contrast, are able to support measures of an unlimitedly leftist character because their revolutionary program is divided sharply into two disparate stages: the violent destruction of the existing social order, then the construction of a new regime. In the first stage, wildly impractical radical measures are grist for the Red mill; in the second, completely authoritarian procedures are imposed to accomplish the task.

The "revolution betrayed" approach also serves to save face for those Americans, in the State Department and elsewhere, who through bad judgment or evil intentions brought tragedy to the Cuban people and diplomatic defeat to America. If future Communist consolidations of power in this Hemisphere are to be dealt with realistically and intelligently, it is desirable that the men chiefly responsible for the Cuban disgrace be eliminated from public office.

DEMOCRACY VS. DICTATORSHIP

One of the reasons that American policy took the wrong turn in the Castro situation is that the State Department and most of American informed public opinion held a simplified view of the Latin American situation. It was assumed that *the* issue in Latin America was democracy vs. dictatorship. It was assumed that only the right-wing governments were dictatorships, thus completely overlooking virtually dictatorial systems of a leftist character which operated through nominally democratic institutions. It was assumed that the dictatorships invariably oppressed the people and were hated by them. It was assumed that the United States gave support to Latin American dictatorships, or, at the very least, failed to take measures to destroy them. It was assumed that the United States thus squandered much of the good will it had acquired during the era of the Good Neighbor policy.

Some of these propositions are false and all of them are questionable. The demand that the United States actively support "democracies" against "dictatorships" is frequently voiced as a smokescreen by philo-Communist groups. The word "democracy" often assumes it Soviet connotations as in the so-called "people's democracies" and deluded American liberals find they are being inveigled into backing pro-Soviet, hate-America regimes which are considerably more savage, inhuman and totalitarian than the old-fashioned *caudillo* dictatorships that they supplant.

As of June 1960, rightwing, militaristic dictatorships were confined to two small, unimportant countries: Paraguay and the Dominican Republic. This suggested that the transition from dictatorship to democracy would be achieved gradually by the Latin American people as they advanced to greater economic, political and educational maturity, became urbanized, developed industries and attained national cohesion. The underdeveloped countries tended to remain largely dictatorial behind facades of democratic institutions which were seldom viable. Yet as an isolated and ignorant peasantry is displaced by an urban proletariat, as the landlord ruling class is supplanted by a capitalist one, the trend is toward more democratic institutions. If the changeover from dictatorship to democracy is caused by institutional processes of a fundamental character, the strength of which varies from country to country, it would seem rash for the United States to rush in and seek to complete the process.

The demand that the United States deny "bread and salt" to the dictatorships implies intervention in the internal affairs of Latin American nations to impose those forms of government which we have found suited to our own national character. The trend in U.S. policy has been away from such intervention since the first inauguration of President Franklin D. Roosevelt. The reasons for this abstention, quite aside from moral considerations, include realization of the fact that intervention generally brings the United States a harvest of hate and belief that the Latin American peoples will best attain political maturity if they are given responsibility and freedom to solve their own internal problems.

In recent years, most of the rightwing dictators have supported U.S. policies. In Central America, according to an intelligent and authoritative study by Martz, the dictatorships have tended to be more orderly, more constructive in the economic field and perhaps more popular than the real and pseudo democracies.

The concept of democracy vs. dictatorship is objectionable because it reveals a narrow conception of American institutions and ideals. To the extent that we wish to transform Latin America in accordance with our own image, we should be concerned with individual freedom and due process of law at least as much as with democracy. In backward countries, these three institutional processes often do not move in parallel directions and the triumph of "democracy" may mean rule by a mindless majority, suppression of dissent, destruction of civil rights, flouting of due process, and oppression of the really creative and constructive members of the society.

Our broad purposes for Latin America would presumably include such other values as economic and political stability, the development of a strong middle class and of a free-enterprise economy, a system that is dynamic and expanding, that is moving into the full light of the modern world and not away from it.

Reluctance to interfere in the internal affairs of Western Hemisphere Republics is a sound attitude provided it does not apply to situations in which one of these nations becomes an agency or outpost of international Communism. In that event, the United States and the other American Republics are bound both by the decisions of the Tenth Inter-American Conference and by their overriding continental interests to work to restore free institutions.

TIME IS NOT ON OUR SIDE

The political importance of Latin America to the United States is greater than its economic or strategic role. Latin America is the one great, underdeveloped region of continental proportions which has been massively exposed over a long time period to some of the basic concepts of U.S. civilization, to North American political and economic doctrines, methods of business enterprise and secular and scientific attitudes of mind. During the past century, there has been a considerable growth of hemispheric solidarity and a corresponding displacement of French and Iberian by North American cultural leadership.

Any serious breach in the wall of hemispheric solidarity must be a severe blow to United States prestige. Communist consolidation of power anywhere in Latin America will inevitably be interpreted as evidence that the United States is stumbling and that the Free World alliance is globally on the retreat.

In the last decade, three Communist-dominated governments have taken power in the Americas—those of Guatemala, British Guiana and Cuba. The Jagan regime in British Guiana was ousted by the British Government; the Guatemalan Communist regime of Arbenz was shattered by Latin American freedom fighters supported by a militant, courageous and dedicated American Secretary of State, the late John Foster Dulles. In the Cuban case, indecision and appeasement prevailed in the State Department during the year and a half which Fidel Castro needed to consolidate his power internally and create a proletarian dictatorship.

SELECTION IV–C

Maury D. Baker, professor of history at Kent State University, has specialized in Latin American affairs with a particular interest in Mexico. This excerpt from his article "DamYankeeism in Latin America," *Social Science*, XXXVIII (October, 1963), pp. 199–204, is reprinted by permission of the author and of *Social Science*.

To the Latin Americans, the United States represents a business civilization that is obsessively materialistic. Its power is economic and political, not intellectual or cultural. Its sense of values is pragmatic; man is not measured primarily for intrinsic qualities, such as goodness or intelligence; he is weighed by actions and results. "To make good," "to deliver the goods," "to bring home the bacon" are characteristic slogans. The philosophy of life of the North American is one of success, with possession of money the obvious sign of success. The ideal type is the successful businessman; the archetype is the millionaire, who is enterprising, shrewd, and, above all, active.

The North American love of action is part of what might be identified as a cult of energy. Muscular activity is always something to boast about; athletes advertise their status in big letters spread across their chests. The cult manifests itself also in enthusiastic dedication to work. North Americans live to work, rather than work to live. This does not encourage the development of sensitivity and perceptiveness and tends to breed a leveling vulgarity and crudeness. The emphasis on deeds rather than moral substance stimulates disdain for the inner life. The contemplative man, the "egghead," is suspect.

Latin Americans feel that the success of the United States in material production and social progress is gained through social self-discipline and conformity, which is characteristic of almost all citizens. Organization, mass production, and standardization have detracted from North American individuality and freedom. The resultant civilization is so complex that its life has to proceed with the regularity of a clock. "Time is money," "to save time," "to have a good time" are expressions commonly heard. People live according to formulae which save time: they walk fast, eat fast, read fast, and even worship fast. Latin Americans find this discipline stifling. They believe it takes its price in terms of human personality, of self-expression, of charm, of erudition. North Americans rob themselves of the opportunity to enjoy life, to savor it. They have, according to Chilean scholar Benjamin Subercaseaux, "renounced an immense amount of the pure animal enjoyment which primitive man possessed and which we Latin Americans would not renounce for any price. North Americans do not regret this renunciation because they have been born into a society of self-controlled people . . . but when we Latin Americans go to live in the United States, we feel that life has lost all its attraction . . . we feel like a Polynesian on whom a missionary has just placed a shirt."

Because of their empty inner life and their intense, exhausting external life, in the opinion of Latin Americans, many people in the United States tend to turn to forms of escapism, ranging from television addiction through theatrical evangelism and frenzied dancing to excesses of alcohol and sex. An element in the existing breach between the two Americas has been a kind of moral revulsion in Latin America against the United States as a country of Hollywood morals, commonplace divorce, and lack of religious faith. One thing should be understood: the Latin Americans consider the people of the United States as less moral than they are. They consider the civilization of the United States to be inferior to theirs. In the words of José Enrique Rodo, written half a century ago, "the torch lighted on the shores of the Mediterranean more than 3000 years ago, which soared to glory in the culture of Athens, a work and tradition of which we Latin Americans form a part, adds up to a sum which cannot be equalled by any equation of Washington plus Edison." Latin Americans fear contamination by North American culture, fear what some call "cocacolazation." They fear that, along with North American automobiles and refrigerators and television sets will come "vices, corruption, false horizons of life and progress." They fear they will cease to be Latin Americans.

*   *   *   *   *

Generalizing about Latin America is dangerous: the area includes many different nations and historic pasts and environments and peoples. It is like trying to describe a jigsaw puzzle by discussing a few of its pieces. Attempting to generalize about the motivations of Latin Americans amounts almost to effrontery. Who can explain human likes and dislikes? Who can assess the influence of the church upon the minds of men in Latin America? Who knows the strength of the Iberian subconscious in Latin America—a subconscious that values the past and resents the twentieth century, of which the United States is so prominently a part? Who can say how much of the hostility toward the United States is compounded simply of the natural envy and frustration felt by people whose lives are difficult for those whose lives are relatively easy?

What can we do to eliminate DamYankeeism? Not much. The United States is the Latin Americans' most convenient whipping boy: should they forget it, the Communists will remind them of it. The Alliance for Progress may lessen the charges of neglect, but it will increase charges of intervention and imperialism. Nothing short of a miracle will halt Latin American criticism and resentment of the United States. Nothing can alter the geographical and racial and historical factors that have arranged the fates of the two regions. Time and need may bring them closer together, slowly, but it is doubtful that the next century will see such harmony that the Latin Americans will cease to think of themselves as Ariel and the North Americans as Caliban. The people of the United States might as well reconcile themselves, with all possible equanimity and grace, to the continuing existence in Latin America—as elsewhere—of DamYankeeism.

13

NATO AND NUCLEAR SHARING

The MLF

I. EDITORIAL INTRODUCTION

Given the number of crises it had encountered in its first years, NATO's survival in 1960 might reasonably have surprised the casual observer. A few crises had been solved, many had disappeared, most receded into the background, dormant temporarily, but liable to create tensions again among the allies. By 1960 the world was resigned to living with an uneasy balance of terror, with the reality of nuclear proliferation, and with discouragement over prospects of disengagement or disarmament, although each of these related issues continued to be discussed. Such changes as had occurred by the end of the Eisenhower administration emerged primarily from a condition not fully recognized by the allies or their enemies: namely, the new power and prosperity of Western Europe. It was not that the Soviet Union had abandoned its hostility; the threats over the U–2 fiasco, the abandonment of the summit meeting of 1960, and the continuing festering of a divided Berlin confirmed the continuing Cold War. But against this constant the European allies appeared to be less afraid of communist invasion, more critical of American seniority in the partnership, and all absorbed in their own burgeoning economies.

In the light of the changing relationships of Western Europe vis-à-vis both America and Russia, new questions were asked. Why should the United States continue to exercise a nuclear monopoly within the alliance, in partial conjunction with the United Kingdom? From this major question developed others, such as the weaknesses in America's leadership, the credibility of America's protection of Europe in the event of crisis, and the charges of a new colonialism making Europe a permanent ward of America to be exploited economically and politically. With the France of de Gaulle increasingly disturbed over "Anglo-Saxon" hegemony and with Germany increasingly uncomfortable at its exclusion from nuclear controls despite its major contributions to the alliance, the United States felt it necessary in 1960 to show the allies that it would share the nuclear deterrent.

This decision, reflected in the North Atlantic Council communiqué of December, 1960, where the United States suggested a multilateral force (MLF) that would employ nuclear weapons (Selection II–A), raised as many problems as it solved. The MLF would have to conform with a Congressional requirement that the ultimate decision for its use be in American hands; it would have to anticipate its negative effect upon disarmament plans and upon hopes of limiting the spread of nuclear weapons; it would have to respect the visceral fears of Germany, the major beneficiary of this plan, on the part of the allies as well as of the Warsaw Pact countries; and it would have to create the illusion of equality while maintaining the primacy of American control.

The plan failed, even though it ranged from vague talk of missile-armed tactical land forces to a Polaris-armed flotilla of twenty-five ships, each ship armed with eight missiles. The MLF collapsed in the wake of French opposition and European suspicions, and its demise, though never announced, may be perceived amidst the pieties of the 1964 Anglo-American communiqué favoring allied nuclear defense but not nuclear proliferation. (Selection II–B.)

The debate over the wisdom of a multilateral nuclear force was not confined to Europeans. From its beginnings the administration was forced to justify the program, if only for the enormous cost involved in the project. Senator Wayne Morse of Oregon wondered at its purpose. The objection to the American veto would still be valid, and if this were a move to put the use of nuclear force to a majority vote of the allies in the future, the United States would be as firm as de Gaulle against the MLF. But even more seriously at the moment, the Europeans did not seem to want the MLF, or even a NATO that would involve additional costs. If this was Europe's attitude, let them defend themselves. (Selection III–A.) The intimations of a neoisolationism in the Senator's statements gave particular force to a plea by Undersecretary of State George W. Ball for the MLF as a means of coping with the change, of adjusting NATO to new circumstances. Even more, the MLF appeared in Ball's view as a vital instrument in promoting unity between America and Europe. (Selection III–B.)

The tensions of a presidential election understandably affected the debate on the MLF, and Europe's skepticism about the reality of sharing under the new plan was clearly expressed in the course of the campaign debates. Congressman Craig Hosmer of California mocked the hypocrisy of the administration's official position that the MLF represented mixed control of atomic weapons when in fact the power rested with the President and the American commander in Europe. And if the French doubted the support of America in a moment of crisis the fault lay with the Kennedy-Khrushchev meetings in which both leaders revealed that the mutual destructiveness of the nuclear power made missile warfare untenable. No wonder de Gaulle was forced to develop his own *force de frappe*. American leadership, Hosmer suggested, had failed. (Selection III–C.)

Whether or not American leadership had failed is still a moot question; the failure of the MLF, on the other hand, is not in doubt. The French in particular, and the other allies, except Germany, in general, found the MLF unsatisfactory. Rather than solving the intra-NATO differences, it had only exacerbated old problems: German interest in the plan only aroused fear of a German control of nuclear weapons; French coldness reflected de Gaulle's conviction that the MLF was only another measure of American control of Europe; the smaller allies were fearful of Soviet response to their participation; and all recognized the element of sham in the "sharing" of nuclear weapons. Under these circumstances the United States permitted the MLF to be shelved.

Professor Robert Strausz-Hupé of the University of Pennsylvania, in speaking before the House Foreign Affairs Committee in 1966, was convinced that the kind of pressure exerted on the allies to accept the MLF damaged the fabric of the alliance, while the "belated burial" did nothing to restore it. The scrapping of the MLF not only angered Germany which was to be its major beneficiary but proved to France that the United States would sacrifice NATO interests in order to reach an accommodation with the Soviet Union. What American foreign policy needed was a sense of coherence that would inform NATO as well as the rest of the world of its course and direction. (Selection IV–A.)

Ronald Steel, a former foreign service officer and an analyst of America's European policies, saw a very different lesson in the history of the Multilateral Force as early as 1963. To him its difficulties heralded the end of an alliance which had once served a purpose but no longer did. The world had changed since a weak frightened Europe requested American help against an aggressive Soviet enemy. The Russians were no longer the threat they had been in the 1940's; Europe was no longer weak or frightened. They did not need the type of tutelage the MLF implicitly reflected; Europe had the capability of defending itself. It was time, Steel urged, that the United States came to terms with the new Europe. (Selection IV–B.)

Since NATO in 1967 has failed to answer the problems of nuclear sharing, has lost France as an active ally, and has increasing doubts of America's leadership, the collapse of the alliance should have been complete. Yet, Thomas Schelling, a Harvard economist, could regard the departure of France in 1967 as an end of the "ideology" of the Atlantic Alliance rather than an end of the alliance itself. The presence of United States troops in Europe is still "the central feature of NATO strategy and the guarantor of Europe's security," while the issue of nuclear sharing is not only insoluble in his view, but also of lesser importance, "a luxury, an intra-alliance problem to be argued seriously only when there is no external threat to command our energies." Nevertheless, Schelling like Strausz-Hupé asked for a foreign policy for NATO in the future, and a concomitant American diplomatic initiative that has yet to be developed by the Johnson administration. (Selection IV–C.)

II. DOCUMENTS

> SELECTION II–A
>
> In the final communique of their Paris meeting, December 16 to 18, 1960, the Ministers of the North Atlantic Council instructed the permanent representatives to study the U.S. proposal for the MLF (multilateral forces). This selection including the above recommendation is taken from NATO Letter, IX (January 1961), p. 13.

The regular Ministerial session of the North Atlantic Council was held in Paris from December 16 to 18, 1960.

2. The Ministers engaged in an extensive review of the international situation—political, military and economic. In pursuance of decisions previously taken, they also considered the question of long-term planning on the basis of a progress report from the Secretary General and suggestions put forward by Governments.

I

3. The Council reaffirmed the solidarity of the Alliance and their dedication to the principle of the settlement of all disputes by peaceful means, without recourse to the use of force or threats. They declared their determination to work for a lasting improvement in international relations, in which freedom, national independence and law would be respected. This would be true peaceful coexistence free from all idea of world domination.

4. The Council deplored the lack of progress during the past year on disarmament, resulting from the communist states' withdrawal from the Ten-Power Conference before even examining the Western proposals. The Council reaffirmed their support for the principles expressed in those proposals as a basis for attaining their common objective of general and complete disarmament by stages under effective international control. They expressed their hope for the early resumption of negotiations.

5. The Council regretted the lack of progress on the reunification of Germany on the basis of self-determination. With regard to Berlin, the Council reaffirmed their declaration of 16 December 1958. In face of the recent

Soviet threats and harassing tactics, they once again declared their determination to protect the freedom of the people of West Berlin.

II

6. In order that the Atlantic Alliance may pursue its constructive purposes in peace and without fear, confronted as it is by the menace of growing communist military strength, the North Atlantic nations must be able to respond to any attack with whatever force might be appropriate. There must be a proper balance in the forces of the Alliance of nuclear and conventional strength to provide the required flexibility. The Ministers, in the light of the Annual Review, took note of the progress which had been made, and expressed their determination to continue their efforts to improve the deterrent and defensive strength of the Alliance.

7. In this connection, the United States Government suggested the concept of an MRBM multilateral force for consideration by the Alliance. The Council took note of the United States suggestion with great interest and instructed the Permanent Representatives to study the suggestion and related matters in detail.

The Council welcomed the assurance of the United States to maintain in the NATO area United States nuclear weapons made available to NATO.

8. At the same time, the Council agreed on the equal importance of strengthening the shield forces of NATO in other respects so that there can be no possibility of miscalculation or misunderstanding of the Alliance's determination and ability to resist aggression by whatever means are appropriate and necessary.

9. The Ministers noted with satisfaction the steps so far taken in response to the proposals made by Defence Ministers in Spring 1960 in the field of logistics and for co-operations in research, development and production of military equipment. They urged all parties concerned to press on with the projects already selected, and to study what further projects are suitable for co-operative action.

> *SELECTION II–B*
>
> The following is the text of a joint communique prepared as a White House press release and issued following the meeting of the President of the United States and the Prime Minister of the United Kingdom on December 8, 1964. It is reprinted here from the Department of State *Bulletin*, LI (December 28, 1964), pp. 903–4.

The President of the United States and the Prime Minister of the United Kingdom met in Washington 7th December to 9th December. They were assisted by Secretary of State Rusk, Secretary of Defense McNamara and Under Secretary of State Ball and by the Foreign Secretary, Mr. [Patrick] Gordon Walker and the Secretary of State for Defence, Mr. [Denis] Healey.

In the course of a wide ranging exchange of views, the President and the Prime Minister reviewed the current international situation in light of the responsibilities which their countries carry for maintaining, together with their allies and friends, peace and stability throughout the world. They re-affirmed their determination to support the peace-keeping operations of the United Nations and to do all in their power to strengthen the systems of regional alliance in Europe, the Middle East and the Far East to which they both contribute.

They recognized the importance of strengthening the unity of the Atlantic Alliance in its strategic nuclear defense. They discussed existing proposals for this purpose and an outline of some new proposals presented by the British Government. They agreed that the objective in this field is to cooperate in finding the arrangements which best meet the legitimate interests of all members of the Alliance, while maintaining existing safeguards on the use of nuclear weapons, and preventing their further proliferation. A number of elements of this problem were considered during this initial exchange of views as a preliminary to further discussions among interested members of the Alliance.

They also agreed on the urgency of a world-wide effort to promote the non-dissemination and non-acquisition of nuclear weapons, and of continuing Western initiatives towards arms control and disarmament. They recognized the increasing need for initiatives of this kind in light of the recent detonation of a Chinese nuclear device.

The President and the Prime Minister reaffirmed their determination to continue to contribute to the maintenance of peace and stability in the Middle East and the Far East. In this connection they recognized the particular importance of the military effort which both their countries are making in support of legitimate Governments in South East Asia, particularly in Malaysia and South Vietnam, which seek to maintain their independence and to resist subversion.

They recognized also that a nation's defense policy must be based on a sound economy. The President and the Prime Minister, while determined that their countries should continue to play their full parts in the world-wide peace-keeping effort, affirmed their conviction that the burden of defense should be shared more equitably among the countries of the free world.

They agreed also on the need for improvement in the balance of payments and in the productivity and competitive position of both their economies in order to ensure the underlying economic strength which is essential for fulfilling their heavy international responsibilities. In this connection they arranged to explore in detail the possibilities of closer cooperation between their two countries in defense research and development and in weapons production.

The President and the Prime Minister reaffirmed their belief in the importance of close allied cooperation in international affairs. They agreed that this meeting was only the first stage in their consultation in which the matters that they had discussed would need to be examined in greater detail. They looked forward, too, to continuing discussions at all levels both within the Alliance and in wider international negotiations in pursuit of nuclear and conventional disarmament and all measures to reduce world tension.

III. VIEWS OF PARTICIPANTS

> ### SELECTION III–A
>
> Senator Wayne Morse, Democrat of Oregon, has been a frequent critic of foreign policy under both Republican and Democratic administrations. In this excerpt taken from the *Congressional Record*—Senate, 88th Congress, 2d sess., June 13, 1964, pp. 10832–33, he airs his views on the MLF.

EUROPEAN DRIVE FOR NUCLEAR INDEPENDENCE

One good which I do see coming out of the whole discussion of a NATO nuclear force is that it will finally compel the United States to face reality and make some basic and long overdue decisions about NATO.

The meaningless cut-and-paste job that came out of the Ottawa Conference is one more stalling device designed to protect our Defense and State Department policymakers from facing the inevitable while they work on something else. But it will not save them for long.

It will not save them, because they are refusing to recognize that now, and for several years past, NATO has been largely a United States-Germany alliance maintained primarily for the defense of Berlin.

The monumental disinterest of France and Britain in this endeavor is being made more clear than ever in the debate over the NATO nuclear force. Like Germany, they see no need whatever to subsidize Greece, Turkey, Spain, Norway, Denmark, and Italy in order to keep the Russians from rolling through West Berlin. That is a folly all the members have all been happy to leave to the United States.

But unlike Germany, none of our other NATO partners has much interest in a nuclear force, even under NATO command and with mixed units that cannot be withdrawn, over which the United States will maintain a veto and which will add little but a new expense to the NATO defenses.

Why do we not face up to the fact that the only purpose in the proposed NATO nuclear force is to give Germany a hand in nuclear weaponry which she is not allowed to have on her own? That is what this is all about. West Germany is forbidden by treaty to manufacture nuclear warheads and missiles. Now that France has decided that NATO no longer serves her primary national interest and is embarking on her own military buildup, including the nuclear one, it is alleged that Germany will soon come to feel that she, too, must have her own such force.

One alternative would be to free Germany from her 1954 pledge. But that is supposed to arouse raging fires of apprehension on the part of the Russians, and among some of Germany's neighbors as well.

FALLACY OF FEAR OF GERMANY

I do not think that there is much to be said about the notion that the former victims of German aggression within the Atlantic Alliance fear nuclear weapons in the hands of Germany. If they truly did, they would be anxious to participate in a NATO force in which Germany was only one of many members, and over which the United States had a veto.

But no. France does not allow any nuclear warheads on her soil because they are under American control.

That is the De Gaulle position. I ask, Is that the position of an ally?

Considering this position of de Gaulle, and the position of de Gaulle on manpower assignments to NATO, on foreign trade, on the Common Market, and on the discrimination against the United States vis-a-vis GATT, we would have a hard time bringing him under the definition of "ally."

I am at a loss to understand why this administration is proposing more concessions to France until we determine the question as to whether de Gaulle is to be an ally again. If he is not, let him "go it alone." We should not support his nationalistic program, or his plan for a French nuclear force, with a single dollar of American taxpayers' money.

Norway and Denmark do not allow nuclear warheads on their soil at all. The Italian Government was recently forced to promise its people that no bases would be made available in Italy for our Polaris submarines. So much for their fear of the possibility of a German hand on a nuclear capacity in which there was no American participation.

While Germany is anxious to have American participation in nuclear force even with an American veto, France is only anxious to have a European nuclear force in which there will be no American participation at all. The rest of the partners, including Britain, are too disinterested or too poor to concern themselves with any appreciable share in it.

AMERICAN PROPOSALS

I do not see anything in either the rearrangements on paper that was put together at Ottawa, or the proposed surface fleet of Polaris vessels, that will bridge this gap, that is really a gap among the Europeans. I do not see any good purpose whatever in putting more American money into a venture that is only a facade to cover up the dissolved foundation of NATO.

At Ottawa, a nuclear command under General Lemnitzer was set up, having at its disposal three U.S. Polaris subs, 180 British Vulcan bombers, and national fighter-bomber forces from 8 other members, many of which are already equipped for U.S. controlled nuclear warheads. A NATO liaison staff will go to Strategic Air Command headquarters at Omaha to take part in planning and targeting operations. However, all warheads assigned to NATO will still be under American control, and any of the assigned forces can be withdrawn at the discretion of the donor country.

The French were right in accepting this arrangement as being nothing new, different, or constructive.

The Secretary of State did not bring out of Ottawa the slightest change in French posture from what it was when the French delegates first sat around the table at Ottawa. Ottawa did not produce any significant commitment on the part of France. The French delegates went back to France, and De Gaulle remains free to travel down his nationalistic road. I say he should be allowed to go, but we should not pay his travel expenses. He should pay them, himself.

The force is proposed to be under NATO command, but not under NATO control. It retains the same objection that the French and many others in Europe regard as the fatal defect, and that is an American veto.

PROPOSED FLEET NOT MULTILATERAL AT ALL

But our proposed nuclear surface fleet maintains the same defect. It also has the added defect of being very costly to ourselves and the Germans, because under this arrangement, we and the Germans would each pay 40 percent, leaving 10 percent to Britain, and 10 percent to any of the other members who might want to participate. France will undoubtedly remain out of it entirely. For its mere 10 percent Britain will also have a veto over its use.

The total cost of this force has not been indicated, but estimates I have heard run from $2.5 to $6 billion. Forty percent of $2.5 billion would put the U.S. share at $1 billion. Forty percent of $6 billion would be $2.4 billion. Even the lower figure is much too high a price to pay for political peace within NATO. That this is a purely political device is generally understood. The force would add nothing to the existing destructive power of the nuclear forces already in the hands of the West.

I do not see how anyone who thinks we and Germany should finance 80 percent of a new nuclear force can consider that force to be a multilateral, NATO force. With Britain financing only 10 percent, it is idle to maintain the fiction that she would be a real partner in the surface fleet venture.

And without France, there simply is no NATO any more, no matter how much we may pretend otherwise. France is too key a country to permit NATO to continue to function without her. It does not matter whether France's reasons for picking up her marbles and leaving the game were sound or not. It is not an issue of wisdom, but an issue of fact. We are all in NATO together, making equal financial and manpower contributions, or NATO is finished. When a major participant declines to fulfill those contributions, that is the end of the organization.

Yet here we are, pushing for a new branch to the organization, this time without France, with only 10-percent participation from Britain, and with insignificant and reluctant contributions, if any are forthcoming at all, from 10 of the other members.

DOES NOT MEET EUROPEAN OBJECTIONS TO PRESENT SETUP

Neither do I see anything in this force that would do anything to overcome European objections to the present arrangement of having all nuclear warheads in NATO under American command. The U.S. veto would remain, and I would be very strongly opposed to any subsequent effort to eliminate that U.S. veto.

What concerns me is that this surface fleet may be only the preliminary step to the creation of a NATO nuclear force to which there will be no veto. Only the doctrine of use of the force by majority vote would overcome the European objection to the present system. Any system that retains a veto in the hands of the United States can hardly remove those objections. So I see little in the surface fleet that will meet the objections to the status quo, unless this is but an opening wedge to a future move to put it under majority vote.

It is quite possible that the military and diplomatic planners who are obsessed with the idea that the United States must be permanently joined with Europe politically, economically, and militarily, think they can advance faster by taking a step at a time than by revealing their true objective at the outset. Perhaps they mistakenly think that once the surface fleet is a reality, and we have sunk a billion dollars into it, Congress will then be more easily persuaded to keep it going by giving up our veto over its use.

SELECTION III–B

Undersecretary of State George W. Ball spoke up for the MLF—in a major speech at Georgetown University, May 7, 1964—when the plan was under heavy criticism in Europe. His address, a portion of which is reprinted here, appeared in the Department of State *Bulletin,* L (May 25, 1964), pp. 826–28.

THE MULTILATERAL NUCLEAR FORCE

The multilateral force we are proposing would be organized within the framework of the Western alliance. To constitute a truly international force, we have felt that it should meet four conditions:

First, it should be assigned to NATO by all countries participating in the force. To meet this condition, we propose that it be collectively owned by the participants and that all participating nations share in the costs of creating, maintaining, and operating it.

Second, it should not be predominantly based on the soil of any one nation. To meet this condition, we are proposing a sea-based force consisting of Polaris-type missiles mounted on surface warships. This force, deployed on the high seas, would operate outside the national limits of any state.

Third, it should be managed and operated by nationals of all participating countries under such conditions that it could not be withdrawn from the alliance to serve the national uses of any participating government. To meet this requirement, we propose that the ships themselves be manned by mixed crews of nationals of the participating nations.

The United States Joint Chiefs of Staff and the Secretary of Defense have concluded that an efficient first-class force can be created in this fashion. SACEUR [Supreme Allied Commander Europe] has stated he would welcome the force as a significant addition to NATO's deterrent forces.

Fourth, the decision to fire the Polaris weapons should be a collective decision of the participating nations. One proposal is that political control be exercised through an executive body representing the participating nations. Obviously this control question is the heart of the matter. We are confident it can be solved.

In an ideal world we could no doubt devise less elaborate means for managing nuclear weapons. But we must work within the limitations of existing political arrangements. Those limitations arise from the fact that Western political institutions have not evolved in pace with the march of our technology. Until the West has achieved a far greater political unity than it possesses today, we believe that the development of a multilateral force is the best available course to pursue.

Not only does it offer the most effective means of dealing with the nuclear problem in the present political framework; it can also make possible a gradual and constructive evolution within that framework. The multilateral force would provide a new opportunity for working toward a greater unity in Europe and a closer partnership between the two sides of the Atlantic.

For the striking progress that has been achieved toward these goals in the past decade and a half has, to a considerable extent, come about from necessity—from the fact that governments have been compelled to cope with specific and immediate problems in Europe and the Atlantic area. And, as we seek to cope with the problem of nuclear arrangement, I have no doubt that we shall—of necessity—make further strides toward a greater political unity in the years ahead.

Over the long pull, it will not be abstract principle but importunate necessity—the urgent need to get hard things done in order that we may survive and flourish—that will move us toward the attainment of the ultimate objective of unity and partnership.

UNEQUAL ALLOCATION OF RESPONSIBILITY

If the lack of political unity in Europe complicates the management of nuclear weapons systems within the NATO alliance, it also limits the development of NATO as an instrument for effective political consultation.

This question of consultation has been a favorite subject for discussions in conferences such as you have been having here today. A strong case can be made—and is frequently made—for greater consultation among NATO members, particularly with regard to world problems that lie outside the scope of the alliance.

The logic of this is clear enough. The member nations of NATO represent 90 percent of the industrial strength of the free world. They are, in Dean Acheson's words, "the central power which will support—if it is to be supported at all—a non-Communist world system."

I do not mean to suggest that, in the modern decentralized world, it would make sense to reserve the management of world affairs to an exclusive board of directors drawn solely from the NATO nations. Such a proposal would be an affront to friendly nations the world over that are playing responsible roles in their own areas. The United States, for example, has military alliances with 28 countries in addition to its NATO partners. At the same time it is clear that unity of policy among the members of NATO is an essential component of free-world power. To quote Mr. Acheson again: "If the center is not solid, relations with the periphery will not provide strength."

Unity of policy should presumably be hammered out through consultation. But consultation—essential though it be—can be fruitful only if all powers concerned are determined to make it so. It can produce little, for example, in the face of rigid philosophical differences such as those we have encountered in attempting to develop a common economic policy toward Cuba. It will also produce little when the consulting parties hold widely differing concepts of responsibility for world problems.

It is this latter point that imposes the most severe limit on the efficacy of consultation today.

Until the Second World War the metropolitan nations of Europe spread their dominance over vast areas of the world through colonial arrangements. But with the crumbling of the great colonial systems and the emergence in their stead of half a hundred new states during the turbulent years since the war, world power relationships have had to be vastly revised.

During this period the world interests of European states have greatly altered; at the same time America has had to devise new concepts of world responsibility.

I mention this dichotomy between interests and responsibility for it is, I think, fundamental to the question of consultation. We Americans have few national interests—in the narrow sense—outside our own territory, but we have assumed vast world responsibility.

The result is an unequal allocation among the Atlantic nations both of responsibility and of the burden of decision that goes with it. This imbalance derives from the imperatives of history—not from deliberate American choice. We are aware that policy and responsibility must not be divorced. We recognize that no nation can be expected to share one without the other.

The United States today is quite prepared to share both with its NATO partners. So far, however, such sharing has been severely limited by differences of attitude within the NATO alliance. The willingness to accept world responsibility—as distinct from the preservation of national interests—is, in our observation and experience, not universal among the NATO membership.

Hopefully this is a passing phenomenon. For the past decade and a half most European nations have been preoccupied with pressing postwar business—the liquidation of colonial arrangements and the building of strong domestic economies. Now this business is largely finished.

Yet this alone will not solve the problem. The problem will never be fully solved until Europe gets on further with the achievement of its own unity, until it organizes itself on a scale commensurate with the requirements of the age.

There are quite obvious reasons for this. The undertaking of world responsibility requires a world view. The discharge of such responsibility under postcolonial conditions must be based on the command of vast resources for defense and foreign aid—and on the will to use them. Western Europe collectively has more than enough resources, but a fragmented Europe cannot efficiently mobilize them in support of a common effort and a common view.

The existing structure of Europe, therefore, sets limits to the effective sharing both of responsibility and decision. But this does not mean that—within the limits thus imposed—we should not continue to improve the present imperfect allocation. In fact, the United States is quite ready to go forward in sharing its responsibilities around the world wherever there is a will on the part of its European partners to share—and this includes a willingness to provide resources to make that sharing effective.

It was this thought which underlay President Johnson's comment in his recent speech to the Associated Press in New York when he said, in speaking of our Atlantic relations:

> We also welcome agreed new mechanisms for political consultation on mutual interests throughout the world with whatever changes in organization are necessary to make such consultation rapid and effective.

THE ULTIMATE GOAL OF NATO

I approach the end of my observations tonight with three general conclusions:

The *first* is that NATO as it exists today—an Atlantic alliance with a unified force in being under a unified command—is an extraordinary peacetime achievement, a platform of accomplishment on which we should continue to build. And we should be wary, indeed, of any actions that might reduce its full effectiveness.

The *second* is that we cannot safely ignore the problem of widening participation in the management of our atomic defense, complicated as it may be by the fragmented structure of Western Europe. And unless you gentlemen are able, out of the collected wisdom represented here, to come up with a better solution than the multilateral force, I strongly urge your support for that proposal.

Finally, if NATO is to fulfill its purpose as the central arrangement for the defense of the free world, it must gradually extend its concern to the larger questions of free-world policy. Here again the limitations that obtain are not hard to isolate. They do not derive from any fault in the institutional structure of NATO but rather from the limited sense of world responsibility —as distinct from national interests—felt by many of our NATO partners.

These, then, are some of the problems for which we must find solutions over the coming months and years. Effective solutions will not be achieved merely by tinkering with the NATO structure but rather by progress in achieving a greater cohesion in relations among the member nations. This, it seems to me, is already in process. It has already produced substantial results, but there is much more to be done.

NATO, therefore, should not be regarded as an end in itself. It should be thought of as one of the pillars in a more comprehensive Atlantic relationship— an Atlantic relationship we must achieve in due course if we are to gain that ultimate goal of which Woodrow Wilson spoke with such prophetic passion—the "universal dominion of right by such a concert of free peoples as shall bring peace and safety to all nations and make the world itself at last free."

> ### SELECTION III–C
>
> During a discussion of the MLF in the House, Representative Craig Hosmer expressed the following views as they appeared in the *Congressional Record*—House, 88th Congress, 2d sess., September 22, 1964, pp. 22466–67. Hosmer, a Republican from California, has been a member of Congress since 1953.

. . . as to the multilateral force proposal, I simply cannot understand what is behind it. Obviously a mixed manned force with nuclear capability, and in this instance it is a strategic force rather than a tactical force, certainly implies mixed control.

Yet mixed control is exactly what Mr. Johnson is denouncing. So a great schizophrenia exists here between the MLF approach pursued by the administration on the international front and the zealous harboring of nuclear control which it pursues on the campaign trail and other approaches. The MLF is just another one of a long series of illusory deals that have been cooked up to try to make the Europeans think they have some substance of control while at the same time withholding it. What must they think, being offered MLF and hearing Johnson's campaign declarations at one and the same time? If it is not a dishonest inconsistency, it is certainly a perplexing one.

The gentleman from Washington had one more question and that was whether or not our policy with respect to NATO and nuclear weapons has influenced the French decision. Of course, the answer to that question is decisively yes. First, it induced that country to develop its own strategic nuclear weapons. Now it impels it to acquire tactical ones. As a matter of fact, the French Government is spending much money and devoting great effort by the year 1970—5 years, 3 months from now—to place its tactical forces totally on a nuclear footing.

Now who will control these French tactical nuclear weapons? We will not. The U.S. President's finger is not on the French nuclear trigger and never will be. General de Gaulle's finger is on it and his successor's finger will be on it.

Why has Mr. de Gaulle been impelled to go about this nuclearization of his tactical forces? Simply because in 1961 he was told by President Kennedy that since the Soviet Union had achieved its massive capability to exchange intercontinental ballistic missiles with the United States, the massive retaliation doctrine was no longer credible as a deterrent against Soviet invasion of Western Europe and therefore something else had to be substituted. Mr. Kennedy and Mr. Johnson had what they thought was a solution. "We will increase conventional forces," they said.

The Europeans viewed that with a great deal of dismay and the greatest of hostility. What we were in effect telling them was that if the Soviet invades Europe, we are not going to run the risk of any destruction of the United States or of any destruction of the Soviet Union—the two of us are going to stand clear from this destruction threat. We will eschew nuclear exchanges. We will let Europe again be ravaged by the holocaust and destructive power of the conventional warfare which laid it to waste in the two World Wars.

General de Gaulle and the rest of the Europeans, faced with that kind of choice, of course, took no steps whatsoever to augment their budgets and build up their conventional forces. It was simply too much to ask them to place themselves in a position inviting that kind of destruction. The result is that today Europe is in greater peril of Soviet aggression than for many years. The only feasible way to change this situation is to stockpile the discreet battlefield weapons I have described, which do not invite escalation and whose consequences are far less severe than the conventional explosives. These are what we have to have. The big question is why President Johnson and his immediate predecessor have failed to have the courage or wisdom to see that we have them. I will say this: During the Eisenhower administration, which the gentleman from California has referred to, these developments were researched and carried to the point where, at the end of President Eisenhower's term, a decision could be made to weaponize them. But when this Kennedy-Johnson administration came in, no such decision was made.

IV. VIEWS OF OBSERVERS

SELECTION IV—A

Robert Strausz-Hupé's statement, "The Crisis in NATO," is here reprinted from *Hearings* before the Subcommittee on Europe of the Committee on Foreign Affairs of the House of Representatives, 89th Congress, 2d sess., May 12, 1966, pp. 152–55.

Strausz-Hupé, professor of political science at the University of Pennsylvania and director of the University's Foreign Policy Research Institute, is a firm defender of a strong military deterrent in Europe.

The effort to categorize strategic thought deserves praise. No nuclear war ever having been fought, we cannot think about it in ways other than by extrapolating from the body of nonnuclear military experience and by designing purely imaginary strategies for various kinds of more or less probable contingencies.

Much given as we are as a people to devising orderly filing systems, it is questionable that filing away various schools of strategic thought under such rubrics as, for example, "Unilateral Disarmers" or "Finite Deterrers" or "Forward Strategists," will gain us deep insights into the great problems of war and peace. These rubrics tell us nothing about the assumptions which underlie these and other strategies or the kind of capabilities needed for fighting or terminating the cold war or for avoiding or winning various kinds of hot war.

My thesis is that all the strategies now being proposed and controverted are based on one or the other of two assumptions about the Communist system: There are those who assume that the Communist system is here to stay because it is a viable or a benign system which we can seek to overthrow only at extreme peril to our physical and spiritual value. There are those who assume that the Communist system is a rotten and perishable system which, by its very existence, endangers the peace of the world, and which, by the application of the right strategies, can be made to disappear.

The latter assumption appears more plausible than the former. It is supported by ample, empirical data. More important still, the validity of this, the second assumption, has been acknowledged by the behavior, though not by the pragmatic statements, of Soviet leadership itself.

The Soviet leaders have confessed to the awful state of Soviet agriculture. For 50 years, the collectivization of Russian agriculture has proven a consistent failure. Although Western experts disagree on the exact figures, they seem agreed on one conclusion: Under virtually any system other than the Kolkhos-Sovkhos system, Russian agriculture could contribute to the gross national product from 50 to 100 billion rubles more than it does now, and the average Russian could be from 50 to 100 percent better off than he is now.

The malfunction of the Communist system as a producer is directly related to its malfunction in politics. It is totalitarian because it cannot risk its existence on the free expression of the popular will. Because it is totalitarian it cannot elicit that spontaneous popular initiative which could get the Soviet economy off the ground. This, in the simplest words, is the Communist dilemma. To seek relief from internal pressures by expansionist ventures abroad has always been the most tempting alternative of despotic rulers confronted with mounting opposition at home.

This, in the simplest words, is the problem which the Communist system poses for us.

What should be the objective of our strategy? It shoud be to bring about the demise of the moribund Communist system without triggering a general nuclear war. If we do not contain Communist expansionism, we will provide the Communist regime with the opportunity of exporting its domestic dilemmas into world politics and of compensating for failure at home by success abroad. If we contain the Communist system too tightly, the Soviet rulers might gamble their survival on an all-or-nothing wager—a bigger and better Cuban-type challenge. If we press too hard, a second Communist revolution might depose the present Soviet establishment, bring to power another team of revolutionary activists, and restore the dynamism of the world Communist movement. How to foreclose either of these two alternatives, i.e., the breakdown of containment or the radicalization of Communist leadership, this task calls for an American statesmanship which knows how to blend toughness with subtlety and perseverence with flexibility.

It is this task which President Johnson appears to have had in mind when, on May 2, he spoke as follows:

> It remains our conviction that an integrated Atlantic Defense is the first necessity—not the last result—of the building of unity in Western Europe—for expanding partnership across the Atlantic—and for reconciling differences with the East.

Thus, President Johnson renewed the pledge which, 2 years ago, he had made in a speech at Lexington, Va., namely, to "build bridges across the gulf which has separated us from Eastern Europe."

In brief, NATO, the integrated power of the Western peoples, is to serve as a bridge to the East.

Unfortunately, NATO, in its present state, cannot serve as a bridge to anything—if for no other reason than that its own bridges are either blocked or down. The pressure which, throughout the early 1960's, the United States exerted on its European allies to pursue simultaneously a conventional strategy and to buy the multilateral force aggravated the long-standing crisis of NATO. The belated burial of the project not only did not repair the damage to the alliance but provided grist to the mills of De Gaulle who, all along, had asserted that the MLF was a propaganda device for isolating France.

The Gaullist critique of U.S. conduct now receives support from the timing of the U.S. anxious bid for a nuclear nonproliferation treaty. This treaty, it appears, can only be concluded by withholding from the Germans that share in NATO strategy which the MLF was to have one day granted them. Whatever can be said for or against a treaty with the Soviets on halting nuclear proliferation, it is difficult to see what the Soviets are prepared to give in return for the reduction of Germany to a permanent second-rate status in NATO.

The Soviets have never intended to give nuclear weapons to anybody, especially not their Warsaw allies. Certainly, the Soviets have always sought, with every means at their disposal, to obtain the demilitarization and neutralization of Germany. Their model of a nonnuclear proliferation treaty provides for the accomplishment of this purpose.

According to official pronouncements, cultural exchange and increased trade is supposed to help in building the bridge between West and East. In fact, this kind of bridge building has turned into a disorderly scramble for Communist bloc markets. For a good many years, the members of NATO deliberated on a common policy for trade with Communist countries. If such a policy ever existed, it now lies in shambles.

We are now told that increased East-West trade will liberalize the economies of the East European countries. No one has yet explained what contribution the export to Communist countries of, let us say, IBM computers or Rolls Royce motors, can make to the freedom of, let us say, individual Poles or Russians. Undoubtedly, these exports will render the economies of the recipient countries more efficient—more efficient to satisfy the requirements of the incumbent regimes. Undoubtedly, this kind of trade will accrue to the profit of select Western commercial interests.

Since it serves no agreed political purpose, and since it merely palliates the built-in deficiencies of the Communist system, it runs counter to that very policy of measured containment which alone can engender the beneficial, nonviolent transformation of the Communist system.

It is no wonder that the Soviets are emboldened. They now seek to exploit the crisis of the Western alliance. A few days ago in Rome, Soviet Foreign Minister Gromyko called for an all-European settlement without U.S. participation.

While the United States and the Western Europeans are building their separate competitive bridges to Eastern Europe and the Soviet Union, Eastern European and Soviet supplies maintain North Vietnam and the Vietcong in fighting trim. In all fairness to the Soviets, it is not they, but their Western apologists, who assert that Soviet and East European ammunition shipments to North Vietnam are intended only for keeping the North Vietnamese Government out of the clutches of the Red Chinese. The Communist press reports otherwise.

The crisis of NATO has not been caused by the failure of any single policy —the ill-fated MLF, the bungled attempt to fit West Germany into a NATO scheme for strategic decisionmaking, the uncoordinated Western policies for trade with the Communist countries, the search for politically ambiguous arms control agreements.

The crisis of NATO stems from the fading of that unifying vision which, for a while illuminated U.S. foreign policy. Because of the fragmentation of its foreign policies, the United States has lost sight of foreign political pri- orities. The relaxation of tensions—incidentally, a term coined by the Soviets some 30 years ago—has become an end in itself rather than a condition to be created by the attainment of an overarching political objective; namely, the transformation of the political system that now weights upon the peoples under communism and, by virtue of its instability, upon the international balance. There is little use in trying to mend fences—to keep De Gaulle out or to keep him in. A patched up NATO, uncertain of its purpose and kept together only by the pressure that the United States cares to exert at the moment, can neither contain nor really bridge.

In order to restore the Western alliance we will have to do many difficult things. Before we can do these many difficult things we will have to learn to see again the world—the West, the Communist states, the Afro-Asian countries—as an interdependent whole.

SELECTION IV–B

Ronald Steel, a former foreign service officer, has been a frequent contrib- utor to journals of national and international affairs and is author of *End of the Alliance: America and the Future of Europe*. This selection, excerpted from his article "The Disintegrating Alliance," *Commonweal*, LXXVIII (April 26, 1963), pp. 128–29, is reprinted by permission of the Common- weal Publishing Company, Inc.

With the American guarantee to defend Europe now thrown into question, the old foundation of the alliance has been eroded. For the Europeans it is no longer the absolute condition of their defense. It is only a conditional American promise which looks less convincing with the closing of each American missile base in Europe. It now offers Europeans only the dubious privilege of furnishing a large land army to back up a nuclear force entirely under American control. In this light it does not strongly recommend itself to a Europe which has become the economic equal of America and which is impatient with its old status of inferiority.

Within the realm of political interests, NATO is not the unalloyed asset Washington may imagine. As the Cuban crisis revealed so clearly, NATO directly involves the Europeans in any quarrel between America and Russia, regardless of their stake in that quarrel. It also showed that the United States had no hesitation to lead its allies to the brink of nuclear war without finding it necessary to inform or consult with them in advance. The Cuban affair, to a good many Europeans, taught that if there is to be any hope for Europe to escape devastation in a war between the two nuclear powers, it could not be achieved by an integrated military alliance with the United States.

Europe today is in no position to break loose from America—not yet. Until they are able, and willing, to build a credible defense force of their own, Europeans must remain dependent on American protection and committed to NATO. However, the economic resurgence of Europe has made a European defense force technically possible. Within the near future Europe will be capable of building a convincing land army and forging a nuclear deterrent force of its own. The question is no longer whether Europe can defend itself, but whether it is willing to do so.

Washington has greeted the prospect of an independent European defense force as a mortal threat to Western civilization. One can only assume, from recent statements of Administration officials, that General de Gaulle is a greater menace than Mr. Khrushchev. The administration's recent succession of blunders—beginning with the Skybolt fiasco, continuing with the Nassau Pact, and now a farcical scheme for loading nuclear missiles on cargo ships— have all been directed toward one end: prevent the Europeans from mounting their own nuclear defense force.

Should the Europeans acquiesce in these proposals, they will be congratulated by Washington for their perspicacity and reasonableness. They will be given no significant role in the determination of American strategy and diplomacy (as the Pentagon has elaborated many times, there can be only one center of nuclear control in the West—the United States) and they will be expected to pay for an increasing share of the alliance's nuclear hardware —that is, to buy more of their weapons from American manufacturers. But in return they would be spared the heavy accountability of being responsible for their defense and their diplomacy. Unfortunately, from the Administration's point of view, the Europeans show no interest in doing this. Inspired by the vision of union, western Europe is shaking itself loose from its long dependency on America.

Europe is becoming a great world power, one ascending over both America and Russia. It is today embarking upon a great experiment in unification, one similar to that which occurred in America nearly two centuries ago. But as this union gathers force, it will become increasingly anachronistic for Europe to remain militarily dependent upon the United States. This goes against the whole grain of European unification; it denies Europe's nascent power. It has come to be considered a land of humiliation, one which we would not endure at the hands of the Europeans, and which we cannot reasonably expect them to accept from us.

No nation, if it has an alternative, willingly places itself under the dominion of another, no matter how friendly. For many years Europe had no alternative. But today it does, and it is already beginning to be exercised. By the end of the decade, when the French nuclear deterrent becomes operational, and put at the service of the European community, the military independence of Europe will have been achieved.

At that point the old structure of NATO will have dissolved. Europe will not need our protection, and we will not be dependent on Europe, since the intercontinental missile will have eliminated our need for European bases to deter Soviet aggression. The defense of America will soon be conducted entirely from the United States itself, or from roving missile-equipped submarines. This will reduce our involvement in Europe to the half-million men stationed on the Continent as our contribution to NATO.

These troops are our hostage to NATO's nuclear strategy; they assure the Europeans that our nuclear guarantee is really credible. But once the Europeans possess their own nuclear deterrent, these troops will have ceased to serve any rational function. They could only involve the United States in a European conflict over which we would have no control. Ultimately the United States will be forced, in the name of its own self-interest, to retire its troops from Europe. No matter how many vows of eternal allegiance are made in Washington today, the military independence of Europe will demand the end of our direct involvement on the Continent.

This re-evaluation of NATO may not be so long in coming as the Administration now imagines. Early this year Wayne Morse told the Senate "the more we find ourselves paying for the privilege of remaining in Europe, the more we find ourselves alone among the major powers in meeting the assigned manpower obligations of NATO, the more independent military establishments that rise up in western Europe, then the more inclination there will be to make a realistic, ad hoc judgment as to whether what has become to us a mere United States military foothold in Europe is worth jeopardizing American cities and American lives."

There is no need to moan and gnash our teeth over Europe's desire to provide for its own defense, to accuse the Europeans of ingratitude—as though nations constructed their diplomacies on gratiude. There always has been, after all, something unseemly about our determination to look with anguish upon the ability of our allies to play a more independent role in their own defense. Was it not the purpose of NATO, back in those almost forgotten days of the late forties, to help the Europeans recover so that they might be able to take care of themselves? Is not Europe's coming ability to do so the mark of NATO's success? Surely it was never imagined by the founders of the alliance, either in the United States or in Europe, that it was to be the instrument for a permanent American tutelage over the Continent.

Rather than fearing the coming equality between Europe and America, it would be more appropriate for us to encourage the Europeans in their efforts to create a strong and independent military force. And even to be gratified that an alliance designed to protect Europe while it struggled from postwar chaos is finally fulfilling its purpose. The permanent dependency of Europe upon America was not the reason for the building of the Atlantic alliance. The passing of this condition should satisfy us as well as our European allies.

We are emerging from the postwar period, one which fixed our diplomacy for a decade and a half. A new confrontation of forces is forming, one based upon the slow transformation of Russia into a status quo, bourgeois state, on the constitution of a powerful European community, and on the cessation of America's long protectorship over Europe. The old premises on which NATO was founded are all passing into history. The alliance, at least in the form we have known it, cannot escape disintegration once it becomes irrelevant to the altered shape of the post-war world. Faced with the passing of NATO, the great task of our diplomacy is not how we turn the clock back on history, but rather how we must deal with a world in which a powerful new force has entered—a uniting Europe.

> SELECTION IV–C
>
> An excerpt from Thomas C. Schelling's "The Atlantic Alliance," *The Virginia Quarterly Review*, XLIII (Winter, 1967), pp. 24–26, 33–35, is presented here. Schelling, a professor of economics at Harvard and a member of Harvard's Center of International Affairs, is also a member of an advisory panel to the Bureaus of European Affairs of the Department of State. This excerpt is reprinted with permission of the author and the *Virginia Quarterly Review*.

Let us turn now to the military part of this alliance, and particularly to the organization of military forces under the North Atlantic Treaty. Here we have the usual problems—force levels and defense strategy—as well as the new and serious problems imposed by France's refusal to let her soil participate in integrated defense preparations. Unquestionably, we shall have to be content with less adequate defense arrangements in the future, and very likely with a smaller defense force. There are going to be arguments about the command structure for NATO troops, the location of NATO headquaters, and, as always, the appropriate rôles of conventional and nuclear ammunition in NATO strategy. Throughout all of these arguments, there should be no question about what has so high a priority that it stands unique as the goal of the organization.

That is the continued presence of a respectable American troop contribution to Western Europe. Whatever else the NATO organization does, it provides and has provided since 1950 a physical guarantee that any significant military engagement in Central Europe will involve the United States in an unmistakable way. Sixteen years ago it was argued before the Senate that the main purpose of the American troop commitment to Europe was to leave the Russians in no doubt that the United States would be involved if they attacked Western Europe. It was to show the Russians that we would be involved whether or not we wanted to be, so that they would have no need to psychoanalyze our intentions to reach the conclusion that they would meet enough United States troops to make it a Soviet-American crisis, not just a European one.

This does not mean that American troops were merely a trip-wire. In the first place, together with European troops, they constitute such a substantial force that they have far outgrown any simple notion of trip-wire. And, second, as has been made perhaps more articulate under Presidents Kennedy and Johnson but was nevertheless quite evident under President Eisenhower, the NATO forces of which the United States element is such a large component are not intended to trigger automatic nuclear holocaust at some identified point in a crisis and to stand idle until that point is reached. Their function is to meet a local crisis as effectively as they can, posing the continual threat that if the crisis continues and enlarges, the danger of intercontinental nuclear war continues and enlarges with it.

Whatever else happens to NATO, it must continue not only to express, but physically to embody, this American guarantee. Of all the things that NATO has accomplished, what is historically most striking is not just that war has been averted for sixteen years but that during those sixteen years the United States has, as a matter of continual unquestioned policy, kept a fine army on European soil in peacetime in order to help preserve the peace.

Whatever the adequacy of the force for defense, we must not let our concern for its defensive rôle, and our arguments about defensive strategies, cause us to forget that the original purpose of 1950 is still the overriding purpose. We may lack strength, we may lack unity, we may lack adequate command arrangements, we may even lack the territory to provide any defense in depth, but what we still have and must keep is the physical presence of American troops in Europe in sufficient numbers to make clear that they are a real force, not a token force, and that in case of military action they are there to fight and not merely to sound an alarm.

There are going to be those who say that with reduced territory, perhaps with reduced supplies, very likely with reduced troop strength, NATO will have to revert to a pure trip-wire strategy and give up any notion of flexibility. In one respect, but only one respect, this may be true. That is that the goal of having enough non-nuclear force stationed in Europe to meet and contain whatever level of conventional force the Soviet Union could assemble and launch westward may have to be dropped altogether. I shall not mind dropping that particular goal. I wish that goal had not been quite so attractive to the American government in recent years, because it came close to identifying what was meant to be a "flexible strategy" with a quite inflexible strategy, an inflexibly conventional one, and one that the Europeans not only disliked but distrusted. The important idea of a conventional *strategy* became too closely identified with the question of conventional *force levels*; and the rôle of conventional force was too often identified as one of massive defense against massive attack. This is only one of the rôles of conventional force in Europe and I believe the least plausible, not just because such an attack seems an unlikely contingency but because it is unlikely that, whatever the plans, a war involving fifty to a hundred divisions in Central Europe could run its course in a conventional way.

If we can abandon the massive-defense criterion as the main rationale for a flexible strategy, we may be more successful in getting our allies to explore with us the serious and more plausible contingencies in which something less than instant nuclear war would be the appropriate response. And an invitation to explore such contingencies will no longer be suspected as a nuclear withdrawal by the United States, or as an attempt by the United States to talk European countries into force levels beyond those they are willing to consider.

It is necessary to emphasize this physical commitment of American troops to Europe because questions about nuclear strategy and the sharing of nuclear authority get so much attention. These nuclear problems are inherently insoluble; no satisfying solution has been found and none is going to be found. It is a sign of NATO's success that the nations of Europe can afford to spend so much of their attention on matters of nuclear authority within the Alliance, matters that have more to do with status than with security. But the central feature of NATO strategy is the presence of American troops in Europe.

.   .   .   .

Let us turn now to the question of nuclear authority in NATO, the edge of which already has been touched in discussing the German nuclear interest. We know, now, that there is going to be no satisfactory solution to this problem. We have tried for years somehow to compromise two principles, that the European countries, especially Germany, should have some authority to launch nuclear weapons and also that they should not. The problem has not been posed in practical terms, but in legal terms. One of the great misfortunes about the discussions that have occurred about multilateral forces and other arrangements is that we have all together confirmed some principles that might better have been denied. The Germans have not had to say that they would seek an independent solution if there were no multilateral solutions, so many Americans and Englishmen have said it for them. In arguing for a multilateral force we have argued that the Germans cannot be expected forever to acquiesce in an inferior status, and we have tended to acknowledge that without nuclear weapons a country's status is inferior. Militarily Germany is superior to its European partner; in the kind of military force that counts, they are the great contributors. Ground troops are an impressive kind of bargaining power, and the French and British nuclear forces matter much less to the defense of Europe than the German ground forces. But nuclear discussions have focused on President de Gaulle's not very impressive nuclear force rather than the impressive German ground forces.

We have now given various solutions a try, and none has really survived. Secretary McNamara is now proposing to give the countries of NATO Europe a greater sense of intimacy with American nuclear planning, nuclear strategy, and nuclear targeting. His proposal is a good one, and my impression is that the initial response has been favorable. But his proposal is a good one whether or not there is a nuclear-authority problem that needs to be solved. And if there is a nuclear-authority problem that needs to be solved, I doubt whether a Special Committee on nuclear problems will solve it. The hope must be that the problem can be redefined, not that it can be solved.

There are limits to what consultation can achieve. Letting Europeans listen in on, or participate in, American strategic planning is bound to be somewhat disappointing to them, because the United States probably does not have a strategic plan for every imaginable contingency. Nuclear plans are only proposals, unless the President and his closest advisors have throught them through in detail and have made up their minds. But there are only twenty-four hours in the day, and part of it has to be used for sleeping, and the President and his closest advisors cannot have thought through every possible contingency and reached a decision in advance. European governments might indeed be better able to anticipate American policy in Vietnam, Cuba, or a potential crisis in Yugoslavia, if there were continual discussions. But they could not anticipate American actions any more than Americans could, and even American officials cannot be sure of what our detailed policy would be in those serious crises in which nuclear options might have to be considered.

What would Allied governments have learned about the United States rôle in the Korean war, had consultations been regularly held in the spring of 1950, about the United States rôle in the Suez crisis or the Hungarian crisis, had consultations been regularly held in early 1956, about the President's likely conduct of a Cuban crisis had consultations been regularly held in early 1962? The answer is that if consultations were based on the correct premise that, for most contingencies, there are no plans that govern decisions, but there are ideas, capabilities, alternatives, and motives that can be better appreciated through exploratory planning, consultation is worthwhile. But it is bound to be less satisfying than many Europeans seem to expect.

Maybe one great advantage of closer consultation with our allies would be, not to make them happy to be "inside at last," but rather to make them realize that they were not missing so much by being outside.

The problem of nuclear sharing and nuclear authority is one we should not try quite so hard to solve. Trying to solve it raises more problems. The whole affair takes attention away from things that critically matter. And taking them as seriously as we do gives these nuclear issues precisely the status and importance that we should deny them. Maybe it is fortunate that

President de Gaulle has given NATO some urgent practical problems that will attract attention, consume our theoretical interests, and take the front stage away from the problem of nuclear sharing. Nuclear sharing is a kind of luxury, an intra-alliance problem to be argued seriously only when there is no external threat to command our energies. Perhaps now we can discuss the location or shape of the North Atlantic Council, and let the nuclear question take the back of the stage for a while. It is worth trying. And if our Allies want to discuss something more portentous, let us see if the Alliance can develop a genuine foreign policy toward Central Europe.

14

CONTAINMENT IN ASIA

Vietnam

I. EDITORIAL INTRODUCTION

One of the lessons taught, if not learned, in the containment of communism in Korea was the importance of avoiding American commitment to a protracted land warfare on the Asian continent. The dangers of alienating allies, of appearing to pit white men against colored, and of becoming enmeshed in the kind of war that could bring no victory were apparent to the leaders of every administration since 1950. Yet, in the fulfillment of the containment hypothesis as it was hardened under Dulles, the credibility of America's resistance to communist expansionism depended upon its loyalty to the war efforts of allies. Dulles' Formosa policy reflected this loyalty. When France lost its control of Indochina, the United States filled a vacuum in South Vietnam, shoring up a regime which could easily have been subverted by communism. The objective was not only to help free people maintain their independence, but also to save neighboring regimes from the same fate. If one country fell, all the others in the area would be shaken, to fall in rapid order as if they were piles of dominoes. Communism would dominate all Southeast Asia, and be in a position to threaten the Indian subcontinent. So went the rationalization for America's involvement in Vietnam as expressed by American secretaries of state from Dulles to Rusk.

Thus the basic decisions on Vietnam were made in the mid-fifties when the United States constructed an alliance reminiscent of NATO which would hopefully withstand the pressures from Communist China that attended the collapse of French power in Indochina. For those countries which for one reason or another could not fit into an alliance, bilateral treaties were made. As the French moved out, the Southeast Asia Collective Defense Treaty, creating SEATO, was signed at Manila in September 1954, pledging self-help and mutual aid in defense against aggression. A special protocol was attached to the Treaty to ensure its application to the new states of Laos, Cambodia, and the free part of Vietnam which had been carved out of French Indochina at the Geneva peace tables. (Selection II–A.) The ambivalence Americans had felt toward the French anticommunist war, also was a colonialist war, now disappeared. Indochina divided at the 17th parallel, appeared to be a reprise of the Korean experience, with President Diem to be supported as President Rhee of Korea had been. The difference was that the defense of the area would be conducted primarily by the Vietnamese themselves with Americans providing financial and technical support in the event of aggression from the North or from insurrection within.

Such was the expectation of the Eisenhower administration. For a time the reforms urged on the Diem government by American advisors seemed to be the answer to the attraction of communism, and the success of Diem in pacifying the different factions in his country presaged a period of political stability during which economic reforms could be effected. But communism remained a threat as China grew stronger; the guerrilla action in Vietnam increased in pace as it received support from North Vietnam; and the government of Diem assumed an increasingly autocratic posture as it became engulfed in corruption and civil strife. By 1963 there was danger that the increasing opposition to Diem would nullify the anticommunist efforts of the country. The previous few years had opened the way to communist domination. What should the United States do? On the one hand was the reality of a civil war in which the United States could be labeled as a foreign invader, and on the other, there was the equal reality of a collapse of Vietnam which might lead to a communist seizure of all Southeast Asia.

President Johnson, unlike Presidents Eisenhower or Kennedy, was forced to pay full attention to the Vietnamese problem. Even before the death of Diem, increasing numbers of Americans were moved into Vietnam to replace Vietnamese soldiers diverted by internal quarrels. The assassination of Diem and his family in November, 1963, did not strengthen the struggle against the Vietcong and against their supporters from north of the 17th parallel; there was no effective leader to replace Diem's rule. The United States found itself caught in the struggle, unable to withdraw and unwilling to assume full responsibility for the war.

Events overtook plans. A North Vietnamese attack on an American destroyer in the Gulf of Tonkin in August, 1964, permitted Americans to make a definite response in the form of a Congressional resolution authorizing the President to take such steps as he deemed necessary to defend the area. (Selection II–B.) On the strength of this resolution, American participation in Vietnam escalated to the point where in 1967 the Americans were waging the major fight while the Vietnamese had still not formed a stable democratic government. Was America therefore involved in another Korea, a war that

might be the prelude to World War III? Was it playing the role of an imperialist aggressor interfering in a genuine civil war, and on the wrong side?
Or was it showing the world the credibility of American promises, thereby
inhibiting communist aggression elsewhere?

This was the "Great Debate" of the Johnson administration. Senator
Frank Church of Idaho spoke for a large body of Americans when he asked
for peace, a negotiated settlement, on the grounds that there was no old-
fashioned victory in sight. More important, he rejected the "domino" thesis.
He claimed that Hanoi had as much to gain from keeping the Chinese out
of Southeast Asia as had the United States. (Selection III–A.)

Responding to this widespread sentiment, William P. Bundy, Assistant
Secretary of State for Far Eastern Affairs, warned America against accept-
ing myths about Vietnam. In particular he attacked the idea that this was a
civil war in which different factions of Vietnamese competed for power. The
Vietcong and the National Liberation Front were only agents of Hanoi.
Negotiations could not be made with them but only with their masters in
Hanoi, and then from a situation of strength. Anything less would invite the
acceleration of communist subversion. (Selection III–B.)

But George Kennan, although disclaiming expertise in Southeast Asian
affairs, doubted the validity of this argument. Given the split within the
communist world in 1966, even a communist Indochina would pursue an
independent course, in his opinion. Without urging a precipitate withdrawal,
the United States, he felt, should attempt to liquidate its involvement irre-
spective of loss of face. Success in a military sense could be as dangerous as
failure if it alienated our friends around the world. The United States should
recognize that there were limits to America's responsibilities for peace in
the world and for the support of particular kinds of governments. (Selection
III–C.)

To the charges that America's involvement in Vietnam was illegal, Eberhard Deutsch, chairman of a Committee on Peace and Law through the
United Nations, asserted that intervention was consistent, almost mandatory,
with responsibilities under SEATO and with the Charter of the United Nations. Questioning the President's legal authority to conduct an undeclared
war under the Congressional resolution of 1964 was without merit. (Selection IV–A.) In rebuttal, William Standard, chairman of a Lawyer's Committee on American Policy toward Vietnam, castigated American action as
opposed to the spirit and letter of the Charter. In his view, the best step
America could take in its plight would be to admit its unilateral intervention,
confess error, declare a six months' cease-fire, and to create conditions for
negotiations. (Selection IV–B.)

To political scientist Hans Morgenthau, America by remaining in Vietnam could lose not only its position in that country, but also its moral
heritage. Examining carefully the fear of losing prestige by withdrawal, he

explained it as a product of an unfounded sense of inferiority. What else is it but realism to withdraw when there is no country to be defended, no honor to be lost, no commitment to be accepted beyond military assistance? Selection IV–C.) In his arraignment there was the implicit charge against America's assumption of world wide responsibilities which James Reston of the *New York Times* called the "Rusk Doctrine": namely, the United States would undertake to defend an area, any area of the world, whether or not it wanted or asked for aid, as long as such action appeared to contain communism.

In the views of Morgenthau and of Kennan, America accepted an image of communism which did not accord with recent historical experience. Ironically, it was the father of containment himself, George Kennan, whose passion against this application of containment in Vietnam led him in his testimony before the Senate Foreign Relations Committee to use the language and presumably the opinions of John Quincy Adams in 1823 when he counseled Americans to keep out of Europe's toils. Were the opponents of involvement in Vietnam in 1966 driven to a neoisolationism that required the Monroe Doctrine for sustenance?

II. DOCUMENTS

> *SELECTION II–A*
>
> Portions of the text of the Southeast Asia Collective Defense Treaty of September 8, 1954, as taken from the Department of State *Bulletin*, XXXI (September 20, 1954), pp. 393–94, 395–98, are presented in this excerpt.

The Parties to this Treaty,

Recognizing the sovereign equality of all the Parties,

Reiterating their faith in the purposes and principles set forth in the Charter of the United Nations and their desire to live in peace with all peoples and all governments,

Reaffirming that, in accordance with the Charter of the United Nations, they uphold the principle of equal rights and self-determination of peoples, and declaring that they will earnestly strive by every peaceful means to promote self-government and to secure the independence of all countries whose peoples desire it and are able to undertake its responsibilities,

Desiring to strengthen the fabric of peace and freedom and to uphold the principles of democracy, individual liberty and the rule of law, and to promote the economic well-being and development of all peoples in the treaty area,

Intending to declare publicly and formally their sense of unity, so that any potential aggressor will appreciate that the Parties stand together in the area, and

Desiring further to coordinate their efforts for collective defense for the preservation of peace and security,

Therefore agree as follows:

ARTICLE I

The Parties undertake, as set forth in the Charter of the United Nations, to settle any international disputes in which they may be involved by peaceful means in such a manner that international peace and security and justice are not endangered, and to refrain in their international relations from the threat or use of force in any manner inconsistent with the purposes of the United Nations.

ARTICLE II

In order more effectively to achieve the objectives of this Treaty, the Parties, separately and jointly, by means of continuous and effective self-help and mutual aid will maintain and develop their individual and collective capacity to resist armed attack and to prevent and counter subversive activities directed from without against their territorial integrity and political stability.

ARTICLE III

The Parties undertake to strengthen their free institutions and to cooperate with one another in the further development of economic measures, including technical assistance, designed both to promote economic progress and social well-being and to further the individual and collective efforts of governments toward these ends.

ARTICLE IV

1. Each party recognizes that aggression by means of armed attack in the treaty area against any of the Parties or against any State or territory which the Parties by unanimous agreement may hereafter designate, would endanger its own peace and safety, and agrees that it will be that event act to meet the common danger in accordance with its constitutional processes. Measures taken under this paragraph shall be immediately reported to the Security Council of the United Nations.

2. If, in the opinion of any of the Parties, the inviolability or the integrity of the territory or the sovereignty or political independence of any Party in the treaty area or of any other State or territory to which the provisions of paragraph 1 of this Article from time to time apply is threatened in any way other than by armed attack or is affected or threatened by any fact or situation which might endanger the peace of the area, the Parties shall consult

immediately in order to agree on the measures which should be taken for the common defense.

3. It is understood that no action on the territory of any State designated by unanimous agreement under paragraph 1 of this Article or on any territory so designated shall be taken except at the invitation or with the consent of the government concerned.

.   .   .   .

PROTOCOL TO THE SOUTHEAST ASIA
COLLECTIVE DEFENSE TREATY

Designation of states and territory as to which provisions of Article IV and Article III are to be applicable:

The Parties to the Southeast Asia Collective Defense Treaty unanimously designate for the purposes of Article IV of the Treaty the States of Cambodia and Laos and the free territory under the jurisdiction of the State of Vietnam.

The Parties further agree that the above mentioned states and territory shall be eligible in respect of the economic measures contemplated by Article III.

This protocol shall enter into force simultaneously with the coming into force of the Treaty.

In witness whereof, the undersigned Plenipotentiaries have signed this Protocol to the Southeast Asia Collective Defense Treaty.

Done at Manila, this eighth day of September, 1954.

> **SELECTION II–B**
>
> This document, H. J. Res. 1145—Joint Resolution of the Congress: Public Law 88–408—approved on August 10, 1964, was passed unanimously in the House and by a vote of 88–2 in the Senate. It is reprinted here from the Department of State *Bulletin,* LI (August 24, 1964), p. 268.

To promote the maintenance of international peace and security in southeast Asia.

Whereas naval units of the Communist regime in Vietnam, in violation of the principles of the Charter of the United Nations and of international law, have deliberately and repeatedly attacked United States naval vessels lawfully present in international waters, and have thereby created a serious threat to international peace; and

Whereas these attacks are part of a deliberate and systematic campaign of aggression that the Communist regime in North Vietnam has been waging against its neighbors and the nations joined with them in the collective defense of their freedom; and

Whereas the United States is assisting the peoples of southeast Asia to protect their freedom and has no territorial, military or political ambitions in that area, but desires only that these peoples should be left in peace to work out their own destinies in their own way: Now, therefore, be it

Resolved by the Senate and House of Representatives of the United States of America in Congress assembled, That the Congress approves and supports the determination of the President, as Commander in Chief, to take all necessary measures to repel any armed attack against the forces of the United States and to prevent further aggression.

Sec. 2. The United States regards as vital to its national interest and to world peace the maintenance of international peace and security in southeast Asia. Consonant and the Constitution of the United States and the Charter of the United Nations and in accordance with its obligations under the Southeast Asia Collective Defense Treaty, the United States is, therefore, prepared, as the President determines, to take all necessary steps, including the use of armed force, to assist any member or protocol state of the Southeast Asia Collective Defense Treaty requesting assistance in defense of its freedom.

Sec. 3. This resolution shall expire when the President shall determine that the peace and security of the area is reasonably assured by international conditions created by action of the United Nations or otherwise, except that it may be terminated earlier by concurrent resolution of the Congress.

III. VIEWS OF PARTICIPANTS

> *SELECTION III—A*
>
> Senator Frank Church, Democrat of Idaho, has been critical of the American position in Vietnam and authored the article "We Should Negotiate a Settlement in Vietnam," which appeared in the *Saturday Evening Post,* 238 (April 24, 1965), p. 14. An excerpt from that article follows, reprinted with the author's permission.

This is a time of ferment. Some of these guerrilla revolts will succeed; others will fail. The outcome, in each case, will depend upon the character of the government challenged, and the willingness of the people to rally behind it. That some governments won't prove equal to the test is no reason for us to panic. The other governments in Southeast Asia are not so many dominoes in a row. They differ, one from another, in popular support and in capacity to resist Communist subversion. We all hope Saigon will prevail, but the argument that "as goes South Vietnam, so goes all of Southeast Asia," is predicated more upon fear than fact. Communism isn't going to take over the world; it is much too poor a system for that.

Whether Saigon can meet the test remains to be seen. Until now, it has been losing its war, not for lack of arms, but for lack of internal cohesion.

The Viet Cong grow stronger, not because they are better supplied but because they are united in their will to fight. This spirit cannot be imported from without. The weakness in South Vietnam emanates from Saigon itself, where we, as foreigners, are powerless to pacify the spoiling factions. Only the Vietnamese can furnish a solution.

This brings us back to the central question: Why did we intervene in South Vietnam? President Eisenhower, who committed us there, expressed the reason, and his successors, Kennedy and Johnson, have faithfully repeated it. We went in, upon the invitation of Saigon (10 governments ago), to give aid and advice to the Vietnamese who were fighting the Viet Cong rebels. We can give arms, money, food, training and equipment, which is all we committed ourselves to do, but we cannot, as a foreign nation, win the war. Ultimately, a civil war has to be decided by the people of the country concerned.

We only deceive ourselves when we pretend that the struggle in Vietnam is not a civil war. The two parts of Vietnam don't represent two different peoples, with separate identities. Vietnam is a partitioned country in the grip of a continuing revolution. That the government of North Vietnam has deeply involved itself in support, or even direction, of the rebellion in the South doesn't make the war any less a civil war. The fighting is still between Vietnamese. The issue is still that of determining what groups of Vietnamese shall govern the country.

It is true, of course, that foreign powers are interested in the outcome of this struggle, China favoring Hanoi, the United States backing Saigon. But, again, the involvement of outside countries, even when it takes the form of limited intervention, doesn't change the essential character of the war.

With the war in Vietnam at a point where neither side can achieve a conclusive military decision, some kind of political settlement has to be worked out. I cannot furnish a precise blueprint for a peaceful settlement. No one can at this point. But I can indicate, in general terms, a form of settlement that lies in that middle ground that both sides must seek out if a negotiated settlement is to be reached. The timing of any settlement must, of course, be left to the President, He alone can know whether or when Hanoi appears willing to bargain.

As for the United States, we can always deal at the conference table from a strength that rests not upon the softness of Saigon but upon our own possession of the sea and air. Therefore I believe we must demonstrate that we cannot be driven out of Indochina, and that we won't bow to a Communist-dictated peace. Our recent bombings should make it clear to Hanoi that we will not quit under fire, or withdraw or submit to coercion.

At the same time we should make it equally clear that we are prepared to negotiate on honorable terms. The judicious use of both the arrows and the olive branch, clutched by the American eagle in the Presidential Seal, represents our best hope for avoiding a Korean-type war on the Asian mainland.

We should indicate our willingness to interpose a neutral buffer zone in Indochina, consisting of Laos, Cambodia and South Vietnam. Such a zone need not create a power vacuum for Chinese armies to fill. This is a more likely result, in the absence of such an agreement, of an expanded war. The integrity of the neutralized region against invasion from without could be guaranteed by the signatories to the agreement. Thus the military might of the United States would remain a deterrent to Chinese encroachment from the north, which is—or ought to be—our primary purpose in Southeast Asia anyway. During its transitional phase such an agreement could be policed by special forces of an international commission, set up to preside over a cease-fire while political arrangements are worked out by the people of each country.

Admittedly, this involves the unavoidable risk that pro-Communist elements may come to prevail, but the war itself—which sees Western forces increasingly pitted against Asians—has become the breeding ground of steadily growing political support for the Communist cause. As Prince Sihanouk, Cambodia's royalist ruler, has pointed out, the risk of Communist ascendancy after a settlement grows larger every day the war is prolonged. If this estimate is correct, and there is mounting evidence to support it, then the time to negotiate is now, while the anti-Communist elements in Indochina still possess authority.

Now is the time, while the jungles and rice fields still belong to the Vietnamese, to strive for an end to the war. Hanoi has reason to bargain, for she covets her independence and has cause to fear China. The same holds true for Laos, Cambodia and South Vietnam. Even the Soviet Union has incentive to work for a settlement that will foreclose a Chinese occupation of Southeast Asia. These propitious conditions, all of which work in our favor, are likely to be the first casualties of a widening war.

> ## SELECTION III–B
>
> A portion of "Reality and Myth concerning South Vietnam," an address by William P. Bundy, is presented here as excerpted from the Department of State *Bulletin,* LII (June 7, 1965), pp. 890–93. Bundy, who is assistant secretary of state for Far Eastern affairs, presented the address before the Dallas Council on World Affairs on May 13, 1965.

THE SOUTH VIET-NAM STORY

In 1954, after the fall of the French stronghold at Dien Bien Phu, the Geneva accords of July 20 signified the end of hostilities and the end of 90 years of French rule in Indochina. The country was roughly cut in half at the 17th parallel, creating the Communist regime of Ho Chi Minh in the North and a non-Communist state in the South.

When the Republic of Viet-Nam was formed in 1955, and recognized as independent by 35 nations, the South was a shambles; 13 years of fighting that ended with the signing of the Geneva accords had left its physical as well as human toll in Viet-Nam. The Government and people of South Viet-Nam had all the aspirations and hopes of any lesser developed country, but they also had more than the usual number of liabilities facing a new new nation. These included:

900,000 refugees who had fled their homes in the North at the time of partition in order to escape Communist rule;

a long-term military threat from the North, which had emerged from the war with large military forces;

a Government nearly paralyzed by long years of war and lacking sufficient trained officials for effective self-government;

acute economic dislocation and lack of Government revenues; and

persisting pockets of southern territory that had long been held by Communists and other dissident groups.

In the face of such problems, hopes were not high for the survival of the fledgling Republic of Viet-Nam. But the Communists had underestimated the most important resource in the South—the Vietnamese people. The people in the South had intelligence and native skill—but, more importantly, the determination to avoid the totalitarian destiny of their fellow Vietnamese in the North.

So, from 1954 to 1959, great progress was made. In Ngo Dinh Diem a stanchly nationalist and anti-Communist leader was found. Against all odds, including the opposition in 1954–55 of old-line military leaders and religious groups, he took hold. Under his rule the nationalist feeling of the newly formed country—which does differ to a significant degree from the North— was aroused, and it soon became and has remained clear that, whatever the extent of their attachment to particular governments in their own country, the great mass of the people of South Viet-Nam do not wish to be ruled by communism or from Hanoi.

On the economic and social front, education was vastly expanded, major land reforms carried out, and the economy grew at a rapid rate, far outstripping what was happening under the Communist yoke in the North. Instead of decaying and dropping by default into communism, South Viet-Nam was in a fair way toward becoming really able to stand on its own feet.

In all this the United States played a major helping role. On the military side we helped to create a fairly decent army almost from scratch, with a normal military assistance advisory group of a few hundred men. That army was never big enough to threaten the North, nor was it meant to be; it may well have been too much oriented to conventional warefare and not to the handling of a sophisticated guerrilla aggression.

Then, beginning roughly in 1959, two trends got underway that are still today at the heart of the problem.

First, the Diem government, instead of steadily broadening its base and training key groups for responsibility, began to narrow it. More and more the regime became personal in character. Opposition parties, which had previously been active in relatively free elections, were driven underground, and there began a process of repression which, while never drastic by the standards we should apply to governments in new nations—much less by those of Communist countries—nevertheless alienated increasing numbers of the all-too-small pool of trained men capable of helping to govern effectively.

Second, Hanoi went on the march. Seeing itself thwarted in both South Viet-Nam and Laos, Hanoi began to send trained guerrillas into the South and increasing cadres to assist the Communist Pathet Lao forces in Laos. In South Viet-Nam there had been from the start thousands of agents and many pockets of Communist influence left behind in the division of Viet-Nam, and as early as 1957 a campaign of assassination of local officials had begun that tallies on the map almost exactly with the areas under strongest Communist control today. In 1959 such activity was stepped up, guerrilla units formed, and the real campaign got underway.

That campaign is sometimes referred to as a civil war. But let us not delude ourselves. Discontent there may have been, and local recruiting by the Viet Cong, largely through intimidation. But the whole campaign would never have been possible without the direction, personnel, key material, and total support coming from Hanoi, and without, too, the strong moral support, and key material when needed, provided by Peiping and, up to 1962 at least, by the Soviet Union. Thousands of highly trained men coming from the North, along with the crucial items of equipment and munitions—these have been from the start the mainspring of the Viet Cong insurgency. This has been all along a Communist subversive aggression, in total violation of the Geneva accords as well as general principles of international behavior.

Indeed the true nature of the struggle has been publicly stated many times by Hanoi itself, beginning with a 1960 Communist Party conference in North Viet-Nam which declared the policy of, as they put it, "liberating" the South.

By early 1961 South Viet-Nam was clearly in difficulty. President Johnson, then Vice President, visited the country in the spring, and we stepped up our military supplies and tried to turn our training emphasis increasingly to the guerrilla front. Then, in the fall of 1961, a series of key assassinations and raids on government centers brought South Vietnamese morale to a critical point. Something more was needed. President Kennedy considered and rejected the sending of United States combat units to fight the Viet Cong. Instead he responded to the request of the South Vietnamese Government for American military advisers with Vietnamese units, and for Americans to furnish helicopter and air transport lift, combat air training, communications, and in short every possible form of assistance short of combat units.

But the military effort was and is only one aspect of the struggle. The economic front was equally important, and a smaller but extraordinarily dedicated group of civilian Americans went into the dangerous countryside, unarmed and often unescorted, to help in the creation of the fortified hamlets that soon became, and remain, a key feature of strategy, and to bring to the villages the schools, fertilizer, wells, pigs, and other improvements that meant so much and would serve to show the Government's concern for its people.

The basic strategy adopted in early 1962 was sound and was indeed in key respects the same as the strategy that prevailed against communism in Malaya, Greece, and the Philippines. It is a strategy that takes patience and local leadership, and that takes learning and experience as well. The Vietnamese and we are still learning and changing today, and will go on doing so.

But even as we recognized that the struggle must be won in the South, and continued to give every possible U.S. assistance to that end, it became clear in early 1965 that something more was needed. Attacks against the North, the source of the aggression, would all along have been justified as a basic measure of self-defense by the South Vietnamese Government and by our own Government acting at its request. By early February we were confronted with increased infiltration from the North and with a stepped-up pace of terror and hostile action that culminated in the attack on several American and South Vietnamese installations at Pleiku and elsewhere.

You all know the result. The President, acting at the request and urging of the South Vietnamese Government, directed that United States aircraft join with South Vietnamese aircraft in a campaign of measured and carefully directed attacks against military targets in North Viet-Nam. This was not a change of policy—it was a change in the measures taken to carry out policy, made necessary by the actions of the other side, in order to show Hanoi, as well as our friends in the South, that we were prepared to see the struggle through so that South Viet-Nam would be free from external interference.

SELECTION III–C

This statement by George F. Kennan was recorded in *Hearings*, Committee on Foreign Relations—Senate, 89th Congress, 2d sess., Part 1, February 18, 1966, pp. 331–36.

Mr. Chairman, and distinguished members of the Foreign Relations Committee, the subject on which I am invited to give my views this morning is, as I understand it, the complex of problems connected with our present involvement in Vietnam. I would like to explain, in undertaking to speak on this subject, that southeast Asia is a part of the world for which I can claim no specialized knowledge. I am not familiar with the official rationale of our policy there except as it has been revealed in the press. I cannot recall that I have ever, either during my official service in government or subsequently, been drawn by the executive branch of our Government into consultation on the problem of our policy in southeast Asia, or even been made privy to the official discussions by which that policy was decided.

I am sure that there are many data, relevant to any thoroughly founded judgment on these matters, which are not available to me; and this being the case, I have tried in recent weeks and months not to jump to final conclusions even in my own thoughts, to remain sympathetically receptive, both to our Government's explanations of the very real difficulties it has faced and to the doubts and questions of its serious critics.

I have not been anxious to press my views on the public but I gladly give them to you for whatever they are worth, claiming no particular merit for them except perhaps that they flow from an experience with Communist affairs that runs back now for some 38 years, and also from the deepest and most troubled sort of concern that we should find the proper course, the right course, at this truly crucial moment.

WISDOM OF U.S. MILITARY INVOLVEMENT IN VIETNAM

The first point I would like to make is that if we were not already involved as we are today in Vietnam, I would know of no reason why we should wish to become so involved, and I could think of several reasons why we should wish not to.

Vietnam is not a region of major military and industrial importance. It is difficult to believe that any decisive developments of the world situation would be determined in normal circumstances by what happens on that territory. If it were not for the considerations of prestige that arise precisely out of our present involvement, even a situation in which South Vietnam was controlled exclusively by the Vietcong, while regrettable, and no doubt morally unwarranted, would not, in my opinion, present dangers great enough to justify our direct military intervention.

Given the situation that exists today in the relations among the leading Communist powers, and by that I have, of course, in mind primarily the Soviet-Chinese conflict, there is every likelihood that a Communist regime in South Vietnam would follow a fairly independent course.

There is no reason to suspect that such a regime would find it either necessary or desirable in present circumstances to function simply as a passive puppet and instrument of Chinese power. And as for the danger that its establishment there would unleash similar tendencies in neighboring countries, this, I think, would depend largely on the manner in which it came into power. In the light of what has recently happened in Indonesia, and on the Indian subcontinent, the danger of the so-called domino effect, that is the effect that would be produced by a limited Communist success in South Vietnam, seems to me to be considerably less than it was when the main decisions were taken that have led to our present involvement.

Let me stress, I do not say that that danger does not exist, I say that it is less than it was a year or two ago when we got into this involvement.

From the long-term standpoint, therefore, and on principle, I think our military involvement in Vietnam has to be recognized as unfortunate, as something we would not choose deliberately, if the choice were ours to make all over again today, and by the same token, I think it should be our Government's aim to liquide this involvement just as soon as this can be done without inordinate damage to our own prestige or to the stability of conditions in that area.

It is obvious on the other hand that this involvement is today a fact. It creates a new situation. It raises new questions, ulterior to the long-term problem, which has to be taken into account. A precipitate and disorderly withdrawal could represent in present circumstances a disservice to our own interests, and even to world peace, greater than any that might have been involved by our failure to engage ourselves there in the first place.

This is a reality which, if there is to be any peaceful resolution of this conflict, is going to have to be recognized both by the more critical of our friends and by our adversaries.

EXPANSION OF HOSTILITIES IS DANGEROUS

But at the same time, I have great misgivings about any deliberate expansion of hostilities on our part directed to the achievement of something called victory—if by the use of that term we envisage the complete disappearance of the recalcitrance with which we are now faced, the formal submission by the adversary to our will, and the complete realization of our present stated political aims.

I doubt that these things can be achieved even by the most formidable military successes.

There seems to be an impression about that if we bring sufficient military pressure to bear there will occur at some point something in the nature of a political capitulation on the other side. I think this is a most dangerous assumption. I don't say that it is absolutely impossible, but it is a dangerous assumption in the light of the experience we have had with Communist elements in the past.

The North Vietnamese and the Vietcong have between them a great deal of space and manpower to give up if they have to, and the Chinese can give them more if they need it. Fidelity to the Communist tradition would dictate that if really pressed to extremity on the military level these people should disappear entirely from the open scene and fall back exclusively on an underground political and military existence rather than to accept terms that would be openly humiliating and would represent in their eyes the betrayal of the future political prospects of the cause to which they are dedicated.

Any total rooting out of the Vietcong from the territory of South Vietnam could be achieved, if it could be achieved at all, only at the cost of a degree of damage to civilian life and of civilian suffering generally for which I would not like to see this country responsible.

And to attempt to crush North Vietnamese strength to a point where Hanoi could no longer give any support for Vietcong political activity in the South, would almost certainly, it seems to me, have the effect of bringing in Chinese forces at some point, whether formally or in the guise of volunteers, thus involving us in a military conflict with Communist China on one of the most unfavorable theaters of hostility that we could possibly choose.

EFFECT OF CONFLICT ON OTHER INTERESTS AND POLICIES

This is not the only reason why I think we should do everything possible to avoid the escalation of this conflict. There is another one which is no less weighty, and this is the effect the conflict is already having on our policies and interests further afield. This involvement seems to me to represent a grievous misplacement of emphasis in our foreign policies as a whole.

EFFECT ON CONFIDENCE OF OTHER COUNTRIES

Not only are great and potentially more important questions of world affairs not receiving, as a consequence of our involvement in Vietnam, the attention they should be receiving, but in some instances assets we already enjoy and hopefully possibilities we should be developing are being sacrificed to this unpromising involvement in a remote and secondary theater. Our relations with the Soviet Union have suffered grievously as was to be expected, and this at a time when far more important things were involved in those relations than what is ultimately involved in Vietnam and when we had special reason, I think, to cultivate those relations. And more unfortunate still, in my opinion, is the damage being done to the feelings entertained for us by the Japanese people. The confidence and good disposition of the Japanese is the greatest asset we have had and the greatest asset we could have in east Asia. As the only major industrial complex in the entire Far East, and the only place where the sinews of modern war can be produced on a formidable scale, Japan is of vital importance to us and indeed to the prospects generally of peace and stability in east Asia. There is no success we could have in Vietnam that would conceivably warrant, in my opinion, the sacrifice by us of the confidence and good will of the Japanese people. Yet, I fear that we abuse that confidence and good will in the most serious way when we press the military struggle in Vietnam, and particularly when we press it by means of strategic bombing, a process to which the Japanese for historical reasons are peculiarly sensitive and averse.

I mention Japan particularly because it is an outstanding example, both in importance and in the intensity of feelings aroused, of the psychological damage that is being done in many parts of the world by the prosecution of this conflict, and that will be done in even greater measure if the hostilities become still more bloody and tragic as a result of our deliberate effort.

It is clear that however justified our action may be in our own eyes, it has failed to win either enthusiasm or confidence even among peoples normally friendly to us.

.   .   .   .

HIGHEST RESPECT FOR U.S. FIGHTING QUALITIES

Now, just two concluding observations: I would like it understood that what I have said here implies nothing but the highest respect and admiration for the fighting qualities of our forces in the field. I have the greatest confidence in them, men and commanders alike. I have no doubt, in fact, that they can and will, if duty requires, produce before this thing is over military results that will surprise both our skeptical friends and our arrogant adversaries. It is not their fighting qualities. It is the purpose to which they are being employed that evokes my skepticism.

UNITED STATES SHOULD NOT SHOULDER POLITICAL BURDEN OF OTHER COUNTRIES

Secondly, I would like to say I am trying to look at this whole problem not from the moral standpoint but from the practical one. I see in the Vietcong a band of ruthless fanatics, many of them misled, no doubt, by the propaganda that has been drummed into them, but cruel in their methods, dictatorial, and oppressive in their aims, I am not conscious of having any sympathy for them. I think their claim to represent the people of South Vietnam is unfounded. A country which fell under this exclusive power would have my deepest sympathy; and I would hope that this eventuality at any rate would be avoided by a restrained and moderate policy on our part in South Vietnam.

But our country should not be asked, and should not ask of itself, to shoulder the main burden of determining the political realities in any other country, and particularly not in one remote from our shores, from our culture, and from the experience of our people. This is not only not our business, but I don't think we can do it successfully.

TIMELY WORDS OF JOHN QUINCY ADAMS

In saying this, I am only paraphrasing and very poorly the words once uttered by one who had at one time been a Member of the U.S. Senate, and who, had a Foreign Relations Committee existed in his day, would unquestionably have been a member of it. This was John Quincy Adams, and I would like your permission to recall, before I close, the words of his that I have in mind. They were spoken in this city 145 years ago on the 4th of July . . . 1821 . . .

Some of you may be familiar with them but they stand repeating at this moment:

Wherever the standard of freedom and independence has been or shall be unfurled, there will be America's heart, her benedictions, and her prayers. But she goes not abroad—

He went on—

in search of monsters to destroy. She is the well-wisher to the freedom and independence of all. She is the champion and vindicator only of her own. She will recommend the general cause by the countenance of her voice, and by the benignant sympathy of her example. She well knows that by once enlisting under other banners than her own, were they even the banners of foreign independence, she would involve herself beyond the power of extrication, in all the wars of interest and intrigue, of individual avarice, envy, and ambition, which assume the colors and usurp the standards of freedom. The fundamental maxims of her policy would insensibly change from liberty to force * * *. She might become the dictatress of the world. She would no longer be the ruler of her own spirit.

Now, gentlemen, I don't know exactly what John Quincy Adams had in mind when he spoke those words, but I think that without knowing it, he spoke very directly and very pertinently to us here today.

Thank you, sir.

IV. VIEWS OF OBSERVERS

SELECTION IV–A

Eberhard Deutsch, Chairman of the American Bar Association Committee on Peace and Law through United Nations, is the author of "The Legality of the United States Position in Vietnam," *American Bar Association Journal*, LII (May, 1966), pp. 440–42, portions of which are reprinted here by permission of the *American Bar Association Journal*.

In its memorandum in opposition to the policy of the United States, the Lawyers Committee on American Policy Towards Vietnam asserts that "the conduct of the United States Government in Viet Nam appears plainly to violate the terms of the Geneva Accords." While the United States is not a party to the accords, it did by contemporaneous unilateral declaration agree, in effect, to respect them. But, as demonstrated above, the Geneva Accords since their inception have been violated continuously by the Hanoi regime. It is an accepted principle of international law that a material breach of a treaty by one of the parties thereto dissolves the obligations of the other parties, at least to the extent of withholding compliance until the defaulting party purges its breach.

It has been suggested that because the power to declare war is vested by the Constitution in the Congress alone, the deployment of United States forces to Vietnam by the President, without a formal Congressional declaration of war, violates the constitutional fiat. When the phrasing of this clause of the Constitution was being considered at the convention in 1787, its original form, vesting in Congress the power to "make" war, was changed to give it the power to "declare" war, "leaving to the Executive the power to repel sudden attacks"—"he should be able to repel and not to commence war" and "to 'conduct' it which was an Executive function."

The President is, under Section 2 of Article II of the Constitution, the "Commander in Chief of the Army and Navy of the United States." Throughout the history of the United States, he has been deemed to have authority to deploy the country's military forces to trouble spots around the world, frequently in combat. The Department of State has a record of some 125 such instances.

In the last analysis, however, the exercise of the President's power as Commander in Chief in deploying forces of the United States to Southeast Asia for the defense of the Republic of Vietnam has had the repeated sanction of the Senate, as well as of the Congress as a whole, so that, although the situation now seems unquestionably to constitute war in its technical sense, a formal Congressional verbal declaration of war as such could not conceivably be essential to clothe the President's conduct with constitutional validity. This Congressional sanction has been evidenced by overwhelming majorities in the Senate's approval of the SEATO Treaty, in the adoption of the Joint Congressional Southeast Asia resolution of August 10, 1964, and in the passage of the appropriations necessary to carry on the defensive actions undertaken by the Executive.

First, as to the treaty. In it (paragraph 1, Article IV) each of the parties "recognizes that aggression by means of armed attack in the treaty area against" any of them or against the "free territory under the jurisdiction of the State of Viet-nam" (protocol) "would endanger its own peace and safety."

The "treaty area," under Article VIII, includes "the general area of the Southwest Pacific not . . . north of 21 degrees 30 minutes north latitude." The United States has historically owned tremendously important and valuable strategic territorial interests in that area. Aside from its trusteeship over the Mariana (except Guam), Marshall and Caroline Islands, the United States owns Guam, Wake and the Samoan group. And yet the Lawyers Committee on American Policy Towards Vietnam has asserted that "SEATO is not a regional agency within the letter or spirit of the UN Charter," because "Article 51 and 53 . . . envisaged regional systems which historically and geographically developed into a regional community—not contemplating a regional system which fused . . . Southeast Asia with a country of the North American Continent"—"separated by oceans and thousands of miles from South East Asia."

In the cited paragraph of the treaty, the United States agreed that in the event of aggression in the treaty area it would "act to meet the common danger." In recommending ratification of the treaty to the Senate, its Foreign Relations Committee reported that "the committee is not impervious to the risks which this treaty entails. It fully appreciates that the acceptance of these obligations commits the United States to a course of action over a vast expanse of the Pacific. Yet these risks are consistent with our own highest interests." The Senate ratified the treaty on February 1, 1955, by a vote of 82 to 1.

In light of all of the foregoing, it seems difficult to find anything in the nature of an adequate foundation for the *ipse dixit* of the Lawyers Committee on American Policy Towards Viet Nam that "the 'Southeast Asia Collective Defense Treaty'—connecting the United States with Southeast Asia, architectured by Secretary of State Dulles, is a legalistic artificial formulation to circumvent the fundamental limitations placed by the United Nations Charter on unilateral actions by individual members."

Undoubtedly the clearest and most unequivocal Congressional sanction of the President's deployment of United States forces for the defense of South Vietnam is contained in the Joint Southeast Asia resolution of August 10, 1964, reciting expressly "that the Congress approves and supports the determination of the President, as Commander in Chief, to take all necessary measures to repel any armed attack against the forces of the United States and to prevent further aggression," and that the United States is "prepared, as the President determines, to take all necessary steps, including the use of armed force, to assist any member or protocal state of the Southeast Asia Collective Defense Treaty requesting assistance in defense of its freedom."

The Lawyers' Committee on American Policy Towards Viet Nam quotes a passage from an article in the *Washington Daily News* of June 4, 1965, by Richard Starnes, read into the *Congressional Record* by Senator Ernest Gruening of Alaska, which states that the joint resolution was "passed in the fever of indignation that followed" the Gulf of Tonkin attacks, and then, again as their own *ipse dixit,* assert that "there is no evidence that Congress thought or understood that it was declaring war."

This statement is simply incorrect. When the President sent his message to Congress on August 5, 1964, recommending passage of "a resolution expressing the support of Congress for all necessary action to protect our Armed Forces and to assist nations covered by the SEATO Treaty," he stated explicitly that he "should now ask the Congress on its part, to join in affirming the national determination that all such attacks will be met, and that the United States will continue in its basic policy of assisting the free nations of the area to defend their freedom."

.   .   .   .

The legal authority of the President of the United States to conduct the present war, for "the maintenance of international peace and security in Southeast Asia," which, as the Congress declared in its 1964 resolution, "the United States regards as vital to its national interest and to world peace," is surely sustained amply by the composite impact of that resolution, the terms of the SEATO Treaty ratified by the Senate and the appropriations made by the Congress to support the military actions in the treaty area.

That the memorandum of the Lawyers Committee on American Policy Towards Vietnam is grounded on an emotional attitude opposed to United States policy, rather than on law, is not only demonstrated by a look at the facts, but is emphasized by the memorandum's concluding paragraph:

> Should we not, twenty years after President Roosevelt's hopeful dream— twenty years after the advent of the nuclear age with the awesome potentiality of incineration of our planet and the annihilation of our civilization and the culture of millenia—Should we not "spell the end of the system of unilateral action . . . that has been tried for centuries—and has always failed"?

Contrasted with the tone and substance of that memorandum is the temperate statement of thirty-one professors of international law from leading law schools throughout the United States, which recites simply that they "wish to affirm that the presence of US forces in South Vietnam at the request of the Government of that country is lawful under general principles of international law and the United Nations Charter. The engagement of US forces in hostilities at the request of the Government of South Vietnam is a legitimate use of force in defense of South Vietnam against aggression."

Contrasted also with the tone and temper of the memorandum of the Lawyers Committee on American Policy Towards Vietnam is the simple resolution adopted unanimously on February 21, 1966, by the House of Delegates of the American Bar Association on the joint recommendation of its Standing Committee on Peace and Law Through United Nations and its Section of International and Comparative Law. The resolution is supported by a brief report, which concludes "that the position of the United States in Vietnam is legal under international law, and is in accordance with the Charter of the United Nations and the South-East Asia Treaty."

These conclusions as to the legality of the presence of the United States forces in Vietnam under the Constitution of the United States, as a question of domestic law, are those of the author. They were not included in the opinion of the thirty-one professors of international law or in the resolution of the American Bar Association.

> ### SELECTION IV–B
>
> In "United States Intervention in Vietnam Is Not Legal," *American Bar Association Journal,* LII (July, 1966), pp. 627–29, 633, William L. Standard of the New York Bar took issue with Deutsch's interpretation of the legality of the United States presence in Vietnam. This excerpt is reprinted with permission of the *American Bar Association Journal.*

Satire and sarcasm often have been weapons of effective, if deluding, advocacy. The article by Eberhard P. Deutsch, "The Legality of the United States Position in Vietnam," in the May, 1966, issue of the *American Bar*

Association Journal (page 436) is a classical demonstration of this technique. The author takes issue with the Lawyers Committee on American Policy Toward Vietnam, as expressed in its memorandum of law, on the following fundamental questions: (1) The right of self-defense under the United Nations Charter; (2) Violations of the Geneva Accords; (3) Sanctions by the SEATO treaty; and (4) Violations of our own Constitution.

But the author concludes with the statement that the memorandum of the Lawyers Committee "is grounded on an emotional attitude opposed to United States policy, rather than on law." He seeks to demonstrate this by quoting the *concluding* paragraph of a 26-page, carefully documented statement of the applicable law, which in peroration states in the very last sentence: "Should we not spell the end of the system of unilateral action . . . that has been tried for centuries—and has always failed?"

The author then wields the weapon of sarcasm by contrasting the Lawyers Committee memorandum with the "temperate statement of thirty-one professors of law from leading law schools throughout the United States." The statement of these professors appears in the *Congressional Record* of January 27, 1966 (page A410), and the entirety of that statement is:

As teachers of international law we wish to affirm that the presence of U.S. forces in South Vietnam at the request of the Government of that country is lawful under general principles of international law and the United Nations Charter. The engagement of U.S. forces in hostilities at the request of the Government of South Vietnam is a legitimate use of force in defense of South Vietnam against aggression. We believe that the evidence indicates that the United States and South Vietnam are taking action that attacks neither the territorial integrity nor the political independence of the People's Republic of Vietnam—action that seeks only to terminate aggression originating in North Vietnam.

This one-paragraph "temperate statement" is not buttressed by a single citation or authority. What is particularly deplorable is that it was issued in November of 1965 as a rebuttal to the committee's memorandum, which was issued in late September, 1965.

The author of the "legality position" article then contrasts the Lawyers Committee memorandum with "the simple resolution adopted unanimously on February 21, 1966, by the House of Delegates of the American Bar Association." This resolution, in a concluding one-sentence statement, asserts that "the position of the United States in Vietnam is legal under international law, and is in accordance with the Charter of the United Nations and the South-East Asia Treaty." The House of Delegates' resolution, too, does not support its conclusion with a single citation or authority.

When the *Harvard Law Record* on March 10 contrasted the memorandum of law of the Lawyers Committee with the "simple resolution" adopted by the House of Delegates, it had this to say: "Viewed against the background of the *sober and erudite* Lawyers Committee brief and Arthur Krock's research, the ABA resolution contributes little to the national dialogue on Vietnam" (emphasis supplied).

The satirical technical of the author of the "legality position" article is worthy of an undergraduate debater, but not of the respected Chairman of the American Bar Association Committee on Peace and Law Through United Nations. He does, indeed, wrestle earnestly with four basic propositions discussed by the Lawyers Committee, and it is to these propositions that I shall address myself.

I. UNILATERAL INTERVENTION VIOLATES U.N. CHARTER

The writer of the "legality position" article discusses the first exception of Article 51 of the Charter of the United Nations, which reads: "Nothing in the present Charter shall impair the *inherent* right of individual or collective self-defense *if* an armed attack occurs against a Member of the United Nations, until the Security Council has taken the measures necessary to maintain international peace and security" (emphasis supplied).

He asserts that "A thesis that members of the United Nations are not permitted to participate in collective self-defense to repel aggression, on the ground that the aggrieved nation is not a member of the United Nations, can hardly be supported on its face, in reason, logic or law." He cites as authority two distinguished writers.

The Lawyers Committee in its memorandum concludes that Article 51 does not permit the United States to act unilaterally in the "collective self-defense" of Vietnam because Article 51 applies only if an armed attack occurs against a member of the United Nations.

This limitation was not inadvertent. It was the result of careful draftsmanship by Senator Arthur H. Vandenberg, who "was the principal negotiator in the formulation of this text" of Article 51. In a statement of June 13, 1945, before the United Nations Commission that drafted Article 51, Senator Vandenberg said: ". . . [W]e have here recognized the inherent right of self-defense, whether individual or collective, which permits any sovereign state among us [*i.e.,* members of the United Nations] or any qualified regional group of states to ward off attack. . .".

Secretary of State Edward R. Stettinius, Jr., noted the following on May 21, 1945: "The parties of any dispute . . . should obligate themselves first of all to seek a solution by negotiation, mediation, conciliation, arbitration or judicial settlement, *resort to regional agencies or arrangement* or other peaceful means of their own choice" (emphasis in original).

Professor Julius Stone states: "The license [of individual and collective self-defense] does not apparently cover even an 'armed attack' against a *non-Member*" (emphasis in original).

Furthermore, the United States has acknowledged that the right of "collective self-defense" applies to Vietnam only if it becomes a member of the United Nations. On September 9, 1957, in arguing before the Security Council for the admission of Vietnam to the United Nations, Henry Cabot Lodge, our representative, stated: "The people of Vietnam . . . ask now only . . . to enjoy the benefits of collective security, the mutual help which membership in the . . . United Nations offers.

This does not mean, of couse, that a nonmember state or entity does not have the "inherent" right of self-defense of that nonmember states may be attacked with impunity. But it does mean that in case of an attack upon a nonmember state it is for the United Nations to decide upon the necessary measures to be taken by its member states and not for any state to decide for itself that it will employ arms for "collective self-defense."

During the Suez crisis President Eisenhower said: "The United Nations is *alone* charged with the responsibility of securing the peace in the Middle East and throughout the world" (emphasis supplied).

And at the same time, Secretary of State John Foster Dulles characterized as "unthinkable" a proposal that the United States and the Soviet Union act jointly to restore the peace in that area, saying that that was the function of the United Nations. He said:

> Any intervention by the United States and/or Russia or any other action, except by a duly constituted United Nations peace force would be counter to everything the General Assembly and the Secretary-General of the United Nations were charged by the Charter to do in order to secure a United Nations police cease fire.

The author of the "legality position" article confuses the right of an attacked nonmember state to defend itself with the lack of right of a member state to participate in that defense in the absence of United Nations' authorization.

The issue is the lawfulness of the actions of the United States, which is both a nonattacked state and a member of the United Nations. It does not follow that because Vietnam has an "inherent" right to defend itself, the United States has an "inherent" right to decide for itself to participate unilaterally in that defense. Professor Hans Kelsen, one of the principal authorities relied upon by Mr. Deutsch, has pointed out this critical distinction: "It is hardly possible to consider the right or the duty of a non-attacked state to assist an attacked state as an 'inherent' right, that is to say, a right established by natural law."

The argument also makes the United States its own judge to determine the occurrence of an "armed attack" in Vietnam, whereas Article 39 of the United Nations Charter provides that "The Security Council shall determine the existence of any threat to the peace, breach of the peace, or act of aggression. . . ." But as Philip C. Jessup, now a Judge of the International Court of Justice, has noted:

> It would be *disastrous* to agree that every State may decide for itself which of the two contestants is in the right and may govern its conduct according to its own decision. . . . The ensuing conflict would be destructive to the ordered world community which the Charter and any modern law of nations must seek to preserve.

State C would be shipping . . . war supplies to A, while State A would be assisting State B . . . and it would not be long before C and B would be enmeshed in the struggle out of "self-defense" [emphasis supplied].

Acceptance of Mr. Deutsch's argument would destroy the concept of collective peacekeeping, which the Charter embodies, in the case of non-member states or areas.

.   .   .   .

There have been instances when the President has sent United States forces abroad without a declaration of war by Congress. These have ranged from minor engagements between pirates and American ships on the high seas to the dispatch of our Armed Forces to Latin American countries and our involvement in Korea. But, except for the Korean War, none of these instances remotely involved so massive and dangerous a military undertaking as the war in Vietnam. And in the Korean War the United States fought under the aegis of the United Nations.

Since Mr. Deutsch assumes that the Tonkin resolution does constitute a "Congressional declaration of war *in haec verba*," empowering the President to act, it is fitting to recall that on May 6, 1954, at a time when the fall of Dien Bien Phu was imminent, then Senator Lyndon B. Johnson criticized the President in these terms:

We will insist upon clear explanations of the policies in which we are asked to cooperate. We will insist that we and the American people be treated as adults— that we have the facts without sugar coating.

The function of Congress is not simply to appropriate money and leave the problem of national security at that.

Congress should, therefore, exercise its constitutional responsibility as a co-equal branch of government of checks and balances to determine whether this country shall continue to be involved in the war in Vietnam. Under the rule of law, compliance with the forms and procedures of law are as imperative as compliance with the substance of law.

> ## SELECTION IV–C
>
> The following is taken from Hans Morgenthau's "Vietnam: Shadow and Substance," *The New York Review of Books* (September 16, 1966), pp. 3–4, and is reprinted with the permission of the author and publisher. Morgenthau, who is the director of the Center for the Study of American Foreign and Military Policy and the Albert A. Michelson Distinguished Professor of Political Science and Modern History at the University of Chicago, has been a major opponent of American involvement in Vietnam.

The comment on our policy in Vietnam most frequently heard in Washington in the summer of 1965 consists of two questions: How did we ever get into this mess, and since we are in it, and cannot get out through negotiations, what can we do but stay? These questions deserve an answer; for the answers will shed light upon the nature of our policy in Vietnam. They will show that we have consistently confounded the shadow of national power with its substance, the prestige of the nation with the actuality of its power, ephemeral public relations with the stability of the national prestige, the prestige of policy-makers with the prestige of the nation. We are here in the presence of a central misunderstanding of the nature of foreign policy and, in consequence, of a persistent dilettantism in trying to cope with the problem of Vietnam. This central fault in our thinking is responsible both for our general predicament and for our day-by-day failures, and it provides a common explanation of certain glaring deficiencies in a foreign policy otherwise inexplicable.

The prestige of a nation is its reputation for power. That reputation, the reflection of the reality of power in the mind of foreign observers, can be as important as the reality of power itself. What others think about us is as important as what we actually are. Thus all nations, and especially those active in foreign policy, must see to it that the mental picture other nations form of their power at least represents faithfully the actuality of their power, if it does not excel it.

It is at this point that the policy of prestige must guard against two pitfalls. If it exceeds that actuality by two much, prestige will become bluff, and a policy based upon such a misreading of reality will fail, as did Mussolini's in the Second World War. On the other hand, prestige that makes a nation appear to be less powerful than it actually is reduces the influence the nation might in fact exert. The impotence of the United States in the inter-war period is a case in point. Thus wisdom lies in seeing to it that the shadow that a nation's power casts in the form of its prestige is neither too large nor too small, but always retains a rational relationship to the substance of power. It is here that our policy in Vietnam is at fault. It illuminates the peculiar immaturity of our relationship to power by erring both ways: it claims both too much and too little in view of the substance of our power.

The prestige of a nation is not determined by the success or failure of a particular operation at a particular moment in history. Quite the contrary, it reflects the sum of a nation's qualities and actions, of its successes and failures, of its historic memories and aspirations. The pages of history record many examples of nations which secure in their possession of great power and recognized as such by their peers, have suffered defeat or retreated from exposed positions without suffering a loss in prestige. When was the prestige of France higher: when it fought wars in Indochina and Algeria which it could neither win nor thought it could afford to lose, or after it had liquidated these losing enterprises? And how much did American prestige suffer in the long run from the debacle of the Bay of Pigs, as thorough and spectacular a failure as one would wish only one's enemy to suffer, and as humiliating a revelation of governmental incompetence as one would not want perhaps even one's enemy to reveal? When France demonstrated the wisdom and courage to liquidate two losing enterprises on which it had staked its "honor," its prestige rose to heights it had not attained since the beginning of the Second World War, and the Bay of Pigs has weighed little in the scales of American prestige, heavy as they are with power and success. To say, then, that we ought not to be in Vietnam but cannot leave because our prestige would suffer, is to confound ephemeral fluctuations of public opinion with the lasting foundation of national power and prestige and to think little of American power and of the American prestige which reflects that power.

Yet the same fear that anticipates a disastrous loss of prestige from a temporary setback engenders an over-estimation of national power, and a need to transform a losing into a winning position. The sense of inferiority, which underestimates our national power and prestige, calls forth a policy of bluff. Obsessed with the fear of the permanent loss of prestige which we imagine would follow a temporary setback, we have become oblivious to the much more serious loss of prestige which would ensue, and has already ensued, from the continuation and escalation of a losing enterprise. Can anyone who has followed foreign public opinion carefully and with at least a measure of objectivity doubt that our prestige throughout the world has declined drastically since the beginning of 1965? Nobody questions our phyical power to destroy Vietnam, South and North. Yet in even so friendly a country as Germany, which depends upon a commitment of our physical powers to its defense, there are people within and outside the government who question our ability to honor this commitment when we have sent the flower of our armed forces to Vietnam without having a chance to win. Everywhere people question, sometimes under their breath and sometimes loudly, the wisdom and morality of the government of the United States. And what will our prestige be if hundreds of thousands of American men are bogged down in Vietnam, still unable to win and unable to retreat?

Unaware as we are in general of the nature and the greatness of our power, we have become negligent of its limits in dealing with Vietnam. Thus our judgments and actions are at odds with empirical reality. On the one hand, our knowledge of reality counsels us to liquidate a losing enterprise, and thus we try to negotiate our way out; but the negotiating conditions we stipulate always limp a couple of months behind reality, and thus our attempts consistently fail. For, on the other hand, our policy makers are dominated by a state of mind combining a sense of inferiority with a sense of invincibility, which has made us decide that we cannot afford to retreat and that we must and can win. Since a rational assessment of empirical reality contradicts this decision, we are compelled to disregard reality and to invent a mythological reality which supports our decision.

.   .   .   .

I have spoken of the prestige of the nation and of the prestige of those who govern it, that is, of the mental image which others have of us. Yet there is another kind of prestige: the image *we* have of ourselves. That image will suffer grievous blemishes as we get ever more deeply involved in the war in Vietnam. This war is a guerrilla war, and such a war, supported or at least not opposed by the indigenous population, can only be won by the indiscriminate killing of everybody in sight, that is, by genocide. The Germans proved that during the Second World War in occupied Europe, and they were prevented from accomplishing their task only because they were defeated in the field. The logic of the issue we are facing in Vietnam has already driven us onto the same path. We have tortured and killed prisoners; we have embarked upon a scorched-earth policy by destroying villages and forests; we have killed combatants and non-combatants without discrimination because discrimination is impossible. And this is only the beginning. For the logic of guerrilla war leaves us no choice. We must go on torturing, killing, and burning, and the more deeply we get involved in this war, the more there will be of it.

This brutalization of the Armed Forces would be a serious matter for any nation, as the example of France has shown. It is intolerable for the United States. For this nation, alone among the nations of the world, was created for a particular purpose: to achieve equality in freedom at home, and thereby set an example for the world to emulate. This was the intention of the Founding Fathers, and to this very day the world has taken them at their word. It is exactly for this reason that our prestige has suffered so disastrously among friend and foe alike; for the world did not expect of us what it had come to expect of others. This is indeed, as Keyes Beech put it, "the dirtiest war Americans ever had to fight," with the sole exception of the wars against the Indians, which, however, were not foreign wars. Cam Ne and Chau Son are not in the line of succession to Lexington and Concord and the other great battles of American history; they give the lie to that tradition. War, the wanton killing of human beings, can only be justified by a transcendent end; this makes a war just. There is no such end and there is no justice here. Those who are so concerned about our collective and their personal prestige might take a moment to reflect on the kind of country America will be when it emerges from so senseless, hopeless, brutal, and brutalizing a war.

15

AMERICA AS A WORLD POWER

Balance Sheet

I. EDITORIAL INTRODUCTION

The record of the past twenty years answers at least one question about the American foreign policy that was raised frequently in 1946: How resolute would the United States be in its participation in world politics? Whatever the wisdom of its actions, there has been no withdrawal into the isolationism of an earlier era. For better or for worse the United States has stood fast as a leader in world affairs, even when its leadership was called to account as bitterly by friends as by enemies. The United Nations remained in New York twenty years later; American alliances ranged from unilateral commitments in Asia to a grand alliance in Europe; American economic assistance extended to nearly every part of the world. Indeed, critics in 1967 were more likely to fault the United States for excessive interference in affairs outside the country, for its assumption that it was responsible for maintenance of peace and security everywhere in the world, than for any tendency to resume isolationism.

The United States had learned its history, particularly the lesson that the absence of an American presence in world affairs in two critical periods in the twentieth century had helped to bring on two world wars. Yet this knowledge has only produced new problems, which none of the administrations since 1946 has been able to solve. What were the limits of American responsibility, of American strength? Must America pursue a *Realpolitik* now that world leadership had been accepted? How much should policy be guided by a moral sense, by the urge to crusade an American conception of a world order? How should America behave toward a world that generally suspects its motives, and is ungrateful for its concern and assistance?

President Johnson provided a point of departure for exploring the ramifications of these questions in his Memorial Day address of 1966. Solemnly listing the names of nine men who had died since 1945 in nine different conflicts, the President asserted that these men and the situations leading to their deaths symbolized America's understanding that peace in the world was a national responsibility. Peace must be fought for, aggression fought against, or else there would be no world community of the future. (Selection II.)

Perhaps the strongest challenge to the commitment that Johnson saw as America's burden for this generation was Senator Fulbright's frequent reminders to the Senate wherein he urged Americans to distinguish between myths and realities. He was disturbed over the direction of American foreign policy. His point of departure was the need to free America from the rigidity that had set in after the successful containment of communism in the 1940's. The world, communist and free, had changed since that time, but the United States still persisted in viewing the outside world as an arena for the struggle between good and evil.

Fulbright saw a "fatal arrogance of power" that could in the future destroy the accomplishments of the past and the good intentions of the present. He was disturbed about many aspects of American foreign policy, not least of which was the inexorable increase of executive power and the attending atrophying of Senatorial advice and consent. This criticism was not substantially different from that of Charles Beard twenty years before, although the angle of observation was by no means identical. His complaint was not the fact of American involvement in Europe and the world, as was the case of Beard; it was rather the nature of that involvement. He saw America caught up in problems which made American leaders prisoners of shibboleths —the indivisibility of communism, or the unquestioned wisdom of the domino theory in Southeast Asia. The consequence could be a fatal entrapment in a suicidal World War III as well as the stifling of dissent in a society dependent upon free exchange of ideas. (Selection III–A.)

Adlai Stevenson, former standard bearer of the Democratic Party and ambassador to the United Nations under both Kennedy and Johnson, has often been identified with the kind of dissent expressed by Fulbright. But in a characteristically perceptive speech before the Commonwealth Club of San Francisco in 1964 he asserted that the administrations of both Kennedy and Johnson were aware of the changing nature of the Cold War. It was important to remember that it "takes two to make a detente," and that the Soviet communist threat was never a mirage. With all the aggravations and shortcomings of the past, the United States, it should be remembered, exercised a leadership that was not based on the kind of coercion Soviet Russia displayed in Europe. The United States has shown its capacity to lead a "world of diversity" by its experience and behavior in leading a world under the siege conditions of the Cold War. (Selection III–B.)

Ambassador Stevenson's concern was with the credibility of American leadership, threatened in his view by the ambiguities of Fulbright's position. But the ambassador shared with the Senator a suspicion of the older language of "victory" in the combat with the present enemy. The most articulate spokesman for a school that accepted the MacArthur heritage of power harnessed to a specific if simplistic goal was Senator Barry M. Goldwater, the Republican candidate for President in 1964. In his stirring call to action in 1962 he rejected wholly the containment philosophy which dominated American policy since the war. Communism was the enemy, and it must be destroyed. America had the power to win the contest, and if that power was not used American weakness would tempt the enemy to start a nuclear war. (Selection III–C.)

Historians looking at the experience of the past twenty years have usually placed their evaluations of the success or failure of American statecraft in the context of the realist-moralist polarity popularized after the second World War. Among Kennan's many services to America's understanding of foreign policy was his message in lectures at the University of Chicago in 1951. One of the running afflictions in American diplomatic history had been the pathetic faith in a moralistic-legalistic approach to American foreign policy. It blinded Americans to the reality of power, oversimplified the problems of policymaking, and left Americans exposed to the isolationism of the past. The object of foreign policy must be the service of the national interest without delusions either about the efficacy of international law or the possibility of "total victory." (Selection IV–A.)

That this tendency to moralism continued in American foreign policy has not only been obvious but was also a saving grace in the view of some observers. But others were concerned that even in the use of the rhetoric of moralism Americans had betrayed their tradition and were engaging in a form of imperialism as obnoxious to the rest of the world as was communist expansionism. Such voices were particularly vocal over the Vietnam intervention. Archibald MacLeish, poet and scholar of the age of Franklin Roosevelt, felt that America had abandoned itself to an unthinking "realism" in which power was exercised without moral justification; indeed, it was exercised, he claimed, without regard for the genuine national interest. Invasion of Cuba, occupation of Santo Domingo, and bombing of North Vietnam were all examples of American indifference to the "opinions of mankind." MacLeish felt that if the United States has become arbiter of the world's conduct, the traditions which distinguished America from the other nations of the world will have been betrayed. (Selection IV–B.)

McGeorge Bundy, former Special Assistant for National Security Affairs to both Presidents Kennedy and Johnson, responded to MacLeish's plaint. Addressing himself particularly to the question whether America in Vietnam or in the Dominican Republic had sacrificed its idealism for a new "realism," he looked to history since 1940 for the answer. He found it. Since 1940 and the fall of France the United States had taken its stand in the larger world; and despite errors and hesitations and temporary regressions America had used its power responsibly in behalf of peace and self-determination. In showing more sophistication in reaching these objectives than there had been in Wilson's day, American leaders recognize that the path is difficult, that popularity is unlikely, and that success can never be clearcut. If this behavior is "realistic," it is joined to the goals which are still "idealistic." (Selection IV–C.)

II. DOCUMENT

> ### SELECTION II
>
> An excerpt from President Johnson's Memorial Day address at Arlington National Cemetery in 1966 follows. The President linked the Truman Doctrine to the defense of Vietnam emphasizing both as parts of America's worldwide responsibilities for the maintenance of peace. Taken from the Department of State *Bulletin,* LIV (June 20, 1966), pp. 962–63.

There is a special roll of honor that I would like to call today:
Lt. Col. Seldon R. Edner of San Jose, California
1st Lt. George B. Smith of Los Angeles, California
1st Lt. Leland Williams of Taylor County, Texas
1st Lt. Revier Harding of Fort Worth, Texas
Staff Sergeant William Goodwin of Tacoma, Washington
Lt. Col. Alfred Medendorp of Grand Rapids, Michigan
Lt. Col. Frank Lynn of Chicago, Illinois
Maj. Rudolf Anderson of Del Rio, Texas
Specialist Fourth Class James T. Davis of Livingston, Tennessee
Who were these men?

Edner was the first American killed in Greece, where in 1947 we decided to help the people of that country resist aggression.

Smith and Williams were killed in the airlift which prevailed over the blockade of Berlin in the winter of 1948 and 1949.

Harding and Goodwin were the first American soldiers killed in the struggle against aggression in Korea.

Medendorp and Lynn were killed on Kinman Island, when in 1958 aggression was attempted in the Taiwan Straits.

Anderson was the airman shot down over Cuba during the crisis of 1962, when an effort was made to place offensive weapons on that island.

Davis was the first American killed in the resistance to aggression in Viet-Nam.

These men represent all those Americans who have risked their lives— and lost them—in the peacebuilding efforts since 1945.

They were sent on their missions because this nation believes that peace is not something that just happens.

Peace does not come just because we wish for it.

Peace must be fought for. It must be built stone by stone.

In the first half of this century we learned that there can be no peace if might makes right—if force used by one nation against a weaker nation is ever permitted to succeed. We have learned that the time to stop aggression is when it first begins. And that is one reason that we are in South Viet-Nam today.

Modern weapons and means of communications, even more than common aspirations, have created a single world community. There is no going back. This is the way it will be as far ahead as any of us can see. We can only go forward to help make that community one in which nations respect the rights of other nations and live at peace with one another.

For the American interest will be well served if our children grow up in a world of independent nations capable of assuming collective responsibility for the peace. Our interest—and the interest of world peace—will not be served if nations continue to violate the independence of other nations.

So, as our men and our allies today fight in Southeast Asia, we are working on many fronts to build a mosaic of peace and human progress.

We are working to strengthen the Atlantic world and, from that firm base, to build bridges of cooperation to the East.

We are trying to assist the governments and peoples of Latin America, Asia, and Africa to work together to lift the burdens of poverty and ignorance and disease.

We ache to turn all our energies—more of our resources—and all our talents to building that kind of world community.

But there will be no community to build if aggression achieves in Viet-Nam what it has been denied from Greece to Korea to Berlin.

III. VIEWS OF PARTICIPANTS

SELECTION III–A

Senator J. W. Fulbright, chairman of the Senate Foreign Relations committee, adapted this paper from one of the Christian A. Herter lectures he delivered at the Johns Hopkins University School of Advanced International Studies in Washington in 1966. With his permission the article, which appeared under the title "The Fatal Arrogance of Power," in *The New York Times Magazine* (May 15, 1966), pp. 29, 103, is presented here. © 1966 The New York Times Company. Reprinted by permission.

To criticize one's country is to do it a service and pay it a compliment. It is a service because it may spur the country to do better than it is doing; it is a compliment because it evidences a belief that the country can do better than it is doing.

Criticism may embarrass the country's leaders in the short run but strengthen their hand in the long run; it may destroy a consensus on policy while expressing a consensus of values. Woodrow Wilson once said that there was "such a thing as being too proud to fight." There is also, or ought to be, such a thing as being too confident to conform, too strong to be silent in the face of apparent error. Criticism, in short, is more than a right: it is an act of patriotism—a higher form of patriotism, I believe, than the familiar rituals of national adulation.

Thus, it is not pejorative but a tribute to say that America is worthy of criticism. If nonetheless one is charged with a lack of patriotism, I would reply with Albert Camus: "No, I didn't love my country, if pointing out what is unjust in what we love amounts to not loving, if insisting that what we love should measure up to the finest image we have of her amounts to not loving."

What is the finest image of America? To me it is the image of a composite —or, better still, a synthesis—of diverse peoples and cultures, come together in harmony, but not identity, in an open, receptive, generous and creative society.

We are an extraordinary nation, endowed with a rich and productive land and a talented and energetic population. Surely a nation so favored is capable of extraordinary achievement, not only in the area of producing and enjoying great wealth—where our achievements have indeed been extraordinary—but also in the area of human and international relations—in which area, it seems to me, our achievements have fallen short of our capacity and promise. The question that I find intriguing is whether a nation so extraordinarily endowed as the United States can overcome that arrogance of power which has afflicted, weakened and, in some cases, destroyed great nations in the past.

The causes of the malady are a mystery but its recurrence is one of the uniformities of history: Power tends to confuse itself with virtue and a great nation is peculiarly susceptible to the idea that its power is a sign of God's favor, conferring upon it a special responsibility for other nations—to make them richer and happier and wiser, to remake them, that is, in its own shining image.

Power also tends to take itself for omnipotence. Once imbued with the idea of a mission, a great nation easily assumes that it has the means as well as the duty to do God's work. The Lord, after all, surely would not choose you as His agent and then deny you the sword with which to work His will. German soldiers in the First World War wore belt buckles imprinted with the words "*Gott mit uns.*" It was approximately under this kind of infatuation—an exaggerated sense of power and an imaginary sense of mission— that the Athenians attacked Syracuse and Napoleon and then Hitler invaded Russia. In plain words, they overextended their commitments and they came to grief.

My question is whether America can overcome the fatal arrogance of power. My hope and my belief are that it can, that it has the human resources to accomplish what few, if any, great nations have ever accomplished before: to be confident but also tolerant, and rich but also generous; to be willing to teach but also willing to learn; to be powerful but also wise. I believe that America is capable of all of these things; I also believe it is falling short of them. Gradually but unmistakably we are succumbing to the arrogance of power. In so doing we are not living up to our capacity and promise; the measure of our falling short is the measure of the patriot's duty of dissent.

The discharge of that most important duty is handicapped in America by an unworthy tendency to fear serious criticism of our Government. In the abstract we celebrate freedom of opinion as a vital part of our patriotic liturgy. It is only when some Americans exercise the right that other Americans are shocked. No one, of course, ever criticizes the right of dissent; it is always this particular instance of it or its exercise under these particular circumstances or at this particular time that throws people into a blue funk. I am reminded of Samuel Butler's observation: "People in general are equally horrified at hearing the Christian religion doubted, and at seeing it practiced."

No one challenges the value and importance of national consensus, but consensus can be understood in two ways. If it is interpreted to mean unquestioning support of existing policies, its effects can only be pernicious and undemocratic, serving to suppress differences rather than to reconcile them. If, on the other hand, consensus is understood to mean a general agreement on goals and values, but not necessarily on the best means of realizing them, then it becomes a lasting basis of national strength.

It is consensus in this sense which has made America strong in the past. Indeed, much of our national success in combining change with continuity can be attributed to the vigorous competition of men and ideas within a context of shared values and generally accepted institutions. It is only through this kind of vigorous competition of ideas that a consensus of values can sometimes be translated into a true consensus of policy.

The correction of errors in a nation's foreign policy is greatly assisted by the timely raising of voices of criticism within the nation. When the British launched their disastrous attack on Egypt, the Labor party raised a collective voice of indignation while the military operation was still under way; refusing to be deterred by calls for national unity in a crisis, Labor began the long, painful process of recovering Great Britain's good name at the very moment when the damage was still being done. Similarly, the French intellectuals who protested France's colonial wars in Indochina and Algeria not only upheld the values of French democracy but helped pave the way for the enlightened policies of the Fifth Republic which have made France the most respected Western nation in the underdeveloped world.

A second great advantage of free discussion to democratic policymakers is its bringing to light of new ideas and the supplanting of old myths with new realities. We Americans are much in need of this benefit because we are severely, if not uniquely, afflicted with a habit of policy making by analogy: North Vietnam's involvement in South Vietnam, for example, is equated with Hitler's invasion of Poland and a parley with the Vietcong would represent another Munich.

The treatment of slight and superficial resemblances as if they were full-blooded analogies—as instances, as it were, of history "repeating itself"—is a substitute for thinking and a misuse of history. The value of history is not what it seems to prohibit or prescribe, but its general indications as to the kinds of policies that are likely to succeed and the kinds that are likely to fail, or, as one historian has suggested, its hints as to what is likely not to happen.

There is a kind of voodoo about American foreign policy. Certain drums have to be beaten regularly to ward off evil spirits—for example, the maledictions which are regularly uttered against North Vietnamese aggression, the "wild men" in Peking, Communism in general and President de Gaulle. Certain pledges must be repeated every day lest the whole free world go to rack and ruin—for example, we will never go back on a commitment no matter how unwise; we regard this alliance or that as absolutely "vital" to the free world; and, of course, we will stand stalwart in Berlin from now until Judgment Day. Certain words must never be uttered except in derision —the word "appeasement," for example, comes as near as any word can to summarizing everything that is regarded by American policy makers as stupid, wicked and disastrous.

I do not suggest that we should heap praise on the Chinese Communists, dismantle NATO, abandon Berlin, and seize every opportunity that comes along to appease our enemies. I do suggest the desirability of an atmosphere in which unorthodox ideas would arouse interest rather than horror, reflection rather than emotion. As likely as not, new proposals, carefully examined, would be found wanting and old policies judged sound; what is wanted is not change itself but the capacity for change.

Consider the idea of "appeasement." In a free and healthy political atmosphere it would elicit neither horror nor enthusiasm but only interest in what precisely its proponent had in mind. As Winston Churchill once said: "Appeasement in itself may be good or bad according to circumstances. . . . Appeasement from strength is magnanimous and noble and might be the surest and perhaps the only path to world peace."

In addition to its usefulness for redeeming error and introducing new ideas, free and open criticism has a third, more abstract but no less important function in a democracy. It is therapy and catharsis for those who are troubled or dismayed by something their country is doing; it helps to reassert traditional values, to clear the air when it is full of tension and mistrust.

There are times in public life as in private life when one must protest, not solely or even primarily because one's protest will be politic or materially productive, but because one's sense of decency is offended, because one is fed up with political craft and public images, or simply because something goes against the grain. The catharsis thus provided may indeed be the most valuable of freedom's uses.

> *SELECTION III-B*
>
> Adlai E. Stevenson was Ambassador to the United Nations when he defended American foreign policy in an address before the Commonwealth Club in San Francisco on April 3, 1964. The following portion of that speech is reprinted here as it appeared in "The Anatomy of World Leadership," Department of State *Bulletin*, L (April 20, 1964), pp. 619-20.

We have heard a great deal about leadership in the postwar world—leadership of the two contending blocs engaged in a struggle described as cold war. It is a simple statement of historical fact to say that for a number of years one side was led unquestionably by the Soviet Union and the other side was led unquestionably by the United States of America.

There was a fundamental difference in the character of the two leaderships: One was imposed by the leader and his Red Army; the other was imposed upon us by our resources and our capacity to act in a war-torn world. We have no apologies to make about our acceptance and performance of that role; indeed, we can be deeply proud of both.

But the days of unquestioned and unchallenged leadership are past. The fear of external threat, which is the cement of alliances, has subsided somewhat—and some of the followers have grown strong enough to strike out on their own.

And again there is a fundamental difference in the change that has occurred on the two sides. Communist China has broken away violently from the leadership of the Soviet Union in a split of unprecedented bitterness. There is hardly a Communist party anywhere in the world which has not felt the devisive repercussions of that schism. Meanwhile, the other members of the old Soviet bloc twist and turn and maneuver to put a bit more daylight between them and the old leader. That is just about the last thing that the Soviet leaders wanted to happen—and they have done their best to prevent it.

On our side an old friend within the alliance now sometimes declines to see things the way we see them for reasons which sometimes seem quite obscure to us from where we sit. Other old friends occasionally disagree—as we do with them—though very often, when we talk things out, we find our way to common ground.

But our differences, even when they persist, do not set us at each other's throats in alleys and villages around the world. A basic purpose of our whole postwar policy has been to help Europe get back on its feet, stand up on its own, and look us in the eye as equals. If we sometimes do not like what they say when they look us in the eye, let us not forget that we know something the Communists don't know: Lasting unity can be attained only among nations that are not dominated by any member of the group. Lasting unity is created not by the overlordship of the strong but by leadership of the strong in a community in which very member is equal because he is free.

As the world of the two great blocs and the unalined states is breaking into a pluralism of power and prestige, the most powerful nation in the world still cannot throw up its hands and resign from a job which it never sought anyway. Leadership always will be needed; leadership always will be welcomed—provided it is the right kind of leadership in the right places at the right time.

What is the right kind of leadership in a world in which the prevailing political passion is national independence? What is the right way to exercise national power in an age when the most powerful nations cannot use their most powerful weapons?

There is diplomacy, of course. There is joint military planning with close allies. There is common trade policy and development policy. There is technical cooperation and the export of science. There is information and cultural exchange. All these—and other tangible things—come to mind.

But what I have in mind is something less tangible than the spending of money and the organizing of resources. What I have in mind is leadership by attitude—and by example.

A wise Asian said not long ago that, in our time, his people would expect Americans to make a great effort to understand them, without themselves making a great effort to understand the Americans. It is not easy for Americans to get used to a world in which they have to try hard to understand the sentiments and feelings and prides and prejudices of others—and then find that those others continue to cherish unfair, false, even outrageous opinions about the purposes and motives of the United States of America.

Put it this way: A man who serves as a leader in his community has to accustom himself to the fact that individual citizens and special-interest groups will often berate him for his actions because they have not considered all the angles the leader must consider before he acts. Much of this criticism the leader will think unfair; yet, while he can never give way to pressure merely because it comes from the weak, neither can he give way to the temptation of responding in kind, of lashing out at his adversaries, of talking or acting as irresponsibly as his less powerful but noisier critics. He has to do what he thinks is best—consulting all the elements of the community, but consulting his own independent best judgment as well. His patience, his restraint, his self-control, his magnanimity, his compassion—in a word, his maturity—will be often and sorely tried. But this is the price of power. He either learns that simple lesson, or he stops trying to be a leader among his fellow men.

So it is with the leadership of a nation, among its fellow nations in a world not yet safe for diversity. We are, quite simply, too strong to react in kind to every ugly street cry, every student placard, every irresponsible act. In this kind of world, wielding our kind of power, real toughness is not bluster but maturity. If we want to know how to act in such a world, we could do worse than to reread Kipling's *If*.

Alongside the mature *attitudes* of the powerful leader, I would place the impact of *example* as an instrument of leadership in the world that is emerging.

> SELECTION III–C
>
> From *Why Not Victory?* by Barry M. Goldwater (New York, 1962), pp. 149–54, 161–63. © by Barry M. Goldwater. Used by permission of the McGraw-Hill Book Co. The former senator from Arizona was the Republican candidate for president in 1964. This excerpt was taken from his book which put forth most of his views on foreign policy.

Strangely enough, I find myself in the position of one who, over the past year, has been challenged to make a *case for victory* in a conflict with an enemy of enormous power whose undisguised aim is to conquer the United States and enslave the world. I have been challenged to explain what victory in the Communist War means, how we could achieve it, and what we would do with it after we won it. This challenge, astounding as it is, comes from the Chairman of the Senate Foreign Relations Committee—Senator J. William Fulbright of Arkansas—who reflects in his statements a policy line now being promoted within the top ranks of the Kennedy administration. Senator Fulbright, and I am sorry to say some others in positions of influence today, believes that victory in the Communist War is impossible, that we must co-exist with an alien ideological power which is using every device at its command to overwhelm us, and that one of the means toward co-existence is "aggressive compromise."

I doubt if any United States Senator or government official—ever before in the history of our Republic—has been called upon to make a *case for victory* in a conflict where everything that the United States stands for today —or ever stood for in the past—is at stake. I doubt if this nation ever before has found itself in a battle for her very existence where any public official or group of public officials automatically foreclosed the possibility of victory and questioned what we would do with it if it ever were achieved.

When I realize that Senator Fulbright speaks for a sizable bloc of influence in our State Department, I begin to wonder what forces are at work among us in this hour of crisis. I wonder whether the entire scope of this protracted conflict and the dire consequences which it holds for our nation and the world's freedom have been correctly understood. I wonder whether the American people actually realize that the failure to proclaim victory as our aim in the Communist War is not just an oversight but a calculated policy of influential men. Let me state this in Senator Fulbright's own words. "Apparently we have not yet fully accepted the fact that . . . *we can hope to do little more than mitigate our problems as best we can and learn to live with them.*" Since that time, Senator Fulbright has made it plain that his method of "mitigation" would be through negotiation and compromise. This is what he proposes in the Berlin crisis, which might well serve as a terminal point in our diplomatic negotiations with Russia. The Senator apparently believes that negotiation and compromise are what we must do to "live with" communism. He assumes that the American people and the rest of the free world want to live with communism rather than risk a test of strength. He also tells us, in effect, that the price of this living is compromise—which is another way of saying that we will yield further and further to Khrushchev's demands.

But I'm getting a little ahead of myself. I believe it is important for the reader to understand how the exchange between Senator Fulbright and myself evolved. It began on June 29 of last year when the Foreign Relations Committee Chairman delivered a speech to the Senate entitled, "Some Reflections Upon Recent Events and Continuing Problems." These remarks were hailed in a certain segment of the press as a major foreign-policy declaration. Now since these "reflections" contained so many arguments for doing nothing in the Communist War but waste more and more money in the name of social reform for other nations, I felt impelled to reply. I did this in a Senate speech on July 14. I challenged the Foreign Relations Chairman to explain why his approach to the Communist War, which boils down to more and more foreign aid, has not yielded results after the expenditure of nearly a hundred billion dollars. I challenged his assertion that a successful American action in Cuba would result in alienating Latin America, Asia, and Africa. I challenged his assertion that communism ninety miles off our southern coast was not "intolerable" to the American people. I challenged his declaration that the erection of missile bases by the Communists in Cuba would not increase the danger to our national existence. And I also said that this nation needs an official declaration stating that our aim in the Communist War is victory.

Now in his response to this, Senator Fulbright ignored my question concerning the wisdom of pursuing a costly and ineffective foreign policy. He ignored quite a few other things in commenting briefly on the Senate Floor on July 24 on what he referred to as "certain themes" contained in my remarks. He was excessively bemused with one of my phrases—"total victory." He seemed to think there was something funny about it. He referred to total victory as a "stirring term with a romantic ring." He ridiculed it as something that "quickens the blood like a clarion call to arms." I suggest that ridicule is a curious attitude for an American to take when discussing victory in a struggle that means survival. It is even more curious when that American holds the influential office of Chairman of the Senate Foreign Relations Committee—and I say this whether he is referring to "total victory" or just plain "victory." There are many details of our conduct in the Communist War which invite scoffing and ridicule, but the subject of our *winning* in this desperate struggle is definitely not one of them.

The Senator from Arkansas says he does not know what victory would mean—as he puts it—"in this age of ideological conflict and nuclear weapons." Perhaps we are meant to believe that victory for the forces of freedom in the world takes on a different meaning because ideology is a factor and weapons are more powerful. If Senator Fulbright finds difficulty in understanding what victory would mean perhaps he should spend a little thought on the question of what defeat—*the only alternative to victory*—would mean. This is a frightening thought—*what would defeat mean?* But, it is one which must be considered—and considered seriously—if our national policy is anything but victory.

This is a conflict where one side or the other must win, and no amount of wishful thinking can make it otherwise. On this question, the decision is out of our hands. The rules for the conflict have been laid down by the Soviet Union through a massive design aimed at destruction of the United States and domination of the world. Against the Communist strategy as it is being pushed today, there can be no middle alternative between *a policy aimed at victory or one that would permit defeat*. There is no cozy twilight zone such as Senator Fulbright envisions where the *status quo* is maintained. We know this from what has happened to the world since the end of World War II. We have continued to delude ourselves with something called "peaceful co-existence" while communism has kept right on gobbling up one country after another. Hundreds of millions of the world's people have fallen under the yoke of communism while we have followed a useless policy of spend and drift. Now we are told that this is the only feasible approach; that we can't hope for victory; that we can't risk a war; that we couldn't cope for victory if we won it. I say this is the most dangerous kind of sheer nonsense.

If there is doubt as to what victory in the Communist War means, let me say that it means the opposite of defeat; it means freedom instead of slavery; it means the right of every man to worship God; of nations to determine their own destiny free of force and coercion. Victory in the Communist War means the sum total of all the hopes of free men throughout the world. It means human dignity, freedom of choice, the right to work. And it means peace with honor for men who prize liberty and do not fear death.

Can victory be achieved without a nuclear war? My vociferous critics would like us to believe that there can be no Communist War victory without the destruction of civilization. This is precisely what the Communists would like us to believe. Their whole line of attack, through propaganda and adroit economic, political, and military moves, is directed toward making us think in terms of fear. They want to make sure that we believe the risk is too great to employ our strength. Their purpose is intimidation and it is working too well.

Indeed, a decisive victory over the Communists is possible. It won't be easy because we have lost too much valuable time and too many golden opportunities. But it can be done with the proper integrated strategy—a strategy that *aims at victory*; that retains our economic strength; that incorporates the principles of political, military, economic, and psychological strength in meeting Communist challenges and in presenting some challenges of our own. Those who argue against any use of strength, against any military risk, against any unilateral action fail to understand that political victory in the Communist War is the only way to avoid a strictly military solution of the East-West crisis. It involves some risk, but experience shows us that this risk is greatly overexaggerated. Every time we have stood up to the Communists they have backed down. Our trouble is we have not stood up to them enough.

.   .   .   .

In the final analysis the choice is not yield or fight a nuclear war. It is: *win, or fight a nuclear war*. For a nuclear war we shall certainly have to fight from whatever beleaguered outpost we are reduced to occupying, if we continue to yield, piece by piece, all over the world. Finally, in desperation, we would see the horrible alternatives clearly in view—a violent act of nuclear aggression or surrender. Our only hope is to proclaim victory as our aim and then to press boldly and unremittingly on all fronts—always *prepared* to fight and making sure the Communists always know we are prepared to fight.

And, in laying that ground work, there are a number of immediate steps we should take to re-orient our policy for maximum United States effectiveness in the Communist War. They include the following:

1. We must stop believing that our primary objective must be to humor the public opinion of neutral or uncommitted nations rather than to defend our strategic interests, cooperative closely with our allies, and advance our positions of strength. This we must do to more readily because much of this so-called opinion which entrances our co-existence proponents is fabricated by the Communists to our detriment. We must realize that we have no proper method by which we can judge what public opinion really is throughout the world.

2. We must stop lying to ourselves and our friends about disarmament. We must stop advancing the cause of the Soviet Union by playing along with this great Communist-inspired deception. We must abandon the illusion that the Soviets, in their disarmament policies, are interested in furthering peace rather than baiting a trap for us. Their objective is to contrive *our* unilateral disarmament while they continue to arm themselves secretly as fast as they can.

It is not "dialectics" but schizophrenia when we increase our military budget by 15 percent and the Soviets theirs by 33 percent while, at the same time, we proclaim that disarmament is our highest goal and a practical method of solving the present conflict. The American people can stand the truth, but they cannot prosper under an official policy of self-deception.

3. We must not again abandon nuclear testing. This is the worst and most transparent trap into which the United States has fallen during the course of the Cold War. A ban does nothing but serve the Soviet Union to improve its nuclear weapons by clandestine testing, to stop our own advances in offensive and defensive nuclear technology and, ultimately, lead to a situation where we wake up confronted with superior Soviet weapons.

4. We must stop negotiating about things that are non-negotiable, such as the rights of our allies, compromises of our security, treaties like the test ban which can be neither controlled nor enforced. We must not deceive ourselves and our friends into believing that nuclear weapons and modern technology can be negotiated out of existence.

5. We must stop helping communism, whether by trade, political concessions, technical disclosures, soft talk in the United Nations, recognition of Outer Mongolia, pilgrimages to Moscow, or support for revolutionaries of the Castro type.

6. We must avoid economic collapse by scaling down extravagant and useless domestic programs, and halt the squandering of our money on unrealistic world-wide aid programs.

In this mortal struggle there is no substitute for victory. The way of strength is not an easy way. It is a hard course requiring determination and difficult decisions involving considerable risk. But it is the way of peace, not war, of freedom, not slavery. It must be the way of all Americans, Republicans and Democrats alike, the way of all free people with the will to remain free.

IV. VIEWS OF OBSERVERS

SELECTION IV–A

In the following excerpt from his book *American Diplomacy, 1900–1950* (Chicago, 1951), pp. 95–97, 100–103, George Kennan drew on his experience in the foreign service to condemn the "moralistic" strain in American foreign policy in the 20th century. The book was based on a series of lectures delivered at the University of Chicago under the Charles R. Walgreen Foundation. © 1951 by the University of Chicago. Reprinted by permission of the publisher.

As you have no doubt surmised, I see the most serious fault of our past policy formulation to lie in something that I might call the legalistic-moralistic approach to international problems. This approach runs like a red skein through our foreign policy of the last fifty years. It has in it something of the old emphasis on arbitration treaties, something of the Hague Conferences and schemes for universal disarmament, something of the more ambitious American concepts of the role of international law, something of the League of Nations and the United Nations, something of the Kellog Pact, something of the idea of a universal "Article 51" pact, something of the belief in World Law and World Government. But it is none of these, entirely. Let me try to describe it.

It is the belief that it should be possible to suppress the chaotic and dangerous aspirations of governments in the international field by the acceptance of some system of legal rules and restraints. This belief undoubtedly represents in part an attempt to transpose the Anglo-Saxon concept of individual law into the international field and to make it applicable to governments as it is applicable here at home to individuals. It must also stem in part from the memory of the origin of our own political system—from the recollection that we were able, through acceptance of a common institutional and juridical framework, to reduce harmless dimensions the conflicts of interest and aspiration among the original thirteen colonies and to bring them all into an ordered and peaceful relationship with one another. Remembering this, people are unable to understand that what might have been possible for the thirteen colonies in a given set of circumstances might not be possible in the wider international field.

It is the essence of this belief that, instead of taking the awkward conflicts of national interest and dealing with them on their merits with a view to finding the solutions least unsettling to the stability of international life, it would be better to find some formal criteria of a juridical nature by which the permissible behavior of states could be defined. There would then be judicial entities competent to measure the actions of governments against these criteria and to decide when their behavior was acceptable and when unacceptable. Behind all this, of course, lies the American assumption that the things for which other peoples in this world are apt to contend are for the most part neither creditable nor important and might justly be expected to take second place behind the desirability of an orderly world, untroubled by international violence. To the American mind, it is implausible that people should have positive aspirations, and ones that they regard as legitimate, more important to them than the peacefulness and orderliness of international life. From this standpoint, it is not apparent why other peoples should not join us in accepting the rules of the game in international politics, just as we accept such rules in the competition of sport in order that the game may not become too cruel and too destructive and may not assume an importance we did not mean it to have.

If they were to do this, the reasoning runs, then the troublesome and chaotic manifestations of the national ego could be contained and rendered either unsubstantial or subject to easy disposal by some method familiar and comprehensible to our American usage. Departing from this background, the mind of American statesmanship, stemming as it does in so large a part from the legal profession in our country, gropes with unfailing persistence for some institutional framework which would be capable of fulfilling this function.

.   .   .   .

These, then, are some of the theoretical deficiencies that appear to me to be inherent in the legalistic approach to international affairs. But there is a greater deficiency still that I should like to mention before I close. That is the inevitable association of legalistic ideas with moralistic ones: the carryingover into the affairs of states of the concepts of right and wrong, the assumption that state behavior is a fit subject for moral judgment. Whoever says there is a law must of course be indignant against the lawbreaker and feel a moral superiority to him. And when such indignation spills over into military contest, it knows no bounds short of the reduction of the lawbreaker to the point of complete submissiveness—namely, unconditional surrender. It is a curious thing, but it is true, that the legalistic approach to world affairs, rooted as it unquestionably is in a desire to do away with war and violence, makes violence more enduring, more terrible, and more destructive to political stability than did the older motives of national interest. A war fought in the name of high moral principle finds no early end short of some form of total domination.

In this way, we see that the legalistic approach to international problems is closely identified with the concept of total war and total victory, and the manifestations of the one spill over only too easily into the manifestations of the other. And the concept of total war is something we would all do well to think about a little in these troubled times. This is a relatively new concept, in Western civilization at any rate. It did not really appear on the scene until World War I. It characterized both of these great world wars, and both of them—as I have pointed out—were followed by great instability and disillusionment. But it is not only a question now of the desirability of this concept; it is a question of its feasibility. Actually, I wonder whether even in the past total victory was not really an illusion from the standpoint of the victors. In a sense, there is not total victory short of genocide, unless it be a victory over the minds of men. But the total military victories are rarely victories over the minds of men. And we now face the fact that it is very questionable whether in a new global conflict there could ever be any such thing as total *military* victory. I personally do not believe that there could. There might be a great weakening of the armed forces on one side of another, but I think it out of the question that there should be such a thing as a general and formal submission of the national will on either side. The attempt to achieve this unattainable goal, however, could wreak upon civilization another set of injuries fully as serious as those caused by World War I or World War II, and I leave it to you to answer the question as to how civilization could survive them.

It was asserted not long ago by a prominent American that "war's very object is victory" and that "in war there can be no substitute for victory." Perhaps the confusion here lies in what is meant by the term "victory." Perhaps the term is actually misplaced. Perhaps there can be such a thing as "victory" in a battle, where in war there can be only the achievement or non-achievement of your objectives. In the old days, wartime objectives were generally limited and practical ones, and it was common to measure the success of your military operations by the extent to which they brought you closer to your objectives. But where your objectives are moral and ideological ones and run to changing the attitudes and traditions of an entire people or the personality of a regime, then victory is probably something not to be achieved entirely by military means or indeed in any short space of time at all; and perhaps that is the source of our confusion.

In any case, I am frank to say that I think there is no more dangerous delusion, none that has done us a greater disservice in the past or that threatens to do us a greater disservice in the future, than the concept of total victory. And I fear that it springs in large measure from the basic faults in the approach to international affairs which I have been discussing here. If we are to get away from it, this will not mean that we shall have to abandon our respect for international law, or our hopes for its future usefulness as the gentle civilizer of events which I mentioned in one of the earlier lectures. Nor will it mean that we have to go in for anything that can properly be termed "appeasement"—if one may use a word so cheapened and deflated by the abuse to which it has been recently subjected. But it will mean the emergence of a new attitude among us toward many things outside our borders that are irritating and unpleasant today—an attitude more like that of the doctor toward those physical phenomena in the human body that are neither pleasing nor fortunate—an attitude of detachment and soberness and readiness to reserve judgment. It will mean that we will have the modesty to admit that our own national interest is all that we are really capable of knowing and understanding—and the courage to recognize that if our own purposes and undertakings here at home are decent ones, unsullied by arrogance or hostility toward other people or delusions of superiority, then the pursuit of our national interest can never fail to be conducive to a better world. This concept is less ambitious and less inviting in its immediate prospects than those to which we have so often inclined, and less pleasing to our image of ourselves. To many it may seem to smack of cynicism and reaction. I cannot share these doubts. Whatever is realistic in concept, and founded in an endeavor to see both ourselves and others as we really are, cannot be illiberal.

SELECTION IV—B

In "What is 'Realism' Doing to American History?", Archibald MacLeish, poet and former Assistant Secretary of State, expressed his concern about the effect of "realism" on American tradition. The following excerpt from that article is from *Saturday Review* (July 3, 1965), pp. 10–11. Reprinted by permission of the author, the *Saturday Review*, and the Houghton-Mifflin Co.

Something needs to be said about the position in which the United States has been placed in world opinion by the events of the last few weeks and months. The events themselves have been discussed at length by critics and defenders of American policy; their effect on the general attitude toward the United States of the peoples of the world is of equal if not greater importance. In its first public act after independence the American nation acknowledged "a decent respect to the opinions of mankind." The reasons which moved the Continental Congress to adopt that phrase in its famous Declaration are still operative today.

What has happened in these months and weeks is simply that the conception of America—the conception, at least, which has held throughout my lifetime—has changed. I do not say that it has changed everywhere, but it has been altered certainly in the minds of many of our friends in Europe and Latin America, in the official statements of one government allied to our own, and in the actions, as well as in the words, of some at least of our own people, particularly the generation now of college age.

It is not easy to put the change into words. No man knows precisely what others think of him or of his nation. Those in my generation, for example, who fell in love with France in their youth were not in love with the same France that Frenchmen think of, and no American can even guess at what the French thought of this republic back in the days of the First World War. We were their allies, yes, and they liked us for that, though they thought we might have come a little sooner. But we were also a nation given to enormous words and lofty ideas and humanitarian theories. We had Fourteen Points on which we meant to build a League of Nations to save the world and we went up to the front talking about a war to end war—a war to make the world safe for democracy. The French didn't smile—not then at least: too many Americans died with those words in their mouths. But they had their own notion of us and they kept it. We were a young nation and we fought quite well once we got the hang of the fighting, but our thoughts were too large for our mouths; we believed too much in humanity and such abstractions as international justice and international organizations and the possibility of universal peace. It was all in Clemenceau's face as he rode beside Wilson through those yelling crowds.

And twenty-five years later, though much had changed, though the war in

1939 was a necessary war to cleanse the earth of an intolerable evil rather than a sordid commercial struggle, though our part was a greater part, though we led now and no longer followed, the conception was much the same. Again we were a nation that fought well—better perhaps. Again we died—more of us this time, many more. But still we talked in the old way about freedom—Four Freedoms this time—about human decency, about the hope for an enduring peace. And this time, when the war ended, we not only proposed an international organization; we presented a plan already hammered out in preliminary talks with our principal allies, and the plan was adopted. We were still the innocents, the idealists. We even believed, for as long as events would let us, in the good will of those on the other side of the Carpathians who had fought beside us to bring Hitler down.

So that the composite picture somehow endured. It survived Hiroshima, though not unaltered. It was enhanced by the Korean War, where the aggressor was self-confessed and where most of the nations of the United Nations were on our side. It was not harmed—if anything it was helped—by twenty years of the most persistent and abusive propaganda from Moscow and Peking; to indict a nation as an "imperialist aggressor" in a vocabulary in which "liberation" means subjugation and a "people's democracy" is a police state injures it neither in its own nor its neighbors' eyes, if I may paraphrase Mr. Yeats.

I do not mean to suggest that this portrait of America, composed by fifty years of history and two world wars, was wholly flattering. No nation is universally admired until time has left it 3,000 years behind, and even then there will be Alcibiades in the stern of the ship and Socrates's murderers. We had our critics—as many critics, indeed, as we had contemporaries. We were too rich. We talked in a rather childish way about brinkmanship, like two boys daring each other to walk out on a railroad trestle. Our principal exports—tourists and Coca-Cola—were not everywhere well received. Nevertheless, the essential figure was still the figure Wilson had presented—Wilson and that innocent doughboy of the First World War. We were on the side of the angels, however far below. We still talked in the vocabulary of the vast ideal and backed it up with enormous gifts of goods and money. And above all, though we had more power than any nation in the history of the world had ever had, we still refrained from the use of power except as a deterrent.

And then the picture changed. It changed first, or almost changed, at the Bay of Pigs, where, at the last moment, we did not use our planes. It changed four years later, first in Vietnam and then in Santo Domingo: we bombed North Vietnam and we occupied Santo Domingo with American troops. In both cases, of course, we explained our actions as preventive. We bombed North Vietnam because we believed the bombing would prevent the further invasion of South Vietnam by the Communists; we occupied Santo Domingo to forestall a Communist seizure of the Dominican Republic. But in both cases our explanations were overshadowed by our acts. What the world saw was the exercise of power: the use of American troops for the first time since the bad old days of gunboat diplomacy to impose our will on a Latin American country; the use of American bombers against a nation with which we were not at war.

With that spectacle the feel of America in the world's mind began to change. It is still changing. And not abroad alone but here as well. The famous "teach-ins" in universities across the country, where our normally silent students spent long, angry nights, were not, as the participants sometimes seemed to think, debates on foreign policy. They were searchings of the national conscience.

Now, of the rights and wrongs of these great questions, of the wisdom or unwisdom of our decisions, of the accuracy of our intelligence, of the effectiveness, in terms of their own purposes, of the measures adopted, the time has not yet come to speak. The necessary information is not available.

But what matters here is the *meaning* of our policy, not how it came to be. What matters is whether America has actually changed for its own people and for the world.

Do Vietnam and the Dominican Republic mean that we are no longer that idealistic nation of the First World War—no longer a people attached to those enormous phrases, those almost inexpressible aspirations which impose their own sometimes quixotic laws of self-restraint? Have our ways of thinking and of feeling altered? Are we "realistic" now? "Hardheaded"? Indifferent to those opinions of mankind which our progenitors put in the first sentence of their first communication to the world?

> SELECTION IV–C
>
> McGeorge Bundy, who had been a Harvard colleague of MacLeish and formerly was advisor to Presidents Kennedy and Johnson, is now the president of the Ford Foundation. He replied to the MacLeish article presented in Selection IV–B in "The Uses of Responsibility," *Saturday Review* (July 3, 1965), pp. 13–14, 47, a portion of which is reprinted here with permission of the author and the *Saturday Review*.

The question that Archibald MacLeish raises is not directed to the particular quality or wisdom of specific present policies. His question is whether the headline events of recent months indicate some kind of fundamental change, either in the behavior of Americans or in their respect for the opinions of others. I am grateful to Mr. MacLeish for raising this question. There is no American whose honorable concern for the quality of our national and international life has been demonstrated at a greater personal sacrifice or over a longer period of time than Mr. MacLeish's. There is no friend whom I value more. There is no colleague whose expressions of concern are more deserving of attention.

Mr. MacLeish puts his question this way: "Do Vietnam and the Dominican Republic mean that we are no longer that idealistic nation of the First World War—no longer a people attached to those enormous phrases, those almost inexpressible aspirations which impose their own quixotic laws of self-restraint? Have our ways of thinking and of feeling altered? Are we 'realistic' now? 'Hardheaded'? Indifferent to those opinions of mankind which our progenitors put in the first sentence of their first communication to the world?"

Mr. MacLeish believes some people think we are much too concerned about our public image, and he associates himself, as I myself would wish to do, with a certain distaste for that phrase and for the way of thinking it represents. Then he comes to a conclusion to which I will return.

Mr. MacLeish's question is understandable. In order to give it an effective answer, it seems to me, we must begin some distance back in the modern history of the United States, because the structure of our contemporary role in the world rises upon rocks that were put in place in the time of Franklin Roosevelt, in the time that followed the fall of France in that terrible spring of 1940. For it is from that moment that one must date the inescapable place of the United States as one of the great centers of power, as one of those nations inescapably drawn to difficulty and to responsibility all over the world.

My own belief is that it was Franklin Roosevelt himself who articulated, not only for his time but for the years that have followed, the three primary elements of a continuing American attitude toward world affairs. The first, and the one without which the others would not operate, was the acceptance by the United States of the responsibility of holding and using power. The great choice of 1940 was the choice to turn outward, not inward, in the face of the conquest of the continent of Europe. Since then, moments of hesitation and uncertainty have occurred, as in the period of pell-mell disarmament after 1945 and again when there was a reluctance to face a need for renewed rearmament in 1949 and early 1950. Moreover, at particular moments in particular places there have been uneasiness and uncertainty; there have been disappointments, and there have been failures. But broadly speaking the acceptance of the responsibilities of world power has existed for a generation now. There is in many, and perhaps especially among those whose concern is for ideas and ideals and those whose hope is primarily for peace and progress, a reluctance to give full weight to the role of power and its necessity in the world's affairs. And often when there is criticism or concern about a particular action from those who have these deep preoccupations, it will be because of a reluctance to recognize and to accept this element in the affairs of men.

The second great strand in the operations of the United States in its relationship to the world dates, once again, from the time of Roosevelt. It is a commitment to peace. He was not the first to have it on his mind, but he was the first to bring into operation responsible American concern and action for the advancement of peace in the world as a whole. The reality of the American commitment to peace in his time is best symbolized by the dominant role played by American policy-makers and by American purpose in the creation and the sustaining of the organization of the United Nations. It is right to understand this country as a country of peace. It is a country built by people who came from struggle and strife in other countries, and while Americans have their own sense of power and of force, while the American tradition of battle and of warfare is strong, the aspiration of the nation, the purpose of its people, and therefore, by extension, the purpose of those who are elected by its people must be peace. What we do when there is need for force, how we act in the control and management of our power, is fairly and correctly understood, I deeply believe, only in the context of the general, sustained commitment to a goal of less war, less struggle, and above all an avoidance of the catastrophe of full-scale warfare in the age of nuclear weapons.

The third strand in Franklin Roosevelt's policy is more complex. It was an instinctive belief that the United States must concern itself with the interests of others, wherever they might be. Nothing human was foreign to Franklin Roosevelt, and as the power of the United States spread, so did his concern to see that this power was responsive to the will and purpose of people whom it reached. This was much more than simply a refusal to impose the American dream on others, more than a rejection of the notion that we could execute our policy in terms of an American century. It was, rather, an active assertion that the dreams of others must have room to come true and that American power must be responsive to that end.

Seen from afar, on the other side of an American decision which is not approved, our conviction that our policy must be responsive to the interests of others can seem no more than cant—merely the protective cover for lower interests and lesser values. And it is certainly inevitable in the conflicts of nations that there should be differences of judgment on one action or another. Yet I would reassert, as a matter of simple fact, that we Americans do accept the obligation to judge ourselves by the results of our activities in terms of the interests of others. And we take it for granted that others should apply this unusually demanding standard to us.

These three strands—an acceptance of the responsibility of power, a permanent, passionate commitment to the ideal of peace, and a readiness to judge ourselves and to be judged in terms of the effect of our behavior on others—have been a steady part of our policy now for a quarter of a century. They continue to be the main strands of our policy today. And they all relate to the basic proposition that we must accept accountability for what we do; we expect it, we ask it of ourselves, and we respect the judgment of others.

We do not expect that there will always be agreement. We used to. That is one of the elements of our earlier approach to international affairs that we have had to discard along the way, and in that sense, as in some others, it may well be that we are now a little more hardheaded, a little more realistic than we were at the time of the First World War. We no longer suppose that because there is cheering for Woodrow Wilson in the aftermath of an armistice, there is wholehearted concurrence with his desire to rearrange the map of Europe as he thinks best.

.   .   .   .

So the answer I would give to my friend MacLeish is that we must expect to have differences about particular decisions and particular problems. But we can, I think, join in two propositions: first, that there is continuity and steadiness in the underlying policy of the United States; and, second, that perhaps we learn as we go along.